# A Liver Runs Through It

The Bourbon-Soaked History of the 4Day
Paddling through an Endless Stream of Stories

River Dick Doc

authorHOUSE®

Photographs: River Dick Doc & the
4Dayers & fellow travelers
Maps: Northland Outfitters
Illustrations: Jonesey aka Bigtimeartguy
Poster Art Creations: the Colonel
Front Cover: the Colonel
Back Cover sign: Maggie
Back Cover photo: Herb Fletcher

*AuthorHouse™*
*1663 Liberty Drive*
*Bloomington, IN 47403*
*www.authorhouse.com*
*Phone: 1 (800) 839-8640*

*Published by AuthorHouse 10/14/2017*

*ISBN: 978-1-5462-0747-4 (sc)*
*ISBN: 978-1-5462-0746-7 (e)*

*Library of Congress Control Number: 2017913831*

*Print information available on the last page.*

*Any people depicted in stock imagery provided by Thinkstock are models,*
*and such images are being used for illustrative purposes only.*
*Certain stock imagery* © *Thinkstock.*

*This book is printed on acid-free paper.*

*Because of the dynamic nature of the Internet, any web addresses or links contained in this book may have changed*
*since publication and may no longer be valid. The views expressed in this work are solely those of the author and do*
*not necessarily reflect the views of the publisher, and the publisher hereby disclaims any responsibility for them.*

# CONTENTS

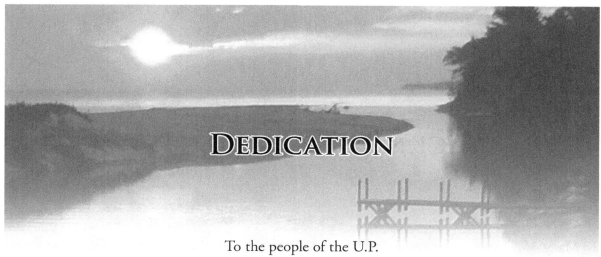

# DEDICATION

To the people of the U.P.

who put up with us,

some years more than others.

# ACKNOWLEDGEMENTS

To Maggie for your love, enthusiastic support & encouragement in my pursuits, and brightening every day of my life. Your ideas, suggestions, and collaboration made this a better book, and by frequently cracking up while proofreading, you brought me even more joy about this project. Thanks for making me laugh by asking why I call it a 4Day when you don't see me for 6 days. As much as I love the 4Day, coming home to you is its' best part.

To my family and friends, for the love and happiness you bring.

To my fellow 4Dayers for the love, camaraderie, and sharing their memories of the trips over the years. There is nothing quite like the re-creation of past 4Day moments by a dozen guys standing on the shoreline, laughing, shouting, and piecing together adventures from long-ago to those of just last night.

To Northland Outfitters for being there from the beginning of it all, and still here today, even as we outlast one set of owners after another. Thank you Tom (R.I.P.) & Carma, Tom & Sally, and Leon & Donna.

To Betsy McCormick and Andy Stachnick, for extending a sincere welcome to us at your bars each and every 4Day. We look forward to hugging you again on the Other Side.

To Carol Watson and Karen. You always made us feel like the Jolly Bar was our home.

To the Good Lord for the Creation with which You have surrounded us, and the 4Day brothers – and a couple of 4Day sisters – with which You have blessed us. Frequently, the 4Day experience feels like a glimpse of heaven.

To distilleries of really bad whiskey for always surprising us with new lows.

To Detroit Tiger pitcher Frank Lary, the Yankee Killer, for being 13 & 1 against the Yankees Suck in 1958 & 1959 combined. Meeting you in 2007 was a huge honor, and the "Yankees Suck" baseball cap you signed that day makes me smile every time I look at it, which is often.

To Jonesey for the fabulous drawings in this book - nobody does it better - and for the line, "It was a dark and snory night."

To Herr Colonel for the fine front cover mosaic & poster art creations.

To Susan Bays, my publisher at Arbutus Press, for indirectly saving this title for the 4Day book. *A Liver Runs Through It* was to be the title of my first book, but Susan changed it to *Weekend Canoeing in Michigan* "because we can't just appeal to drunks". I told Susan that I don't think she fully understands the size of that demographic.

## PLAUSIBLE DENIABILITY OR DENIABLE PLAUSIBILITY

The 4Dayers listed in this book are real, unless they are not.
The stories told in this book may be fictional or non-fictional.

*"… then there would be a time of riotous living with most of the community drunk and wandering about in an aimless daze until the purchased rum was gone. After that, the residents sat moodily in the sun and waited for something to happen."*
from "Wind From the Carolinas" by Robert Wilder

# Northland Outfitters

## Wilderness Canoeing & Camping

M-77, P.O. Box 65
Germfask, MI 49836
906-586-9801

## Manistique River

Northern Pike & Walleye Fishing

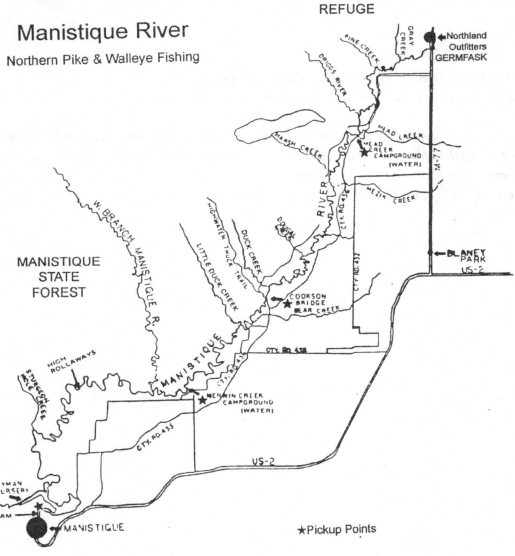

SENEY
NATIONAL
WILDLIFE
REFUGE

★Pickup Points

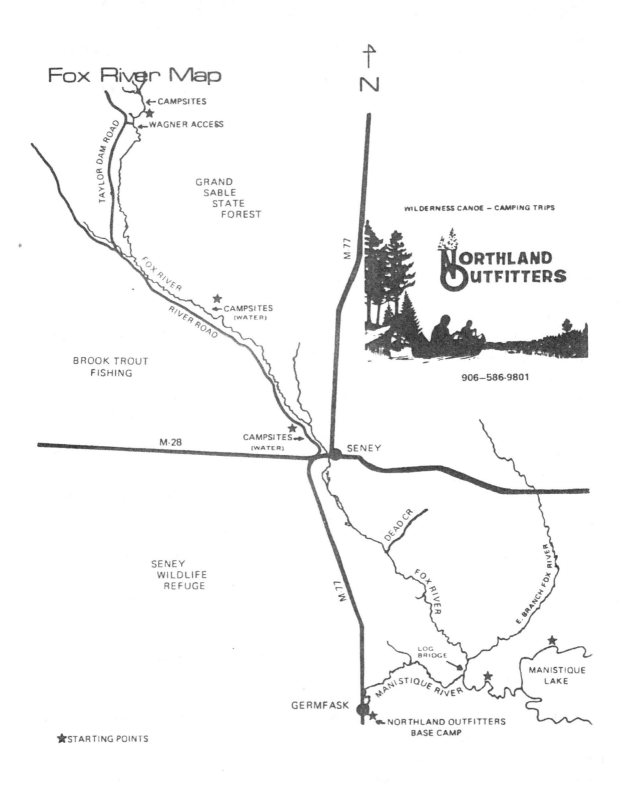

# Fox River Map

← CAMPSITES

★ ← WAGNER ACCESS

TAYLOR DAM ROAD

GRAND
SABLE
STATE
FOREST

↑ N

FOX RIVER

RIVER ROAD

★ ← CAMPSITES
(WATER)

BROOK TROUT
FISHING

M-77

WILDERNESS CANOE — CAMPING TRIPS

# Northland Outfitters

906–586–9801

M-28

CAMPSITES ←
(WATER) ★

● SENEY

SENEY
WILDLIFE
REFUGE

DEAD CR.

FOX RIVER

E. BRANCH FOX RIVER

M-77

LOG
BRIDGE

★

★

MANISTIQUE
LAKE

MANISTIQUE RIVER

GERMFASK ●

★ NORTHLAND OUTFITTERS
BASE CAMP

★ STARTING POINTS

# A Liver Runs Through It:
## The Bourbon-Soaked History of the 4Day Paddling thru an Endless Stream of Stories

Gather round rookies, there's a few things you need to know about the 4Day...

*The road to the 4Day runs through a Friday night in the U.P. town of Curtis and bellies up to the bar at Betsy's Mc's Tally Ho.*

The 4Day is the great annual summer getaway, where men travel to the Upper Peninsula, act like boys, paddle down and take long breaks on gorgeous Northern Michigan Rivers, smoke cigars, drink beer and cheap bourbon, tell and retell stories, laugh at each other's jokes, sing songs, reacquaint ourselves with the U.P. and our friends there, and have an aura of warmth come over them as they cross north over the Mackinac Bridge.

The 4Day is an attitude, an escape, a dream, a longing. It is a celebration of the Upper Peninsula, the spirit of John Voelker, the spirit of Betsy McCormick, the spirit of Andy Stachnik, the spirits of friends who've gone before us, and of friends in the river with us now.

The 4Day is a place of transformation...

Paul becomes a Colonel, Gary becomes a Moth, Pat becomes a Gomez, Frey becomes a madman, Doc becomes a Pop as in "What are we gonna do about Pop?", and northern invaders from Jacksonville, Florida become the Four Horsemen.

The 4Day is table top shuffle board at Mc's Tally Ho, the Keyhole Lounge and, on one 1984 night, in a dive bar in Watersmeet. It's sipping a fifth of bourbon that cost $9.99 or less while on the river, and downing shots of Dickel as we're swapping stores with Andy at his Seney Bar. The 4Day is harmonizing to "Men" while taking a river break during a rainstorm, or "Dang Me" & "Chug-a-Lug" during a night in Betsy's bar, or singing *"The... Old... Log... Bridge"* with gusto as we stand on that same bridge, or in later years its replacement, the new steel bridge.

The 4Day is steering through the rushing Fox River current, squeezing through openings narrowed by Tag Alder bushes leaning in from each shore, brushing against both of your arms. It's shouting "River Dick!" to warn following boats of fallen trees/branches/debris dangerously lurking ahead of them, just below or above the water's surface.

The 4Day is passing fifths at Russell's Corner, it's a rot gut liquor called "P.M." in the A.M., it's chasing $2.99 a fifth Mister Ed bourbon with Jungle Juice, it's finding your dry shoes the next morning buried in the mud or river shoes the next evening at Andy's Seney Bar.

The 4Day is life in the woods, setting up camp, Craigo's ribs – the best we've ever had, Northern Lights above us on the Seney Township Campground island, and buzz euchre on the Peninsula, while dinner cooks and we get fried.

The 4Day is the drive north, stopping on the way to meet friends at the US23 and M59 truck plaza, braking for Blatz at the Nottingham or for Frisbee throws at rest areas or for a round of golf, and a night at Betsy's tavern.

The 4Day is excitement and anticipation, the exchange of phone calls, later emails, and even later texts among the brothers, and staging gear & provisions as the upcoming one draws near. And it's counting down the days to the next 4Day as soon as the current one comes to an end.

This book aims to tell the story of the 4Day, as best our bourbon-soaked brains can recall. It is dedicated to dear friends who've been part of the 4Day experience with us and who have left us for the Other Side: BJay, Goobs, Wayne-O, Marquis, Chucky, Tony Barney, Gillam, Geno, livery owner "Old" Tom, and barkeeps Betsy & Andy. We love them all, God bless 'em.


SHOTS!!!
River Dick Doc

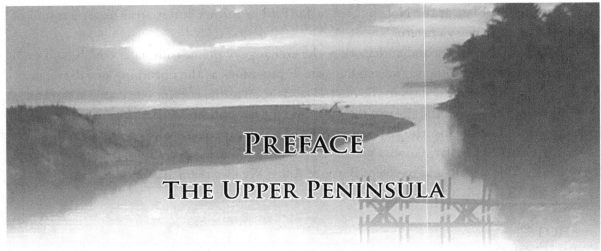

# PREFACE
# THE UPPER PENINSULA

**"Michigan Lost Toledo but Won Paradise"**

*Saturday Night, in Toledo, Ohio is like being nowhere at all*
*They have entertainment to dazzle your eyes*
*You can sit in the bakery and watch the buns rise*
*(Saturday Night in Toledo Ohio by Randy Sparks)*

In 1835, the Territory of Michigan and the State of Ohio engaged in an almost bloodless (one casualty) war over Toledo. When the primarily-political war was over and Ohio had won, Michigan was surprised to find out that Ohio's main war demand was to *obtain* Toledo. It was assumed by all in Michigan that the fight was to see who would get *stuck* with Toledo. When this demand was made of the Michigan delegation during the peace assembly, the Michigan folks asked for and were granted an overnight recess. They could barely contain their astonishment...

*"Did I hear them correctly – they* <u>want</u> *Toledo?!" "Can that be?" "Is this a clever ruse to confuse us?" "I don't think it is." "How should we proceed in tomorrow's negotiations?" "Let's play the contrite, defeated souls, and allow them to carry the conversation. God knows what else will come out of their silly Ohio mouths."*

When the talks between the delegations resumed, Ohio smugly informed Michigan, "And we want you to take the Upper Peninsula off of our hands. It is a wilderness of waterfalls, rivers, lakes, and forests. We cannot be bothered with it." Several Michigan representatives soon had blood trickle down their chins from biting hard on their lips to stop from exploding in laughter.

The Toledo War peace settlement, with Ohio giving their Upper Peninsula land to Michigan in exchange for the disputed Toledo territory, is considered the most lopsided trade between the 2 neighbors (even *before* the U.P. discovery of billions of tons of copper and iron ore), barely edging out the 1960 trade that sent from the Detroit Tigers Steve (not even Don) Demeter to the Cleveland Indians for Norm Cash.

*Author's note:* Steve played in 4 games for Cleveland in 1960, batting 5 times, getting no hits, and retired from the game in May of 1960. Norm, who immediately became the Tigers everyday first baseman, a position he held for 15 years, was the only American Leaguer with over 20 homers every year from 1961-1969, and retired with 373 homers in a Tigers uniform, at that time second to only Al Kaline. Oh yeah, and in 1961 Norm hit .361 with 41 home runs and 132 runs batted in. It's worth repeating that Steve (not even Don) Demeter retired in May of 1960, barely a month after being obtained by Cleveland.

The Upper Peninsula contains 30% of the state's land mass, only 3% of the state's population, and an incalculable piece of its bliss. The U.P.'s long winters retard the over-development that plagues some sections of the Lower Peninsula, and its uncluttered scenery grants a peaceful, warm-your-soul escape. A reawakening of the heart grabs those on the way to the 4Day with the first glimpse of, while still in the Lower Peninsula and 5 miles to its south, the Mackinac Bridge.

That feeling envelopes you while crossing above the Straits on the Mackinac Bridge, every foot driven north on the lovingly-known "Big Mac" a promise realized of the nirvana that is the Upper Peninsula – *Vista del Norte*: wide open spaces, flowing rivers, thick forests, surrounding lakes, Pictured Rocks, Tahquamenon Falls, and damn - no traffic jam!

Go west young man, go west, on US2 out of St. Ignace, as the road pulls wonderfully near and parallel to the northern edge of the Lake Michigan shoreline, sun glistening off of the Big Lake's waters. As far as the eye can see, the pavement meanders beautifully, just like the flow of the Fox River hugs the next bend, while beach sand dances on the highway's edges, your sun glasses perched above a big ole grin.

The delightful drive ends only when the 4Day-eve bar, either a mortar 'n brick pub or a virtual saloon with the boys huddled around the campground bonfire, is reached. 4Day Tales of Yore and bottles of nasty bourbon are passed among the fellers with relish, as the anticipation builds to make more memories in the morning, the morning of "the first day, the first day, the first day of the 4Day!"

Sharing deep thoughts one 4Day eve night at Mc's Tally Ho Bar in Curtis was brother Gomie: *"The 4Day means a lot to me. I love the outdoors... the U.P. is a very sparse and unpopulated area. I'm not uncomfortable with drinking, that's to be said, and it helps that the people that come up here is a very easy group to share the wilderness and have a good time with. The 4Day is a great place to be, with good people".*

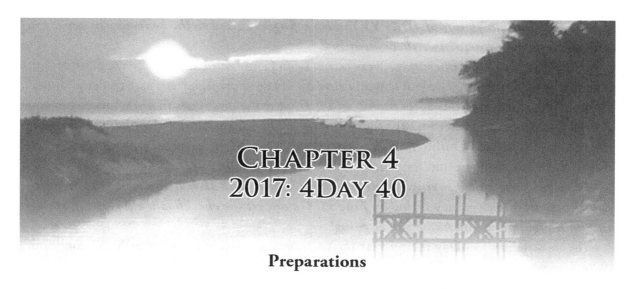

# CHAPTER 4
# 2017: 4DAY 40

### Preparations

*Michigan seems like a dream to me now*
*It took me four days to hitchhike from Saginaw*
*I've gone to look for America*
*(America by Simon & Garfunkel)*

**In 1716, Antoine de la Mothe Cadillac gave his views of the men of the Upper Peninsula...**

**"A certain proof of the excellence of the climate is to see the old men there, whose grandsons are growing grey. It would seem as if death had no power to carry off these spectors. They have good hearing and good sight, but their memory often plays them tricks. They tell tales and recount events which they maintain happened at the time, which is not credible, but they have this advantage that there is no one who can contradict them or call them liars except by inference."**

**300 years later, 4Day brother Captain Johnny shared his view on paddling the Upper Peninsula, "If it doesn't have beer on it, it's not a real boat."**

The 4Day is a continuous trip, not a destination. The trip is the sum of the people participating. Spending 4 days on the waters of Northern Michigan, camping in the woods, sharing stories during river breaks and around the evening's bonfire, with brothers who have the bond of this shared adventure, forms an irresistible lure drawing back each 4Dayer year after year.

With 100 days to go 'til 4Day 40, Mad Dog Chris sums up the timeless 4Day allure...

***A Lake Superior sunset followed by a Lake Superior sunrise, both can be seen in the reflection of the Heart.***

***Tested rookies become seasoned veterans become wisened elders all become brothers.***

***A young Crow drinking Old Crow is chased by a Mad Dog.***

***Each beach holds the treasures of camaraderie and nature's gifts.***

***The chill of the river and the warmth of the fire are equally refreshing for the soul.***

***Our kindred spirits who have passed too soon make their glorious presence felt.***

***Every morsel of food is a gourmet buffet because "chow time is important".***

*The harmonious shouts of 4DAYYYY, with 4 fingers raised to the heavens are never too loud or too few and never lose their meaning.*

In the Northland Outfitters' van, livery owner Leon Genre drove us to that day's put-in point. Listening to our excited discussions about next year's 4Day 40 plans, he tells us, "You guys should plan to stay at my campgrounds for the 40th." "Leon, we're the same guys that you kicked out and banned from your campsites in 2012 for being too loud." "Yeah, I know that, but I'd like your 40th to be at Northland Outfitters." "But how about your other customers camping there?" "I'll reserve the whole campground for you."

*I can hear the voices saying, "Hell yes, there is NO WAY that I won't be 4Dayin' with y'all this year!" Your money is due by June 1st. Go on, git the checkbook, envelope & stamp and do it right now! You know you're going!*

The most fellers to 4Day in any year up 'til now was the famous 23 men & 37 coolers of 1996. This year, very appropriately, 40 brothers will participate in 4Day 40. The U.P. will be well-protected, as our group includes 3 Marines (Jimmy, Rookie Spencer, Mailman), 1 representative each from the Army (Chumley), Air Force (Rookie David), Navy (Mad Dog Chris), & Coast Guard (Rookie Terry), as well as one unaffiliated Colonel. The Upper Peninsula can fend off any attack this July.

*"Jimmy bought the liquor, I bought the cups and ice" from Great Rain by John Prine*

The boys sign up for a meal to create and serve, part of a 4 or 5-man cook crew for either a group breakfast or a dinner, as well as camp gear (shelters, tents, stoves, etc.) they can contribute. Flights are booked & long drives mapped out. Guys from Florida, (the state of) Washington, North Carolina, and Utah will arrive in Michigan the evening before the Great Drive North commences.

*"Because I suspect that men are going along this way for the last time, and I for one don't want to waste the trip;*

*Because only in the woods can I find solitude without loneliness;*

*Because bourbon out of an old tin cup always tastes better out there." John Voelker*

The 4Day journey starts in the 70s with 4 (there's that number again) restless 23 year-olds looking for an adventure get away Up North. From a hint of civilization the first night on the river, boats launch the next morning into the wilderness for 3 days without a cell phone (gasp!) or any way to restock supplies, contact fellow human beings, or find out if the Detroit Tigers won last night. With no past experience to guide us, two canoes loaded with tents and minimal provisions traverse through the Great Michigan Forest, the voyage occasionally allowing a glimpse of wide, riverside sandy beaches that reveal themselves as the two boats round yet another bend, each shared back-country moment strengthening the brotherhood bond.

**Boys, we are paddling through God's cathedral.**

The single 1970's U.P. trip became a 4-decade long journey. From the Beginning…

# CHAPTER 4

## In the beginning

It was a dark and snory night…

# CHAPTER 4
# 1978: 4DAY 1

### Manistique River w/ Ricki, Goober, Stover and Doc

*If the real thing don't do the trick,*
*You better make up something quick*
*You gonna burn, burn, burn, burn, burn to the wick*
*Oooo, Barra-Barracuda, yeah*
*(Barracuda by Heart)*

With Heart turned up loud, the ringing phone was barely audible. The pounding beat of the Wilson Sisters music was no match for the persistent ring wielded by James Richard "Ricki" Rice, a brother for just shy of 5 years. Ricki, one of many newly-minted brothers and sisters from the Eastern Michigan University campus in Ypsi (no college student or townie called Ypsilanti MI by its full name), and I were sophomores upon meeting in 1973 at our temporary home on the 3rd floor of the Phelps-Sellers dormitory. It soon became apparent that Ricki was a man of wisdom and vision.

Back then, with a newly-acquired skill at the wildly-popular card game of euchre, I could seldom pass by his dorm room on the way to class without hearing Ricki's siren call of "we need a 4th for euchre – interested?" That and the cold beer proffered in my direction got me to thinking that fat, drunk, and stupid might be an underrated career path.

Fast forward to June of 1978, 2 years post-graduation. Little had changed since college days: with Ricki calling, I figured a fun adventure was brewing. I figured right. "Doc, you want to go to the Upper Peninsula and canoe, drink and party for 4 days in July?"

Since we spent much time with our brothers and sisters of ETT (a fraternity-sorority in our hearts and in whatever space we gather) drinking and partying, and since Ricki knew that I'd recently fallen hard for canoeing, I figured his question was asked as kind of a courtesy, in line with Ricki's North Carolina/Old South upbringing.

Having awakened a love of canoeing 2 months earlier on the Pere Marquette River, I was motivated to organize a group trip to meander along the Pine River just one month later. The river junkie was born, hook, line, and paddle. *I just dropped in to see what condition the river was in. Yeah. Yeah. Oh yeah.* These two floats in the northwest quadrant of Michigan's Lower Peninsula were weekend trips, wonderful 2-day experiences, and the idea of paddlin' and partyin' for *4 days* sounded like a great idea, cementing Ricki's reputation for good thinkin'.

By 1978, I was fully employed by Duracell, my benevolent corporate employer circa 1976-2006. Q: How to make time for this upcoming U.P. adventure? A: By getting ahead of my workload. Over the next 2 weeks, sleep was minimized, the pedal put to the metal for all things Duracell, pushin' deep into the night. Stamina is not much of a problem when one is 23. ETT brothers Dave Guba, lovingly referred to as Goober aka the Goobs, and John Stover signed on after hearing the 4 day trip pitched, accepting in less time than it took Bluto Blutarsky to chug a fifth of Jack on the Delta's front lawn. The fact that both the first 4Day and the movie *Animal House* debuted in the same year of 1978 is a case of outstanding symmetry.

the original 4Day fellers: Doc, Goobs, Ricki, Stover

Goobs is a dear friend and fellow alum of Bedford High School, home of the Kicking Mules. Rare is the man loved as much as Goobs, the very definition of the phrase salt-of-the-earth. Humble, quiet, and immediately likeable with a laugh that made anyone within earshot of that laugh happy. *Milwaukee's Best* or *Red, White and Blue* are his beers because they are the cheapest — it just makes good sense. Goobs' river essentials are kept in his metal "Yabo box", kind of a pin-up girl in name only. When Goober has the right amount of beer and/or bourbon in him, his baseball cap will be slightly askew, like a mailbox flag turned up, alerting all that spirits were high.

Johnny Stover completed his tour of duty in the Marine Corps just in time to paddle. From his station in Okinawa, we would receive Richard Nixon postcards, often sent from a brothel, telling of rooms too dark see the woman or find his wallet. A fellow EMU Huron, Johnny was the only guy we knew with quadraphonic sound in his dormitory room. Dr. Sheldon Cooper would've approved of the placement of Stover's bean bag chair as the perfect album listening post. Many buzzed nights were spent taking turns reclined in that bean bag chair listening to the swirling electronics in Edgar Winter's *Frankenstein*.

A look at Johnny's dorm day's checkbook would've shown the same daily entry, line after line, page after page: "$5 Domino's Pizza". Stover is a bit of a pirate. Think D-Day from Animal House. As the viewer is told what is in store beyond the flick's conclusion for each Delta frat brother, for D-Day are only two words: "whereabouts unknown". In Johnny's case, he joined us for only one 4Day. The fact that his only 4Day was also the first, and that he lives a somewhat incommunicado life on his sailboat, paints him in an aura of mystery.

Organizing a 4Day was never easier than in year one, mostly because we had no real idea of what was needed. After two weeks of brainstorming, from states stone sober to altered, we realized nightly shelter would improve the off-river experience, you know, Justin case...

*This here is Jed Clampett. Are you the weatherman?*
*I am the supervisor of meteorological observations for this area.*
*Oh well, I was wantin' the weatherman.*
*You're speaking to him. I am Justin Addison.*
*Well shucks, don't feel bad about that, I'm just a Clampett.*

Since none among us had a tent, we leaned on resources from good ole' EMU in the form of Bob England, the head of Eastern Michigan's intramural office. As the signer upper of numerous intramural teams from freshman through senior years, I had much cordial contact with Bob over the years, and he was willing to overlook the fact we were no longer EMU students, a usual requirement to rent a university-owned tent. One tent for four guys, all young and skinny. No problem.

Our 4Day destination: Germfask, a tiny U.P. village harboring the Manistique River and, as we later discovered, the Fox, a designated wild & scenic river. To begin the journey, Goobs drove north from Lambertville, Michigan, a small town bordering Toledo, Ohio, for 50 minutes to Ypsi. There, the 4 of us piled into Stover's van for the 6 and one-half hour drive north. The journey began at 9PM. 9PM is later today than it was in 1978.

Several pre-trip malted-barley, hops, yeast, and THC-enhanced brainstorming sessions somehow convinced us that a visit to the Flint Kmart, a destination that upon reflection has always seemed strange, on the way north would be the ideal stop to supply us with needed supplies. Purchased provisions comprised a few camping and river supplies including cheap champagne, beer, beer, beer, and vodka. Cold cuts and bread rounded out the drink & food purchases. We were men of simple needs. "Pop that cork and let's head out, boys".

4AM found us on the Mackinac Bridge, the fantastic 5-mile long engineering feat that spans Michigan's Lower and Upper Peninsulas. Our heighten senses were entranced by the towers soaring above the bridge at its half-way point. Stover pulled over, parked his van in the northbound right lane, and we all got out to gaze up at these behemoths. Under dreaming spires, to Itchycoo Park, that's where we've been. While standing in the middle of the Big Mac in the pre-dawn darkness, a state police car pulls up next to us. "Boys, what are you doing?" Nodding at the officer, we point upward. "We're just staring up at this tower." "Ok, have a good night". How can you not love the 70s?

Dreamily crossing the Big Mac, Stover then drove the boys west on US2 for an hour, made a right on M77 and continued 15 miles north until arriving 530AM in Germfask. Too early for canoe livery Northland Outfitters to be open, we grabbed breakfast at an old restaurant, shuttered since 1979 4Day 2, on the SE corner of M77 and Ten Curves Road.

The Northland Outfitters livery, owned by Tom and Carma Gronback, has an office the size of a large closet, sporting a table, a chair, and a money lock box. Bug spray and rain ponchos are the lone items to purchase.

"Do you think we need additional bug juice?" the young 4Day pledge class asks. Chuckling, livery co-owner Tom passed on this opportunity to sell us more Deet, assuring us that with the monsoon-like down pour anticipated, no mosquitoes would likely survive in the open. Whew, that's a relief.

We abdicate the paddle mapping, being first timers on the Manistique, to livery man Tom. While respecting livery owners for numerous reasons (attention to safety, river knowledge, doing the heavy lifting to keep the rivers clear of debris, etc.), we did learn an important lesson this first 4Day. While Tom had us ending day 1 at his livery, making for easy camping, his mapping also had us canoeing across Manistique Lake to get to the beginning of Manistique River. Mental note #1: do NOT begin future Manistique River trips by paddling for what seemed like forever on the lake *without a current at our backs* while heading to the river outlet.

Day 1 features the forecasted torrential rains. A badly needed paddling break is made, seeking shelter beneath a bridge, and a deck of cards produced for a round of euchre while we dry out. Play takes place by pulling the two canoes together, legs straddling the canoes, feet dug into the river's sandy bottom to keep our euchre "table" stationary.

After 30 minutes of euchre, beer, and the last of the 22 smokes rolled for the trip (naively thought sufficient to last for the *entire* trip but finished early on day 1), Goobs exuberant play sent one of the cards into the river. Euchre sucks with 23 cards. Mental note #2: bring a second euchre deck on subsequent 4Days.

Drying out in any form proves impossible, and as the rains grow heavier, we dig in, seemingly paddling hard enough to pull skiers behind the canoes, determined paddling never again to be witnessed on a 4Day. Rising to a chant, the curse uttered around each bend is "Where is that <u>damn</u> livery?" Finally, there it is on our right. No tent set-up this night, as the thoroughly soaked victims pull the boats ashore & without breaking stride dive into the arid heaven that is Stover's van. A dry euchre deck is found, sandwiches chowed down, beers guzzled, doobs rolled for tonight and the next 3 days, and stories told until all pass out.

The monsoon of the first day gave way to sunny skies for the rest of the floating party. The Manistique River shoreline yielded sandy beaches as yet unmatched in 4Day lore for size of each and total number, as if large sections of the Lake Michigan beach had been barged in and scattered about for our visual delight. The sandy shores provided enticing paddling break opportunities and at day's end camping spots, where huge bonfires pierced the black evenings.

Jugs of vodka and O.J. on the 2nd night of river camping heralded a 4Day tradition of at least one man per trip *re-living the magic* aka bringing up lunch. Appropriately, the man who organized the first 4Day was also the man who kicked-off the ritual, as Ricki heaved with vigor on the third morning. I see you enjoy pulp with your orange juice, sir.

4Day One covered 50 lake 'n river miles, putting more mileage on our canoes than in any

4Day since, and it's not even close. Not only did we start by paddling across Manistique Lake for the first and last time, upstream from the usual Ten Curves Road launch, but this was also our only Manistique River trip that ended downstream from the Cookson Bridge access. From Cookson Bridge to the take-out at Merwin Creek is 4 hours. In another 8 hours, the boats would've touched the waters of Lake Michigan.

After partyin' hard on day four (and one, two, and three), we reached the end of the first 4Day at the Merwin Creek access, moved our gear from the canoes into Stover's waiting van, stopped at the first pay phone to alert the livery that their canoes were in, and drove home that night. The energy of youth is fascinating to ponder in life's rear view mirror.

On the road home, framed with an incredible sunset to the west to fit the buoyant mood, one story after another is thrown around the van, using the remaining brain cells of the 4 brothers to re-create the unique experience. It was hours of back-and-forth chatter and non-stop laughter. When it finally got quiet for a minute, a sad thought hit me, "Ricki, this 4Day idea was genius, equal to the concept of twi-night double headers at Tiger Stadium. You may never come up with a better idea". Ricki thought about it for a few seconds, and then suggested, "Well, why don't we do this again next year?" "Ricki, I stand corrected."

# CHAPTER 4
# 1979: 4DAY 2

## Fox River w/ Ricki, Doc, rookies Chucky & Big Guy

*There was beer all over the dance floor*
*and the band was playin' rhythm and blues*
*You got down and did the gator, and half*
*an hour later, you were barfin' all over your Girlfriend's shoes*
*(The Greeks Don't Want No Freaks by the Eagles)*

"Let's get another beer — we can chug it down and <u>still</u> make the first pitch!" Chucky was on a roll and the boys were being happily mesmerizing by his hyper chatter. Downtown Detroit's Greektown had become our go-to grub 'n grog pre-game stop before an evening of fun at Tiger Stadium (Hoot Robinson's post-game, of course), and Foster Lager beer in 25 oz. oil cans had been drawing us to the Golden Fleece Restaurant like a moth to a bonfire.

"This is crazy. I've never dated a girl with multiple personalities." Chucky's stories made us almost forget about the Detroit Tiger game that awaited. "She asked me if I wanted to see soft-spoken Sue or Judy, the girl who likes to give head." I said, "C'MON JUDY!"

This created an explosion of laughter that had Ricki and Doc doubled over and Big Guy's beer a geyser shooting thru his nostrils. Ricki motioned for the waiter, "Sir, we're gonna need a mop over here".

Chucky was fired up, "We gotta take some Foster Lagers with us on the 4Day!" Ignoring the rough mumbling under the breath of the young Greek called upon to clean up Big Guy's regurgitated beer, we unanimously thought that a fine idea. Having Foster Lager oil cans in our coolers was suddenly an indispensable part of 4Day 2, one that seemed so obvious.

On the menu for Ricki, Chucky, Big Guy aka Biggie, and Doc this evening was making plans for the second annual 4Day, in the hopes of having one-half as much fun in '79 as the July 1978 experience. Young 'n eager, we weren't quite sure if we could wait a whole year between the first and second 4Day.

"I hate having to wait until July to get to the U.P." Big Guy's restlessness was finding its' voice, "I have nothing going on between now and then, except waiting… and checking the sports page each day for Yankees' updates". Ricki shot a look at Big Guy, "Big Guy?" "Yeah?" "THE

YANKEES SUCK!" The stunned look on Biggie's face had Chucky shaking his head, "Big Guy, you didn't see that one coming?" (Biggie's blind spot to the group's Yankees-Suck attitude would reach its apex on the 25th 4Day).

The growing impatience to get to the U.P. was unanimous, and living in a moment 30 years before the advent of Smart Phone Calendars would not inhibit finding an early departure solution. The calendar in my head was eliminating the quandary with each flipping page. "Ok, Biggie's date book is wide open" I began, then addressed the educator among them, "Chucky, when do your classes wrap up?" "Not until late-June, but I have some vacation time to burn – what are you thinking?" "Well, how about if we leave the Thursday after Memorial Day and…"

"We're IN!!!" was the shouted chorus that made finishing the statement unnecessary.

4Day rookies Chucky and Big Guy had been hearing continuous telling and re-telling of the stories from the inaugural, and were chompin' at the bit to get up to the U.P. Their bit could be spit very soon. With an early 4Day getaway date set, the mood in Greektown became joyous. Ricki had to interrupt the jocularity and remind us of why we were in the Golden Fleece in the first place, "Boys, chug those Foster Lagers 'cause it's time for *Tiger baseball!*" Our dear Bird was on the mound tonight. Maybe Fidrych was finally healthy again and would be the Bird of 1976. If that happens, new manager Les Moss just might lead the Tigers to the pennant in his first year, and have a long, successful run here in Detroit.

"Big Two Hearted River" was Ernest Hemingway's 1924 classic, delightfully stranded on the figurative Upper Peninsula sandbar, written in-part about the Fox River while borrowing the name of another sweet U.P. stream for the book title. Maybe it was the opportunity to paddle down this river that Hemingway spent so much of his youth camping 'n fishing at, or maybe it was just the dreaded thought about repeating the 1st 4Day paddle across Manistique Lake, but whatever the motivation, rather than repeat the 4Day One Manistique River trip, I suggested that we make the 2nd 4Day river the Fox, and presented my case to the boys…

| | |
|---|---|
| "The Fox is a more challenging stream than the Manistique" | *Uh-huh* |
| "It's much more narrow than the Manistique" | *Yep* |
| "… and faster with tight turns" | *Okay* |
| "and…" | *Ah, Doc?* |
| "Yes?" | *Will we be in the U.P.?* |
| "Yes" | *For 4 days?* |
| "Yes" | *with beer and doobage?* |
| "Yes" | *You sold us – let's go!* |

Departing Ypsilanti in the gloomy, damp twilight, we four crossed the Mackinac Bridge at 3AM, entering the rain-soaked village of Germfask before dawn broke. We parked next to the darkened restaurant, waiting patiently for the structure to come to life, while occasional snores cut the patter of rain drops on the car roof. Finally, the lights flicked on, the door opened, and the eating began. As best we could calculate, factoring in our post-dining trips to the dumper, it seemed a net loss for the establishment owner, once the cost for the roto rooter man was deducted from our breakfast bill.

Bellies full 'n loads lightened, we drove a few hundred feet north on M77 from restaurant to the Northland Outfitters' livery. "You boys brought the rain again this year, did ya?" wasn't the greeting that we dreamt of from N.O. owners Tom and Carma, but it beat the hell out of a day working for the man. While Ricki flirted with Carma, Rookie Big Guy tested out his fishing gear, I reviewed the Fox River map with Tom, and Rookie Chucky was his usual self, adding color to the soaking gray with stories that had us all in a fine mood, the hell with the weather…

*"Marquis and I were going down I94, Marquis driving, while I was vomiting out the passenger side window. Just about the time I was thinking, it can't get any worse than this, I felt a thud on my left shoulder – Marquis had passed out while driving".* It was a well-known fact among our group of friends that Marquis, suffering from our laymen diagnosis of "Marc-o-lepsy", could fall asleep under any circumstances. Fortunately, Marquis snapped to quickly when the vomit-stained Chucky barked at him, and safely (?) returned to driving.

Later, it would prove to be ironic that Chucky was entertaining us with a vomit tale.

Tom suggested and we agreed to launching at the Fox River Campground, 4 paddling hours upstream from Seney. Chucky and I decided to paddle together on day one. Funny how a small decision like this can have a big effect on your day.

5 minutes into the first day of 4Day 2, we paddled around a bend and came upon a fallen pine tree that completely blocked the Fox from shore to shore. Our options were (1) paddle through the branches of the tree and hope for the best or (2) pull the canoe out of the river and portage around the tree.

Chucky and I were the lead boat, about 50' beyond Ricki and Biggie, and we made a snap decision to plunge right through the tree. With heads down and eyes closed, Pine needles were snapping machine-gun style all around us. An amazing amount of carnage occurred in the 5 or 6 seconds it took to emerge on the downstream side of the tree… both of us were covered in yellow pollen, Chucky lost the only pair of glasses that he'd brought with him – no glasses the last 99% of the trip for a man near blind without them – and somehow one river shoe got sucked off of my foot and lost to the Fox.

*(Flash forward to the year 2016: Chucky has departed this earthly plane, and I'm working at my desk on this book. As I'm writing the previous paragraph, I wasn't 100% sure in my mind if it was my foot or Chucky's foot that the river shoe was sucked off of — so I sought Chucky's help from the Other Side & spoke aloud, "Chucky, I don't know how involved you want to get in writing this book, but… if it was my shoe that was pulled off, would you turn my desk light off and back on?" Immediately I heard a clicking sound, and my desk light flicked off and back on. I could only smile and say "Thanks Chucky")*

Day one turns into night and gets even better. We camped at one of the DNR sites upstream from Seney Township Park. Two-fisted and glassy eyed, we entertained ourselves by seeing how many cans of Foster Lager (they were empty) that we could stack on Chucky's head (turns out its 3). I had salami sandwiches in the cooler for dinner. Guess I should've zip-locked 'em: after pulling the wet bread off the meat, I laid the pieces of salami on a tree branch to let 'em dry. Corn was part of the campfire dinner, worth mentioning because of how the night progressed.

As on 4Day One, the only tent for the four of us was an EMU rental. When we turned in, a tent wall was on my right and Chucky was on my left, with all 4 of us pressed in pretty tight, shoulder-to-shoulder. After getting a few hours of sleep, the Fosters and Yukon Jack began to take its toll on Chucky. He woke us, or at least me, up with a gurgling sound. That gurgling sound was a promissory note that soon vomit would be following. Chucky couldn't or wouldn't leave the tent to spit up, but just laid there and threw up on himself and, worse yet, on me. In a little bit, there's that gurgling sound again and damned if Chucky again didn't move and, again, splash on himself and send a little my way. Gurgle, chuck, splash, repeat.

*Author's note:* the night gave birth to our version of the term "upchuck". When Chucky would begin to gurgle through his nose & mouth, my imploring cries of "Up, Chuck!" had no effect on our sauced brother.

After round two, I became adept at picking up the first telltale signs of imminent up-chucking. When the third gurgling came around, I quickly sat up, and in one fluid motion unzipped the tent with my right hand, grabbed Chucky by the nape of his neck with my left, and stuck his head out of the tent. This process worked well for each gurgling warning bell that went off the balance of the night.

When we woke up the next morning and unzipped the tent, there waiting on the ground just outside was the result of (1) Chucky's heavy-on-the-corn dinner and (2) me sticking his head outside of the tent for his last several barfs: a pyramid of corn, as if someone had opened a can of Niblets and emptied it on the ground. Morning has broken.

Chucky had thrown up so hard that he blew out all of the blood vessels in his eyes. His pupils were floating in a sea of bright red for the next 10 days or so. Since he was back teaching in 4 days, Chucky must have scared the hell out of the kids when they first saw him. Hopefully, the children saw the humor in it that his 4Day brothers saw.

Poor Chucky did get the shit kicked out of him on 4Day Two. Besides being covered by yellow pollen, losing his glasses right out of the chute, barfing all night and blowing out his blood vessels, besides all of that, there were the mosquitoes. The southern Italian blood coursing through Chucky's veins is very attractive to skeeters, which makes Chucky kind of a human Shell no-pest strip. The bonus of canoeing with Chucky (besides him being loveable, funny, and all) is that the bugs will have no interest in you 'cause they're too busy coming at Chucky in waves. We counted 18 bites on his back alone.

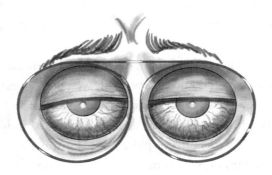

Despite Chucky's wild adventures, as we paddled our canoes alongside the ramp at Northland Outfitters and the 2nd 4Day came to an end, every one of us – including Chucky – said that this 4Day was fantastic (a trend is developing) and couldn't wait to get back to the U.P. for 4Day #3. Rookies Big Guy and Chucky posed with Ricki and me on the livery deck for what became the first 4Day "famous final scene". Of all of the smiles in that photo, the biggest by far was Chucky's.

# CHAPTER 4
# 1980: 4DAY 3

Fox River w/ Chucky, Ricki, Doc and rookies BJay, Matthew & Craigo

*When I die let my ashes float down the Green River*
*Let my soul roll on up to the Rochester dam*
*I'll be halfway to Heaven with Paradise waitin'*
*Just five miles away from wherever I am.*
*(Paradise by John Prine)*

*"Dooocccccccc!"* You couldn't see him, but you knew he had arrived. *"Dooocccccccccc!"*

From inside of my new abode on Nancy Street in Ypsi, Craigo's shouts as he strolled up the sidewalk were as invigorating to the boys gathered in the living room as they were annoying to my new neighbors. We'd be happy to see Craigo burst through the front door at any time, but especially today as the arrival of this 4Day rookie meant that all 6 of this year's 4Dayin' brothers were present, accounted for, and ready to roll north: veterans Ricki, Chucky, and Doc, accompanied by the rookies 3, BJay, Matthew, and Craigo.

Even before Craigo's appearance, the house was loud with anticipation and energy. Chucky, who had moved into the condo with me from our EMU-campus area apartments, had been teaching himself some new songs on the guitar. BJay and Matthew arrived a few minutes apart and, after loading their gear into my station wagon, BJay brought his guitar inside for a jam session with Chucky, strummin' some John Prine tunes.

Ricki soon pulled up to the curb, hopped out of the car and announced, "I thought I'd add something new to the 4Day this year, the Yukon Challenge!", sending a little 4Day tease our way, deciding to save the details 'til we got Up North.

Ricki and Yukon Jack, a nasty, sweet tasting, whisky liqueur, had become good friends. Upon waking each morning, Ricki would walk in the kitchen, pull a fifth of Yukon Jack out of his freezer, and take a healthy pull off of the bottle. The Ricki full-body-shake that immediately followed, left me years later with the suspicion that the creator of those giant dancing windsock guys had been present one morning in Ricki's kitchen.

The label tells you that the "100 proof whiskey and honey based liquor possesses a bold, yet unexpected smooth flavor". The *next* taste off this self-described "Black Sheep of Canadian Liquor family" that's smooth will be the *first*. If it's possible that an experience can be fun while at the same time leaving a bad taste in your mouth, the Yukon Challenge will surely be it. Wisely, we've packed a great deal of Stroh's to serve as chasers.

We 6 drove through the night to our goal of breakfast in Germfask. Last year's restaurant had become someone's house, not such an unusual event in the great northern wilderness, and a new good eats place had popped up across from the Jolly Motel. The sign in the window could've said bad eats without scaring us away, having crossed the Straits of Mackinac on the wings of an empty-stomach-and-munchies perfect storm.

The Fox River was a blast last year, so let's do it again, once more in late-May.

While driving a van full of 4Dayers, coolers, tents, and other gear to the Day 1 Fox River Overlook starting point, Northland Outfitters' Tom mentioned, "When you guys come up here next year, you should give some thought about canoeing around Isle Royale, out in Lake Superior. There's a series of lakes and bays that you paddle around and…"

*BJay, "No current at your back Tom?"*
*Tom, "No, but there's some great wildlife, so you want to bring plenty of film to…"*

*Matthew, "Is there a bar?"*
*Tom, "No, but the scenery is as good as at the Boundary Waters and…"*

*Chucky, "Are there any book stores on Isle Royale?"*
*Everybody, "What?!?"*

*Craigo, "How do we get to the Island?"*
*Tom, "I have a small puddle jumper that I can pilot you guys over in and..."*

Apparently, I'd stated my strong distaste for air travel sufficiently over the years so that the quiet laughter after Tom's first answer had built to a crescendo with the introduction of small aircraft into the equation. Tom figured out quickly what was going on, and when Ricki said, "Tom, we'll get back to you on this one", even Tom started laughing, adding, "Guess we'll stick with the rivers then".

Taking all of our gear on the river with us, the 4Day 3 plan was to paddle Day 1 from the Overlook to one of two DNR sites, both on elevated ground behind a wooden fence on the right bank, then Day 2 down to the Seney Township Campsite. Day 3 was to anyplace that looked good for camping, as there are no designated and/or maintained campgrounds between the Seney Township site and the final take out at the Northland Outfitters livery. On Day 4, we bring it on home through the merger with the Manistique. That merger takes place about a football field beyond an old wooden foot bridge, known to the boys through a little ditty we thought up as *"The... Old... Log... Bridge"*. After the bridge, it's on to the trip's end at the livery.

Years later, we would pre-stage our gear (when the logistics allowed) at the planned camp site downstream, driving there at the start of each day, to lighted the canoe load, eliminate the possibility of soggy sleeping bags AND to have the already-set up tents waiting for us after a long day on the river. But, that wisdom was yet to come.

Launching in a light mist, the first beer took place as skies darken, and by the time the first fifth of bourbon was polished off, the clouds emptied everything that they had and seemed to borrow additional rain water from an unknown source. The 2 DNR sites that we were to choose from for night one camping were barely visible through the deluge that engulfed the river. We briefly pulled over at the base of the 2nd DNR spot, but even if we were willing to pitch tents in a downpour, the slopes we had to negotiate with all of our gear was a slick mud patch. Onward gentlemen, and you fellers, too.

The torrential rain gradually eased and, as the Seney Township Campsite came into view, ceased for the day, allowing us to pull the boats ashore and pitch our tents (multiple tents make their first 4Day appearance) in fairly dry conditions.

The next morning, Ricki prepared breakfast for us, "Are you boys ready to take the Yukon Challenge?" We were hoping for eggs, but this should scramble us pretty good. "One fifth of Yukon has been in a cooler of dry ice, and another sitting out warm. You take a hit from each bottle, and then state your opinion of which of the two serving methods is best." The fact that there was 100% participation in the Yukon Challenge without anyone questioning the decision may be the best indication of the type of people who attend the 4Day.

The grimaces elicited from both sides of the issue made it clear that the winning Yukon serving method would be settled by a razor-thin margin. Dry ice or served warm made as much difference as sterilizing a needle for a lethal injection, and about as desirable. The best use of Yukon Jack turned out to be medical: Ricki successfully treated a cut on his hand by pouring Yukon on the wound, then set it aflame to cauterize it and stop the bleeding.

BJay was the one person willing to take Ricki's Yukon Challenge a 2nd time, just for fun.

The world makes happier rotations with off-beat individuals like BJay Wright inhabiting it. A few years back, BJay and Chucky entered a restaurant, setting their coats on chairs at a table before proceeding to the counter to place their orders. In the pocket of his coat, BJay had brought along his two 6" long baby alligators. While at the counter, they heard a lady scream, "Gators!" as tiny reptiles ran across the restaurant floor. BJay turned to Chucky and asked, "Do you think they're mine?"

With the Yukon Challenge (dry ice Yukon wins by a crystal) and breakfast behind us, we launch Day 2 on the Fox. Within 20 minutes, we've reached the M28 Bridge. Oh, we have another good idea: let's pull over about 100' past the bridge, fill up empty cans of Stroh's with river water, and hurl 'em back towards the bridge (thrown upstream to ease empties retrieval). The one who throws the closest to the bridge wins our admiration. We'll call it the *1st Annual Stroh's Throw*. One of Craigo's throws lands <u>on</u> M28. We hadn't expected one to travel that far. Fortunately there's no vehicle driving where it landed. This Stroh's Throw is tricky business.

The Fox River Spreads... has there ever been a more wonderful stretch of any river? Beginning 45 minutes from the Seney Township access, the Spreads begin as the Fox splits in two... and then splits in two again... and then again. Within 30 minutes, all of these river fingers reconnect as one. It's a *blast* (a truly fine word that merges Blatz w/ Pabst) to paddle through. While traversing the spreads, the river narrows to the point where you can reach out right and left and touch both banks simultaneously. The more the stream tapers, the more it accelerates as you fly through rushing S-curves.

The sun pops out, we're loving the Spreads' experience, and then the shouting begins, "Hey, what do we do now?" Soon there is a flurry of voices trying to identify what the problem is, a complicated chore since it could be coming from anyone of several river splits. Even if the voice is coming from the same river split that your canoe is on, unless you're standing up in your canoe, all you can see in the winding, narrow stream is the 3' tall reeds within inches of both sides of the boat.

The shout, "We ran out of water!" echoes across the Spreads. What? Ran out water? "Chucky" I said, "Matthew and Craigo are canoeing together, and it didn't sound like either of them", then Chucky spun around from the bow, "No, that's BJay and Ricki!"

1980 was the year that something happened to us in the Spreads that never happened before or since: a canoe took a fork that ran out of water. At one of the Spreads' river splits, Ricki and BJay took a left fork that narrowed more 'n more 'n more 'til there was no water left. I stood up in the canoe to see over the reeds, and saw Ricki also standing in the distance, scouting the terrain. Using a term of endearment, I got Ricki's attention with, "Hey, dribble dick!" "Hey, Doc!" came right back. I was surprised that Ricki would respond to that moniker without adding an obscenity to my name in reply, but people react differently when in an unexpected situation. BJay and Ricki backed up their canoe until they reached the split, floated right and we had another fine story to tell.

One of the unique features of early 4Days (through 1992, the year of Jimmy's dry shoes), was that there were a larger number of attractive places to camp downstream from the Seney Township site than there were in later years. Was it improved access from higher water due to the downpours of those first few years that made it so? Possibly. Their later disappearance could be simply nature re-taking the land. In any case, in 1980 nights 2 and 3 we found wide, flat clearings with gorgeous stands of birch trees to camp under.

It was during the heavy rains of the early 4Days that I learned to love birch trees. The presence of a campfire was spiritual on dry evenings, but a wonderful comfort after a day of paddling through rain storms, and you could always start a bonfire using birch bark, it seemed even in the wettest of conditions.

The higher river levels consistent with the 70s 'n 80s precipitation & snow pack melt allowed us to float over many of the fallen trees and various debris encountered over several hours of paddling downstream from the Spreads. The chore of working our way through this stretch of the Fox in what would be considered "normal" (lower) water levels, revealing more logjams, was a treat yet down the road.

Dawn broke the 4th day, finding the fellers standing at the morning fire. Chucky spoke for all of us, the disappointment in his voice, "Man, every year somebody throws up, but a year is going to go by with no one puking", when we hear a tent unzip, and here comes Rookie BJay crawling out on all fours, vomiting, to a rousing round of cheers from his 4Day brethren. Now we can break camp with a happy heart, as we launch our canoes into the waters of the Fox River.

Paddling downstream for a couple of hours, Chucky & I are within shouting distance of Ricki & Rookie BJay, but had not seen the canoe of rookies Matthew & Craigo in the last hour or so. We were badly in need of a break when a glorious sight appeared around the bend: not every man's fantasy, but it was Craigo and Matthew above the river on the Old Log Bridge, Matthew smoking a stogie and grinning ear-to-ear, looking every bit like Winston Churchill on V-E Day, and Craigo leaning against the railing, waving us in with a fifth of Old Crow and the last of their Stroh's.

As we climbed up on to the bridge, the sun broke through the clouds, staying with us for the final two paddling hours that remained. Floating slowly downstream the rest of the way, the sunshine glistening off of the water, we used our paddles only when absolutely necessary, stretching out the remaining river time as long as possible, while the smell of cigars and the sounds of opening Stroh's enhanced the peaceful ending to 4Day # 3.

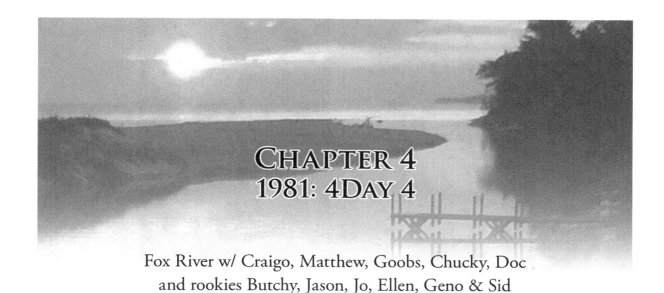

# CHAPTER 4
# 1981: 4DAY 4

Fox River w/ Craigo, Matthew, Goobs, Chucky, Doc
and rookies Butchy, Jason, Jo, Ellen, Geno & Sid

*I'm growing older but not up*
*My metabolic rate is pleasantly stuck*
*Let those winds of change blow over my head*
*I'd rather die while I'm living than live while I'm dead*
*(Growing Older But Not Up by Jimmy Buffett)*

"Doc, where are the bathrooms?"
"Anywhere you want 'em to be Geno."

Geno emerged early on day 1 from behind a clump of trees in a prancing, upbeat mood, "That's the first dump I've ever taken in the woods!" His excitement from the experience lightened not only his load, but also the mood of the now giggling canoers beached on the riverbank. It's nice to know that as you near the age of 30, there are still some firsts out there waiting for you and, thanks to Joseph Gayetty's 1857 bum-wipe invention, Geno could wilderness-defecate as our forefathers did, but with a softer ending.

Geno's inaugural blessing-of-the-birch was only one of the firsts for this 4Day: two of our *sisters* are floating the Fox River with us, Ellen West and Geno's sibling, Joanne Golles. We met Ellen and Jo in the dorms at EMU in 1974, where they started the party sorority Phi Kappa Buzz. Comfortable with the wilderness and fun, urban *or* rural, overhearing stories of the first 3 4Days done got the girls riled up and desiring to Go North. These are strong gals along the lines of Irene Sember (70-ish wonderful lady we parked with at Tiger games; there's nothing like watching Irene save spots for her regulars by barking at and chasing away uninitiated young-ins 50 years her junior). Comparing anyone to Irene is high praise, indeed.

Ellen brought her boyfriend, a fella we'd not met before, Jason Brown, a man likely to tell you a bird's Latin name and mating habits when you ask what color it is. He's a traveling man, citing adventures from Colorado to New York City, and friends with Harold C. Black, the sometimes conga or tambourine player 'n primary bagman for the marijuana-infused band David Peel and the Lower East Side. At the New York City book release party celebrating Abbie Hoffman's "Steal This Book" (with Abbie in attendance), the Lower East Side band, with Jason on congas, entertained the attendees.

Representing Lambertville and rounding out the '81 pledge class are a couple of guys that Goobs and I graduated with: Bedford High class of '72 members Dennis "Sid" Siedlecki and Butchy Byers. Sid is best-known for his Lazarus-like ability to rise from the dead at cards, awaking from chin-on-chest passed out, and then produce a winning hand late in a poker or euchre game. Butchy is our resident outdoorsman, most content when roaming a forest, tossing a baited line in the water, or floating down a river.

We've taken a liking to this Fox River, paddling it for the 3ʳᵈ year in a row AND with a big crew: 11 including the 2 ladies among the 6 rookies. Day 1 was a debris-filled, longer than usual, 6 hour paddle from the Fox River Campground to the Seney Township Campsite.

"Damn, do you guys <u>always</u> eat this good on the river?" rookie Sid inquired. Ah, from the mouths of the inexperienced. "Sid", Goobs replied, "not… even… close". Rookies Jo & Ellen served us a dinner of lobster tails (*lobster tails?*) and potatoes tossed in garlic, lemon, pepper and butter wrapped in aluminum foil to be cooked on the campfire. During lunchtime each day, Jo & Ellen passed around a magic Tupperware container that never seemed to empty of roasted chicken, salami, cubed cheese and raw veggies. Amplifying Goobs' comments to Sid, I shared the oft-told story of recent 4Day dining, "2 years back, I pulled a dripping-wet salami sandwich dinner out of the cooler, slowly separating the soaked bread from the meat, and hung the meat slices on tree branches, hoping they would dry a little".

I took an early morning Day 2 walk into town to get the latest news (2 days old when in Seney) on what seemed more probable each day, a baseball's players strike. There have been plenty of player-owner meetings, but no settlement seems likely. The Tigers are playing pretty good ball – this is no time for a strike, damn it. Gibby is having a breakout year, sitting among the league's top 5 while hitting .330, well into the high rent district.

Although this years' 4Day offered some new wrinkles, our old friend torrential storms moved into the area and stayed awhile. Chucky & I were paddling Day 2 during a steady 5 hour rain storm when rookies Joanne and Jason paddled up to us. Poor Jo looked miserable and asked, "What do we do now?" Rookie Butchy overheard this as he floated by, reached in his cooler, grabbed a beer, and very un-rookie-like said, "Open another Busch!", one of the most memorable, brilliant pieces of home spun wisdom ever uttered on the 4Day.

Butchy's advice probably didn't bring the answer that Joanne was looking for to boost her spirits, spirits that were about to dip a bit deeper. Jo was in the front of the canoe, Jason handling the steering from the stern, when their boat ran under a thicket of tree branches and flipped over. "Jason! What are you doing?!? I've *never* been on a canoe that's tipped over before." Jason smiled and said, "Jo, look on the bright side. You look like you'd do great in a wet t-shirt contest right now." He showed much better judgment with his next move: before Joanne was able to extricate herself from the branches digging into her ribs, and then strangle Jason, he was in Geno's canoe, having switched places with Ellen at a speed we wouldn't have guessed he had, and was soon well downstream from Jo's wrath.

While Jason was creating special memories with Joanne, Butchy was making friends with everyone. Always in good humor, with a laugh that was contagious, he was someone you wanted to paddle with or alongside of, telling jokes as he caught some nice brook trout in the Spreads.

Butchy, always ready with Mad Dog

Just when it seemed Butchy's stock couldn't go any higher, we pulled over for the night into a drenched camping spot. Surrounded by soggy from the day's unrelenting rain, he disappeared into the woods with his hatchet, amazingly emerging with an armload of dry fire wood. Stunned 4Dayers shook of their sedentary amazement and followed Butchy back into the woods, helping bring out additional supplies of fuel for the evening fire.

A man among men and some women, Butchy then cooked for us those fine brook trout he caught earlier, along with bear burgers from a black bear hunt he'd recently been on.

"Is it too early for Mad Dog?" Matthew asked with a big grin as our last canoe launched into the Fox for Day 3. We couldn't say no to Matthew's enthusiasm and, after all, it is Chucky's 28th birthday today! 10 or 11 Strohs downstream, chased with Mad Dog and Yukon Jack, had the celebrating birthday boy crawling on all fours in an unsuccessful search through the low riverside brush for his brain cells. Once upright, pie-eyed and of faint smile in his wind-swept rain pancho, Chucky looked like our very own Green Manalishi (*"now when the day goes to sleep, and the full moon looks"*).

The 4Dayers met another day of rainfall with good cheer, working together to get each other through the fallen trees blocking our way, keeping their strength by marching in the parade of alcohol circling our boats.

The frequency of portages this 4Day was greatest on today's journey, and while we slogged through each stoppage as a team, Craigo was Rhett Butler to the Scarlett O'Hara that was Ellen and Joanne's canoe. He often paddled ahead to the next logjam, would lie hidden in his boat beneath shoreline branches, popping up to extend a hand as the ladies approached.

One of those hanging branches punched a hole in the bag protecting Craigo's sleeping bag, and by the time we reached "the Peninsula", our campground for the night, it was soaked. His evening was spent holding the sleeping bag over the evening campfire in a partially-successful effort to give him something dry to sleep in.

Rookies Ellen and Jo set up the evening bar, asking, "Upside-down cocktails anyone?" To all interested it was head back, mouth open, then the ladies administered first vodka, 2nd triple sec, 3rd a drop of Rose's lime juice, 4th swallow. Although Butchy had slipped from consciousness in his hammock, the girls made sure that he received his scheduled final upside-down cocktail of the night. Neither rain, nor victim's sleep, shall stop the appointed rounds.

The cocktails relieved Goobs of any inhibition, and he followed Jo around the campfire while barking like a dog. Joanne shook her head, "I haven't showered in days, and I am <u>still</u> getting hit on."

In an era of Billy Jean King versus Bobby Riggs, Joanne and Ellen's participation on the 4Day was first-hand proof that women can be as tough as men. We love them both and it was fun to have the ladies on the river with us. It was also cool that in Geno & Jo we had the only brother-sister team in 4Day history. Despite all of that, the 4Day has become a closed boys club. The inclusion of the fairer sex changes the dynamics. Exhibit A was Goobs barking around Jo at the campfire when 4Day pursuits such as telling and re-telling stories, jokes, and movie quotes, talking Tigers, or singing "Men" or "Sixteen Tons" should be pursued.

Wonder if we'll ever see that Jason fellow again?

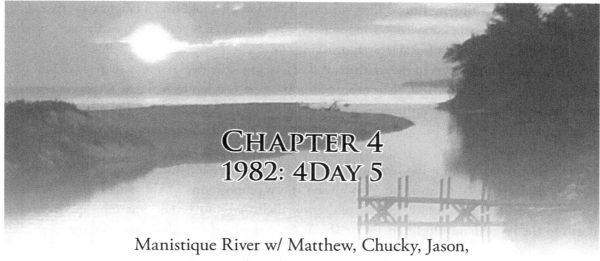

# CHAPTER 4
# 1982: 4DAY 5

Manistique River w/ Matthew, Chucky, Jason,
Doc and rookies Jimmy & Patti

*Let it rain, let it pour, let it rain a whole lot more*
*'Cause I got them deep river blues*
*Let the rain drive right on, let the waves sweep along*
*'Cause I got them deep river blues*
*(Deep River Blues by Doc Watson)*

"Jason?"
"Doc?"

We hadn't seen or had contact of any kind with Jason since we met him at last year's 4Day. Maggie and I were walking the aisles of the Ypsilanti Meijer store on the eve of 4Day 5, buying food that would go well with beer 'n bourbon. Just as we were turning the corner at the frozen food section, there was Jason standing right in front of us.

After a 4Day brotherly greeting, Jason's inquiry, "What have you been doing since the 4Day?" couldn't help but bring a smile. "Well, funny that you should ask. Since you last saw me I've been counting the days until tomorrow – the *next* 4Day" "What?!? It is?" "Yes it is." Jason immediately asked, "Can I come with you?" From such chance encounters history is made.

10PM the following day, with my company station wagon and passengers Matthew, Chucky, and fellow Meijer-shopper Jason already loaded, we pulled into Rookie Jimmy Vollmers' driveway. We'd been trying to get Jimmy to come 4Day with us for a few years, and he was now primed 'n ready to head north for the 4Day experience. What experience Rookie Patti, Jimmy's girlfriend who came along, expected is a mystery to this day.

Jimmy had not long ago completed an active tour of duty with the Marines, a "Semper Fi" man through and through. Post-active duty, Jimmy enrolled at Eastern Michigan University. His first class was a biology lecture, finding himself sitting next to a full-bearded man, our dear brother and fellow 4Dayer BJay Wright, also recently discharged from the Marines. The two bonded instantly, with BJay suggesting that Jimmy come on out and join our EMU intramural softball team, the conduit bringing Jimmy into our lives. Quick with a joke and a laugh, self-effacing, a man with wide-ranging knowledge and interests, a friend who has your back, easily meeting the 4Day criteria of being comfortable with drinking, Jimmy is a very well-liked fellow.

Dawn broke as we entered the southern end of Mackinac Bridge. A gorgeous array of blues & oranges crept over the horizon, their beauty almost severe enough to make us forget how much we craved breakfast, and elevating how happy we felt on the US2 drive west. The steel gray clouds and impending rain that has always been a promise of the 4Day was nowhere to be seen. How strangely fantastic.

Happily, the restaurant in Germfask, across M77 from the Jolly Motel, was still in business <u>and</u> open. As we'd come to learn, two always dicey propositions in this small town. With a ravenous breakfast stop under and stretching our belts, we drove the remaining quarter mile north to the Northland Outfitters livery. If you need any further paddling encouragement, the livery roadside sign provides it, enticing you with a painting of two canoers gliding between the pines with a rising or setting sun (depending on your view of life) ahead on the river of no return.

It's always nice to see livery owners Tom and Carma. We invariably learn something new when we chat with those two. Today we learned that last night the Tigers broke their 10-game losing streak, hallelujah! When Mike Ivie gets a hit, you know things are going your way. The amazing thing is that after a 10-game losing streak, the Tigers are still 7 games over .500, but they were sitting so nicely at 36 and 19. Oh well, it's only late-June and Sparky seems to have a team of young, talented players that could do big things if not this year than in the next few.

Invigorated by the good news from Michigan & Trumbull, we launched on the Manistique for the first time since 4Day One, which means it's the first time ever on the Manistique for everyone except me. Matthew loved it. "The Fox is great, but this river is so laid back, and there's not much chance of tipping over when you're trying to pass a drink to another canoe." Chucky talked about how nice it would be to toss a fishing line in the Manistique, but with a Stroh's in one hand and an unknown bourbon (the label was scratched off) in the other, he got nowhere near his angler's gear let alone his paddle.

The sun was shining the most on Jimmy's smile, "Boys, this... is... wonderful! I am SO glad that I made the trip." Jimmy was lying back, using his paddle for nothing more than steering & occasionally pulling in the bourbon, Mad Dog, or smokes being passed his way. Patti seemed a little bored but satisfied to be in the front of Jimmy's boat.

The clouds began to shroud the sun, but not the fun. *"Fris-bee!"* the shouts went out, so the boats were beached and the disk flipped among us. "46... 47... 48... ok, that's 49 catches in a row... oh no!" A general moan arose. "Jason, how could you drop that!?!" The good-natured shouting back and forth temporarily obscured the fact that one of us didn't venture out of the boats to join in. Patti stayed in the canoe and... is she *painting her toe nails*? The absolutely foreign nature of this had us all laughing and shaking our heads.

2 hours upstream of the livery, the Fox River merges from the right. 200' before the confluence of the slower Manistique and faster Fox waters, the Fox gloriously flows beneath (and sung with gusto) *the... Old... Log... Bridge.* Paddling downstream from the two rivers merger, our first visual of the livery grounds are the cabins along the right bank, with 14 shaded acres alongside 1,400' of the Manistique River. We eschewed the rustic, cozy cabins and the well-maintained bath house with showers to set up camp among the pines as Day 1 ends all too soon.

Launching Day 2 from the livery, in a few minutes we're floating though the Seney National Wildlife Refuge. The Refuge provides breeding grounds for, among others, eagles, woodpeckers, loons, and Sandhill Cranes. Walking last night's campground as the sun arose, picking up empties, disposing of trash, and starting the process of loading our gear into the canoe, my contemplation of the wildlife viewing that awaited on the second day was suddenly interrupted...

"Doc, I can't see!" My brother from another mother sounded concerned. Chucky had just woken up in the tent we shared, with both eyes swollen shut from spider bites suffered during the night. "No problem Chucky. You just sit on the bottom of the canoe, I'll handle the steering and let you know which side of the boat to reach out from when someone is handing something fun your way." This plan seemed to put Chucky at ease and over the course of next couple of hours his eyelids gradually opened up and our boy was back to his normal, animated self.

On the journey to the second day take-out and campsite at Mead Creek, a lazy 4-hour float downstream from the livery, we passed below the bridges at Ten Curves Road (2 miles west of the Ten Curves access) and M77. The river beyond M77 takes you into the Seney National Wildlife Refuge. With each passing Pabst Blue Ribbon, the scenery becomes more and more delightful... birds flocking in large numbers, thick gorgeous forests, turtles, and deer.

Once inside the Refuge, we paddled by 3 Manistique River tributaries, each merging from the right and marked by a sign with the tributary's name:

*Gray's Creek*, today's one-third point

*Pine Creek*, today's half-way mark

*Driggs Creek*, 15 minutes from the Mead Creek ending

Unfortunately, the Mead Creek campground includes a fair-amount of poison ivy that bit me this year. The result was particularly irritating post-4Day, back in the real world, sitting in waiting areas for meetings in my capacity as a Duracell salesman, in the one business suit I owned, a wool suit, hot, in July, with oozing poison ivy on my legs, wrapped in towels and encased in plastic. Yuck.

Awakening on Day 3, Patti made her discomfort known. Camping out in the wild had lost its charm. As we canoed downstream, Patti repeatedly asked Jimmy, "How far is it to the nearest motel?" I asked Jimmy if he'd explained to Patti that camping in tents is part of the 4Day. "Yeah, I *told* her" said the mildly-irritated Jimmy.

The Day 3 plan was to paddle about 3 hours downstream from Mead Creek, find a sandy beach big enough for 3 tents and a bonfire, and camp for the night. Remaining on Day 4 would be another 2-3 hours until arriving at the Cookson Bridge take-out, and the trip's end.

The combination of bourbon 'n beer running on empty, steady rain, hungry skeeters, and Patti's laser-focused mantra for indoor lodging, "I'm cold, I'm wet, I'm done", pushed us past any desirable camp spots, through a seemingly endless series of river bends, until we heard Matthew in the lead boat shout, "There's the Cookson Bridge – one day early". Thus, the first 3Day took place. Chucky later admitted to Jimmy that he was secretly glad that Patti pushed the issue, under cover of "Well, we gotta take care of the girl."

After paddling hard as the rain fell for most of today's 6 river hours, we hastily tossed our gear into the waiting vehicles, drove the 30 minutes to the Jolly Bar in Germfask, and drank 'n ate ourselves into an upbeat, happy mood. Even Patti got into the spirit of it all, forgetting her awful nights forced to sleep outdoors in a tent, sharing stories about the fun we were surprised that she had. Despite perking up in the bar, it was Patti's high-maintenance attitude those 3 days on the river that was the tipping point in the decision that the 4Day going forward would be a closed boys club.

Passing out as our heads hit the pillows at the Jolly Motel next door, we slept the sleep of the satisfied, (most of us) dreaming of future 4Days. Still, fun was yet to be done *this year* since we'd only spent 3 days on the water the past week, so...

Neither rain nor bleating mantras nor lack of a river should stop the 4Day from completing its appointed rounds. To put the "4" back in 4Day, Matthew, Chucky & I decided to soldier on, becoming pioneers of sorts, as the first 4Dayers to spend a day of the 4Day on dry land (and create a sentence with four 4s in it... er, make that six 4s... ok, an endless amount of 4s). We celebrated the fourth day of the 1982 4Day by crossing the Straits of Mackinac to spend quality time in a Mackinaw City bar called... *the Straits of Mackinac*. Ah, and what a celebration it was, sharing stories and laughs while lifting glass after glass in honor of our fellow 4Dayers, to the glory of the Fox and the Manistique Rivers, and to our unique discovery of how to complete a 4Day when the canoe and river is missing: spend an afternoon Up North in a pub with a nautical theme while enjoying the company of 4Day brothers.

# CHAPTER 4
# 1983: 4DAY 6

Fox River w/ Craigo, Goobs, Matthew, Chucky, Doc and
rookies Slovik, Schmidt, Clevidence, Timko & Puppy Casey

*I woke up this mornin' with the sundown shinin' in*
*I found my mind in a brown paper bag within*
*I tripped on a cloud and fell-a eight miles high*
*I tore my mind on a jagged sky*
*I just dropped in to see what condition my condition was in*
*(I Just Dropped In by the First Edition)*

Driving Up North on a Friday night, the radio tuned to Ernie and Paul on WJR, and these young and coming-on-strong Tigers putting a 10 to 1 whuppin' on the 1ˢᵗ place Orioles – is there any better way to enjoy the road trip up to the 4Day? Enos "Old Dude" Cabell had 3 hits while Juan Berenguer and Doug Bair combined on a 3-hitter. Tram & Lou are blossoming into annual all-star-caliber players, turning easy double plays, both hitting well over .300 to ensure runners are on base to be knocked in by Parrish, Gibby, Herndon, Chester, and Glenn Wilson. Tommy Brookens, who plays anywhere needed, was able to give Trammell a breather at short in the blow-out win. During the Tiger broadcasts, Ernie has taken to calling Quaker State native Brookens "the Pennsylvania Poker". God bless Ernie and Paul.

Crammed into my station wagon was Chucky, Matthew, Goobs, me, and a whole lot of gear. Side mirrors have never been more important. Following close behind on I-75 was a car load of rookies: old friend Slovik with 3 of his buddies - Schmidt, Clevidence, Timko and his dog Casey.

Blazing a trail through the late night and early morning hours, on the drive from Ypsilanti to Germfask, and arriving as the sun arose over the Northland Outfitters livery in Germfask, was the modus operandi the first 5 years of 4Dayin'. 1983 was the year that we decided to try something new: getting a good night's sleep before hitting the river.

Rooms were rented for our late-Friday night arrival in Mackinaw City at a little Ma 'n Pa Motel, the Wa-Wa-Tam. An old timer by the name of Elmer was the proprietor, a friendly, reserved fellow. Elmer was agreeable to staying up for our 10PM arrival. To repay this gesture, it seemed like the kindest thing to do was to move our ruckus away from his motel and home to a tavern in town, at least until the call to "drink up people!" closed the pub.

Walking into a place called the Keyhole Lounge, located on Mac City's main drag, is near the top of the list of outstanding moves in 4Day lore. The Keyhole has a fine watering hole look about it with, can it be? "There's table top shuffleboard along the right wall!" an enraptured Craigo declared. Rookies Timko and Schmidt immediately challenged Craigo and rook Slovik to a game, the players' focus heightened as Slovik set the stakes, "Losers buy shots of Beam for the winners". Fine call rookie. Occasional townies' challenges were repulsed as all nine 4Dayers took turns controlling the table 'til closing time, the constant stream of winners' "SHOTS!" somehow enhancing their performance.

Goobs, suddenly an excitable boy, exclaimed, "The 'Rodeo Song' is on this juke box!" The expletives-included song had become a big favorite of Goobs in the last year, frequently played by him tonight, and impossible to forget by any patrons who shared the Keyhole with us on this evening. At the other end of the musical spectrum was a song that I fell in love with this night, to always be associated with Keyhole/4Dayin' fun, "A White Sport Coat" by Marty Robbins. Marty's fabulous crooning of being "all alone in romance" makes listeners never so happy to be in a "blue, blue mood". The boys vote was unanimous: the juke box at this joint is fantastic!

Stumbling back to our Wa-Wa-Tam Motel rooms, the fellers fell into a deep sleep, passed out some might say, with dreams that began, *"Well, it's 40 below and I don't give a fuck, got a heater in my truck, and I'm off to the rodeo..."*

Your all-inclusive 1983 4Day resort getaway includes beer, all the mind-altering diversions you can/can't handle, beer, food that runs out by the end of the 3rd day, beer, stories that crack us up at the moment but we'll never remember later, beer, and an inclination to want to jump off every piling, bridge, & stone embankment that we come across. Oh, and a little canoeing.

Launching Day 1 at the Fox River Campground, the section of the Fox upstream from the Seney Township Campsite treated us to the usual number of fallen trees and various debris to be negotiated, brief interruptions to canoeing the narrow, windy, fast-flowing current as tag alder bushes brushed both arms.

Added to the 4Day culture this year is the rookie lunatic fringe.

Clevidence and Timko are enjoyable company, veterans at paddling & camping, sliding easily into sharing stories and jokes. Slovik is an old friend, adding spark and energy to any of our gatherings, with a gleam in his eye & a smile that hints at walk-on-the-wild-side adventure we're happily sucked into. And then there is Schmidt.

Observing Schmidt for a few hours prompted Goobs to say, "And I thought that Slovik was crazy". We have a new winner! Coincidentally, much of this 4Day's lunacy and elevated mind-altering took place in Schmidt's presence. As darkness enveloped the first evening, Schmidt celebrated the events of the day by sitting in the campfire. Butt on the ground. Literally. Backing into the fire, knees bent, flames wrapped around his feet and rising up around his butt and legs as he lowered himself into it, avoiding serious burns a major mystery.

While Schmidt fire-squatted, Slovik told the story of Schmidt entering the reputed meanest, roughest bar in Harlem, a white speck in a dark sea, blowing through the front door, wearing a full-length fur coat, bellying up to the bar, laying lines out that covered its width, snorting the product, and departing without saying a word, leaving the barkeep and clientele in jaw-dropping, stunned silence.

This night, Schmidt proved his brain was in the nether regions. While shouting, "Happiness is Cleveland in my rear view mirror!" Schmidt decided to drive into town taking the most direct route. Over Chucky's tent. With Chucky in it. *"Chucky! Chucky! Get out!"* Chucky dove out just in time to avoid being flatten, a truly dangerous situation barely avoided. Perhaps Schmidt would've stopped at the last minute. Perhaps. *"Is there someone else up there we can talk to?"* P.S. amazingly, the tent was repairable.

The Day 2 rising sun revealed steam rising off of the river and smoke rising off of Schmidt. Prior to enjoying another fantastic run through the Spreads, we stopped at the M28 Bridge. The fellers said, "Chucky! Don't jump! Chucky! Noooooo!" Chemically impaired judgment said something else. Fortunately, he jumped off the bridge feet first into the knee deep Fox, Chucky's right heal absorbing most of his weight. It would bother him in future years each morning when he first awoke, especially when rain was comin', exhibit A to stick with beer, bourbon and Mary Jane. Rookie Schmidt traveled the 30 minutes through the Spreads with only a floatation cushion between him and the river.

Chucky's jump, although ending painfully, inspired leaps of faith by the rookies at what felt like each and every mid-stream elevation we paddled to, including logjams, of which there is a tremendous amount in the several hours between the Spreads and the Fox-Manistique merger. The smile, head shake, and catch phrase among the veterans was, "Rookies, God bless 'em".

In our concern for the rookies' zealous illogic, we created the first 4Day rule: never let a solo canoeist go last. The boys' goal was to bring 'em back alive! Seemingly at loggerheads with rule one, rule two was created: no bourbon may be brought on the 4Day that sells for over $9.99.

Overlooked was the need for a 3rd rule: make sure that we bring enough food to last as many days as we'll be in the wilderness. The last of our morsels was swallowed Day 3 around the evening campfire at the Peninsula.

Singing, laughing, and story-telling in the spectacular Day 4 sunshine was a thing of beauty, the lack of food be damned. Craigo's refrain, over and over, was sung with gusto, "I can't deny that I LOVE IT! I got this thing for Up North!" paraphrasing Jimmy Buffett's "Perrier Blues" lyrics. After several 4Dayer renditions of Jerry Reed's "Amos Moses", Slovik said he'd like to listen to an entire cassette tape of nothing but this classic (so, for a future Slovik birthday gift, Maggie and I made a 120 minute tape of exactly that: Amos Moses continuously played over 50 times, audible after each 2 minutes & 17 seconds play is the lifting of the needle and placing it back to the start of the song).

Shouts of "Land Ho!" emitted from the boys as we pulled the canoes up on to the landing at Northland Outfitters, concluding one of the strangest of the 4Days. After livery co-owner Carma photographed our Famous Final Scene, Slovik's suggestion to grab a beer down the street at the Jolly Bar was vetoed by stomachs void of food since yesterday, and buried under the cry, "on to the Fort!" Mackinaw City's *Fort Restaurant* had become a post-4Day favorite stop, with an all-you-can-eat buffet dinner cheap 'n overflowing. Each year found us seated by the hostess at the corner table, 4Day-scented bodies positioned directly beneath the Fort's finest ventilation fan.

*Post-4Day: July 17…*

Stretching out that 4Day feeling a week after it ended, Matthew, Chucky, Goobs and I piled into my station wagon looking for adventure. What we found instead was a delightful but somewhat sedate afternoon of Frisbee flipping and beer drinking at Silver Lake in Pinckney. With the sun setting on a gorgeously sunny day, and Roxy Music on the cassette player as our soundtrack, we wrapped up the pleasantly uneventful afternoon with a drive back to my Ypsilanti condo.

Turning south on US23 as it splits from M14, on the north rim of Ann Arbor, we saw a police officer standing by a stopped car in the northbound shoulder, about to give a ticket or a warning to the driver of that vehicle. Giving it minimal thought, I rolled down my window, extended my beer outward, and yelled as loud as I could, "Hey cop! That Bud, that's beer!" The officer looked at me, said something to the driver, and ran back to his cop car. Oh-oh. As I accelerated, in my rear view mirror I spied the officer of the law wheeling his patrol car down into the valley of the grassy median, emerging in the same southbound direction us, hell bent to hang my ass. Occupants in the cars ahead of us were about to have a little unexpected excitement on the way to their early-evening destinations.

To this day, I do not know what speed my station wagon reached, as the speedometer does not register beyond 90 mph. What I do know is that, as we wheeled over to the mercifully obstacle-free shoulder of the road, the frightened faces of the drivers we rocketed past (didn't expect me on your right, did ya?), with their unheard cries of *"Save the children!"*, became blurred dots, and their vehicles seemed to be standing still. My directive to the boys was clear, "Get all of the empties out of the car NOW!" They complied enthusiastically, and seemed saddened when the impressive stockpile of beer cans was no more.

*"No we won't forget, the Thrill of it All"* blasted on the speakers (the musical accompaniment could not have been planned any better) as we careened somewhere beyond zoom down the US23 shoulder. We were on a big bend to the right, and there was no sign of the cop in my rear view mirror. Suddenly, an oasis in the late-afternoon was a roadside sign that read, 1 mile to the Geddes Road exit. Oh c'mon, can we make it? Can we make it?

On two wheels we took that Geddes Road exit with gusto. Halfway between US23 and the end of the exit ramp, the cop was now in sight – he did not exit! – rocketing by southbound, cop lights screaming, all other drivers the Red Sea to his Moses, damn near airborne in his quest to string me up. Holy crap! He must not have seen us exit here, OR maybe he DID see us, but too late to exit, and would be coming back for us soon. Paying as little attention to the Geddes Road speed limit as I did that of US23, a roadside sanctuary came into view: Concordia College.

Turning my steering wheel so fast that my fellow Stooges slammed into the passenger side doors, I raced for the back of the campus main building, found an appropriate spot, and backed the car in it as deep as I could. I dared not leave, as the by now fire-breathing officer would pistol whip and jail me if he was cruising Geddes Road and saw the car emerge.

The nervous tension in the car was broken as Matthew grabbed and shook my shoulders with religious fervor. "Doc, this is the ***BEST*** time that I ever had!!" Chucky and Goobs were howling. I was nervous as hell, at that moment finding little relief in their euphoria. After waiting for only a fraction of what seemed like an hour, I threw fate to the wind, and eased out towards Geddes, my head swiveling from side to side, searching the landscape for my tormentor.

Goobs, Chucky & Matthew relived the adventure, with a joy I was unable to allow myself, on the 20 minute drive from Concordia College to the condo. As we arrived home, the boys stayed with me in case bail was needed and, of course, not wanting to miss a possible dramatic ending. They told and retold the story to Maggie, who seemed to get a kick out of spending an evening seeing how her husband was going to get out of this one.

So five of us sat and 4 of us watched the USFL title game between the Michigan Panthers and the Philadelphia Stars. Bobby Hebert and Anthony Carter were the heroes of the game, as the Panthers won by a score of 24-22, but I could never get comfortable, for surely the officer had seen my license plate number, and the knock on the door would come any second, if not tonight, then maybe tomorrow. But it never did, and I was eventually able to fully enjoy the day that bad judgment resulted in one helluva story. I felt bad for that possible poor stiff somewhere down US23, maybe around Milan, who was handcuffed and hauled away to jail for doing 56 in a 55 by one mad-as-hell policeman.

Over the years, the well-known story has been shared at many a group function, sometimes with extra details. Big Guy, as an example, has inserted himself into the station wagon, spinning an entrancing version of the adventure, but so far afield that it wasn't until 10 minutes into the yarn that any of the 4 actually involved recognized it for the experience that it really was. Big Guy's adornment does, however, honor the story, much like the one million people that were at 50,000 seat Tiger Stadium that 1976 Monday night when the Bird beat the Yankees 4 to 1.

# CHAPTER 4
# 1984: 4DAY 7

Ontonagon River w/ Butchy, Craigo, Goobs,
Chucky, Big Guy, Doc and rookie Tom

*When I'm dead and in my grave,*
*No more whiskey shall I crave,*
*And on my tombstone shall it be wrote,*
*10,000 gallons run down my throat*
*(Cornish Men of the Upper Peninsula)*

### *"4Day!" "Tigers!"*

Those are the shouts and the main topics – the *only* topics – as the boys arrive at our house for the annual caravan north (though Yankee-fan Big Guy & Indian-fan Goobs are a bit muted). With the Tigers starting the season a record-setting 35 & 5, it ensures that there'll be a heavy dose of baseball talk nudging its way (even more than usual) into the 4Day chatter. Although losing to Texas last night, the Tigers still hold a 6 game lead with 2 games remaining 'til the All-Star Game weekend. Further warming the hearts of Tiger fans was the amazingly large number of Olde English D caps seen at this year's Kentucky Derby.

Invited by Chucky to join in the fun this 4Day is Rookie Tom. A pleasant sort, Tom teaches in the Garden City school with Chucky. Although quiet, he is clearly excited about being a part of the great annual 4Day adventure. He is not alone in this eagerness.

The early 7AM caravan start time could not contain our enthusiasm: in addition to the normal 4Day buzz and Tiger-talk, there is an extra high: this year the 4Day crew is tackling a new Upper Peninsula river, traveling further west than ever before. The 10-hour drive will take us to the tiny western U.P. town of Watersmeet for a canoeing journey down the Middle Branch of the Ontonagon River.

For most of us, this will be our first time west of Manistique in da U.P. Westbound US 2 takes us past the towns of Escanaba and Iron Mountain before motoring into Wisconsin for a brief spell, then back into Michigan for short cruises through Crystal Falls and Iron River prior to being greeted by the "Welcome to Watersmeet: Home of the Nimrods" sign.

The Nimrods name was adopted for the school teams back in 1904, when its meaning was a little bit different than it is today. In the Book of Genesis, Nimrod was a "mighty hunter before the Lord", and Watersmeet, located within the Ottawa National Forest, is prime hunting land, so the name made sense. Among ESPN's top 10 high school nicknames, Nimrods is #3 (should've easily beaten out the top 2 names, Syrupmakers & Beetdiggers). ESPN ran an ad campaign celebrating the social & cultural importance of athletics in school; one ad ended with the line, "Without sports, who would cheer for the Nimrods?" Not long ago, the school body was asked if they wanted to change the name. The kids replied, "Nimrods Forever!"

Having checked into our Watersmeet motel, we took the short stroll to the only bar in town, and are settled in for a night of drinkin' and pool playin'. After apparently finding the bourbon that Minnesota Fats favors, Butchy is beginning to call and hit with astounding frequency double 'n triple bank shots. Laughing like a maniac after each "how the hell did he do that?" shot, Butchy ran the table until deciding to use it as a mattress, where he stretched out suddenly unconscious, before we carried him away to his bed next door.

Research told us that the Middle Branch of the Ontonagon was a river full of rapids, most of them found in the lower, or last half, of our planned journey. Research didn't say a damn thing about the infestation of insects. Deer Flies chomped on us from early morning until the shift change at dusk when the skeeters' hunger took over.

In the early stages of the river trip, launching north of US2 near the livery, the rapids are nowhere in sight, the paddle a peaceful one through flat water. The quiet didn't last long. The warning came from Craigo, canoeing solo in the lead boat and now shouting, "Hey, that looks like a Moose! It *is* a Moose! Come in slow!" We'd never encountered a moose while paddling the Fox or the Manistique Rivers. This western U.P. is an exciting place!

The moose is standing midstream, water to its bony knees, a magnificent cork-in-the-bottle on our paddling route. The animal is a good 6' tall, it's antlers from tip to tip the same. It stopped to quench its thirst with river water, then lifts its head, turns it towards us, and looks like he might relish an encounter, should we be silly enough to try to canoe around him.

Maybe later in the day, with higher levels of liquid courage flowing through us, maybe then we would have plunged forward. However, we choose patience, beaching the canoes at least 100' short of the moose, getting out of the boats and tossing the Frisbee, waiting out the great beast. Rookie Tom, sitting in his canoe, grabbed the misplaced first throw, his only catch, which was followed by 211 more consecutive Frisbee catches. The moose did not share our enthusiasm for this Frisbee achievement, wandering off about 20 minutes in, up the left bank into the forest and out of sight.

At the Buck Lake Bridge, we found good flat ground for our tents, and made camp for the night. While gathering firewood, Goobs quietly scanned the area, asking, "Where'd Big Guy go?" We shouted his name and got no reply. Oh crap! We've seen a moose, maybe a bear grabbed Biggie. And then the laughing starts. It is coming from Butchy who is doubled over, tears running down his cheeks, unable to speak. He lifts a hand from his knee and points a finger towards the river. All we could see is an open mouth and a set of nostrils above the water line. In an attempt to avoid the deer fly bites, Big Guy has taken to the river, his large frame underwater except for a mouth and nose gasping for air.

All is quiet around the next morning's campfire until Craigo begins to imitate Big Guy's alligator-like efforts of yesterday to seek relief from the bugs. Butchy is the first to cave, heaving with laughter at Craigo's re-creation, and soon the silence dissolves into a group crack-up, with even Big Guy eventually seeing the humor in it all.

Launching Day 2 from the Buck Lake Bridge, the rapids' promise is soon realized. The river picks up speed, taking us through 5 challenging class 2 whitewater runs over the day's 3 hours, evoking a series of ***"Yee-ha!"*** shouts from the boys. Even when you can't see our other canoes, you can hear the 4Dayers whoopin' 'n hollerin' as we fly around bends featuring fast water drops and waves pounding against the rocks peeking above the surface.

In a rare moment of patience before plunging ahead with life, Chucky asks, "Where are we supposed to go now?" a question rarely put forth when on a river – you go where the current takes you. The rapids, however, have come to an end, replaced by marshy waters; multiple tributaries appear & begin to run parallel with the main body of the river. When the tributaries start to cross over the river, it's easy to stray off the river on to a tributary, in our case, on to a tributary that became increasingly narrow until it eventually disappears and has us completely surrounded by a field of tall reeds.

"Doc, I thought you said you researched this river." Big Guy is riding me, appropriately so, as it now felt as though we are sitting in canoes in the middle of a field, not canoeing in the traditional sense. Nevertheless, we soon find it easy to paddle thru the reeds & reconnect to the main body of the Ontonagon. While we find our way out of the reeds, eagles appear, soaring through the skies above and entertaining the boys.

The sign tells us Tamarack Creek is merging into the river, serving as the 15-minutes-to-go landmark. Chucky's suggestion, "Let's get one more break in before camping!" met with no opposition. We pulled the canoes over where the riverbed is impressively rocky, and dig out a fifth to pass around. The very blasted Goobs pops out of his canoe, staggers several feet, and mumbles about the struggle to walk here, "Boy, these rocks would really be hard to walk on if you were hammered!" Big Guy kicks the laughter up a notch when he replies to Goobs, "Yeah, I guess we'll just have to use our imagination on that one, Goobs".

The Burned Dam Campground lines the right riverbank. Alongside the campground, the river flows into the Mex-i-mine Falls, a class 3 rapids run that only the most skilled paddler should take on, and listed as a State of Michigan waterfall. Most folks portage here, but most folks haven't consumed as much vodka as Goobs has today, nor are as crazy as his paddling partner Craigo. The invulnerability of youth didn't hurt, either.

The Mex-i-mine Falls rapids are very fast and very boulder-infested. Before Goobs and Craigo run these rapids, they empty their canoe of all gear, and the rest of us line the river banks every 50' feet to act as spotters, and to salvage the boys' bodily remains. It is go time for the two.

Craigo's inquiry, "Are you ready Goobs?" is met with a response of, "Let's DO IT!"

The first two attempts end with the boys flipping the canoe over and slamming themselves into the Falls' boulders, creating pain that will be felt much more the next morning. The third time through is the charm, to approving shouts from the spotters. Later, livery owner Bob told us not to run the Mex-i-mine Falls with his equipment, as he himself had busted up a few canoes trying to paddle through. Bob really should've mentioned this *before* our trip began.

The wild ride through the waterfall is the talk of the campfire. Rookie Tom, thinking it was the coolest thing he'd ever seen, inquires "You guys don't feel <u>any</u> pain from crashing into those boulders?" Craigo answers for him and his partner, "Hell no, we feel GREAT!" As the evening camaraderie rolls on, Goob's 3-sheets-to-the-wind-laughing-for-no-apparent-reason provides additional fireside entertainment, Sunday becomes Monday, and nobody was ready to turn in.

"Damn, what hit me?" is Craigo's rhetorical question when he joins us around the next morning's campfire. Banging boulders was bound to have some cost, delayed though it was.

"There's only one way to shake it off," the 4Day chorus repeats, "get back out on the water". Packing up from Burned Dam Campground, we hit the river and are immediately into churning whitewater. We'd been told that during today's 6-mile paddle the river floor would drop over 40', but until you're in the middle of it, you don't fully comprehend how fast and furious this kind of a drop would make the trip. There are 7 fabulous sets of rapids the river winds through today, and each flat water break between the rapids sees huge smiles and laughter from the paddlers. This is awesome!

There is one rapids, though, with one particularly big rock that is a bit tricky…

"The Rock" is located midstream at the end of a straightaway. The piece de resistance at the conclusion of a wild, downhill 4 minute rapids ride, while the entire time the floor of the Ontonagon is falling away below, the Rock awaits. Big Guy and I are canoeing together and, under the heading of poor judgment, Biggie and the greater weight is in the front of the boat. We are pulled towards the Rock like a magnet and I am unable to steer us away from the coming collision. Our canoe runs up the side & on top of the boulder, turns sideways and begins to tip as rushing water fills the boat. All of our gear is jettisoned into the river and floating downstream.

Shaking off alcoholic inertia while hurriedly beaching their boats on the shore and screaming instructions to each other, Goobs, Butchy, Tom, Chucky and Craigo run down the riverbank a couple hundred feet ahead of us. Once there, they lock arms and form a human chain stretched from the shoreline out to midstream, just seconds before our overturned boat and its contents, including Big Guy and I, arrive. Their efforts bring us to safety and scoop up our canoe, paddles, pads, cooler, bagged-up tent, clothes & sleeping bags. In the 4Dayer's world, it is the rescue of the decade.

Day 4 is mostly flat water, a chance to float slowly for several hours with the canoes side-by-side, from the previous night's Interior Bridge camp to our take-out. The final approach to the take-out requires 30 minutes of serious paddling to get across the lake that the Ontonagon River has become. This lake is more difficult to cross for one canoe than any other. In the front of the boat that he shares with Chucky, Tom cannot figure out why, as hard as he is paddling, all the other canoes are pulling away from his – until he looks back and sees that Chucky, instead of stroking, is dragging his paddle in the lake, his altered state mesmerized by the lines the drag creates on the lake's surface.

Pulling in at the sandy beach ending, we're waiting for the livery folks to pick us up at the appointed hour. With some time to spend, we build a final fire, drying out some still damp clothes and tents, and enjoy a little Frisbee tossing (107 then 196 consecutive catches – damn, we're hot!). The lake that we'd paddled across is known as the Bond Falls Flowage, featuring gorgeous Bond Falls, a waterfall with a 50' drop, one that not even Craigo and Goobs would try to paddle through.

On the way home, after crossing the Mackinac Bridge, Goobs, Big Guy and I decide to break up the drive and spend a night in the tiny town of Alger. The only pub in town, the Alger Bar, is about a 100' walk from the only motel in town, the Alger Motel. Mm… let's get a room at the Alger Motel and go to the Alger Bar, which also seems to be the only restaurant in town.

After many rounds, Goobs put his head down on the bar and passed out. Heavy. Like a rock. The bar owner made sure that we knew of one of the tavern's policies, "Hey, we can't have anyone dying in my bar". Biggie tells him, "Our buddy's not dead, he's just a heavy sleeper." That piece of reassuring information did not seem to help with the bar owner, "Well, you gotta get him out of here." We tried once more, "No, you don't understand, he's a real HEAVY sleeper!"

Goobs' friends have seen this movie before. At a Michigan State football weekend last year, Goobs passed out, becoming an immovable object in the backseat of a car. We can't get him out of the car and into the motel room 'cause he knows some ancient Korean trick allowing him to increase his passed-out weight by 10X normal. The only practical application of this trick seems to be in avoiding being kidnapped while unconscious.

Jimmy & never-been-on-a-4Day Ricky Callahan stopped by our MSU room, chatting for a while before Jimmy asks, "Where's Goobs?" I informed him, "Passed out in the car. We tried moving him for hours, no luck, got that ancient Korean thing going." Jimmy proudly says, "We have two Marines here, we'll get him out." Ok, good luck guys. 20 minutes later, covered in sweat, Jimmy said, "Jesus! We can't budge him!" Big Guy laughed, "Yeah, we were sayin' that unless Jimmy and Ricky got themselves a crane out there, they ain't comin' back with Goobs".

As entertaining as this tale is, sharing it does not sway the proprietor of the Alger Bar, who demands Goobs removal from his establishment. At this point, it is our good fortune that Goobs' head lifts up from the bar, and we 3 start making the short walk back to our motel room. Big Guy & I, after making sure that Goobs is safely tucked in, sit outside in a couple of chairs provided by the motel, watching the occasional vehicle drive by, kicking back with a final beer and a few new 4Day stories to re-live.

*Post-4Day: Monday, September 24, 1984…*

The Detroit Tigers clinched the American League East last week, and will open post-season play Tuesday, October 2, versus the A.L. West champion K.C. Royals. This is the culmination of an unbelievable season, the wire-to-wire Tigers never out of first place, a Jack Morris no-hitter, the 35 & 5 start, the team's 104 victories setting a single season club record… Wow!

9 days before that October 2 date, I'm working in my home office, the small TV on my desk turned to the noon news. The lead story is that, at 7AM tomorrow morning, tickets for both the American League playoffs AND the World Series will go on sale at Tiger Stadium. I jump up from my desk and shout downstairs, "Maggie! Maggie! MAGGIE!!! Tiger playoff and Series tickets…" is all that I get out. "When?!" she shouts back. Within 15 minutes, we collected funds and miscellaneous items needed for an overnight stay in line, are out the door and eastbound on I-94. By 1PM, 18 hours before the tickets go on sale, we are the 100th and 101st people in line at the Corner. As we take our place, a reporter for USA Today interviews the 50th person in line, while Marquis and Chucky slide in line behind us.

We while away the time with small talk, reading, telling stories, and meeting folks standing closest to us. By midnight, a football game breaks out among those in line. With our shared experience, a fraternity of sorts has formed among the ticket seekers, and an honor system is in place allowing those who've been there for hours to step out and join the football game without losing their place once the playing is done.

As the night time temperature drops to the mid-30s, Maggie stretches out on a chaise lounge we've brought, burrowing beneath several blankets in an effort to keep warm. We haven't eaten in a while, so I head over to the nearby White Castle, and bring back a couple of sacks of sliders for Mag, Chucky, Marquis, and me. Maggie is still buried under the blankets an hour or so after ingesting the Whities, when she turns over on her side. This untucks the blankets, freeing the pocket of Whities' gas that had been ripening beneath her. The impact on the pick-up football game was immediate. The guy closest to us had been going out for a pass, which sailed over his head when his knees buckled as the aroma assaulted his nose. Several "What in God's name?" were issued, and I recall this being the first time I'd ever heard the word "malodorous" used by someone other than a college professor or a janitor.

Eventually, the air cleared and, at 7AM, the ticket windows opened. It took another full hour to get to the window, place our order of 4 tickets together (one per person limit) to each of the potential post-season home games, and have our tickets in hand. 19 hours passed from arrival to walking away from the ticket window, every moment worth it. In 20 days, Kirk Gibson will deposit a Goose Gossage fastball into the rightfield upper deck & the final out of the 1984 World Series will settle into the glove of left-fielder Larry Herndon, clinching for the Detroit Tigers the 4th Series title in their history! Bless You Boys!

# CHAPTER 4
# 1985: 4DAY 8

## Fox River w/ Goobs, Chucky, Big Guy, Jimmy and Doc

*In the Upper Peninsula of Michigan state,*
*Where M77 meets M28,*
*Some get there by canoe, some get there by car,*
*They're all lookin' for Andy's, Andy's Seney Bar*
*(Doctoones 1985)*

A month before paddling the oldest mode of transportation down the 4Day river, several guys flew the newest transportation mode east to New York City, so we could cheer on our Tigers during a weekend series in the den of iniquity, aka Yankee Stadium. The Tigers took 2 out of 3 from the despised Yankees Suck, but the real show was our dear boy Chucky.

The Friday night Murphy's Tavern fun (Jimmy next morning, "How the hell did I spend $120?") resulted in the 10 motel room items that Chucky threw up on or in besides the toilet: Big Guy's pants, Jimmy's jacket, Doc's tote bag, the bedroom floor, the walls, the ceiling (what tha?), the sink, the bathroom floor, the base of the toilet (getting closer), his hand (a last second miscue), and finally (bingo!) the toilet itself.

Strolling Saturday through Central Park before the game, Chucky's normally weak eyes spied a bikini-clad young lady sunning herself on a blanket 100 yards away. Chucky sprints over to the lady, lays down on the blanket next to her, chats her up while coolly propped up on one elbow, then springs to his feet and sprints back to us. Breathlessly, he explains, "She needs a cigarette – who has a cigarette?" Reluctantly, Big Guy gives one up, and we watch Chucky race back to the damsel, stretch out next to her, and proffer the smoke to fair maiden. Within seconds, Chucky is once again on his feet, back to us in a flash, explaining, "She needs a light – who has a light?" In the laughter and good feelings that Chucky's performance inspired, we momentarily forget that our personal items were befouled by him the night before.

Trekking to the Upper Peninsula was the smallest group to 4Day since 1980, a tight knit assembly of five old friends: Jimmy 'n me and the 3 brothers that stood up at my wedding – Chucky, Goobs, and Big Guy. This Fox River adventure would be one of the special ones. Besides these participants, we met for the first time two folks who would put a huge imprint on 4Day folklore:

Betsy McCormick, new Germfask motel and bar owner, and Andy Stachnick, owner of Andy's Seney Bar. Andy used to drive a big rig, transporting logs/power poles mostly, from Traverse City north to Munising, work Andy found tedious. Then one day, his guardian angel stalled Andy's truck just down the road from a bar in Seney, a bar 200' east of the Fox River and with a "For Sale" sign in front of it. Andy jumped at the opportunity to change his life, and bought the bar in 1978, the same year as the first 4Day. Amazingly, despite paddling and camping the area during 6 of the first 7 4Days, 1985 would be our first time stepping into Andy's Seney Bar.

Somehow we squeezed 5 guys, 3 coolers, 2 tents, several bags of gear and ammo boxes (home for a long river list of everything BUT ammo) into my van for the Saturday morning departure.

3 long Frisbee breaks at I75 rest areas created a happy compliment to the party rolling down the highway, and added a couple of hours to our road time. Waiting for us at the end of our normally 4 hour drive north were overnight accommodations at the Wa-Wa-Tam Motel in Mackinaw City, the lodging we discovered two years earlier, proprietor Elmer holding 2 rooms for us.

After checking in, the boys strolled to an evening of merriment and tom foolery at the Keyhole Lounge. Jimmy put his quarter down on the table top shuffleboard ledge, shouting above the music, "G-o-o-o-o-bs!!! Let's play the winners!" his deep baritone going through the bar's clientele on its way to echoing off the tavern walls. Goobs and Jimmy ran the table for a good hour, the soundtrack to their success the outstanding Keyhole juke box. Old classics by Johnny Cash & Patsy Cline crossed paths seamlessly with new songs from Tears For Fears announcing *Everybody Wants to Rule the World* & A-Ha singing *Take on Me*.

Many a glass was lifted to the memory of recently-passed Harry Harcourt. Harry is the brother of Johnny Harcourt, a future 4Dayer and dear friend. Johnny told us quite a few Harry stories over the years. A favorite has Harry pulled over by the Roseville Police. The cop asked Harry, "You been drinking?" *Yes* "Then why are you driving?" *I'm too drunk to walk* "Get out of the car, sir" *What car would that be?*

Suddenly, just about the time we gave consideration to calling it a night and wandering back to our motel, the dark street outside was brightly lit by lightning bolts thundering down from the skies. I called to our waitress, "Another round of shots 'n beers, please", and we settled in for additional story-telling, even getting some friends involved who couldn't make it…

*Marquis said he'd heard Monte Clark was going to be replaced as Lions coach by Linda Lovelace. He said she will no doubt blow a few, but she won't choke on the big ones.*

*At the ballpark near his North Carolina home, where the local Asheville Tourists minor league team plays, Ricki sez they have 6 Thirsty Thursdays a year when beers are .25. The team did not have Thirsty Thursday on the 4th of July this year, explaining "we can handle the drunks and we can handle July 4 fireworks, but we can't handle them together".*

*Laz is doing his Detroit hometown proud in his new California home: although his hockey team only came in 3rd place, Laz lead the league in penalty minutes. This news was met with many smiles and nods of approval around our table.*

*Maggie figured that Soviet Premier Chernenko couldn't meet with the Greek Premier because he's too old to bend over.*

*This feller KB, whom we met at Kathy's new Jacksonville digs in May, prophesized, "you're only young once, but you can be immature all of your life".*

Chucky, who didn't want to be left out, asked "Did you hear the new song in Ethopia? He Ain't Heavy, He's Lunch?"

The hard rain became a sprinkle as the lightning moved east, and we eased off the bar stools to make our way out the Keyhole door to the Wa-Wa-Tam and shut-eye, but not before one final quarter found its way into the juke box, allowing Marty Robbins to take us home with *A White Sport Coat & a Pink Carnation.*

Morning broke and last evening's grey was replaced by a bright blue. I notice that Biggie is wearing a cool lookin' purple Keyhole Lounge hat. "Hey Big Guy, when did you buy the hat?" "Oh, the owner gave it to me last night 'cause we spent so much money there". Big Guy is well-known for keeping a figurative titanium padlock on his wallet, only opening it for Haley's Comet sightings and leap-year celebrations. Steaming sarcasm would best describe my reply, "Because WE spent so much money last night? WE?!?" Knowing that we were about to embark on the 4Day, a belief in karma, and the knowledge that we now had another Big Guy story to tell, all helped to cool me down.

After the 4Dayers stuffed themselves with breakfast at new favorite restaurant Audie's (two big draws: Audie's is near the Wa-Wa-Tam <u>and</u> is open early), we crossed the sun-splashed Mackinac Bridge for the 75 minute drive to the tiny village of Germfask.

"Hey, where you guys been?" said livery owner Tom Gronback, teasingly as last year we were 4Dayin' 4 hours to the west of Germfask, on the Middle Branch of the Ontonagon River in Watersmeet. "We missed you, too, Tom", as well as the town, not realizing to what degree until standing in front of the livery store.

Herding 4Dayers & their gear into the livery van, Tom drove us to the Fox River Campground launch site. Standing at the top of the campground cliff, with its expansive view of the river valley below and the pine-covered hills rising above it, heightened the joy we felt to be back on the Fox after our absence last year.

Despite the sunny skies above, we traversed the Fox under a low-budget rainstorm of Canada House Whiskey & Milwaukee's Best beer, with a couple of cases of less modestly priced Busch beer (this week's special at Flick's Market in Lambertville) thrown in by Goobs and Big Guy.

Pulled over during a late-afternoon paddling break, the toasted Goobs stood ankle deep in the Fox while facing the sandy shore. Finding a need to relieve himself, Goobs held his pud in one hand and a Busch beer in the other. As soon as Goobs starts to pee, he starts to weave. The boys are frozen in place, watching in fascination as Goobs begins a slow-motion, face-first plunge. Gradually picking up speed, but never taking his hands off pud or beer, not a drop of brew is being spilled. On the way to a nosedive into the dirt, the gyroscope in Goobs brain is now in control and he is constantly turning the can of beer so that it is always perpendicular to earth. Neither of his hands are free to minimize the jarring impact that quickly takes place, much too fast for intervention, divine or otherwise. Pulling Goobs up from the ground, we are amazed that the only beer missing is the initial pull taken from the freshly opened can. Shouts of "nice job Goobs!" is broken by the hysterical laughter as we now look down & see pronounced indentations in the sand of Goobs face, hand, pud, and the ring from the beer can bottom.

Paddling around the day's final river bend, the Seney Township Campsite came into view. It was early evening by the time all gear had been brought up from the canoes and tents set up. Before settling in with a nightly campfire, we decided to take a trip into town for a visit to the bar in Seney. While driving us to the start of today's canoe trip, Tom talked about the bar's burgers, and his morning comments had our stomachs thinking all day long out on the water.

From our camp, it was about a mile and a half to Highway M28, over the Fox River Bridge, to Andy's Seney Bar. There we met Andy, a 40-something fella with an outgoing personality that, along with the comfortable feel of his watering hole, made strangers judge themselves welcome. That campfire never did get started on this evening, since we spent the better part of 8 hours enjoying the night and early morning hours at Andy's establishment. This wonderful experience was the first of many 4Day nights at Andy's over the years, and it motivated me, before heading home, to take pencil to paper to capture this initial Andy's visit…

*In the Upper Peninsula of Michigan state, where M77 meets M28,*
*Some get there by canoe, some get there by car*
*They're all lookin' for Andy's, Andy's Seney Bar*

*His daughter serves pizza from across the street,*
*With shots of cheap whiskey the stuff's hard to beat*
*At one-fifty a pitcher your money goes far,*
*But we still dropped fifty at Andy's, Andy's Seney Bar*

Chorus…
*Hey Andy! More Black Jack – we want it straight up!*
*Hey Andy! Toss a towel – we got onion ring slop!*
*Hey Andy! More Beer!!! – bring it before we drop!*

*Andy will refill your pitcher & clean your card table*
*Where's Goober? He's hittin' on a bar wench named Mabel*
*Goobs tells her she's the best that he's ever seen,*
*'Cause he's drunk blind & eyesight ain't too keen*
*Ya might say he got pie-eyed at Andy's, Andy's Seney Bar*

*Chucky's stomach lost a fight with Andy's cuisine*
*He crawled to the car, his face kinda green*
*Was it the burgers? The pizza? Or something between?*
*We only know it was something from Andy's, Andy's Seney Bar*

repeat chorus

*The Big Fella, Chucky, Jimmy, the Goober and Doc,*
*Had their fill of drinkin', and it was 3 o'clock*
*And then as from their livers came a voice from afar:*

*"You can get wet on the Fox River*
*But you can drown at Andy's,*
*Andy's Seney Bar"*

Over the entire 4 days on the water, Goobs was enjoying his new camera (sent to him as a bonus for subscribing to Newsweek), taking all sorts of photos. While never wanting to rush a 4Day, he was excited to get home, develop the rolls of film, and see what took place while he was at play and his memory center was napping. After the Fox was absorbed by the Manistique, Goobs continued shooting photos late on the 4th & final day, not wanting to miss capturing on film the gorgeous late-afternoon colors glistening off of the water. For reasons unknown, maybe freeing up a hand to open a final Milwaukee's Best, Goober had set the camera down on top of Jimmy's cooler as we floated together down the calm waters of the Manistique River. Our little flotilla continued downstream from the big A-frame, the structure located 15 minutes from the trip's completion, cigar smoke floating above us as we soaked in this year's last few moments.

Canoeing by the first cabin on the livery's property, the 20-minutes-to-the-end mark  takes you where the river bends left. Suddenly, the trip's only serious rapids are upon you. It was then Big Guy shouted: "Jimmy! You got Goobs' camera!" It was still sitting atop Jimmy's cooler. He negotiated the rapids beautifully, and the camera never budged. Whew! Then, beyond a midstream island, a fallen tree surprised us. Jimmy swung his paddle from left to right to steer around the tree and, like Darrell Evans feasting on a hanging breaking ball, his swinging paddle sent Goobs' brand new camera rocketing into the river. All 3 canoes pulled over, the guys walking and swimming the area, feeling along the floor of the river, but couldn't locate the camera. Jimmy was apologetic, but he was not at fault and Goobs acknowledged that fact, taking it in stride, only bringing the subject up to talk about how skillfully Jimmy cleared the rapids with the camera intact.

With farewells & see you next years to Tom and Carma at Northland Outfitters, we headed down the street from the livery and checked in at the Germfask motel. The town's Jolly Motel and

Jolly Bar had undergone name changes this year, renamed the Foxx Motel and Foxx Bar. While checking into the motel, we met in passing-only Betsy McCormick, the new motel and bar owner, with just a few pleasantries exchanged. We would come to know and love her after an unexpected 1994 evening in another U.P. bar she owns, Mc's Tally Ho, in nearby Curtis. It was not until a few years after the 1994 night that we came to realize this was the same Betsy that operated the Jolly Motel and Jolly Bar in Germfask from 1985 to 1987, both under the name Foxx, in honor of her husband's saying "Tally Ho the Fox!" when heading out the door for the day, an English phrase for good luck when fox hunting ("good bye, we're off").

# CHAPTER 4
## 1986: 4DAY 9

Fox River w/ Jason, Goobs, Chucky, Big Guy,
Jimmy, Doc and rookie Wayne

*They come from the cities*
*And they come from the smaller towns*
*Beat up cars with guitars and drummers*
*Goin crack, boom, bam*
*(R.O.C.K. in the U.S.A. by John Mellencamp)*

Preparation for the prodigious amount of beer drinking on the 4Day should not be overlooked. A tour of the Stroh's Brewery in downtown Detroit, including all the free ale we could quaff, the week before the 4Day, was the ideal exercise to get in indulging shape. 4Dayers drinking one Stroh's after another before the annual paddling trip is the equivalent of Detroit Tiger batters hitting ball after ball over the outfield wall in batting practice before a Tiger victory. Our Stroh's Brewery host showed us a number of classic Stroh's commercials while we drank, then asked us if anyone knew why Stroh's was the best beer, eliciting several shouts of "cause its free!"

This year, it was our good fortune to have Jimmy's brother Wayne join our merry band of 4Dayers. Jimmy told us that Rookie Wayne would meet us along the highway on our drive to the Upper Peninsula, in a rest area along I-75 north of Flint. As we pulled into the designated rest area, an oak tree of a man, perhaps a NFL offensive lineman visiting our state, towered above all others. Jimmy cleared it up for us, "Guys, meet my brother Wayne".

During the introductions, Wayne walked up to one of us, looked down, and with an amused smile, said, "So they call you the Big Guy". With wide eyes and an audible gulp, Big Guy extended his hand upward and replied, "Yes Sir". Watching his hand completely disappear into Wayne's paw, Big Guy's 6 foot, 270 pound frame suddenly seemed insignificant, dwarfed by Big Wayne's mass.

Prior to departing the rest area, the subject of lunch came up. It was suggested that we stop to eat in Mackinac City, 3 hours away. That's when Wayne made a statement that immediately became a catchphrase with his new 4Day Brothers, "Guys, I wanna make one thing clear: *Chow Time is important*". Wayne told us in no uncertain terms that we would be stopping at the very next exit that had a Burger King. Nobody argued with this rookie.

With the arrival of Wayne, the days of soggy salami sandwiches for camp dinner & occasionally running out of food before the 4Day concluded, were over. He brought along the world's biggest cooler (how it fit into a canoe is one of the great 4Day mysteries, causing us all to review the definition of the word "impossible"), home to roast beef, potatoes, and all the fix-ins, besides an impressive quantity of beer. Rookie Wayne opened our eyes to a new world of happy culinary camping, and 4Day dining never was the same again.

As day one dawned, Wayne said that Goobs was gonna be his canoe partner. Wayne had taken a particular liking to this smallest guy in the group.

Nobody on that trip will ever forget the sight of 430-pound Wayne in the back of the canoe, little Goobs up front, the weight differential causing the canoe to stick out of the water at a 45 degree angle (the angle seemed impossible, but that word no longer applied to Wayne once we saw his cooler fit into a canoe), as if a big outboard motor was at work in the stern. Goobs' fingers were holding on to the front of the canoe as he peered over the edge, only his eyes and forehead visible to those of us looking back, the Wayne-Goober bow half-a-foot out of the water. The rest of us were skimming over the obstacles just beneath the water. Goobs first indication that there was anything just below the surface would be when Wayne and the back of the boat would slam into it, and Goobs would catapult off of the front of the canoe, landing a few feet downstream.

"Double-Doobie Break!" Wayne called out whenever we pulled the boats over for a little river recess. A new 4Day tradition was suddenly born, once again courtesy of Wayne-O, leaving us with shit-eating grins, crispy around the edges, easily dissolving into laughter, and in a chatty mood…

"Hey, did you guys know that Chucky has become a High School English teacher?" "How's that goin' Chucky?" "Well, they told me I'd have an honors class and teach Tennessee Williams. Turns out I have a remedial class and I'm teaching Little Abner." Chucky said the class is at Detroit's Osborne High, 90% black, and he's teaching Romeo & Juliet by having the students learn it "Rap" style. Jason thought that brilliant, and the boys showed their agreement with a round of head-nodding admiration and tugs from a fifth of something cheap 'n brown.

The warm weather and sunny skies had guys hanging off the back of their canoes, bodies immersed in the cool river, for long stretches of downstream floating. No one wanted the day to end, 'cept Goobs: we lost count of the number of times this human cannonball shot off the bow of the canoe he shared with Wayne, and no one was happier than Goobs to see the camp ground as we rounded the final day 1 bend.

Turns out that Wayne's call for a "Double-Doobie Break!" wasn't just at paddling stops. We started each morning herding all hands into a tent, and blowing shot-guns 'til you couldn't see the man next to you. With attitude adjustments in place, we took to the Fox River once again.

The day 2 Spreads on the Fox were as wonderful as ever. The midstream fields of fallen trees downstream from the Spreads were plentiful and particularly challenging this year. What a fortuitous time to have Big Wayne-O with us.

The sight of this playful mountain man, standing alone on top of a giant fallen tree blocking our paths, telling us to just, "come on up… come on up", grabbing the front of each incoming canoe with one hand, dragging it over the obstacle, then setting down gently a boat fully-4Day loaded on the downstream side of the tree, was amazing. Seeing Wayne pull Big Guy's packed-to-the-gills, heavily-weighted, canoe over a wall of downed trees, seemingly around every other bend, with such ease is burned into our memories.

Wayne shared stories about his time in Vietnam, wading with his platoon through waist deep water, guns 'n gear held high above their heads, never knowing when they might be fired upon, and at the end of the day forced to set up camp in these conditions. No wonder Wayne doesn't recognize the word impossible.

Wayne told us about working post-Vietnam days with the phone company. He was up on a telephone pole in a ladies' yard on a particularly hot day, dripping with sweat. Descending the pole, he was greeted by the homeowner w/ a pitcher of lemonade. Wayne was very appreciative, thanked her, and she disappeared into the house. When she came back out, she couldn't believe that he drank it all – she'd brought out two glasses, thinking that they'd each have a glass full. Wayne just figured that someone finally brought him out a properly-sized drinking mug.

Wayne had one joke after the other that he'd tell us on the river or around the campfire, the best of them, "Bunga-Bunga"…

"Three guys are captured by a tribe of natives, and brought before the tribal leader. He tells them *do you want death OR bunga-bunga?* The first guy says, *hell, I'll take bunga-bunga.* The tribal leader says good, and a dozen tribal members line up and give it to him in the butt. The second guy gets the same choice. He says *aw man, bunga-bunga is pretty bad, but it's better than death, so I'll take bunga-bunga.* 100 tribesmen line up and give him bunga-bunga. The tribal leader gives the same choice to the third captive. He thinks it over... first a dozen, then 100 guys butt-buddy you. *Heck with it, I'll take death.* The tribal leader says *good: death... by bunga-bunga*".

About once a half-hour the balance of the 4Day, someone said "death by bunga-bunga", and it never stopped being funny. Wayne had blessed us with another 4Day catch phrase.

Around the day 3 campfire, I told the boys about a recent Duracell business trip to Parkersburg, W. Va. One night at the bar, I had a Michigan shirt on and a fella named Tim Parks walked up and said, "I bet you never seen anything like this in Michigan" and proceeded to take a bite out of his beer glass and started chewing on it. He smiled and asked me, "What do you think about that?" I told Tim, "I think your mouth is bleeding".

The campfire conversation shifted to movies...

Big Guy said, "*The Natural* is one of my favorites. Old Tigers 3rd baseman Phil Mankowski has a small bit where he takes a grounder in the pills. Now that's fine directing!" Jason asked, "I wonder if he got a chance to read the script beforehand, or if they just surprised him?" Chucky figured, "Based on Mankowski's defense with the Tigers, he probably knew it was coming but couldn't stop it." "Chucky", I asked, "you don't think Mankowski is a worse infielder than Chico *I got a hole in my glove* Fernandez, do you?" "No, but it's a toss-up between Mankowski and Enos Cabell." A chorus of "Old Dude!" welled up from the 4Dayers in honor of Enos' nickname.

Jimmy asked, "Chucky, didn't you see the *Color Purple* recently?" "Yeah, Whoopi Goldberg playing an ugly black woman, gutsy casting. Now *Runaway Train* on the other hand... you have a Russian Director directing American actors from a Japanese screenplay produced by Hebrews. Is this a great country, or what?"

On the final morning, Wayne announced that he wanted to canoe with Chucky that day. Suddenly Goobs going airborne when the back of the boat was slammed below the surface wasn't as funny to Chucky. "Goober, I'll give you whatever you want if you'll paddle with Wayne again today. Do you want my credit card?" Goobs just laughed, "I need a day off Chucky".

The 4Day will never be the same as before Wayne Thomas Vollmers joined the brotherhood. What a damn good thing that is.

# CHAPTER 4
## 1987: 4DAY 10

Fox River w/ Slovik, Jimmy, Wayne, Jason, Big Guy,
Goobs, Chucky, Doc, and rookie Johnny Steck

*These moments you're left with, may we always remember*
*These moments are shared by few*
*There's wind in our hair, and there's water in our shoes*
*It's been a Lovely Cruise*
*(Lovely Cruise by Jimmy Buffett)*

Chucky & I spotted Faz sitting in the 3rd row behind home plate at Tiger Stadium a few days before the 4Day. He told us that his pizza shop, closed for 2 years, would be re-opening in September. What wonderful news! How can any EMU student in the 70s and early-80s ever forget the famous "Faz" fold over pizza? It was guaranteed to burn the roof of your mouth on the first bite, but tasted so damn good, better than any calzone we've ever had!

While still living in the dorms, we met Faz in 1973 at his campus pizza shop on College Place, around the corner from our favorite watering hole, Hungry Charlie's Bar on Cross Street. Faz Pizza featured "Free FAZT Delivery!" and Ypsi's most memorable phone number, 481-1111. Back in '73 and '74, Detroit Tigers Bill Freehan and Mark Wagner were occasionally seen in Faz' pizza shop, at least once when the smell of burning hemp was in the air, purely coincidental.

Faz is instantly likeable and seems to be friends with *everyone*. He was the only Muslim delegate to the 1984 Democratic National Convention, and what a thrill it was for all his family and his many friends to see Faz interviewed by Dan Rather during the convention. Faz ran for Ypsilanti mayor in 1985, taking out a full page ad in the Ypsi Press that included photos of Faz with George Bush, Gordie Howe, Danny Thomas, Muhammed Ali, Jimmy Carter, Henry Kissinger, Sugar Ray Leonard, and several others. There was even a photo of Queen Elizabeth in the ad – no Faz next to her, just Queen Elizabeth. His popularity did not translate into an election-day victory, selfishly good news for us as Faz could now keep focusing on making pizzas.

Speaking of good eatin', a special part of every 4Day are the good-bye, have fun, and be safe brownies (all ingredients legal) that Maggie sends me off with each year. The quantity is enough to share among all 4Dayers with a sufficient amount to often last 2 or more days. Since this is the

10$^{th}$ 4Day, Mag made an *extra* big batch. Despite that, it's amazing that any brownies survived the drive north, as the boys called for them at each rest stop and bar break taken.

A round of 9 holes at the St. Ignace Golf Course was on the 4Day10 Eve agenda, prior to an evening at the Keyhole Lounge. Before crossing the Big Mac for the St. Ignace course, we pulled into Mackinaw City and the Wa-Wa-Tam Motel to grab our rooms for the night. New owners, Garey & Roberta, are quite a change from the staid Elmer. They are happy, personable folks and fun to chat with. Their genuine joy in our arrival, and happiness in the part that their Ma 'n Pa operation played in our 4Day10 celebration, made us feel very comfortable. Garey is a bit of a scamp. He'd recently received a warning from the Mackinaw City police for flying his small plane <u>beneath</u> the Mackinac Bridge, a warning that he told us about with great satisfaction!

Last year, we golfed for the first time as a group the day before the 4Day, just a casual couple of hours on the St. Ignace course. This year the stakes were raised: in a 9-hole competition, the losing team picks up the entire dinner/drink tab at the Keyhole Lounge post-golf. Teams were picked by luck of the draw, with Wayne ending up on Big Guy's team. Wayne has a care-free attitude about golf, and had an enjoyable time on the course last year despite shooting 117 for 9 holes. Hmm... maybe Big Guy will pay for his free Keyhole Lounge hat from 1985 after all.

Midway through the round, it was pretty clear that the team with Big Guy and Wayne would be picking up the Keyhole tab. About the time this realization kicked in, the winning team was having problems finding golf balls they'd just hit down the fairway. Turns out that Big Guy, playing ahead of us, was attempting to bury our Top Flites by stepping on them. It didn't change the outcome, but did make winning that much more pleasurable.

Post-golf at the bar, there was an awful lot of grumbling emitting from beneath that free Keyhole Lounge hat, the loser's bill steadily rising with the serious grub 'n gulp binging taking place. The waitress seemed to be on a tether, wearing a footpath into the wooden floor from picking up our drink orders at the bar to delivering them to our table. The imbibing was partially driven by the frequent toasts to the Mobil Lounge Softball Team & Beer Swiller Club's (aka MLST&BSC) first championship season, clinched this past month. Whatever drove the alcoholic intake was a boon to Chucky's smokin' hot table-top shuffleboard performance, a performance that reminded Jason of a W. C. Fields quote, "Always carry a flagon of whiskey in case of snakebite, and furthermore always carry a small snake". The bar manager's edict that we depart the premises at 2AM found an authoritarian analogy in Slovik's world, "I've never passed the State Police Post in Lima, Ohio without giving them the bird".

The noteworthy through-the-night Keyhole imbibing slowed the next morning's departure to a crawl. As a result, the hour & 15 minute drive across the bridge to Germfask started a bit later than planned. Arriving near the noon hour at Northland Outfitters, livery owners Tom & Carma greeted us with a sign reading, "10th Anniversary – Jeff and Friends". The couple's good cheer under sunny skies, with a beckoning river several feet away, served as a much needed adrenaline shot to the bleary-eyed party boys.

The Fox River, for the 7th time in the 4Day's first 10 years, would be our river of choice. This narrow water highway was as exciting and challenging as always, forcing quick decisions when confronted with obstructions around so many tight bends, with little space to maneuver around each.

The river trials were not the only 4Day aspects that felt familiar. On day 1, Wayne and Goobs repeated their paddling partnership of 1986, with little Goobs & the canoe's bow sitting at a 45 degree angle above the waterline, the result of water displacement from man-mountain Wayne in the stern, giving Goober an aerial view of the Fox normally reserved for birds and winged insects while providing priceless amusement for the spectators; Chucky had his left eyelid swollen shut by a skeeter/spider bite (pick one); and Jason got drunk, he claimed for the first time in 2 years although not a single 4Dayer was in agreement with his assessment (Jimmy noted, "If Jason had a 2-year drinking hiatus, it was well camouflaged on last year's 4Day").

The tardy arrival at the livery meant a late start to canoeing and the canoe flotilla didn't pull into the Seney Township campsite until early-evening. No one felt like cooking, so we made the 20 minute walk to Andy's Seney Bar for Andy burgers and beers.

Goobs was bellied up to the bar, having a real pleasant discussion with an old timer, 'til Goobs told of having a friend who had family in the area about 100 years ago. "Friend's last name is Harcourt. Does that sound familiar?" As soon as Goobs said the name, the old timer turned his back to him and never said another word.

The ancient mariner at Andy's was fighting a longtime battle. In the town of Seney during the late-1800s, there was a feud on the level of the Hatfields and the McCoys: the Harcourts and the Dunns. In 1891, Steve Harcourt was tending bar in his Seney tavern when he was shot and killed by Dan Dunn. Dunn then fled Seney to the Lower Peninsula, with Steve's brother, Jim Harcourt, in pursuit. Jim caught up to Dan Dunn near the town of Flint, where he took Dunn's life in revenge for Steve's shooting. Jim Harcourt was arrested, brought back to Seney for trial, convicted and served 3 years in jail for Dan Dunn's murder. Upon his release in 1894, Jim was elected Township Supervisor for the first of nine consecutive terms, the Seney town folks' way of weighing in on the feud. Today, Goobs' ex-drinking buddy took the opposing viewpoint.

After breaking camp Day 2 morning under cloudy conditions, we were beneath the M28 Bridge in a half-an-hour, Andy's bar a couple hundred feet to the east. We had our heads on a swivel, hoping that Goobs old drinkin' compadre from last night didn't still want to fight the Harcourt-Dunn feud. The Spreads were only 15 minutes downstream from M28 as the skies above were turning as nasty as old Dan Dunn's disposition.

At the upstream edge of the Spreads, we usually take a break, pull the boats over and toss the Frisbee for a bit while popping open a Stroh's. BUT, these skies looked as ugly as ugly gets, so before the rains began, we decided to get beyond the 30-minute Spreads' journey, to where the tall trees form a canopy overhead, providing limited downpour shelter. We hadn't cleared the Spreads when all hell broke loose. Talking later about his rookie year, Johnny said, "The skies turned a purple I've never seen before, ugly skies, but beautifully ugly. 12 guys got under a tarp and the boats pulled up next to each other where the Spreads widen out." The tornado-like clouds swirled overhead, and the purple skies now turned a fantastic greenish-purple as torrential rains pounded the thin plastic tarp that struggled to keep us moderately dry.

Today was an 8-hour experience on the river, battling the usual number of fallen trees between the Seney site and our favorite campground, the Peninsula. Big Guy and Goobs were canoe partners, and for just about all of those 8 hours, Goobs was in a puckish mood, barking Yankees Suck-chatter at Big Guy: *"Hey Big Guy!"* "What?" *"The Yankees Suck!"* Near the end of the paddle, Goobs finally passed out, giving Big Guy some peace. The rest of us had made it to camp, tents set up, as the late-day colors began to fade, and here comes Biggie paddling in, Goobs sound asleep in the bow. From our camp site, I yelled down to the river, "Goobs!!! Goobs!!!" till his chin left his chest, "What do you think of the Yankees?" Goobs got off one final, *"THE YANKEES SUCK!!!"* easily his loudest of the day. The nasty look that Big Guy shot my way, with daggers in his eyes, had the whole camp laughing. The story of Goobs, Biggie, and "Yankees Suck!" was repeated over & over at the evening's bonfire.

Echoing down the river all of day 3 was Chucky imitating lines from Mel Brooks *History of the World Part 1*, including impersonating Mel Brooks as Moses holding 3 stone tablets: "The Lord has given us these 15 (drops one of the tablets)... these 10, 10 Commandments". Chucky also did a great parroting of Mel Brooks' King Louis XVI character, messing with Harvey Korman's Count de Monet. "Count de Money!" with the exasperated Korman replying, "No, no, it's *de... mo...nay*, de-mo-nay!"

We found open, flat riverside ground an hour or so upstream from the *Old... Log... Bridge* and pitched tents for the night. Around the campfire, Biggie was giving his views on perfect womanhood, "I see a chick goin' by in a pick-up truck, a lotta dirt on it ("it" being the truck, we believe), and I know that's a girl I could carry on a conversation with, not some dolled-up babe." Wayne-O talked about his first date with some lady, driving down Gratiot in his van, "and she's complaining about the van's curtains, saying I probably use these 'cause I have a lot of girls in here. I'm not gonna listen to this shit, so I stop the van in the middle of the road and tell her, get out". Recalling how it all happened got Wayne to laughing, "She says *what*? I said *get out!* This gal is asking what do I need all this noise for? My stereo's too loud. She's telling me about her nice stereo back home, and asking me, the curtains – what's all this? So I told her, 'Hey, you don't like it, you don't have to ride in the mother f_____er!' So I turned around on Gratiot Avenue, pulled into a restaurant parking lot, opened the door for her and said, 'Get out! I'll call you, don't call me'. She said, 'What's the matter?' I said, 'Conversation over – out!'"

The campfire conversation switched gears and, although this doesn't quite sound right, the boys started singing instrumentals, perhaps better characterized as howl-alongs. It started with the Moody Blues song "Procession", mimicking with sounds guttural to high-pitched the flows of the tune's instruments. Sticking with the Moody Blues theme, the 4Day choir began to do acapella work on the band's various album intros, of particular fun was the "Ride My Seesaw" opening. The fire seemed to rise as the voices did. Once past the first verse, recall of the lyrics disintegrated, the singers settling for a disjointed "New York, New York" that sounded better to our liquored selves than it likely was.

Chucky had turned in for the night a while ago, and we were trying our best to prompt him to re-join us. Jimmy resorted to lines from *History of the World Part 1*, "and here he is... Count de Money!" A few moments of silence passed, then from his tent, a faint, distant Chucky voice came back with, *"de-mo-nay"*, and the 4Dayers exploded in laughter. Further baiting with, "the return of Count de Money!", did not draw Chucky back to the fire, so we offered Jack Daniels, a bit of a Hail Mary as whiskey is likely is what lined the path to his sleeping bag (although trying to entice a drunken man with liquor has worked in the past).

Jimmy then appealed to brotherhood, "Chucky, company by the fireside!" Although Jimmy was unsuccessful, his plea lead to Big Guy's cry, "To the final night of the 4Day". When this was echoed by Jason, it seemed every voice jumped into a spontaneous rhythmic cadence without missing a beat,

> *The final night of the 4Day*
> *The final night*
> *The final night*
> *The final night of the 4Day*
> *The 4Day, the 4Day*
> *The final night of the 4Day!*

And so it was Jimmy and Big Guy's efforts to entice Chucky to the campfire that lit the fuse of this revered 4Day sing-a-long.

The *final night of the 4Day* chant was halted when sounds came from Slovik's tent, sounds different than the snores that had flowed from his tent the last couple of hours. Shouts of "Tommy's up!" was met by silence from Slovik aka Tommy Tutone, so the boys began an impromtu 4Day version of Woodstock's *Rain Chant* shouting, "Tom! Tom! Tom! Tom! Ta-ah-ah-ah-om! Tom! Tom! Tom! Tom! Tom!" When this failed to rouse Slovik, it was pointed out that he had already made a post-pass out appearance, emerging from his tent to senselessly kick a log *out* of the fire (where logs don't burn as well), only to silently disappear into the darkness and towards his tent once again. So, maybe it was ok that our exhortations didn't rouse Slovik.

4Day post-script: 1983 one-year-only 4Dayer and lunatic Schmidt joined us at Joe Louis Arena for the Great Lakes Invitational hockey tournament this December. Schmidt took a post-game walk on the roofs of cars stopped at the Jefferson Avenue traffic light in front of the Joe, stopping at one car to lay on the roof, head hanging over the driver's side window to chat up the gentleman driving. This was the last known sighting of Schmidt, who – before the light turned green - climbed down from the car and walked off into the night.

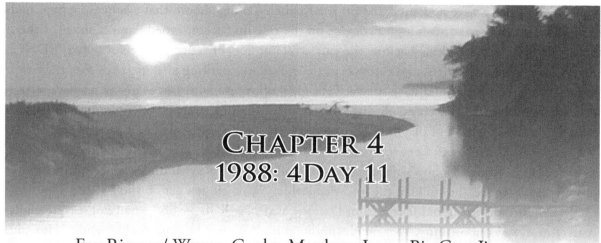

# CHAPTER 4
# 1988: 4DAY 11

Fox River w/ Wayne, Goobs, Matthew, Jason, Big Guy, Jimmy, Johnny, Chucky, Doc, and rookies Rusty Vollmers & Bob Vollmers

*Last night I dreamed that I passed from the scene*
*And I went to a place so sublime*
*Oh, the water was clear and tasted like beer*
*Then they turned it all into wine (awwww)*
*(I Like Beer by Tom T. Hall)*

"Doc, I'm coming in for the 4Day!" Matthew was calling from his Philadelphia home with the great news, "It's been too long. I need this badly!" It had been 5 years since Matthew's last 4Day. Moving from Michigan to Pennsylvania in the interim had stunted his participation, and five years is an eternity when you embrace the adventure as much as Matt does ("I've always considered being part of the experience one of my better decisions").

4Day-eve lodging was at our home-away-from-home, the Wa-Wa-Tam Motel in Mackinaw City. After checking in, we headed over to Audie's, a family restaurant that seats 60, for their buffet, before making a night of it at the Keyhole Lounge. 7 of us grabbed tables at Audie's Restaurant, arriving several minutes before the slower-moving but chow-time focused four of Big Guy plus Vollmers Brothers Wayne and rookies Bob & Rusty. In girth units, these 4 averaged 300 pounds plus, with heights between 5'11" and 6'5".

The sun was setting in such a way that it came in low through the windows at Audie's front door - until the final four arrived. Those big fellers stepped into the restaurant and blotted out the early-evening sun, immediately sending the room into a brown-out situation. The Vollmers Boys and Biggie scanned the room, their eyes coming to a screeching halt on the buffet, involuntary smiles curling the corners of their mouths. They were lined up much like Wyatt Earp, Doc Holiday, and gang at the O.K. Corral shootout, and every bit as serious. Initially paralyzed into silence, the patrons soon understood what the arrival of these 4 meant, and bolted to the buffet, much as a drowning man grabs the last seat on the dinghy floating by.

Were the boys local residents, Audie's would've been faced with the option of a severe buffet price hike or closing their doors. An impressive chow base was built in each of us, leaving the boys believing that they were now prepared for the Keyhole Lounge booze that awaited. Perhaps had the boys not imbibed to such a great degree on the ride up (as concerned parents shielded their children's eyes, hustling kids back to the cars while no longer sober 4Dayers shouted "4Day!", drank from open containers, and threw Frisbees in rest area parking lots), perhaps *then* the bases built at Audie's buffet would have survived the alcoholic onslaught. But as it was...

Tequila 'n bourbon 'n beers, oh my! An alcoholic tsunami wrapped itself around a night of table top shuffleboard, and playing and re-playing the odd couple mix of *Lunatic Fringe* and *A White Sport Coat & a Pink Carnation* on the outstanding Keyhole juke box. "I should have done this years ago!" Rookie Bobby Vollmers said over and over. With a year under his belt, sophomore Johnny Steck smiled the smile of the knowledgeable, "Wait 'til you get on the river!"

Matthew ran into an old friend from Detroit, Matthew Kline, who he had not seen in eight years. Jimmy saw opportunity, "Bar maid, another round! We need a toast to old friends!" Hearing that Matthew Kline's sister-in-law owns the Keyhole, Jimmy hopefully added, "And pour 'em on the house!" His hopes were dashed, but we drank to his disappointment. As the night ended, our Matthew climbed into the bed of his long-lost buddy's pick-up truck, and caught a ride to the Wa-Wa-Tam, while the rest of us staggered back. By the time the one mile trip ended, Matthew had to be rolled out of the back of the truck and assisted into his motel room.

"Up and at 'em boys, it's time to start drinkin'!" was my message as I went door-to-door, letting all know that it was time to get rolling to Northland Outfitters & the Fox River. Dressing for the day, in his pocket Matthew found a Keyhole Lounge coaster with his old friend's name and address on it. As a bonus, Goobs' address was on it, too. "If we get moving within the next 30 minutes, we have time for breakfast" is a time-tested way, I found, to start the parade.

Seeing us file through the front door, Audie's owner was thankful that he decided not to repeat his dinner all-you-can-eat buffet as a breakfast special. Surprisingly, although they were already seated when we arrived, our table was served before the table of Wayne, Rusty & Bob Vollmers (whose previous night arrival at the buffet put fear into the hearts of dinner patrons). Even more surprisingly, the three brothers did not seem to mind that their meals were not delivered until 10 minutes after ours. When the bills arrived, their totaled was $29.87 for 3, even though a good-sized Audie's breakfast cost about $5. "Guys", I suggested, "you should check with the waitress, she messed up your bill." "No she hasn't Doc," Wayne informed me, "we ordered again." By the time we were seated, Rusty, Bob, and Wayne had eaten a full breakfast, had their plates cleared away, and then placed a 2nd food order.

*Splash!* Rookies Rusty and Bob tipped over at the second bend, now forever to be known as "Russell's Corner". "Who let the rookies go in the same canoe?" Their fellow 4Day brothers gathered the gear floating downstream, helped the rookies right their ship, and repeated the process a few more times today. On the occasion of the third flip, Bobby popped up from the water shouting, "Alright then! On to the next dunking!" That's the spirit, rookie.

Goobs and Matthew were canoeing partners for most of the trip, with Goobs constantly asking Matthew to paddle faster whenever they lost sight of Big Guy's canoe. "Why Goobs?" "So that I can get close enough to remind him that *the Yankees Suck!*"

The first day on the river, Matthew was getting extremely drunk, rocking the canoe he shared with Goobs. At the next break, Goobs asked Big Guy, "You want to paddle with Matthew for awhile?" Acquiescing, within 5 minutes Matthew's playful rocking had deposited Big Guy into the drink – in less than 6" of flat water. Twice within 50 yards. Big Guy's gear was soaked, and he… was… steaming. Matt tried to calm him down, "What are you complaining about Big Guy, *my* stuff is dry." Matthew then went on a several minute belly-laugh jag that was contagious for all but Big Guy.

1st night on the Fox, the boys were sitting around the campfire telling stories, except Rookie Rusty. He just sat there pleasant, quiet. Next to him was a comic-book-large, bursting at the seams, trash bag, quite possibly the largest trash bag known to man. I assumed it held Rusty's tent, sleeping bag, dry clothes, and any other miscellaneous gear he might want handy on the river. I was wrong. When Rusty opened the bag, it appeared that every product the good folks at the Hostess Co. ever thought of, and perhaps a few items yet in the testing stage, were visible: Twinkies, Ho-Hos, Ding Dongs, Suzie-Qs, Mini Muffins, Snoballs, Cupcakes, Rusty-Cups (test-stage item), and on and on and all for his own consumption.

Rusty began to open up a little after tugging on the bourbon being passed around the bonfire. After an extended amount of tugging, it was apparent that the dam holding back Russell's words had burst open. The Quiet Man was now holding court, while we sat with mouths open, regaling us with stories about the fun he was having on the river and his life story, until, *"Russell! Bed!"* Wayne bellowed. Rusty said not another word, and crawled into a nearby tent. I didn't know if it was <u>his</u> tent, but felt immense relief knowing it wasn't mine.

Although it was our third consecutive year as witnesses, the incredible amount of food that Wayne prepared and ate each night on the river never failed to amaze us. "Wayne brought 3 giant coolers of food," Chucky said on our final night of camping, "and he ate it all – I can't believe it!"

Creating 4Day "fern leaf hats" was tangible proof that we were looking for previously untried ways to stretch out the final day of paddling. Standing on shore, fern leaves sticking out of our hats, the first people we saw this 4Day paddled by us, a 2-boat family outing. In the first canoe a Mother & Son cruised by us. They waved and we waved back. In the 2nd boat was a Father & his 15-year old Daughter. They waved, we stared. Hard. The Father looked very nervous and began to furiously paddle… far, far away from us.

Heading home after pulling the boats out of the water at Northland Outfitters, we drove about 3 hours when it felt like time for a break a little south of West Branch at an old friend just off I-75 exit 202, the Alger Bar. Goobs is well beyond feeling great and wanders into the bathroom. Chucky is sitting in one of the stalls and hears a loud scratching noise on the other side of the stall wall on his left, like a large squirrel is climbing it. "What tha…?" a startled Chucky says as Goobs' head suddenly hangs over the top of Chucky's stall. Goobs is staring down and then, in his outdoor voice, shouts, "Hey he's takin' a SHIT!" Everyone in the bar has heard Goobs pronouncement, and Big Guy is turning red from laughter, "That's Goobs!" Ironically, Goober had what could be called a shit-eatin' grin as he emerged from the dumper, with Chucky shaking his smiling head a few steps behind, a flushed conclusion to 4Day 1988.

# CHAPTER 4
# 1989: 4DAY 12

Fox River w/ Chucky, Johnny, Jason, Big Guy,
Wayne, Rusty, Bob, Jimmy and Doc

*Just sittin' around drinkin' with the rest of the guys*
*Six rounds bought, and I bought five*
*I spent the groceries and half the rent*
*Like fourteen dollars and twenty-seven cents*
*(Dang Me by Roger Miller)*

Chucky, future 4Dayer Mister P, and Father of the 4Day Ricki Rice, visited Secretariat a couple of months before this year's 4Day. The 3 traveled to Claiborne Farms in Paris, Kentucky, the home of, arguably, the greatest race horse of all time. Chucky posed for a photo with Secretariat, 16 years after attending his first Kentucky Derby back in 1973, the year that Secretariat won the Run for the Roses in a record time of 1:59. Chucky never cashed his winning Derby ticket from that day, preferring to keep it as a souvenir. Secretariat's win the next month at Belmont secured the Triple Crown, as he finished an amazing 31 lengths ahead of the 2nd place finisher. This champion horse passed away in October, 5 months after the guys' visit. At Secretariat's autopsy, it was found that his heart was twice the size of that of a normal horse.

Once back from the Secretariat visit, Chucky joined us at Ypsilanti's Spaghetti Bender to get in drinkin' trim for the upcoming 4Day. He lined up 5 shots of Jack on the table. "Ok, who's going to time this for me?" he asked. Maggie handled the time check, and gave Chucky the go signal. It took him a mere 30 seconds to knock down all 5 shots. Chucky later listed this accomplishment as one of his more notable, along with being hired as the first teacher in the City of Detroit's autistic children program, meeting Secretariat, and refusing to let the child within him go.

Driving rain and strong winds played havoc on Frisbee tossing, limiting rest area stops to calls from nature, and shaving 90 minutes off the usual time required to reach our 4Day eve home in Mackinaw City. The flooded conditions kept us off the St. Ignace golf course, pushing us with little resistance into the Keyhole Lounge pub at earlier hours than usual, hours that meant the presence of a family-oriented crowd, a presence that initially seemed to have a negative effect on the 4Dayers conversation...

*Chucky asked, "Does this shirt make me look fat?" Wayne-O assured him, "No Chucky, 20 years of beer drinking makes you look fat."*

*Bob Vollmers wondered, "How do those dead bugs get into enclosed light fixtures?" "What?" "No really, I've always been curious about that."*

Before anyone places an order for tea and scones, or sashays out the front door to peruse the nearby shops in search of doilies, let's get out of this discourse death spiral. "Waitress, we need your assistance!" Doctor Fletcher prescribes a double round of shots and change for the juke box. It's time to heat up the bar with a little Wang Chung *Everybody Have Fun Tonight*, Kenny Loggins *Danger Zone* & the Pretenders *Message of Love*, kicking off a run of rock 'n roll that sent electricity through the tavern, sent families out the door to more sedate locales, and sent us to a late night of beers, shots, sing-a-longs, and table top shuffleboard.

It wasn't easy getting the boys up, fed, and on the road in a timely fashion the day after this long Keyhole evening, but somehow we were able to make it to the livery in Germfask by our 11AM target. Once we were paddling down the Fox River, the conversation turned to the incredible, rough 'n tumble history of the area we were canoeing through.

Seney had its start in 1882 as the logging center for several companies that began to cut down the gorgeous stands of white pine blanketing the area. With that many loggers in one spot - an estimated 3,000 - it didn't take long before the support staff set up shop: Seney became home to 21 saloons, 5 blind pigs, and 5 bordellos.

Seney earned the name "the Sodom of the North", attracting all sorts of scum-dogs, including Leon Czolgosz. After losing his job as a Seney railroad hand, Leon drifted east where, after getting riled up listening to a speech given by anarchist Emma Goldman, he assassinated President William McKinley in Buffalo in 1901, thus elevating Vice-President Theodore Roosevelt to the Presidency.

And then there was P.K. Small, self-styled meanest 'n ugliest lumberjack in America. Getting into a bar fight during a drinking binge, P.K. had his nose bitten off, and was the recipient of frequent face stompings (known as "logger's small pox") from caulked boots of fightin' partners. P.K. Small would greet folks arriving in town on the train by picking them up and turning them upside down, shaking from their pockets a "loose offering", before setting the victims free. His logging days done, P.K. became a full-time bar regular, earning free drinks and the nickname "Snag Jaw" by biting the heads off of live frogs, toads, and snakes.

"The Sodom of the North" lasted about as long as the Third Reich: by the mid-1890s, the area's white pine forests were reduced to stumps, the lumbermen moved north to Grand Marais, and Seney's population shrank from 3,000 to less than two hundred, about what it is today.

After sharing these stories on the river, we decided that, once we canoed to our Seney Township Campsite, we would be taking a walk to Andy's Bar to feel the town's history up close and personal. When the 8 of us walked in, Andy was holding court and filling drinks for the only two folks at his establishment. Seeing us, Andy's face lit up, and he said, "It's good to see you boys! Let's do a shot together!" as he poured out a round that was good because of the company and because it was on the house. Many, many shots were on the house and, if being 3 sheets to the wind allowed us to reach out and touch Seney's history, then P.K. Small was walking right alongside as we staggered back to camp and into our tents.

The boys were standing around the 2nd morning breakfast fire when they heard a tent unzip, and turned to look in the direction of the noise. "Lord!" "Oh my God, take a look at Johnny" "Hey Johnny, you ok?"

It's rare when someone looks rougher the morning after a 4Day night than Johnny Steck. Despite that, Johnny has a favorite saying, "I'd quit my job before I'd miss a 4Day". 1989 marks his 3rd year of paddling with us, and 4 years since Jimmy introduced him to our group of friends. Back in 1985, our softball team was in need of a couple of players. Jimmy stepped forward, "I have two guys in mind", bringing Johnny and future-4Dayer Vid to the next game.

Johnny is quiet, an entertaining physical comedian (he does great Stanley Laurel impressions), is an outstanding athlete and, except for certain mornings on the 4Day (like the morning after a night at Andy's), is almost always smiling. From his days at Pioneer High School in Ann Arbor, Johnny holds most of the tennis team's records. Until 1981, he kept busy earning a living giving tennis lessons, while looking for something a little different.

In 1981, Johnny and Vid opened a candy store together in Ann Arbor. They spent the early years of their lives in New Castle, Pennsylvania, where their families were friends before moving, at different times, to Michigan. In Oil City, a town near New Castle, Johnny's grandfather George Steck opened Mary Ridgway Sweets (named in honor of George's aunt), selling candy treats that he created. 50 years later, Johnny decided to use Grandpa George's recipes and, with his partner Vid, opened a brand new Mary Ridgway Sweets shop, at a house purchased in '81 by Vid's family on Ashley Street in downtown Ann Arbor. Their sweet creations built a loyal following of regular customers but, due in part to candy chain stores moving into Ann Arbor, Mary Ridgway Sweets closed this past year.

4Day Monday is Vid's 37th birthday, and he's yet to be part of this adventure. We probably should've never told him about early-4Day dining on wet salami sandwiches or the time we ran out of food the final day on the river. Chow time is very important to Vid. Hell, it's important to us all, but it's more of a religious fervor for Vidder.

Johnny was struggling a bit as we tore down camp Day 2 morning. I figured hair of the dog was just the ticket for him, and cracked open a fifth, took a long tug, and offered it to Johnny. He was unenthusiastic, but I put my arm around his shoulder and assured him that "the bottle I'm passing to you is not as bad as the grimace on my face would indicate". Much to my surprise, Johnny was receptive to this pitch, nodded, took a respectable hit, and before you know it had a little giddy-up in his step. The packing continued and we were soon back on the river.

2 hours into today's journey, the joy of paddling through the narrow and fast-flowing Spreads met its end with an exclamation mark as we arrived at the first of a dozen logjams downstream. With Wayne as the main muscle and a supporting cast of the rest of us, we worked together to move every boat over each fallen tree, splitting the labor-force into 2 groups: the first exerting the brute strength required to raise the boats out of the water and over the midstream debris, the second handling the lighter load of catching these newly-freed canoes & pushing them on to dry land; the groups would alternate to keep fresh our mobile coalition and maintain esprit de corps.

After 8 hours of paddling and pushing since leaving the Seney site, the High Ground camp never looked so inviting. Tents went up, dry clothes went on, new layers of Deet were applied, and the ravenous 4Day crew gorged themselves on the wonderful chicken, corn-on-the-cob, and baked potatoes spread put out by the Vollmers Boys, with exhausted snoring heard from all tents within an hour of dinner clean-up.

Awakening with sore muscles all-around, the schedule for Day 3 was welcome: a laid-back, two-hour jaunt with few logjams from the High Ground to the Peninsula. Jason, the man who once he started 4Dayin' reset his calendar so that the first day of the 4Day is New Year's Day, considers the Peninsula the greatest campground he's ever had the pleasure to pitch a tent at, including sites camped in Montana, Wyoming, Colorado, New Mexico, and Arizona. "They all have nice campgrounds, but none to match the Peninsula".

The sun-drenched day was ideal for multiple canoe-breaks of swimming and Frisbee tossing. Jimmy & Biggie went off on their own to get in some fishing. Jimmy said, "We were just getting a few nibbles, nothing too big. If we wanted to be serious about it, we'd do it more often." Big Guy had a different take on it: sitting around the evening campfire at the Peninsula, he opened a new fifth of something brown, and told of his & Jimmy's day of fishing. Rusty said, "Every time Big Guy takes a pull off the bottle, the fish he caught and released gets bigger and bigger." Then Wayne chipped in, "Based on what's left in the bottle, he must have started with a goldfish".

With our gear packed, we bid adieu to the Peninsula. 4 hours of paddling remained until we came ashore at Northland Outfitters and the 4Day's end. There was quite a bit of good-natured teasing of Big Guy regarding his growing fishing claims of the previous evening. Chucky said, "*I'm going fishing* really means I'm going to drink myself dangerously stupid and stand by a stream with a stick in my hand while the fish swim by in complete safety."

As we unhurriedly floated downstream, Jimmy taught us some fine sing-alongs including a tear-jerker called the *Ode to Ted Kennedy…*

Oh… your mother is old,
And your father is dead,
And your brother is dead,
And your brother is dead,
And your brother is dead,
And your wife is a drunk,
And your kid has one leg,
And your car doesn't float.

And an old TV ad about *Thunderbird Wine* that was easy to remember…

What's the word? Thunderbird!
What's the price? 44 twice!
What's the reason? It's drinkin' season!

Exiting the river at the livery deck, the songs of Ted Kennedy and Thunderbird Wine that would now forever be a part of 4Day lore bounced around in our heads while we counted down the days until the next annual great Up North experience.

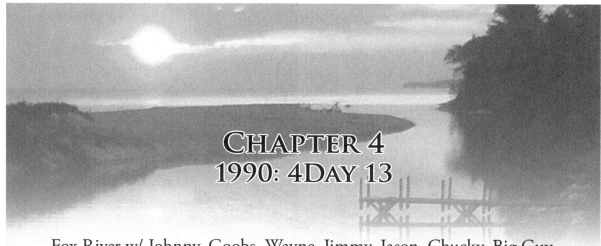

# CHAPTER 4
# 1990: 4DAY 13

Fox River w/ Johnny, Goobs, Wayne, Jimmy, Jason, Chucky, Big Guy, Doc and rookies Kenny, Chris, Paul aka the Colonel, and Z-Bob

*But fortunately I have the key to escape reality*
*And you may see me tonight with an illegal smile*
*It don't cost very much, but it lasts a long while*
*Won't you please tell the man I didn't kill anyone*
*No I'm just tryin' to have me some fun*
*(Illegal Smile by John Prine)*

We embarked on 4Day 13 with a group of 12, the largest contingent to date, including a rookie class of four...

Rookie Kenny "Cherry Jack" Umphrey, 45 years young, the new elder statesman of the 4Day. I'd met Kenny 13 years prior, while we both worked for Duracell, a few months after I was hired in October of 1976. Duracell started me as a trouble-shooter, filling in on field sales as needed. On a January '77 Saturday, Maggie and I had just eased into an altered state with the Moody Blues "On the Threshold of a Dream" at my Ypsi Apartment, when the phone rang. "Hi Jeff, this is Ken Umphrey, Duracell District Manager down in Indianapolis". It was the first time I'd ever spoken with Kenny. In his charming southern Indiana drawl, Kenny continued, "Jeff, there's a vacant sales territory in Indy, and we could use your help for a few weeks". I'd leave Ypsi for the 6 hour drive each Sunday night, come home Friday afternoon, was enjoyably helping out, calling Kenny to check in weekly, yet after a month or so we hadn't met.

Kenny sez "You can't put a price on $5.60 whiskey"

One day I stopped at Duracell's largest Indy customer, though I knew Kenny was handling this one, just to say hi and see if I could be of any assistance, when I ran into the man himself – our initial face-to-face. After taking care of business and on our way out the door, Kenny suggested that we take the afternoon off and have a beer or two. I put up no resistance, followed his car to the local Holiday Inn bar, where we grabbed a table and ordered a round. The waitress returned with 4 beers. Kenny said, "Sorry, but we only ordered two." She informed us it was "Wicked Wednesdays" and all beer orders were 2 for 1. Over a canoe-load of 2 for 1 rounds, we talked about my Maggie, his Pat, families & friends, life experiences (the man climbed Mt. Rainer!), a shared-love of Steve Martin's comedy, and nothing about work. After much beer over the dam, and agreeing to meet for breakfast tomorrow in order to cover at least *some* business, Kenny excused himself to meet a buddy for a racquetball game. He arrived the next morning with a few visible cuts 'n scrapes 'n 14 stitches on his lip. "Kenny, what happened?" "Well… I don't think I'll play racquetball after Wicked Wednesdays anymore."

Rookie Gary "Z-Bob" Zablocki, a man we'd never met, was a good buddy of Kenny's from Indy. After a 4Day-eve night of drinking at the Keyhole Lounge, it hit Chucky, "I went to high school with this guy. That's why he looks familiar." Turns out that after East Detroit High School, Z-Bob spent a lot of time in the Northern Lower Peninsula at his family's cottage in Pellston, until he and his buddies accidently burned it down to the ground. He said his folks were pissed. No sense of humor.

Rookie Chris "Mad Dog" Weaks, 22 years old, Marquis and Craigo's baby brother, is fresh off a tour of duty as a Navy man. Before entering the Navy in 1985, Chris was one of the two 18-year old, rocket-armed, young guns in our Mobil Lounge Softball Team outfield (along with future 4Dayer, Eric aka E), providing the 4Day with an abundance of youthful, unbridled energy.

Rookie Paul "the Colonel" Braun completes the 1990 4Day rookie squad. Paul arrived in the U.P. without his nickname, yet would earn it before he even got into a canoe.

### And then there's the story of Jason "Willie T. Ribs" Brown...

Friday night was all-you-can-eat ribs 'n perch at the Keyhole Lounge. After the chow-fest, Jimmy observed, "I grew up in a home with 4 brothers that were *serious* eaters, some pushing 400 pounds. I remember Thanksgiving dinner tables that were nothing but a blur of arms grabbing food, but I've never seen one man eat as much food in one meal as Jason did tonight." We had no idea at the time, but Jason's eating binge would greatly affect the entire 4Day, and indirectly contribute to Rookie Paul's future nom de guerre.

2AM and another wonderfully joyous evening at the Keyhole comes to an end. Rookie Chris, two blocks shy of the Wa-Wa-Tam Motel, grabs a ride the rest of the way on the running boards of Jimmy's Bronco. As Jimmy makes the turn into the motel parking lot, Chris flies off of his running board perch, breaking the fall with his face. Due to the evening's beer 'n whiskey, Chris won't realize what has happened until the next morning.

The sun comes up and it's time to get the boys moving for the drive to Germfask when I knock on the door of the room Chris is sharing, "Up and at 'em fellers!" Chris is lying in bed with the left side of his face on the pillow. As he lifts his head, the pillow is right there with him, the dried blood from last night's crash acting as an adhesive.

In the room Jason is in, he's sitting up in bed and does not look good. "Jason, what's wrong?" "Doc, is there a pharmacy nearby?" "Sure Jason" "Could you get me something for my stomach?" "No problem. Any thought about what you'd like?" "Hmm... is there a hospital near here?" "Yeah, in St. Ignace. Do you want me to take you there?" "Yes, please."

Rookie Kenny is observing what's going on, "Man, this river is technical. We're not even on the water yet, and one guy's ripped his face up and another is heading to the hospital!"

Jason & I drive north across the Mackinac Bridge to the St. Ignace Hospital, confer with doctors and get him checked in. I then cross south on the Bridge to rendezvous with the boys and check ourselves out of the Wa-Wa-Tam, cross north again on the Big Mac Bridge, returning to the hospital for a check on Jason's status. The first nurse encountered, seeing Chris and his bloodied face walk through the front door, assumes that he needs a doctor. "No, I just been 4Dayin", Chris assures her, declining a physician's care. As an unexpected treat, one of Chucky's all-time favorite movies, "Barfly", is on the lounge TV. A doctor soon enters the lounge, "We're going to keep your friend overnight to run some tests".

The boys, figuring Jason is just suffering from a temporary rib 'n perch back-up, decide to head west a few miles to Lake Michigan's Hiawatha National Forest Campground. There we would stay overnight to wait out Jason's anticipated massive bowel movement, the next morning free him from the hospital, and then start the delayed 4 (now 3) Day.

Lake Michigan cuisine, courtesy Rookie Kenny, is cherries soaked in Jack Daniels for one year, with a dash of sugar for good luck. Kenny extracted the now-hallucinogenic cherries from the whiskey, passing them out among the 4Day crew. Altered states soon follow and a buzz Frisbee game breaks out.

A fifth of $5.60 "Colonel's Pride" is what campers are forced to drink if they drop the disc in the buzz Frisbee game. Rookie Paul has hands of stone on this day and is taking pull after pull off of the *Colonel*. Perhaps due to Paul's determination to avoid any more of the canoers overwhelming choice as the nastiest concoction to ever come in a bottle (Kenny noted, "You can't put a price on $5.60 whiskey"), he began making NFL-quality Frisbee catches, including a sparkling diving grab that took him weeks to recover from. Kenny said, "Look! He's *skipping* across those big rocks!" Paul's many hits of Colonel's Pride hit back in the middle of the night, as he crawled out of the tent for late-night up chucking.

I took some extra tent time before starting the next day, lying there listening to the fellas chat around the breakfast fire. They were talking about "the Colonel" as if the whiskey was a person. It was then that I realized what they were referring to: since the Colonel's Pride whiskey got Paul to puking, he was now and would forever be known as "the Colonel".

Ricky Callahan once said, "I'm not scared of paddling on the 4Day, I'm scared of when you're not paddling. That's when people get their nicknames." Paul Braun can give a knowing nod to Ricky's assessment. And what about Paul Braun? What if, during the buzz Frisbee game he participated in, the whiskey had been, say, "Fighting Cock"? Or "Loose Stool Bourbon"? The Colonel is a pretty damn good name, everything considered.

Better grab up Jason so we can get this caravan moving to the river. Driving back towards the Bridge, it was 8 miles to the nearest pay phone. Placing a call to the hospital, a nurse answers:

"St. Ignace Hospital/Jason Brown?/We have no Jason Brown here" "Ok, how about J. Brown?" "No, no J. Brown" "Let's try James Brown" "Nope... maybe your friend went home." I let her know that Jason had no car and his home was 344 miles away, so I was pretty sure going home was not on his agenda. Getting no satisfactory answer, I drove the final 8 miles to St. Ignace & entered the hospital. Fortunately, the doctor who tended to Jason walked by the front desk and overheard my inquiries. "From the tests run on his heart, we decided to transfer him to Petoskey (an hour southwest) due to their superior facilities." His HEART? He had a heart attack? Ain't no dump, no matter how much ribs 'n perch it moves through the system, is gonna fix that.

The St. Ignace front desk gave me the phone number of the Petoskey Hospital, and I was patched into Jason's room. He was in good spirits, but had indeed suffered a heart attack, and the doctors would keep him the next several days for more tests and observation. All of Jason's river gear was in my car, and he wouldn't be needing any of it where he was. Jason made sure that I knew where his party supplies were, and asked that they be consumed in his name. It shall be done.

Getting started on the Fox one-day-and-several-hours later than usual, we launched at the Seney Township Campground, the normal Day 2 starting point. Once below the M28 Bridge, a couple hundred feet west of Andy's Seney Bar (wow, some DO get there by canoe!), a sound was heard like nothing previously discerned on 4Day waters. It was music! While taking a river break (it <u>had</u> been 20 minutes since launching), Rookie Z-Bob pulled a cassette player out of his dry bag and was playing Hank Junior's "High Notes". The song *If Heaven Ain't Alot Like Dixie* has been a personal favorite to this day, and committed to memory should we ever get caught in a bar brawl way down south.

*Author's note:* for anyone under 30 years old, a cassette player is a device used to play music from audio tape cassettes.

*Author's note 2:* an audio tape cassette is a small (3" x 2") case containing a magnetic tape that runs between two reels.

*Author's note 3:* a magnetic tape is, ah, never mind.

The experience traveling through the Spreads (Dickel-driven this year) was, as usual, amazing as the river split & split again, the boats taking any one of several watery fingers, then rejoining 30 minutes downstream where all channels merge together. On the flip side, downstream from the Spreads, the 6-hour drudgery of dragging our fully-loaded canoes over one fallen tree after another was almost overwhelming as darkness began to fall, and no end seemed in sight... and then... finally, the High Ground on the left bank was in front of us. A steep '6 rise that must be negotiated to get all boats and gear to the site – yes; swarming mosquitos – yes; but a place to set up tents, build a fire, feed our hunger, and rest our weary bones.

Day 2 was a short but obstacle-filled challenging 2 hours from the High Ground to the Peninsula, christen by Rookie Chris as, "the finest camp site the Lord has ever made". Although only 2 hours of river were behind us this day, you do not pass up the chance to camp at the Peninsula where the Fox forms a giant oxbow around the land. There is access on both sides, flat ground with plenty of space for 10 or more tents, no shortage of fire wood, and gorgeous views of the river from the site. A joyous party broke out, one giant ye-ha. Somebody passed out cans of Lite Beer, and all were in such a happy, drunk mood that disparaging remarks about watered-down beer were few and all Lites were consumed.

The Day 3 (normally Day 4) stop at the *Old... Log... Bridge* found the fellers in a festive and reflective mood, thinking of all that had transpired since leaving home: Jason's heart attack, Colonel's new name, Chris' new face, the cherry jack, the brotherhood. Bottles were passed, cigars smoked, and vows taken...

- Johnny renewed his vow to quit any job that would interfere with future 4Days.
- Rookie Kenny vowed to begin soaking cherries in Jack as soon as he returned home, and have a new batch of the hallucinogenic cherries ready for 4Day14. The cherries had become a fan favorite.
- Chucky and I vowed to find a new nasty liquor, or blend, that might spawn another nickname, like *the Colonel*, at 4Day14.
- Jimmy vowed to continue dating.

At the conclusion of the 4Day, Goobs & Big Guy continued to the northern-most reaches of the U.P., stopping for an evening at a tavern in the town of Curtis, a tavern we would all meet in 1994, the two returning weeks later with more tales to tell. The rest of us accepted Z-Bob's invitation to drink beer and stay overnight at his family's trailer in Pellston – where no one smoked. The next morning, the 4Dayers invaded Petoskey to see the hospitalized Jason. He survived the heart attack, was released a week later, and would be able to look forward to many more 4Days.

Amen.

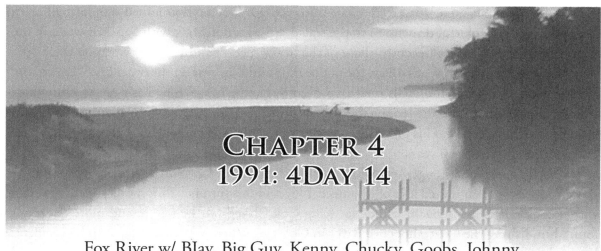

# CHAPTER 4
# 1991: 4DAY 14

Fox River w/ BJay, Big Guy, Kenny, Chucky, Goobs, Johnny, Jimmy, Colonel, Wayne, Doc, and rookie Doctor Bob

*I want to know that you'll tell me, I'd really love to stay*
*Take me to the river, drop me in the water*
*Push me in the river, dip me in the water*
*Washing me down, washing me*
*(Take Me to the River by the Talking Heads)*

This March, a spiritual 4Day brother passed away. John Voelker, pen name Robert Traver, was a Northern Michigan University grad, State Supreme Court Justice, writer (including *Anatomy of a Murder*), but most of all a U.P. native and lover of its waters. He was concerned about potential over-crowding of the Upper Peninsula. When asked to attend the 1957 Mackinac Bridge grand opening ceremony, John begged off, saying it would conflict with his duties on the "Bomb the Bridge Committee". Here is his "Testament to a Fisherman" (the Canoer's wilderness cousin)...

*"I fish because I love to; because I love the environs that trout are found, which are invariably beautiful, and hate the environs where crowds of people are found, which are invariably ugly; because of all the television commercials, cocktail parties and assorted social posturing I thus escape; because, in a world where most men spend their lives doing things they hate, my fishing is at once an endless source of delight and an act of small rebellion; because trout do not lie or cheat and cannot be bought or bribed or impressed by power, but respond only to quietude and humility and endless patience; because I suspect that men are going along this way for the last time, and I for one don't want to waste the trip; because mercifully there are no telephones on fishing waters; because only in the woods can I find solitude without loneliness; because bourbon out of an old tin cup tastes better out there; because maybe someday I will catch a mermaid; and, finally, not because I regard fishing as being so terribly important but because I suspect that so many other concerns of men are equally unimportant - and not nearly so much fun".*

One man makes up the 1991 rookie class, Doctor Bob. Maggie has long said that, concerned about Up North excesses, "you should be taking a doctor with you on the 4Day". Although an Optometry Specialist wasn't what she had in mind, I did point out when we imbibe heavily, our eyes – bloodshot, slits, etc. – were the first things to go. Doctor Bob joined our softball team last year, adding a colorful dimension to the squad, filling a notebook with Sanskrit when in the dugout and hearing voices (recently, those of the heavy metal band Pantera) when on the field.

A few days before this year's 4Day, the phone rang and BJay was on the other line, "I'm comin' 4Dayin' this year. Something tells me that I need to see the boys". BJay has been teaching kids biology & physical science in Georgia the last few years, had not been on a 4Day since 1980 - this is only his second one - and his presence is special, especially to his fellow EMU Hurons that have known him for almost 20 years.

With BJay in the passenger seat while leading the caravan Up North, we listened to Jimmy Buffett, discussing our shared love of his music. BJay said this summer almost every evening ended with a cook out on his hibachi while Nat King Cole played on the stereo, and most weekends found him fishing the Chattahoochee River in Georgia. When in nature, BJay is in his element. If a bird flew by, most folks might say, "Hey, a bird flew by." BJay would tell you its' origins and breeding cycle. Although it's been several years since he's been back in Michigan, it feels like we'd just been with BJay the day before.

When we stopped to eat at the infamous Tony's Restaurant in Birch Run, BJay placed a double order for Texas Toast. Even Wayne "Chow Time is Important" Vollmers tried to warn BJay about the already-enormous size of Tony's legendary servings, but he said he was hungry - not enough, however, to finish off the half-a-foot tall pile of toast placed in front of him, where the bacon serving size is measured in pounds, not pieces.

Departing Mackinaw City after next morning's breakfast, the 4Day crew crossed over the Big Mac Bridge and arrived in Germfask around 11AM. There were warm greetings all around when we saw livery owners Tom and Carma. Once Wayne had wrapped up a round of playful flirting with Carma, he opened up the back of his van. The equivalent of a small village rolled out, including a barcalounger that Wayne intended to take on the river. It took a few of us to convince Wayne that no amount of positioning could allow a barcalounger to fit on a canoe.

After an outstanding day of flying down the Fox River, running a little high and mighty fast due to the elevated water level from the rains of the past week, we pulled ashore at the Seney Township Campground late-afternoon. We caught a break as the skies cleared, allowing tent set-up in dry conditions.

Once camp was set, we strolled into town for an evening at Andy's Seney Bar. Andy was in fine fiddle, welcoming our walk through his door with a "Damn, you fellas back here again?" and then insisting on doing a shot with us. BJay, having brought his guitar north, was invited to play some tunes with a regular at Andy's known to everyone there as Banjo Bob. Mister & Missus Banjo live in the nearby woods, where Andy regularly runs out packages of food to them. Banjo Bob plays his instrument in a band that Andy brings into the bar to play once or twice a month. Andy said, "Banjo keeps asking if I'll book the band more often, but they only know 5 songs, so I hold off bringing 'em back 'til my regulars forget those tunes."

BJay and Banjo Bob start into a couple of Hank Snow songs, and everyone in the bar is toe tappin' and smilin', while a few folks start dancing. Chucky was impressed, "Man, BJay really sounds good up there!" The 4Dayers are laughin' and high-fivin' at BJay's performance. It was about that time that Banjo stopped playing. Chucky summed it up, "Ooh, ouch! I guess Banjo was carrying him."

With some fine Andy-time under our belts, we picked up a dozen pizzas from the restaurant next door before staggering back to camp. On the walk, we entertained the few souls within earshot with renditions of Martin Mull's "Men", Tom T. Hall's "I Like Beer", and T.E. Ford's "Sixteen Tons". We probably could've used Banjo Bob to give us cover.

Around the camp bonfire was a 4Day happy meal of pizza, beer and bourbon, enjoyed while reveling in BJay's time in the musical spotlight, the rough patches in his guitar pickin' briefly forgotten. Around midnight, the heavens opened and rain pounded the campsite, extinguishing the flames and chasing the boys into their tents, but only after emptying a final fifth of something brown.

Kenny awoke to dawn breaking and some rattling around outside his tent. On a river break later in the day, he shared with the boys what he observed. "This morning, I unzipped my tent and saw Doc with the trash bag, throwin' in it bottles, cans, cigarettes, whatever, napkins, setting someone's wet socks on a rock, just general clean-up. Then he picked up the pizza boxes one at a time, there were about 12 laying around the fire pit, looking into 'em, then throwing 'em into the bag. It was barely daylight - he'd probably already walked 2 miles - when he opened up one box, peaked inside, closed the lid, and tipped it to the side. He didn't *drain* the water out, he *poured* it out, like dumping out a pitcher of water. He opened the box back up and I thought, well, that's kinda strange, since I figured after he dumped the water out, he'd throw the pizza box away. Doc then let go of the trash bag, put one hand underneath the bottom of the pizza box, opened it up, and then reached in with his other hand. I thought, this isn't right. There must be some kind of a reptile in there that he's going after. He comes out with a pizza slice, it was limp, he had to hold it up above his head, and then lower it into his mouth. God… I just kinda zipped up the tent, oh my goodness."

The encore to the Day 1 rains were 3 days of sunny skies. BJay brought along an $11.95 half-gallon of Barton's American Whiskey for the river. While we paddled through the Spreads, I noticed that his arm from the elbow on down was below the surface of the Fox River. I asked him about it, and he smiled, then raised his arm up and brought to the surface the whiskey half-gallon with its cap missing. BJay explained that he thought it'd be good to "cut" the Barton's a bit with some Fox River water.

After negotiating one of the many logjams over the next 2 days, the boys stopped, exhausted from dragging canoes over so many obstructions. While we took a badly needed break, BJay hopped out of his canoe with his anglers' gear and waded downstream, searching for a good fishing hole. By the time we caught up with him, BJay had caught a couple of brook trout and was closing in on a few more. Cleaning 'n cooking his catch at our Peninsula campground that night, BJay shared the trout with the 4Dayers, turning the taters & roast beef dinner created for us by chefs Jimmy, Wayne & Johnny into a surf 'n turf delight.

Absorbing the beauty of our surroundings early on day 4, Colonel said "I've been to a lot of places in this country, and I've never seen them equal the natural beauty of the U.P." Johnny smiled at the comment, nodded and offered Colonel a bottle asking, "Wanna do a shot?"

Taking stock on the final day finds there's a fair amount of Canada House Whiskey remaining. Goobs took charge, "I brought this shit here, and there ain't no way I'm bringing it home! Start drinking!" implying that the 20 bourbon & tequila fifths consumed thus far was a sad showing.

After the 4th day on the river, the 4Dayers spent a final night in the U.P., camping along Lake Michigan. The next morning, before packing up for the long ride home, BJay was cooking us up some pancakes when his Coleman stove suddenly caught fire. I ran towards the stove & Chucky thought to himself, "What a hero!", 'til he saw me grab my gear off the burning picnic table and get the hell out of there. The stove and the breakfast on it went up in flames 2' high. Kenny said "BJay mighta pulled the nozzle out a *little* too far. The Coleman looked like a flamin' pancake."

Post-4Day, BJay hung around Michigan for several days, spending time with some old friends at familiar haunts. Chucky, Marquis, Craigo, BJay, Jimmy and I caught a Tigers game at Michigan and Trumbull, enjoying a wonderful pre and post-game at Hoots, before sending BJay off to his Stone Mountain, Ga., home with love, hugs and laughter.

4 weeks after the 4Day, a large group of friends had returned from a weekend at a lodge in northwest Michigan. Maggie and I were at Jimmy and Lisa's house when the phone rang. The caller said that BJay had been fishing near Atlanta on the Chattahoochee River with a buddy, when a lightning storm suddenly developed, the guys pulling their canoe out of the water as they sought shelter on a midstream island. As BJay leaned against an island tree, a lightning bolt hit the tree and took his life. On August 11, 1991, our dear BJay aka B. Jay Wright aka old Dribble Dick, passed away at 38 years young.

Jimmy hung up the phone and the room was filled with stunned sadness and disbelief. Maggie said how perfect it was that BJay died doing something that he loved so much, fishing on a river, referring to it as a "Viking Funeral". We were so thankful that "something" had moved BJay to come and 4Day with his buddies one last time.

In honor of BJay, his friends donated money to the Defenders of the Wildlife in his name. The Defenders of the Wildlife were chosen because, as it was explained over the phone by a staff member, "Defenders' adherents love of and interest in nature made it likely they would want to take off their clothes and run through the woods with the animals". Sounds like our BJay.

BJay had a favorite saying, "It's good for the soul". Having a friend like BJay certainly is.

# CHAPTER 4
## 1992: 4DAY 15

Fox River w/ Big Guy, Jimmy, John, Dr. Bob, Jason,
Colonel, Doc and rookies Vid and Marquis

*Go right to the source and ask the horse.*
*He'll give you the answer that you'll endorse.*
*He's always on a steady course.*
*Talk to Mister Ed.*
*(Mister Ed $2.99 a fifth tribute)*

**Before there was the 4Day, darkness covered the earth.**

**In the Garden of Eden, man may drink beer, wine, scotch, tequila – but he may NOT crack open the fifth of bourbon.**

**Man was in Paradise: at table-top shuffleboard everyone made great shots, at softball no one ever made an out, the rivers were made of beer, the canoes were made of waterproof (and delicious) pizza, and the women were limited only by man's imagination.**

**Paradise would always be man's. Unless he cracked open the fifth of bourbon.**

**(crraaacckk!)**

**"Marquis!!!!"**

**"What?"**

"Rookies!" Though the veteran 4Dayers shouted this greeting to the two newbies, those words just didn't sound right. Vid and Marquis were professionals when it came to the sciences of imbibing and general partyin', so although it was their first 4Day, it felt like they got a real big running start.

Vid had heard the 4Day stories since he joined the Mobil Lounge Softball team in 1985, loved the tales told and camaraderie spoken of, but would have none of associating with an event that sometimes ran out of food before its completion. Once Wayne started 4Dayin' (1986), a presence that made sure grub would always be plentiful, Vid was drawn in, but only after several years of Wayne-O's influence on the event. Initially introduced to the group (along with Johnny) by Jimmy to join our softball team, this bundle of energy quickly became a dear brother. He owns a generous soul, is an outstanding story-teller, and accomplished party animal. Vid & Johnny were co-owners of Ann Arbor's Mary Ridgway Sweets, and their candy creations were delicious.

And then there is Marquis Weaks, the other half of the rookie class of 1992. Probably no one in this group is more beloved, or has a bigger heart than Marquis. His laugh is infectious, and when he giggles, it warms your innards more than a bottle of Early Times. Marquis is outstanding at impersonations, the most succinct of them catch phrases echoed up and down the river by Marquis' 4Day brothers, usually in an effort to get Marquis to do his parodies. Detroit Mayor Coleman Young is his main target *("Who the fuck are the Friends of Belle Isle? All they did was plant a few fuckin' trees!").* Marquis does Coleman better than Coleman does Coleman. He is a fellow EMU Huron, met by many of us our sophomore year while we all resided in the Sellers Hall dorm. Certainly, no one can hold more bourbon than Marquis, an ideal choice for him at any time of the day.

A 4Day-eve tradition has fallen by the wayside. In the desire to immerse ourselves in the Upper Peninsula as quickly as possible, to venture forth beyond the safety of the mitten, to recover that part of our souls awaiting in the woods of the Yooper rabbit-belly… well, theatrics aside, most importantly, to eliminate the 75-minute hung-over, 1st day of the 4Day, morning drive, the boys decided to bypass Mackinaw City and lodging at its Wa-Wa-Tam Motel, opting for a longer 4Day-eve drive (6 vs. 4 and 1/2 hours) from SE Michigan to the U.P. town of Germfask. What we had no interest to eliminate was a visit to Mackinaw City's Keyhole Lounge, where we stopped for food, a few rounds, table-top shuffleboard, and many songs from their outstanding juke box, before crossing the Mackinac Bridge for the evening's Upper Peninsula destination.

In the village of Germfask, we shoehorned this year's nine 4Dayers into two reserved Jolly

Motel rooms. Once checked in, we strolled next door to the Jolly Inn pub. "What should the first round of shots be?" Jimmy asked. After a few options were kicked about, Rookie Vid shared his feelings on the subject, "I'll drink anything that isn't blue or on fire." His declaration didn't really eliminate much that we were considering. We landed on an evening of several rounds of Fleischmann's, in a salute to Marquis' presence since this was the whiskey with which his Grandpa Daisy began each morning, and a whiskey that seemed to go well with the Red Baron Pizzas the waitress kept bringing to our table. Grandpa Daisy is 90 years old and still full of vim 'n vigor, so his daily rock glass-sized example seems worth following.

As the Jolly fun continued, every couple of beers I took to clenching a full glass in my teeth, lifting it off the table, tilting my head back and gulping it down without using my hands, a talent refined during many Thursday nights, post-softball, at the Mobil Lounge. One time this evening, the glass was tilted down to my mouth but I lost control and the glass fell, breaking on the floor. While Jimmy was bent over cleaning it up, I leaned over him, grabbed his glass with my teeth, lifted it up, quickly downed the beer, set the empty glass back where it was just before Jimmy sat up, leaned back with an ear-to-ear grin of satisfaction, and Jimmy was none the wiser.

Big Guy headed back to the motel earlier than the rest, a mistake if the idea was to get away from drinking. Vid and I followed him a few minutes later, with Vid stopping by his cooler to get, for the Big Guy's enjoyment, a fifth of Mattingly & Moore, a bourbon creation by the good folks in Bardstown, Kentucky.

With Biggie being, unfortunately, a Yankees Suck fan, and with Don Mattingly being a Yankee, and with us being drunk, it was obvious to Vid & I that Big Guy would want to drink a whiskey that features the name *Mattingly*. Big Guy didn't see it that way, and told us to shove the fifth someplace dark. Vid wasn't about to do that, especially knowing that Big Guy secretly wanted us to push him. "C'mon Big Guy! Hit the bottle!" Biggie's bark, "Get out of here, you drunks!" only convinced Vid that he was playing hard to get. "C'mon Big Guy, its' *Mattingly & Moore*! If it was Kaline & Stargell, I'd drink it!" (Vid being a Pirate fan besides a Tiger fan) "Wee-sus! How long are you going to push this?" Vid hesitated for a moment, then figured Biggie was tossing a trick question at him. Vid smiled and replied, "Til the bottle's empty".

Although paddling the Fox River for the 12th time in 15 4Days, this trip had a very different feel to it. Missing were comrades-in-arms of many floats through the Spreads: Goobs, a 10-year man including the very first 4Day, Chucky, who had not missed since 1979, and BJay, who passed away when struck by lightning on a fishing trip a month after last year's 4Day.

While paddling on day 1, we commemorated BJay by sacrificing in his name a Jamaican-sized bomber and indulged in his 4Day14 drink of choice, Barton's American Whiskey. Upon hearing of our plans to empty a half-gallon of $11.95 Barton's in celebration of BJay, Vid said, "Well, I never really KNEW the man".

Big Guy shared a favorite BJay story during a river break...

*"After pulling into the Wa-Wa-Tam 4Day-eve last year, Goobs and I take his truck over the bridge for supplies. BJay, Jimmy, and a couple others hop in the back of the pick-up. We pull into a general store when BJay announces he's going next store to get some corn for bait. We tell him "we'll wait right here for you after we shop", then go in spending 30 minutes looking around tourist-style, clowning,*

*checking out the liquor. We go outside. No BJay. We tell a few stories, smoke a few cigs, hit the Early Times. We've got a dilemma - still no BJay! We decide to drive the US2 strip and search for him. Just as we try to pull out on to 2, a car swerves in front and cuts us off. We're about to raise hell, when out from this car pops BJay looking traditionally dazed. BJay had somehow lost his bearings going next store, thought we had left him and got picked up hitchhiking to go back across the bridge when he saw us. Most of us, even in inebriation, didn't follow this thought process, but were glad to have him back. Now that I think about it, I don't remember seeing any corn".*

There was great anticipation as we paddled downstream Day 1: Andy had previously announced that he would be hosting a pig roast at his bar this evening, the tavern a short mile and a half walk from our campsite. The all-you-can-eat price was right at $5 per person, with entertainment by country music and polka bands, plus Banjo Bob himself!

Arriving at the Seney landing, with the pig roast on our minds, we hurriedly set-up camp and hoofed it into town. Turning the corner from Fox River Road to M28, Andy's is still over a quarter-mile away, but Vid immediately knew something was amiss. "Where's the cars? I don't hear any music. I don't smell any pig". We walked the rest of the way to the bar, stepped inside, and saw no pig, no bands, no customers, and no Andy. A waitress we didn't know, perhaps brought in as a shield to absorb the wrath of the disappointed (much as the Piss Boy had been placed on the throne of King Louis XVI during the peasants' uprising), said the pig roast had been postponed to a later date.

We ordered Andy burgers, but when you're expecting a pig roast, it's not quite the same.

The next morning, we walked into town for breakfast at the short-lived restaurant across the street from Andy's. A local at a table nearby heard us talking about the promised pig roast that wasn't, and said, "If Andy tells you it's raining, you'd best look outside".

Packing up camp after breakfast, we hit the Fox Day 2 under cloudy skies and, a little before noon, arrived at the foot of the Spreads. Then, all hell broke loose as storms pounded the area. Colonel said, "That's BJay talking to us". "I wish he'd whisper!" was Vid's quick reply. We pulled the boats together and took cover beneath plastic painter's drop cloths for the 20 minutes it took the violence to move on.

As the skies cleared, Bobby - last year's rookie - took the cap off the first fifth of the day, tossed it into the river and, smiling at Marquis and Vid, said, "Go get it rookies!" With an incredulous look on their faces, they replied as one, "Why? Let's drink!" Certain that with the cap gone this crew would pass the bottle until it was no more, Bobby became a divin' dog, amazingly locating the whiskey's seal.

Maybe it was the knowledge of what the bottle contained that spurred Bobby's dive.

While down in Jacksonville 6 weeks pre-4Day, we found the ABC Liquor store offered a fifth of something brown at an intriguing price: $2.99 for a bottle of Mister Ed. At that price, better get a couple. The art on the label looked to be that of a horse's head drawn by a preschooler. New to us, the cheapest 4Day liquor ever, and likely nasty, Mister Ed seemed like the perfect treat to bring north. If there was any question before the river, the first pull confirmed this was not sippin' liquor, and it required a chaser, with Jungle Juice the popular chaser choice, a custom blend of alcohol and juices.

Hmm, something is not quite right. As the day's fun built, we noticed that Jimmy was changing the drink 'n chase protocol: he would hit the Jungle Juice, then chase it with Mister Ed. To the sober (and us), this was clearly the wrong order. Not only did this drinking method not result in the involuntary grimace to his face that it should have, but Jimmy noted several times that *"Mister Ed taste __GREAT__!"*, a sure sign that his internal clock was pleasantly stuck at drunk-thirty. As Kenny famously once said, "There's those that have, and those that will". This was Jimmy's "have" day.

Late in the afternoon, as occasionally happens when paddling for hours through the wilderness, we found that one great camp site never to be found again. It was land with a sweet expanse of flat ground, about 80' x 40', enough space for 5 tents, but not enough to hold one who'd been chasing Jungle Juice with Mister Ed most of the day. Jimmy was too wobbly for the campground to hold him, almost falling into the river when slamming his knee into a tree angled from the shore to just above the water line. The injured knee would keep him off of the softball diamond for a couple weeks.

As the evening's festivities heightened, Jimmy was starting to sway on the pickle buckle barrel he'd settled on for his camp seat. Vid noted, "In a sea of drunks, Jimmy floated to the surface". Vidder & Biggie were betting on whether he'd fall right or left. He fooled 'em all and fell backwards. Rising from the dirt, Jimmy started staggerin' in a broken line towards Bobby. Responsible for next morning's breakfast, Bobby sat on a milk crate in front of his tent, tomorrow's eggs just inside.

The inevitable crash was a cartoon come to life, a tumbling tangle of bodies, broken egg shells, and torn fabric. Jimmy fell straight forward into Bobby, knocking him off the milk crate into the tent and on to tomorrow's breakfast, taking down the tent and crackin' the egg shells before their time. It was the first time we ever saw Bobby mad. Jimmy said later, "I was a half-drunk son of a bitch!", and he was half-right. That night, Jimmy snored thru a pounding rainstorm, a good 6 hours or so of thunder and lighting. He rose blurry-eyed the next morning, squinting out over the drenched campsite, asking, "Did it rain last night?" His question elicited laughs and good-natured ribbing, but not as much as his next question did, "Anybody seen my dry shoes?" "Yeah, you see those shoelaces sticking up out of that mud pile? Your dry shoes are right below those." "Oh."

When going uncontrollably downhill, floor it. Kenny chose this moment to break out the cherries that he had been soaking in Jack Daniels for the last year. Over these 12 months, the alcohol was absorbed by the fruit, leaving benign liquid and hallucinogenic cherries. Thoughtfully, Kenny brought along plenty for everyone, making the tearing down of camp and the loading of the canoes funnier and more challenging than usual.

Paddling downstream, we were treated all day-long to the natural high of listening to Marquis' impression of Lucille Ball's Cuban-born husband, Ricky Ricardo…

*"Luuuu-cy, you got some' splainin' to do"*, *"Ba-ba-looooo!"* and *"Hey Fred!"* in honor of Lucy & Ricky's neighbor, Fred Mertz. Ricky & Fred had to make dinner in one episode, Ricky asking, *"Fred, what do you know about rice?"* Fred told him, *"Well, I had it thrown at me on one of the darkest days of my life."*

The 3rd evening, we set up camp at the Peninsula. Jason decided to empty a fifth of Jagermeister by himself, and ended up howlin' banshee-like primal screams at the moon that night and into the very early morning hours, while we tried to sleep. Repeated requests from the tents to "Shut the fuck up!" had no effect.

This was the year that we began signing up for meals before heading north. The plan was, you prepare one feeding for the entire group, and then you don't have to cover any other meals, except bringing some river snacks. Your food prep is one-and-done. Jason signed up to handle breakfast on the 4th morning but, and a much bigger issue than effecting our sleep the prior night, he could not be woken from last evening's Jager-binge to cook for us.

Jason snored through his breakfast responsibilities, and through breaking down camp. As we stood at the edge of the river, canoes packed and ready to go, the only item still left on the Peninsula was Colonel's tent with the snoring Jason in it. We called his name, but got nothing. Debating what to do next, Johnny asked, "Colonel, just how much did the tent cost you?" Brilliant! We all agreed to chip in, buy Colonel a new tent, and paddle away, leaving Jason behind in the now old tent. Just then, Jason woke up. The boys gave him 15 minutes to pack before shoving off. He was in a boat just under the time allotted.

Back home a couple of days later, I related this story to Maggie, who seemed surprised, asking, "You were going to leave without Jason, and let him paddle until he caught up?" "Oh no. We weren't going to leave a canoe. He could follow the shoreline downstream just like the critters do." Don't mess with 4Dayers' chow time. This incident directly lead to a new rule: no more Jagermeister on the 4Day. The cut was much too deep.

Once off the river, the final night of the 4Day was spent in Mackinac City at our favorite lodging spot in town, the Wa-Wa-Tam Motel. The fellas grabbed their rooms while I chatted with owners Garey & Roberta, whose pleasant dispositions once again made us feel at home, reminding us how much we missed them on the way up.

A few of the boys had headed to the Keyhole for dinner 'n beers, and I noticed that Big Guy was not among them. I stopped by his room to see if he wanted to join us. The door was slightly ajar. I knocked, called his name, but there was no answer. Pushing the door open, I recoiled in shocked horror! *"Argh!!! Oh, Lord!"* I quickly averted my eyes, but it was not quick enough to avert the permanent imprint on my memory of Big Guy lying buck naked, covered in Noxema head to toe, stretched diagonally across his bed, toes left, head right, his butt facing me. His buttocks were not sublime.

Once I was able to gather my wits about me, the questions were many. Beyond "Why was God punishing me so?" I asked...

1. "Why was Big Guy covered in Noxema?"
2. "Where did he get that much Noxema from?"
3. "Why would Noxema market their product in industrial-sized oil drums?"
4. "Why would the village of Mackinaw City have such quantities on hand?"
5. "Why were my retinas not burned out?"

Biggie claimed he had sun poisoning from the last 4 days, and the Noxema was needed to soothe the pain. I suggested that he leave the Noxema on (since he wasn't riding in <u>my</u> car) for a couple of weeks, reapply Noxema as needed, and go to work wearing only mirror sunglasses with a long scarf draped around his neck, while passing out his phone number, 'cause chicks dig guys without a trace of self-consciousness.

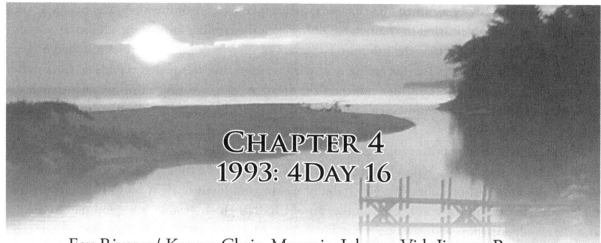

# CHAPTER 4
# 1993: 4DAY 16

Fox River w/ Kenny, Chris, Marquis, Johnny, Vid, Jimmy, Rusty, Jason, Colonel, Ricki, Doc and rookies Moth and Huff

*In the middle of the night*
*I go walking in my sleep*
*From the mountains of faith*
*To a river so deep*
*(The River of Dreams by Billy Joel)*

"I can drink you boys under the table" was how Debbie Muir aka Missus Moth greeted the guys as they arrived at Vid's surprise 43 birthday party, the month before the 4Day. Although Debbie was the most expansive, *all* of the ladies at the celebration were in a fine mood, 8 of them moved to line up and remove their bras for the birthday boy's viewing pleasure. Vid could recall gazing upon only 3 sets of hooters, due to deliberate appreciation that led to quality, not quantity, study. Later, sitting on a chair in the backyard, the bras piled on Vid's head like a tall bonnet, backlit by the setting sun, he presented an amazing visual. I ran to grab Johnny Steck, "Johnny! Johnny! You gotta see Vid – he looks like Betsy Ross!" "What?!?" "It's Vid! He has the girls' bras piled on his head, and he... well, just come and look!" Johnny followed me outside, "Damn, he <u>does</u> look like Betsy Ross!"

Rookie Moth aka Gary Muir told us how the evening ended for him and his bride, once they returned home from Vid's party. "Debbie was buck naked, on her knees and hanging on to the toilet, puking." ("Somehow," Vid noted, "Moth saw this as a green light for sex"). I stumbled towards her and tripped, too drunk to lift my arms to break the fall, landing on my forehead. I only stopped sliding on the tile floor when my forehead hit the base of the bathtub. Deb looked over at me for a couple of seconds, then turned her head and went back to puking." Future 4Dayer Gomie observed, "This lesson was from the Gary Muir School of the Art of Seduction."

Rookie Moth had the wisdom to wed Miss Debbie Boyd, a sweet girl that is the love of his life. Getting this young lady to accept his proposal is his finest accomplishment.

Rookie Moth was one of the first people I'd met when I began my Duracell career in 1976. When first we were introduced, his name was Gary Muir. Then in 1992, late in the day and in front of an audience of half-in-the-bag canoers, he jumped over a bonfire along the banks of the Rifle River. Although clearing the flames, his didn't stick the landing quite right, alighting wobbly on his heels, falling back into the inferno. To shouts of *"Gary's on fire!"* he quickly rolled out of the bonfire, sweats aflame, friends racing over with water trying to squelch the blaze. One well-meaning soul poured Echo Springs bourbon on to the sweats, creating mini-fireballs that rose up with an audible *swoosh* from Gary's clothing. Soon after this incident, Gary was much better known by his new name, the Moth, i.e., "like a Moth to a flame".

Immediately likeable, this rookie gives the teasing back as good as he gets it, and boy does he get it. As a member of our Mobil Lounge Softball Team & Beer Swillers Club, post-game at the bar he has a several-shots-along-the-way habit of passing out in an upright position at our team's table, arms folded on his chest, kind of like an old Indian chief ("today is a good day to die"), and then suddenly pop wide awake, ready for action. After one such awakening, he announced to the team that he was going home to "tap the old lady" before heading out the door. A phone call I placed to Debbie revealing his plans strangely put the kibosh on them, confirmed the next time we saw him. "How'd that tapping go Moth?" "Not so good".

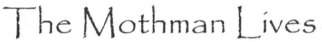

# The Mothman Lives

The boys hit the road to the 4Day the morning after a long Thursday night of softball followed by closing our sponsor bar, the Mobil Lounge. There is an extra reason to celebrate: Ricki Rice, Father of the 4Day, is in town for his first 4Day in 13 years. The party begun Thursday continues Friday on the drive north, with several Frisbee stops at rest areas sprinkled among two extended bar stops: 1st at the Nottingham Bar in Houghton Lake, a watering hole almost half a century old but new to us, and then an old favorite, the Keyhole Lounge.

Crossing over the Mackinaw Bridge, it is early evening before the caravan finally pulls into Germfask. After a quick check-in to our Jolly Motel rooms, it is a fine ye-ha evening at the Jolly

Bar. As the sun shines into our motel room the next morning, I begin to quietly rise from the bed, figuring that all around me are still sleeping. That's when Rookie Huff, lying next to Kenny, speaks up from his bed, "Doc, I thought you were gonna piss on Kenny." "What are you talking about?" "Well, in the middle of the night you stood up and peed on the floor between our beds." "No way." I bend over and press my palm against the floor. "Sonofabitch, I almost DID piss on Kenny!" While I commence to handling clean-up, we decide to henceforth consider this Jolly Motel room to have a bath and a half.

It is with awe that we stand, two paddling hours upstream from the Fox River Campground, at the top of the well-named Fox River Overlook, this year's launch site, with its spectacular view 150' above the winding river valley below. We talk of how, almost 2,000 years ago, this view must have affected the Native American Ojibwa, *les Ojibwes*, when they first walked to the edge of this cliff. Silence falls over the boys, a rare respite from jokes 'n stories, as they absorb the scene... the pines across the valley and tag alders crowding the Fox below, the river's gorgeous dark reddish-brown color the result of tannins, the decaying leaves and other vegetation along the riverside.

"Aw, Moth, that's disgusting!" Rookie Moth lights up a giant novelty cigar as we launch Day 1. The disgusting part takes place at our very first stop, where he puts out the cigar, shoves the unsmoked half in his mouth and commences to chewing, as brown juice covers his teeth and runs down the sides of his mouth. As a rookie's first impression goes, this is in a class by itself.

The other half of this year's rookie class is Huff. Rookie Huff is a southern Indiana gent, a man of impressive girth, and a friend of Kenny's to whom we quickly take a liking. An outdoorsman, woodsman, hunter, and fisherman, you could drop Huff into the early-1800s and he'd be very self-sufficient, thank you. As I learned while awakening at the Jolly Motel this morning with a puddle on the floor, though he is quiet, when Rookie Huff speaks, you should listen.

The sunny skies under which Moth repulsively drooled the end of his stogie evolve to black clouds, and have us scrambling for our rain ponchos as a downpour engulfs the flotilla. Paddling breaks are at a minimum in the deluge, resulting in reaching the Seney Township Campground a bit earlier than usual. We choose to hold off setting up camp until the showers cease, waiting them out on bar stools at Andy's Seney Bar.

Andy's waitress and the 2 regulars on hand are mildly entertained as our frequent calls for *"SHOTS!"* echo off Andy's walls. A couple of hours in, Rookie Moth passes out, face down on the bar. That's when the waitress begins tapping on his head, announcing the sporadically enforced Andy's policy of, "You can't sleep here". This elicits zero response from Moth, so the waitress begins to tap rapid-fire, her taps and laughs (ha-ha-ha-HA-ha) reminiscent of a Woody Woodpecker cartoon, as she giggles at Moth's condition (let's see her drink as much as Rookie Moth did and stay conscious).

When one of the two Andy's regulars pulls up a bar stool and asks, "Where you from son?" Moth finally stirs, slowly lifting his head up from the bar. His eyes narrow and gradually focus on the Pabst bottle in front of him, and he slurs with conviction, *"Milwaukee!"*

The rain halts just before dark, allowing us to pitch our tents in dry conditions. With the tents up, guys are now trekking into the surrounding woods, searching for branches dry enough for a fire. Enjoying a bag of Andy burgers, we're waiting around the bonfire for late-arriving 4Day brother, Rusty, due to roll into camp 9PM tonight to join us for Days 2, 3 and 4. 9PM becomes 10PM which becomes 11PM, and still no Rusty. Even at this point, Rusty's big brother Jimmy is only mildly concerned, "Rusty isn't known for rushing into things."

Finally, at midnight, the slightly askew headlights of a car appear on Fox River Road. As the car belonging to those headlights turns into the campground, we can clearly hear straining 'n grinding sounds coming from the vehicle. "Yeah, that's Rusty," Jimmy tells us, "and his '74 Lincoln Continental Town Coupe. From the rough sounds it's makin' and the look of the headlights, something other than the usual reasons are responsible for his being sidetracked."

The car pulls up next to the fire, front end damage made visible by the flames, the vehicle emitting a few rattles before being turned off, and Rusty steps out with a story to tell. "I had made it to the U.P. early enough that I should've been here at least 2 hours ago, but I hit a deer on US2." "Damn," Colonel asked, "did the deer survive?" "No. Part of it is still on my front grill." A couple of flashlights were quickly produced, and what they illuminated elicited a loud "Whoa!" from Marquis, "There's critter hair on the grill! A lot of it!" Within minutes, 1993 became forever known as the 4Day when "Rusty brung a deer."

Rusty continued, "The deer got up and ran off. I wandered a ways into the woods looking for it, figuring one of you guys would know how to dress the deer and add venison to the dinner menu. It must have had enough adrenaline to escape into the forest, but it wouldn't survive a collision with a Lincoln Continental."

Rusty finished his deer story, "Hitting the deer banged up the car and damaged the radiator. The radiator started leaking pretty bad, and I had to stop a few times for refills from the gallon jugs I keep in the trunk. After using the last of my water, the radiator had to be quenched again on a pitch black stretch of road near Blaney Park, but there was a distant light way off the road.

When I got close, I could see it was a small rental hall, knocked on the door, and a lady opened it. There was a wedding celebration going on. They allowed me to top of the radiator from the hose and fill my two gallon jugs for the road, then offered me wedding cake and beer. I took the cake, told 'em there will be plenty of beer where I'm going, and wished them a happy marriage." There were chuckles around the campfire, as we envisioned the reaction of the wedding party to the sight of this unexpected, 6'5", 300 pound reception guest at their door.

Amazingly, the business nearest to our edge-of-the-wilderness camp is Fox River Automotive, less than a mile away. Before we shove off from land on Day 2, Rusty drops off his car for the needed repair work, mechanics assuring him the vehicle will be ready when we return in 3 days. Yesterday, 6 canoes were rented for 12 paddlers. With Rusty's arrival, the livery dropped off a 7th canoe for us this morning. 7 canoes for 13 4Dayers means there will be one unaccompanied paddler, Johnny, the empty bow of his solo ship a 4Day garbage barge/excess storage area.

We decide today to bypass the High Ground campsite, 6 hard hours of canoeing, and paddle all the way to the Peninsula, an effort that will take 8 hours and then some. Despite what lay ahead, 45 minutes into the day we halt for a break at the edge of the Spreads. A fifth is cracked open, cigars lit, and it was time to share some stories…

*Kenny came up with a future 4Day t-shirt idea, "You been drinkin'? Now <u>there's</u> good thinkin!"*

*Talk of rookie Moth's big day yesterday, eating half of his cigar and passing out later at Andy's Bar, reminded Marquis of a story, "The police pulled Uncle Steve over while Big John was vomiting on to the passenger side floor board. The cop asked Steven, "Have you been drinking sir?" Uncle Steve, pointing at Big John, said, "Yeah, but not as much as he has."*

*Marquis was on a roll now, with a few impersonations of Coleman Young and Ricky Ricardo sprinkled in among the stories. He then switched gears to a favorite 4Day topic: food. "Chucky and I were at the White Castle and this blasted guy was standing in line behind us. When the cashier asked for his order, he said that he was too drunk to make a decision, so he pointed at me and said he'd take whatever I ordered."*

*Ricki weighed in on the subject, "On my first ever trip to a Whities, 3 drunken black folks walked in, the one female with a very short skirt on. One of the black guys stuck his hand up her skirt just before she vomited on the floor." The Colonel had just taken a long hit of Jim Beam, and when he heard this story, he laughed a stream of brown through his nostrils.*

*Rusty said, "On my first 4Day we were at the campfire. Goober was talking about White Castle and said you guys went out and bought 100 of 'em one night, and he didn't know what happened next 'cause he was drinking Mad Dog". The 4Dayers started laughing, in large part 'cause it was cool that the usually quiet Big Man was laying one story after another with us.*

*Jimmy and Vid tag-teamed a great Whities story that included a heavy-drinking, non-4Dayer, a man with an ever-present jug of whiskey, Morrie. "We walked into the Ann Arbor White Castle with Morrie. In a couple of minutes, two State Police Officers got in line behind us. Mo sees the cops, runs out the door to the car, and lays down on the back seat floor. We're all watching this, and the cops ask, is your friend ok? No, not really. When we get back to the car with the bag of Whities, we asked Morrie why he ran. He said, 'I was trying to diffuse the situation'. No, Morrie, you <u>were</u> the situation."*

All this Whities talk got the boys stomachs to grumblin'. They now paddled harder and worked together with an extra crispness of effort at the logjams (we counted 10 today), in order to get fed as quickly as possible. 8 hours of work-hard/play-hard later, we arrive at the Peninsula campground where Ricki, Jason & I have dinner responsibilities. On the menu tonight is Pasta-on-the-Peninsula. Although praise is heaped on the pasta, we could've served just about anything to the 4Dayers after this long, hard day on the Fox. Once the stomachs are full, exhaustion from the day catches up to the boys, and satisfaction settles itself quietly on the camp. After the first of us slowly wanders to the comfort of his tent 'n sleeping bag, the rest follow one-by-one in a soft parade spaced out every 10-15 minutes until the last man puts out the campfire and turns in.

As the sun rises Day 3, tents began to unzip, and fellas wander into the Peninsula's woods to make room for breakfast. Yesterday's lengthy, rugged effort left only 4 hours of paddling with two days to complete it, allowing us the luxury of relaxing in camp all day long and staying on the Peninsula a 2nd night. Some do canoe, but nothing serious, paddling either upstream or downstream a few bends and then back. Most river activity involves hours of Frisbee tossing or taking a walk against the current, carrying a floatation pad, then laying back in the current while hanging on to the pad, only head-hands-feet above the water, and letting the current slowly bring you back to camp. As the sun begins to set on the day, a fantastic feast of chicken, potatoes, and veggies is created for us by Rookie Moth and two of the Sons of Marian Vollmers, Jimmy and Rusty, the perfect end to the perfect day.

The Day 4 half-way point is a long cigar 'n bourbon stop at the new steel bridge, a Norm Cash roof-top home run short of where the Fox and Manistique Rivers merge. It is noted that Moth shows signs of experiencing a physically rough rookie year, with a series of wounds in the form of cuts, scrapes & bruises, with one colorful bruise that wraps around his side and on to his back the size of an album, by Deep Purple perhaps. This leads to suggestions that other nicknames for Rookie Moth, maybe Bruise or Wound, be considered, but the name Moth holds firm.

The call for *"SHOTS!"* on the bridge gets the bottle moving through the crowd again, and elicits a story from Jimmy. To preface this tale, know that last year Moth was in his 7th season with our softball team, aka the Mobil Lounge Softball Team & Beer Swillers Club, and in those 7 years had over 500 at bats without ever hitting a triple. Jimmy said, "Johnny is not only our team's Most Valuable Player, but possibly the greatest hitting coach in history: when Moth walked up to the plate in a game last year, Johnny told him, *Hey Moth, why don't you hit a triple.* And he did! Wow! It's a different kind of called *SHOT!* but still as impressive."

I start, "On the subject of baseball…" when the pleasantly obnoxious Moth interrupted, "We were talking softball, Doc." "Well, close enough. Did you guys see this year's Tiger's Old-Timers Game? It was a 25-year anniversary celebration of the 1968 World Series Champions. Dick Tracewski was talking to a reporter as he reminisced about '68, saying that Dick McAuliffe was the real leader of the team. Mac was standing nearby & replied, *Well, they always followed me into the bar, if that's what he means.* There is another great line in the book I just finished reading, Thomas MacLean's "A River Runs Through It": *In Montana, drinking beer don't count as drinking."*

With Ricki living back in his home state of North Carolina, he's getting a steady diet of Country songs on the radio. He was telling us about some of the song lyrics, "I waited on her hand & foot and it cost me an arm & a leg", "You must have been built in Detroit City 'cause someone recalled your heart", "You said you were out jogging when you were really running around on me" and "She ain't much to see but she looks good through the bottom of a glass".

Heading out from the bridge, we paddle for home as the 4Day armada spreads out over several bends. Late-afternoon morphs into early-evening, the sun-drenched colors of the river and forest at their most vivid. There's enough water in the canoe bottom to cause empties to float and click together when rounding a bend. You have that light, sunburnt warmth, the cigar's half-smoked, and the river appears to have no end.

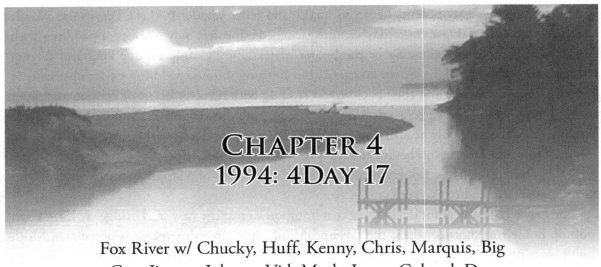

# CHAPTER 4
# 1994: 4DAY 17

Fox River w/ Chucky, Huff, Kenny, Chris, Marquis, Big
Guy, Jimmy, Johnny, Vid, Moth, Jason, Colonel, Doc
and rookies Gomie, Jonesey and Captain Johnny

*We were laughing in a daydream*
*With the world beneath our feet*
*And the sun shined on the water*
*Where the skies and the ocean meet*
*We were spellbound, ohhh spellbound*
*(Daydream by Robin Trower)*

RIP April 1994, the odd trinity of Goobs, Kurt Cobain, and Richard M. Nixon. One of the greatest political t-shirts ever was, "Tanned, Ready, and Rested: Nixon '92".

Goobs favorite musician was Robin Trower. With several friends in his parked car, spanning the evolution from 8-track to cassette player, many evenings were spent in altered states listening to the car speakers blasting out "Bridge of Sighs", "Too Rolling Stoned", or any number of Trower classics. Late the night of his 1993 bachelor party, I drove home the happily tanked Goobs, who was stretched out in the passenger seat, shoulders straight back, legs locked in place, butt lifted off the seat, while air-guitaring his way through one Trower song after another.

1979 was the one year that I had season tickets to Meeechigan Football - Goobs and I had seats together. Holding our tickets to the Indiana game, he drove the 45 minutes to my Ypsi apartment from his Lambertville home. As Goobs was just about to knock on my door, he remembered that he'd left the tickets at his house, and raced home to get 'em. Since he didn't actually knock on my door, and since this was before cell phones, I'm pacing in my apartment, watching the clock tick off to kickoff, wondering where the hell Goober was. Then my phone rings. Goobs relays the whole story, and we agree there's not enough time for him to get back to Ypsi and us then to Ann Arbor to see much, if any, of the game. So... as I'm listening to Bob Ufer call the last play on the radio, 6 seconds left/UM tied with Indiana/45 yards from the end zone/Johnny Wangler flings the ball to the streaking Anthony Carter, who outraces the defenders to the end zone as time expires, in one of the greatest, most amazing finishes in UM football history. I'm alternating between "YES!!" and "F-in' Goobs!!" for the next several minutes. The Greatest Game we never saw, but it sure was fun to hear Bob Ufer call it. The victory was worth 12 blasts by Ufer on the "Bo George Patton Schembechler scoring horn", the actual horn from General Patton's jeep.

One of the ladies attending Goobs' funeral said, "I've never seen so many men crying". Talking to my Dad about the blessing of having a brother like the Goombino, he said, "You have many acquaintances in your life, buy only a very few that you could count on to get you out of a Turkish prison." Goobs was one of those few.

The cause of death was a brain tumor diagnosed as untreatable. Many old friends participated in 'round-the-clock shifts to be with Goobs and administer pain-killing drugs at the appointed times. Around the hospice bed set up in his living room, a few of us were there as Goobs lay on his stomach, the end near. He hadn't said anything for the last day or two when the ringing phone broke the silence. It was Wayne calling. He and Rusty were on their way over to see their little buddy. "Goobs" I said, "you got big Wayne comin' over to pay you a visit. He's always had a gleam in his eye for you, so you might want to flip over on to your back". Goobs uttered the last words any of us can recall him saying, leaving us laughing and with a new catchphrase, "Good thinkin' Lincoln", before turning over on to his back.

Goobs and Wayne shared the same birthday and a special relationship that transcended even the brotherhood of the 4Day, both salt of the earth folk, creating immediately a strong bond. It was appropriate that they shared a birthday, Goobs born the day that Wayne turned 7, on 10/21/54.

"Dirty White Boy! What's happenin'?" It was my brother from another mother, Johnny Harcourt, on the other end of the telephone line, calling in from the Jacksonville home he shares with his bride of two years, our sweet sister and fellow EMU Huron, Kathy Harcourt nee LoCricchio. I'd taken to calling Johnny by his Dirty White Boy nom de guerre, borrowed from the song by the rock band Foreigner, shortly after meeting Johnny in 1978. That year, Maggie worked with Johnny's 1st wife (he has since traded up to Kathy) who invited us to a house party that wife #1 was throwing with Johnny.

Entering the Pleasant Street house in St. Clair Shores, I first encountered Johnny. He'd mixed this night's party music, and I was receiving a lesson in how to create a cassette tape in such a way that your guests, upon hearing the tape, cannot sit down. The living room was packed shoulder-to-shoulder with dancers bouncing (along with the speakers) and dripping with sweat, as Johnny & I found ourselves standing in the doorway leading from the living room gyrations to the hallway. Until the party's end, we never moved from that spot, but for bathroom breaks, beer refills, and occasional forays squeezing between the other dancers. We talked about life, family ("Grandma Harcourt paid $175 to have the family tree dug up, then immediately paid $150 to have this history re-buried."), friends, music, history, the State of the Union, Tiger baseball, and a goat named Guy (rhymes with "key").

I'd met the goat mid-party, after the 10 numbers from my doobie case had gone up in smoke while standing next to Johnny, necessitating the rolling of additional spliffs from the back-up ounce in my pocket (it's all about planning). The goat stood next to my backroom work table, quietly watching me go about my business, except for occasional bleating emitting from between his scraggly beard and rounded horns. The friendly fella sitting on the adjacent chair seemed to know the goat, so I sought information from him, "Is that your goat?" "Yeah, we've been together for a few months now." "What's the goat's name?" "Guy." "Guy?" "Guy." "Why Guy?" "I'm a hockey fan, and a big fan of Guy Lafleur." "Oh, nice to meet you and Guy."

"Hey Johnny, I just met a goat." "Yeah, that's Guy." "Well okay then."

A life-long friendship was born. Not with the goat, although a fine goat, but between Johnny and me. 16 years post-Guy, Johnny was calling to confirm that 3 Jacksonville rookies would be 4Dayin' this year: Pat Carroll and Keith Jones were coming north with Johnny.

The 1992 wedding of Johnny & Kathy Harcourt was the first opportunity that many of us had to meet their two Jacksonville friends and now 4Day rookies, Pat and Keith. The fellas liked these southerners right away – it was impossible not to. Pat is always ready to pitch in, whether it's helping 4Dayers get through/over/around logjams or to gather fire wood in camp. He gained a 4Day name at the very first river break we took this year, Gomez or Gomie, due to his striking resemblance to Gomez Addams of the Addams Family (the John Astin-version, and with the same devilish charm). Keith already came with a fine moniker, Jonesey, an easy one with a last name of Jones. Jonesey is a warm-hearted soul, a good story-teller (a valued 4Day trait), an around-the-country follower of the band Widespread Panic, and an exceptional artist, a talent he exhibits both in bars and around the campfire. The 4Day name for Johnny also predates 4Dayin: Captain Johnny, in honor of the respect he inspires & from his days transporting ships for their owners among various Caribbean Islands. It could be argued that the Kurt Russell's Captain Ron ("a diesel loves her oil same as a sailor loves his rum") is a mild take-off on Captain Johnny.

The Florida Boys arrived at Metro Airport Thursday evening, about 12 hours before we were to begin the 4Day drive north. With our Thursday night softball league on a 2-week hiatus, the usual post-game drink-a-thon at the Mobil Lounge was eliminated, and we were able to get in a good night's sleep before our Friday morning departure.

Friday was a gorgeous, sunny blessing of a day. 14 of this year's 16 4Dayers – biggest crowd we've ever had - caravanned to Lansing, there turning straight north on US27 to the Houghton Lake exit, the half-way point on today's 6-hour journey to Germfask. In Houghton Lake we took a break at the Nottingham Bar, our 2nd year at this road-to-the-4Day watering hole, where we met up with Kenny and Huff, coming up from southern Indiana. Shortly after walking into the bar, Kenny greeted us with the news that he'd been soaking cranberries – a twist from the usual cherries - in Jack Daniels the last 12-months to share on the river, and passed along one of his latest pearls of wisdom, "You know what they call a deer with no eyes? No-i-d-er."

3 hours post-Nottingham, we arrived in Germfask. The Floridians suggested that the caravan north was going a mite fast, 100 mph was a number thrown about, with Captain Johnny mentioning that after clearing the Big Mac Bridge, back-seat Jonesey asked what that "little bump" was back there.

Captain Johnny told us that Jonesey expressed concern to him about his "speech pattern", asking "Do I really sound like I'm from the South? I don't want to have a Southern drawl." Johnny assured Jonesey that any drawl was minimal, but he might want to say, "How ya doin', eh?" when greeting folks up here. Jonesey is practicing this phrase as they drive north. Stopping at a party store, Jonesey brings a 12-pack to the counter, and asks the big gal at checkout, "How ya doin', eh?" She replies southern-sweetly, "Ahm fine, how hew?"

4Day-eve found us at our Germfask tavern, the Jolly Bar, enjoying beers 'n shots and getting hungry. The gent running the bar this evening told us the kitchen was closed, so I called Stop Pizza in Curtis, the nearest place for carryout. Chris & (not Captain) Johnny made the food run, and Johnny comes bursting through the Jolly front door with a stack of pizza boxes. The bar fella tells us "You can't bring those in here". Johnny starts laughing, figuring he must be kidding. He is not. "But your kitchen is closed," we tell him. "Doesn't matter." I explained to him that these guys are going to spend $250 bucks, easy, but you don't want our business?" "No! No pizza in here!" So, we 'n the pizzas left the bar and continued the party outside of our Jolly Motel rooms.

Well, not all of us continued the party outside the rooms. Marquis had stepped into his room and passed out on the bed. He was now starting to sit up while dozing, almost elevating himself above the mattress, and talking in his sleep... *"Merry Christmas!"... "No Gilda, no!"* Marquis' well-known ability to fall asleep under any circumstances, his Marc-o-lepsy, had struck again.

It turned out that the Jolly Bar guy did us a huge favor. When the closed kitchen in Germfask forced Chris & Johnny to make the pizza run, they discovered what a cool little town Curtis was. Not wanting to deal with the Germfask bar fool again at the end of the 4Day, we canceled our Tuesday night rooms in that town and spent our 4Day closing night in Curtis. Thanks to some advance scouting by Captain Johnny, we knew just where to go when we got there. The night of our Germfask bar dispute, the Captain recalled his brother Bill telling him of a favorite pub in Curtis. A visit to that bar was uninspiring, but he was drawn by the Johnny Cash songs booming out the front door of another town tavern, the Mc's Tally Ho, where the Captain met its owner, Betsy McCormick. Betsy is in her 60s, an engaging individual, with a personality clearly made for owning a tavern. It is the general consensus that we have found our new 4Day home.

Launching on the Fox the next morning, Big Guy and Captain Johnny were the lead canoe. On the second riverbend downstream, 5 minutes into the trip, they pulled over on to a sandy beach to await the other 7 canoes. 5 minutes, it turned out, was too far to go.

Vid and Johnny Steck were in the next boat, turning their canoe sideways in the narrow first turn, creating a virtual cork in the bottle, halting all remaining boats, and starting the party. 30 minutes later, Vid and Johnny turned their canoe and all followed downstream. Big Guy and the Captain were waiting around the next bend. "What were you guys doing?" an annoyed Big Guy asked. Vid replied, "We stopped for a doobie." Biggie looked into the canoes and barked, "You guys emptied TWO fifths!" "Well, it was a BIG doobie," said Vid, "Doc had written *War & Peace* on the side of it."

Vid was a day-long bundle of energy, whether dancin' like a leprechaun during paddling breaks, telling stories on land or while afloat, and always spreading good cheer. On one riverside rest, Vid had his arms wrapped around Florida bookends Jonesey and Gomie. I asked the 30-year old Jonesey how old he thought Vid was. "I'd guess about 30 or so." "Nope, he's 44." "Jonesey was incredulous, "*What?* He's *how* old?" "Yep, these 4Day waters, 'n the beer 'n the bourbon, while sharing stories with friends in the wilderness, keeps you youthful."

Reaching the Seney Township campsite, we set-up tents and then headed for Andy's Bar, a must visit for these Florida rookies. Andy was in high spirits, about as tanked as we've ever seen him. Captain Johnny was the first in the door, and Andy bellowed, "How the hell are ya son?" After a little conversing, Andy said, "You're one of them Harcourts, eh? I knew them all. Listen, you gotta stick around, we got live entertainment. This band is called Karaoke."

Captain Johnny was pretty sure that Andy had never met a Harcourt in his life, and felt if he had, Johnny wouldn't be allowed to stay in the bar too long. We had seen first-hand in 1987, when the old-timer stopped talking to Goobs once our friendship with Captain Johnny Harcourt came up, that the Harcourt-Dunn feud from the late-1800s is alive and well in Seney.

Post-Andy's, it was said that my tent could be seen flapping from the snoring by 9PM, the sun not even down yet. This was taken as an ominous sign for some of the rookies, maybe an astute observation. Jonesey had brought a swimming pool raft to sleep on in the tent, and on his first 4Day night ever, with a nice 'n chilly 34 degree temp, the raft popped a hole, leaving Jonesey sleeping on a cold, hard ground. He was heard saying "Fuck!" many times, but not by me.

At the Day 2 breakfast, Chucky created a special dish that he christen Blueberry-Jim Beam-pancakes. Maybe it was the morning-after hunger or maybe they were just that good, but the boys said they'd never had a better 4Day meal.

When we weren't dragging each other's canoes over multiple logjams, a wide variety of "drinks of the day", the only common denominator being all dirt cheap, were grabbed from the coolers and shared among the group. This was the day that Pat aka Gomez aka Gomie won the rookie of the year voting. Beyond energetic work in assisting at each obstruction encountered, he showed a willingness to drink – with gusto – any kind of rot put in front of him, cursing at each swallow.

Several hours of logjams and drinkin' later, Gomez started entertaining us at each stop with some mighty fine buck-dancin', still from the waist up while his legs were flying, an old southern style of dancing that's a cousin to clogging.

With so much time spent waist-deep in the river, wrestling the canoes through the obstructions, Jonesey was lookin' a might chilled. "Hey Jonesey," Vid shouted, "the water ever get this cold in Jacksonville?" "Yeah," Jonesey frowned, "in our coolers."

Marquis' impersonations included one of a fella he worked with named Junior Burns. He told us that Junior walked into work one day with his glasses on a diagonal across his face. When asked what happened, Junior told 'em, "Somebody musta hit me in mah face, when I wasn't lookin."

The sunlight was starting to fade when the traditional 2$^{nd}$ night campsite, the High Ground, came into view. The Jacksonville 3 rookie squad was responsible for dinner tonight, all delicious except for one head-scratching entrée: boiled peanuts. The cooks assured us northerners that this was an acquired taste, a possibility not one of us could see.

Heavy consumption and hard work took their toll on the Moth. He was upright unconscious and catching flak. Big Guy said, "Lookit Moth, he's passed out sitting up, somebody put him to bed." Chucky piled on, "The buzzards are circling. Hey Moth, I wonder who's home tappin' the old lady now, it sure ain't you." The abuse was quickly overtaken by the boys shouting *"4Day!"* louder and louder. Big Guy shook his head, "Guys, loosen up, would ya?"

Debate swirled about who are the best rock 'n roll singers… Jim Morrison – great choice, Ann Wilson from Heart – those sisters rock! Oh - Paul Rodgers of Bad Company & Free, Steven Tyler – yes, yes; but, in honor of Goobs, we all agreed to tip our hats to Robin Trower's lead singer, James Dewar. The shouts of "To Goobs!" rang out, leading to toast after toast.

The wonderful, short Day 3 trip from the High Ground to the Peninsula allowed our tents to be set up and a bonfire going well before dinner time. Vid and I took on rookies Jonesey and Gomie for a round of buzz euchre. We got our butts kicked, leading to many drinks & recriminations…

*"Vid, how could we lose to these rookies?" "It's not my fault. We shoulda drank the good stuff." "We don't have any good stuff." "Doc, I think someone was cheating. Gomie has shifty eyes!" Rising wobbly from my cooler seat, Vid added, "I told you we shoulda played closer to the tent."*

Captain Johnny's alter ego, Asphuc Biggins, showed itself after the bourbon made extensive rounds at the fire, spoutin' philosophical on us, "No matter how much it looks like you, deny it" he advised. Biggins spoke of long, late-night, conversations with a bartender named Lloyd, who told him that his money was no good here. Biggins seamlessly spanned subjects as varied as they were difficult to follow.

There were stories of smoking cigars in the fancy seats at the Jacksonville Suns ballpark, and Trevor the usher who wanted to know if there will be any trouble. Then Biggins recounted a recent Florida afternoon that his slightly less crazy side, Captain Johnny, and I spent along the Intracoastal at a place called the Cove…

*A nice spot was secured on the water's edge & the show begins. When first getting the attention of the waitress, Mister Fletcher can be sooooo smooth, but somewhere around the 5th or 6th shot of Jose, there is a subtle change. Doc, "Johnny, want another shot?" Johnny, "emembmbottob!" Doc, "Yeah! Yeah! Somebody get me that wench! One of you laggards get me that wench! Shots now! Get that little slacker over here!" Johnny (throwing up into the Intracoastal Waterway), "ememmemboblob!" Doc, "I'm struggling with the Tigers. Sparky sucks and the staff can't pitch." Johnny, "Yooois right Dooc, they shoulda kept that Jeff Komlo kid." Doc, "Johnny, that's football." Johnny, "Doc, the Tigers don't play football, ask Isiah Thomas." Doc, "Johnny, you are really messed up." Dennis the host, "You guys are filling the waterway to the top with your empties. If your damn tab wasn't so high, I'd throw you the hell out of here." Johnny, "I agree with you completely Dennis, now go away — you are standing right where I'm going to throw up next."*

*Asphuc Biggins continued, "The crowd slowly grew throughout the evening and by 11 or so the Beaches community knew of the brothers FletchCourt and their uncanny ability to avert the law, angry wives, and that nasty newsboy who keeps demanding money.*

On our final day canoeing the Fox, we arrived at a point one hour short of the livery take-out. The boys pulled over to a fine, long sandy beach for a final 4Day break, getting some Frisbee flippin' in, which always gets the fellas thirsty, as does breathing. Chris couldn't believe that all of our coolers were empty, "Does ANYONE have any beers left?" Colonel had some happy news, "Yeah, I have a few", bringing cheers from the group, until the Colonel's cooler was open. In lieu of ice next to his beers there was dead fish — exactly how the warm beer tasted. As a result, some of the boys were only good for one or two brews.

As the canoes shoved off for the stretch paddle home, Moth decided to get a final swim in. Diving into the water head first, his cranium crashed into a large tree root embedded into the river's floor. Staggering to his feet revealed a large forehead gash had opened. Shouts of, "We got a wounded Moth here!" turned the departing canoes around, returning to the beach.

Stretching Moth out on the sand, with a canoe pad beneath his head, blood from the wound now began to stream off of his wet forehead and fill up his ears. A few small twigs protruded from his split-open temple. Huff, a man of the woods used to handling injuries absent physicians, pulled out an impressively-sized blade ("now THAT'S a knife!"), ready to remove the offending twigs. No disrespect to Huff's surgical skills, but should there be a slight err and we bring Moth home with a lobotomy, his wife Debbie might not be her usual sweet self. On the other hand, it would be quieter in their house… hmm… but, no, no thanks Huff.

From a First Aid Kit, we were able to bandage Moth's head and stem the bleeding before helping him into the canoe he shared with Vid. "Please be careful paddling, Viddy", Moth pleaded. A tad to the rough side of Clara Barton, Vid replied, "Screw you Moth! Were you careful before diving into the river?"

Arriving at the Northland Outfitters landing and the trip's end, I drew the short straw to drive Moth 30 minutes to Newberry where the nearest hospital was located. While not too keen about driving a half an hour less than sober, the leech bite picked up today did allow some river water into my ankle, swelling it up pretty good, so we could make this visit a two-fer.

The good news is that Moth isn't driving. As soon as the attending doctor got one look at Moth he said, "No more bourbon tonight son", having noticed the eyes spinning in different directions, significant head wound bleeding, bourbon breath infiltrating the hallways, and sweat the color of Jim Beam brown rather than clear.

The Newberry medical team wrapped Moth's wound and gave me a $90 antibiotic script to take care of my leech bite swelling. The antibiotic better come with 5 pizzas and 2 cases of beer for $90. While the staff's efforts took care of Moth's bleeding, the "cure" given me backfired. By the time I'd arrived home the next day, my ankle was the size of a melon and extremely painful to walk on. The doctor who wrote the script might be descended from the person who decided to put an "s" in the word lisp – a cruel bastard. While I entertained Maggie with the just concluded 4Day details, she drove me to the local hospital where a competent physician gave me a $5 script that overnight took care of the swelling.

Once back home, Colonel conveyed his appreciation to the Moth, "I'm not sure I ever thanked you for finding that log with your head that day. Were it not for your skills and talent, one of us might have stubbed our toe on it, and that is something nobody likes. So, here's the official *Thank You*".

*Speaking of none of that…*

11.16.94, 4 months after the 1994 4Day ended, marked my 40th birthday, noteworthy as this was 20 years to the day that I first saw Maggie. November 16, 1974 was early in my junior year at Eastern Michigan University and my 20th birthday. Alone that afternoon in my Ambassador East campus apartment, the TV was tuned to the University of Michigan game, a 51 to nothing defeat of Purdue, as Maggie walked by my window. I had never seen her before… she had a blue jacket on, toting a green backpack, long hair flowing down to her butt. I was mesmerized, literally falling over backwards from my seat on the floor. After walking by the window, this lady – whose name I did not yet know - turned into the building, providing hope that she lives in these apartments, too.

4 of us shared the apartment: Jimmy Mong, charming with a Hercules-like stature, the man all women loved and men admired, 4-years-down-the-road Father of the 4Day Ricki, future 4Day class of '92 rookie Marquis, and me. We agreed to invite everyone in the complex to a holiday potluck dinner in our apartment on the first Saturday in December. Since the dinner would be between Thanksgiving and Christmas, we christen it "Thanksmas".

Jimmy and Ricki were to extend the invitations with a visit to each apartment. I'd told them about seeing the girl with hair to her butt, asked that they look for her while knocking on doors, and make sure to invite this vision of loveliness. They reported back that they saw her, told me the lady's name is Maggie, and that she & her roommates had accepted the Thanksmas invite.

Maggie had seen me tossing a Frisbee with the boys on the street in front of Ambassador East, and was likewise interested. Unbeknownst to each other, Maggie and I intended to sit next to one another at the Thanksmas table. Totally out of character for both of us, we stepped outside the apartment after dinner, and were making out on the landing steps. Oo la la!

Once Maggie's dowry included a 1980 Triumph Spitfire, I proposed to her in May of 1981, and she accepted. We were married on the banks of the Huron River at Riverside Park in Ypsilanti, near the EMU campus, on 8.1.81. Attempting to upstage our wedding day, Prince Charles and Princess Diana were wed the same week. Although their nuptials received more media coverage, our marriage lasted longer. Karma baby.

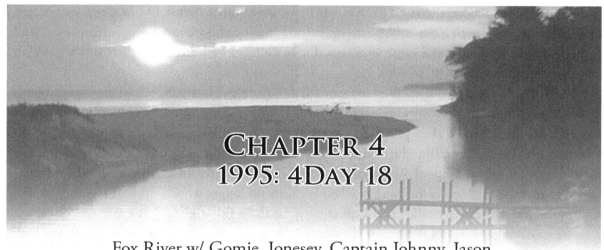

# CHAPTER 4
# 1995: 4DAY 18

Fox River w/ Gomie, Jonesey, Captain Johnny, Jason,
Colonel, Marquis, Dr. Bob, Chris, Moth, Johnny, Vid,
Chucky & Doc and rookies KB, Tony Barney & Frey

*His head smashed in*
*And his heart cut out*
*And his liver removed*
*And his bowels unplugged*
*And his nostrils raped*
*And his bottom burnt off*
*And his penis split and his...*
*"That's... that's enough music for now, lads"*
*(Brave Sir Robin from "The Holy Grail" – Monty Python)*

From the mid-70s through last year, a trip to Tiger Stadium wasn't complete without a pre-game and/or a post-game visit to Hoot Robinson's Bar across from Gate 1. Hoot passed away last December 15, and gone with him was one of the last links to long-ago Tiger legends and Hoot's customers, like Hank Greenburg and Rudy York. To quote the Detroit Free Press, *"The death last week of Hoot Robinson, 87, who put a smile on the faces of everyone who entered his famous bar & grill for more than 60 years, brought a tear to the eyes of his fans & customers. Baseball greats from Babe Ruth to Kirk Gibson enjoyed visiting Hoot, who closed his bar September 2. Won't seem the same around Tiger Stadium without him."*

The 4Day caravan north met 9AM at the US23 & M59 Truck Plaza junction. Immediately a party broke out, likely not what the property owners had in mind when building the truck plaza: Frisbees were in the air, fifths tipped and passed, cigars lit, and the brownies Maggie made for us were devoured. 9AM is later than it used to be.

Absent from the festivities this year is a member of the 4Day class of '79, Big Guy aka Biggie aka Mark Alwood. We'd met as 12 year-olds in 1967, after our families had moved from the Detroit area to Lambertville, a small town just north of Toledo, Ohio. I can't emphasize this enough: Lambertville is located in Michigan, NOT in Ohio.

Biggie and I attended the same church, where we were both acolytes. In our teens, we became close friends, were each other's biggest competitors for neighborhood lawn cutting jobs, and in high school worked at the same McDonald's. In college, we both helped pay our ways with summertime factory jobs in Toledo.

In the late-70s, post-college, Big Guy worked at Lansing's Harley Hotel, where I stayed once a month while traveling for my employer, Duracell. I would arrive in town when Big Guy's work day ended, and we would then party at Lansing area pubs 'til closing time. Each monthly trip to Lansing, I had a 7AM meeting the next morning with a customer named Capitol Wholesale. The first year of calling on Capitol Wholesale, I would see them after an evening of hard carousing and very little sleep. Then came the day when Big Guy no longer worked in Lansing and, for the first night before the 7AM call, I had a quiet evening and a full night's shut-eye.

After arriving at Capitol Wholesale the next morning, the buyer greeted me with a funny look on his face. "Did you have surgery?" I was asked. "What do you mean?" He pointed towards my face. "Your eyes, did you have an operation to fix your eyes?" Apparently, at all of our previous meetings, my eyes were _so_ bloodshot that, with the red now absent, the buyer assumed that I had resorted to a surgical remedy to correct the inflamed eyeballs. I less than cleverly answered "no" when the better answer would've been, "Why, yes I did sir. The entire surgical team, the interns, and the nursing staff were all taken quite by surprise that the procedure also eliminated the overwhelming scent of bourbon escaping my pores, noticeable during visits to your office."

In his absence, picking up Big Guy's slack is this year's rookie class of KB, Frey, and Tony B...

Keith Romig, better known as KB, is an Ohio native, which we hold against him every once in a while, who migrated to Jacksonville. While visiting Kathy (at the time, Captain Johnny's future wife) LoCricchio in 1985, we met KB at a USFL Jacksonville Bulls football game. KB sat in the row behind us. We started a running conversation with him, hit it off right away, and encouraged KB to join us on our next day's travel to St. Augustine. KB accepted and he's been part of the group ever since, even on days Michigan or MSU plays Ohio State.

Frey is friends with Chris, from their naval duty days serving together on the S.S. Saratoga. He repeatedly tells us, "Call me Frey! Call me Frey!" so Frey it is. His 3 4Days years will have a memorable conclusion in 1999.

Tony B., aka Tony Barney, is a man that Moth and I have had the privilege of working with at Duracell in the 1980s. Tony B. has a good heart, is self-effacing, with a fine sense of humor and a ready laugh that makes you feel good when you hear it.

On I-75 North, we look in Gaylord for the 47' tall replica of a beer bottle, landmark for a lunch 'n beer stop at Big Buck Brewery. The Jacksonville Boys are entranced by how Big Buck's toilet seat paper cover automatically advances each time the toilet is flushed, a modern convenience only dreamed about in the Old Confederacy. "You gotta see this!" Vid overhears and thinks that they are all together in the stall looking at a giant dump. "You sick Florida bastards!" KB picks up the Big Buck tab and is immediately declared rookie-of-the-year. Chris, supporting rookie & fellow Navy veteran Frey, argues, "That's not the American way", which meets with a universal response, "What are you talking about, that's exactly the American way!"

The temperature was 70 when we left southeast Michigan, and had dropped 30 degrees by the time we arrived in Gaylord. After eating, the Jacksonville boys go into Big Buck's gift shop to look for sweatshirts. *$50?!?*" Fortunately, the Norman's store in town has them for $5.

By early evening, the train of vehicles pulled into our new 4Day eve U.P. home, the Season's Motel in Curtis, Ray & Rachael proprietors. Last year's 4Day eve run-in with the tool managing the Jolly Bar in Germfask prompted the lodging move to Curtis. The town's Season's Motel is perfectly positioned, no more than 50' from the Mc's Tally Ho bar.

Once between the tavern walls, the boys were in a rollicking mood, pounding beers, their cries of *"SHOTS!"* filling the air, and singing along with the juke box: *"Love… is a burning thing… and it makes… a fiery ring"*. When a little bad language seeped out, owner Betsy made sure we understood one of her rules at Mc's Tally Ho: "There's no fuckin' swearin' in this bar!" Yes ma'am. Chris turned to Tony B., KB, and Frey, "Stop cursin' you damn rookies, and fetch us another round of beers!"

The lodging may change, but the same pain exists when I knock on each room's doors at 7AM to get the 4Dayers moving. With surprisingly little delay, the boys gathered in the Season's Motel courtyard, with one exception. "Where the hell is Moth? MOTH!!!" The final door opened, and out he stepped, with a new look. In honor of his head-crashing dive last 4Day into a large branch embedded on the floor of the Fox River, a bloody incident at (what will now be forever known as) Moth Landing, and due to strict instructions from his wife Debbie, Moth this year is wearing a construction site hard hat each day on the river.

At today's first break on the river, the initial bourbon bottle passed around is christened "Hard Hat Bourbon".

THE 4 HORSEMEN

Jonesey shared with us a picture he'd drawn of the four-man Jacksonville contingent of 4Day brothers depicted on horseback & labeled "the 4 Horsemen: Stench (Captain John), Pestilence (KB), Death (Jonesey) and Gomez (Gomie)". When KB asked the artist, "Hey, why didn't you put a big dick on my horse?" Jonesey replied, "I did".

We spent the first day's evening at the familiar surroundings of Andy's Seney Bar. One of the locals looked us over and asked Vid, "Are you the guys who rode a horse through the bar in Newberry?" Since there were a few U.P. hours that Vid could not account for, he had to reply, "I'm not really sure."

The Moth, Captain Johnny and I found ourselves sharing a table with 3 entertaining regulars: George, an 80s-something elder with well-grounded, Goobs-like wisdom, Ed, who told us that <u>he</u> was the man who rode the horse through a Newberry bar, serving 10 days in jail for the incident, and Dale, a man with a dangerous streak (yes, more dangerous than riding a horse through a bar).

After a few rounds, Moth passed out on his bar stool, arms folded, chin on chest, rotating back 'n forth in half-circles. Horse rider Ed grew concerned, "Say buddy, do you think your friend will fall off the bar stool?" I assured him, "Nah, he does that a lot and almost always stays upright. Hey, how 'bout we buy you fellers a round?" and I order 6 shots. Dale has a quizzical look on his face, "Yer buddy is passed out – why'd you order 6 shots?" "Oh yeah, he's passed out now, but he'll wake up for a shot." The barmaid sets a shot down in front of Moth, and Captain Johnny & I work on waking him up, "Moth! Moth! MOTH!" He does a little moan, lifts his chin off his chest, squints his eyes to focus on the shot, tosses it down, and goes back to sleep. The regulars are impressed. 80-ish George tells us, "Damn! If I hadn't a seen it, I wouldn't a believed it." He then starts telling us that his older brother has never been south of the Mackinac Bridge. Now it's our turn to be impressed, "You got an *older* brother?! Who's alive? Wow! How old *is* he?"

As Day 2 broke, so did a lot of wind. Last nights' Andy burgers were making a return visit. The gas cloud hovering above the Seney Township Camp prodded a relatively early camp breakdown and river launch.

In under an hour, we entered the Spreads, home to one of the favorite 4Day break spots, Boot Hill. Deadfall often accumulates at Boot Hill's river bend and, once the canoes are pulled over these obstructions and secured, the 4Dayers climb 10' to the top of Boot Hill for drinking and its outstanding elevated view of the Spreads. There is a deep hole below the water's surface, maybe 7' to 8' deep, at the base of Boot Hill, and it was here that Captain Johnny arrived when he shouted to the boys congregated above, "Can I get out here?" Dr. Bob provided a technically correct answer, "Yes, you can." When Johnny stepped out of his canoe, he slipped completely underwater, his Detroit Tiger cap floating on the surface, outlined by motion rings, the only marker of where he entered the Fox.

Once we lent a hand to get the Captain out of the depths and up on to the hilltop, we began to pass a freshly-opened fifth of bourbon. Shouts of "Boot! More Boot! " rang across Boot Hill. The "boot" is a miniature boot-shaped shot glass that the marketing department at Jim Beam has begun shrink-wrapping to each fifth. This marketing ploy hit the bullseye with the 4Day crowd. As the boot 'n bottle made the rounds, it was noticed that someone was missing from the sippin' circle. "Who let Marquis sit down?" Marquis was leaning against a tree, snoring as marc-o-lepsy had overtaken him one more time.

Back on the river, KB was talking about his recent visit to White Castle, "You think your shit don't stink, but your farts give you away." Expanding on that subject matter, Bobby was going downstream with his naked butt hanging over the back of his canoe, dumping a load. Vid said, "Bobby, those turds are coming out of you like a Baby Ruth dispenser." After several remarks about how nasty this activity was, Bobby said, "It's ok, they're going downstream!" Vid replied, "Bobby, *we're* going downstream".

*18 years of 4Days and it took a sober man to lose a canoe.* It happened between two of today's many logjams, when we pulled ashore for a break from dragging canoes over and around the fallen trees. Chucky and I recounted the story over the evening campfire on the High Ground…

Chucky, "My first year sober, first time anyone ever lost a canoe." Doc, "We're all standing there, a little break goin' on, I look around. Hey, we're missing a canoe. Who's missing a canoe?" *silence* "Chucky, where's your boat?" Chucky, "I'm sorry." "What?!? You're *sorry*?" "So I hopped in my boat with a rope & a long bungie cord, paddled around a couple of bends and there it was, rattlin' around heading downstream. I roped it on to my canoe and paddled back to you boys. You'd finished the fifth in my absence, so I made you open a new one, damn it!"

Chucky had some river gear next to him at the campfire. In Big Guy's absence, he had sent his 4Day backpack with Chucky. In it was a booklet Biggie put together entitled *Big Guy Readings* that he asked us to "read it on the Seney Campground stooper (i.e. dumper)". Wrapped around two stories, "A Big Two-Hearted Pilgrimage" and "Brook Trout in Traver Country", were Big Guy 4Day-related notes including…

*Chucky! I love you buddy! Your mission, should you accept it… (1) toss the cap in a river and enforce a rookie retrieval and (2) at an appropriate time monitor a full-fledged double-bubbler by the Moth, and then ready the first aid kit – doh! – it's in my backpack. Think Bukowski. (Chucky wrote* "Mission Accomplished – C.P.") Author's note: a double-bubbler takes place when you drink so much from a bottle of liquor that two bubbles emerge inside the bottle.

*Don't canoe past the first bend or you might miss Doc's 4Day doob!*

*Chris, you da man on the portages – SHOTS! – toss the line in for the little Brookies – use crawlers and catch us some dinner.*

*Jason, flora and fauna are you – but if you raise a hatchet or a Jager, there'll be hell to pay!!*

*Absolutely NO Viking Funeral without me.* Author's note: in 1992, when Jason drank too much Jagermeister to attend to his next morning breakfast duties, we considered setting him afire and dumping him into the river for a Viking Funeral, possibly after he's dead. Also, Jason has been a bit wild tossing hatchets when drunk in camp.

*"The Harcourt family originated in Ireland and were a fearless lot who would fight at the drop of a hat!" from "Incredible Seney" by Lewis C. Reimann.*

*At the Curtis Mc's Tally Ho Bar: have John the Bartender set-up a round of "Roostertails" and drink to my shameful absence!* Author's note: no money was attached.

The "Big Guy Readings" did make for fine campground stooper reading, just as he had hoped, and Biggie left room for us to write about anything 4Day for his reading later, so he got abuse, fun, and love – just as if he was with us on the water…

*Big Guy! F-in' Yankees Suck! (writer unknown, but speaking for us all)*

*Biggie, Corn Squeezins! from the 16 4Dayers (under a drawing by Jonesey of the 16 1995 4Dayers)*

*Can you say "Bourbon in a tin cup?" Vid*

*Missed your presence. Missed your wit. Missed your smilin' face. Oh… hell… Love Ya Big Guy! Take Care, Chucky - P.S. Thanks for the reading material.*

Day 3 presented several logjams in the first 30 minutes, requiring us to work together to get all boats downstream, then 90 minutes of easy canoeing. Whether paddling the challenging or laid-back of today's journey, the goal for all was to stay within earshot of Marquis' canoe. He was assuming the role of Coleman Young, who retired last year after serving two decades as Mayor of Detroit. Marquis was nailing Coleman's accent and mannerisms, "I was boarding an aero-plane for my Hawaiian vacation, when one of those TV2 reporters stuck his microphone in mah face, asking if I had anything to say to the people of De-twoit. I told him *Aloha mutha-fucker!*"

Chucky mentioned "It's my first year sober", letting the guys know that he decided to get into AA & NA programs this year, feeling the need to get clean. Later, as I was paddling solo, visible at the end of a long straightaway was the Chucky-Tony B. canoe. Chucky was up front, turned towards Rookie Tony, too far away for me to hear what they're saying, but it looks like they're having a good time heading downstream together. Oops, I may be wrong. Chucky just threw a can of pop into Tony's chest. Chucky later explained, "He kept asking me over & over, don't you miss the drinking and smoking?" "YES! OF COURSE I DO! Now stop reminding me!"

Night 3 camp was on the Peninsula. The sun had not yet set, and Moth was perched on a cooler in front of his tent, a couple bends downstream of toasty. He was working on a bag of chocolate chip cookies, shoving the cookies into his mouth at a pace beyond what his jaw was capable of processing, the jaw's motion more and more sluggish. The boys had been standing by the river, telling stories, but they now quieted and turned their attention towards the Moth, spellbound by his performance. A chunky, brown stream of liquid cookies was running out of Moth's mouth, down his chin and neck.

Rookie KB's inquiry, "Gary, what are you eating?" received no answer. Moth's full focus is on chewing, swallowing, and avoiding choking-death-by-Chips-Ahoy, and the boys are howling! Gomie asks, "Moth, how can you be in sales?" After several failed attempts to clear his throat,

Moth's reply of, "Cause I got the greatest fuckin' personality in the world!" resulted in a camp-wide explosion of laughter. Moth's quote was instantly inducted into the 4Day Hall of Fame.

On this night, Rookie Tony has earned his 4Day name, Tony Barney, for bringing his son's *Barney the Dinosaur* pillow case on a 4Day. The pillow case was sacrificed in the name of bad judgment at the evening bonfire.

Despite the loss of his son's pillow case, Tony B. was basking in the warm glow of an evening on the Peninsula. The good feelings led him to a 2$^{nd}$ bad decision as Tony announced, "There's no way that you 13 veterans can throw we 3 rookies in the river." Upon hearing this, Frey & KB quickly disappeared into the woods, and quiet fell over the camp, the calm before the storm. Chris firmly suggested, "Put your wet clothes on Tony, you're going swimming." Tony suddenly is very nervous. "Doc, can you do something?" I give it a little thought, "Hey Chris, if Tony can roll enough doobs to equal the long length of your cooler, can he avoid being tossed into the river?" Chris says yes, Rookie Tony can avoid a dusk dip in the Fox if he can do that – within 10 minutes. With Chucky's assistance, who in his haste to beat the clock at times includes dirt in the smokes he rolls, Tony B. met the objective Chris gave and stays dry.

Gorgeous sunshine accompanied our relaxed flotilla on Day 4. The Fox had widened out, river dicks were few, and the canoers floated next to each other as we slowly made our way down the stream. The boys were sharing their favorite Detroit Tigers' stories when Johnny Steck spoke up, "Halftime at a UM football game, I was there with Fat Bob the Singing Plumber 'n Norm Cash." Marquis said, "That's the best Tiger story so far." Then Johnny said, "There's more – Norm asked me to leave the stadium to make a beer run." Colonel asked "Wow! Did you?" "Did I what?" "Did you make the beer run?" "Of course – Norm Cash asked me!" A series of "Johnny! Johnny! Johnny!" chants were interspersed with "Norm! Norm! Norm!"

"Oh, oh, Colonel's gonna blow!" During a break on the river, the Colonel was bent over the edge of his canoe, looking extremely nauseous. Knowing that I could not ease his pain, at least I could record it, and ran over to his canoe with the camera. The Colonel moaned, and I clicked – false alarm. Damn. He moaned and I clicked. Nothing, false alarm. The third moan was the charm, the vomit recorded mid-release, the fish were fed, and the moment saved for 4Day posterity. And, to the Colonel's eternal credit, at no time in this process did Colonel ever set his beer down, a man among men!

Resuming our meandering downstream, I had another story "This isn't a Tiger tale, but it's a fun one. Mag, Christine and I took a trip back in time this April…" "Time travel is good" Matthew interjected. I continued, "…attending the Hash Bash for the first time in 20 years. T-shirts were being sold with President Clinton's face above the line *Inhale to the Chief.*" "Great t-shirt!" Chris said. "Yeah, and the mood of the day called for wandering Ann Arbor in a daze, so we ended up on Vid's front porch, waiting for him to get home from the paint store, then played some euchre washed down with Labatt's." The thought of euchre and beer glazed over the boys' eyes, or maybe it was the 4 days of bourbon.

Off the river, we made the drive on Ten Curves Road to our rooms at the Seasons Motel in Curtis. The boys moseyed over to Betsy's, Colonel assuring us he just needed a little time to clean up, and would be joining us shortly. At the bar, we struck up a conversation with a local who asked how many miles we'd paddled over this year's 4Day. When told 30 miles, he replied, "Hell, gravity will get you here in 4 days." True, but the effect of gravity is diminished when 3/4s of the time you're standing on the shoreline drinking and smoking.

Captain Johnny was bellied up to the bar with a huge grin of satisfaction on his face. "I can think of few things finer than ratting on the river for four days then catching a hot shower and strolling into Betsy's and catching that tavern smell, the juke box thud, and the scent of her great burgers on the grille."

At Betsy's, there was one last entry made into the "Big Guy Readings"…

*Big Guy, well, the sadness of the 4Day, the inevitable end has come. All the toasts, the spirits (both distilled and those above us), the river dicks, are gone till next year. I hope for many returns, yours of which is highly regarded on my list. Lastly, the only other thing I can think of is, Tony you f-in' asshole, keep on rolling the G-damn joints or get your f-in' swim trunks on mother f-ker. Yours forever, Marquis*

We departed Curtis 8AM the next morning, eager to get the one hour trip behind us for breakfast at Audie's in Mackinaw City. After filling our bellies, Moth was paying his Audie's bill and he asked the checkout gal for a pound of taffy to go, "because Debbie loves it." Vid, seeing an opportunity with Mrs. Moth, wasted no time in loudly proclaiming, "Then give me <u>two</u> pounds!"

# CHAPTER 4
# 1996: 4DAY 19

Manistique River w/ Big Guy, Chucky, Jimmy, Vid, Marquis,
Johnny, Moth, Matthew, Jason, Colonel, Chris, Frey, Tony
Barney, Wayne, Rusty, Bob V.,Gomie, Jonesey, KB, Kenny, Doc
and rookies Lutostanski, Rookie Dave, & puppy Brittany

*Men Men Men,*
*It's a ship all filled with Men*
*So batten down the Ladies Room*
*There's no one here but Men*
*(Men by Martin Mull)*

With Colonel's *blowing of the chunks* last year captured on film, that photo was the center piece of the 1996 4Day invitation. Above the frozen-in-time barfing was the line, "Relive the Magic" and below it, "4Day 1996". Using vomiting as a lure to come 4Day is a strong statement about the mind-set of folks who attend. The 23-man turnout for this year is the largest yet. Apparently, Colonel's magical experience done got the boys fired up.

23 men, 37 coolers, and one gal – Chris' puppy, rookie Brittany. This is a dog who's repeatedly been photographed next to Pabst Blue Ribbon beer cans. Brittany will feel right at home here.

*Back on the Manistique!* The river that we paddled in 1978 for 4Day One, and once again in 1982, is where we'll experience the U.P. this year. Unlike the Fox, the Manistique is slow 'n wide, obstructions on the river are rare, with frequent sandy beaches to break at or camp on.

Matthew will be with us this year, his first 4Day since '88, to celebrate his 40th birthday. I first met Matthew in the MSU dorms, while on a 1974 visit to see Big Guy. Matthew & his guitar had a room, full mostly of co-eds, enthralled and laughing as he gave a folk-rock tinge to a number of current & past TV commercials including…

*Burger King - Hold the pickles/Hold the lettuce/Special orders don't upset us/All we ask is that you let us/Serve you your way/We can serve your whole beef whopper/Fresh with anything on top her/ Anything you think is proper/Have it your way-Have it your way-Have it your way at Burger King.*

For the 2nd year in a row, 4Day eve was spent in the town of Curtis, lodging at the Seasons Motel and enjoying another tavern evening of beers, burgers, *SHOTS!* and sing-alongs at the motel's neighbor, Mc's Tally Ho pub, proprietor Betsy. Gomie & Chucky were running the table top shuffleboard, the several regulars present putting up with their dominance and the presence of 23 loud folks from down below the bridge. After several hours of fun, 22 of us stumbled back to the Season's. The 23rd 4Dayer to leave had a story for us over breakfast in town the next morning.

With the early day sun filling Stamper's Restaurant, Gomie was telling us how his night ended, "I was putting up with just drinkin' beer, doin' fine, then Doc started feeding me shots. Next thing I know I was just sittin' at the bar drinkin', looked around, all 4Dayers gone and only Betsy was there. Next thing I know, we're staggering across the road to the Shipwreck Bar, we walk in arm-in-arm, holding each other up, locals gossiping back 'n forth - who's this younger man that Betsy's strolling in with? Betsy holds her own you know, a young woman at heart, comes in with a young man spicing up the place a little bit. We're dancing around, I can't say for sure, but there might have been some bumping 'n grinding out there on the dance floor. The lady that Betsy is, she helped me across the road, back to the Seasons Motel - I needed a lot of help getting across the road - she helped me to my room, dropped me off. This morning I woke up as hungover as I've ever been in my life, but knew I had a great time." Based on the twinkle in Betsy's eye every time Gomie would walk into the Tally Ho on subsequent 4Days, it is possible Gomie may have been too drunk to recall *every* moment of their time together.

For the first time in 14 years, the 4Day launched on the Ten Curves Road access along the Manistique River. There are 12 to 13 paddling hours between the start of Day 1 and the Cookson Bridge take-out at the end of Day 4. The first day would be a 2 & one-half hour paddle, ending where we'd set up our tents in advance early this morning, at the Northland Outfitters livery. Today's initial hour would be the slowest of the entire trip, picking up speed only when merging with the quicker Fox River at the new steel bridge.

Watching the long 15-canoe armada snaking its way downstream reminded you of playing the old Centipede video game, a long, continuous, winding line of boats that stretched as far as the eye could see until it disappeared around the distant bend.

Paddling a river we'd been away from for over a decade got Jason thinking back to early 4Days and how the times have changed, "I used to bring tequila and cocaine. This year I brought Maalox and club soda."

During this gorgeous sunny day on the river, we were getting to know the rookies:

Chris brought along two, his dog and a friend. Rookie Brittany the puppy is a sweetheart, great at fetching Frisbees and, with her presence alone, making you smile. Rookie Dave is the 4Day name bestowed on Dave Kniaz because, well, everything about him shouts "rookie!" He is quiet, friendly, helpful, and throws up a lot. Rookie Lutostanski was brought along by his buddy, Rusty Vollmers, and has been given the 4Day name of Fedorov since (1) that's the name on the Red Wings jersey he wears each day & (2) the name Flounder was already taken by Kent Dorfman. He doesn't say much, doesn't smile much, doesn't help out much, and is running 4th in early rookie-of-the-year voting behind Brittany, Rookie Dave, and a smiley-face Frisbee.

The extremely long river breaks during the day meant that the last canoe did not get off the river until just before sunset. After a short nap, Moth stumbles out of his tent, spied a cooler to his left, sat down on it, and rested his head on his left fist, suddenly becoming Rodin's "the Drinker", much to the hilarity of the boys. From a distance of approximately 25', I began tossing empties at Moth, but was slightly off, the beer cans sailing to the left and right of him. Matthew was entertained by my attempts, laughing and said, "Doc, there's no way you can hit Moth." "Want to make it interesting, Matthew?" "Sure, what do you have in mind?" "A buck says I nail him on the forehead with the next empty." "You're on." My throw seemed to float in slow motion, on a line for Moth's head, but then petered out and hit him in the leg. There was no movement from Moth – his Rodin the Drinker persona seemed cast in stone. We went double or nothing on a second throw. I hurled the empty, a Pabst in which I put great hope, but alas the drained PBR hit Moth's arm, too low to win the bet. The $2 check made out to Matthew with its memo of *Missed Moth's forehead twice* remains uncashed and on his office wall 2 decades later. Author's note: there persists until today some question if one of the PBRs directed at Moth was a full beer can.

Early on Day 2, we were loading our canoes and securing the gear in each when livery owner Tom walked up to me. Scanning the enormous amounts of coolers, bags, cooking utensils, etc. that was going downstream with us, he was thinking ahead to the big job of picking up all of this plus 23 men, 1 dog, and 15 canoes from Cookson Bridge at the end of Day 4. Tom said, "Doc you gotta pare down." Just then Chris walked by with 2 full half-gallons of Beam. Nodding towards Chris, I replied, "Tom, we're drinkin' 'em as fast as we can". Tom shook his head and slowly walked away.

Southerner Jonesey asked, "Mead Creek is where we're camping tonight?" Vid replied, "Yeah, you know, Mead Creek as in General Meade. You boys ran up to a Gettysburg ridge in 1863 and he kicked your ass – *Mead!*" "Damn, I can't believe you're pulling Civil War crap on us."

The day was paddled through a steady rain. All down the river, the Jonesey-Gomie canoe was engaged in battle with the Moth-Vid canoe, the southerners versus the northerners, a modern day re-enactment of the Merrimack versus the Monitor, aluminum crashing into aluminum, the four warriors clad in yellow rain slickers, the encounter fueled by beer 'n bourbon. Remember boys: *if the enemy is in range, so are you.*

The combatants were soon in need of a break, and a truce was called as they paddled up to the other 13 canoes. The gently meandering party was making its way down the laid-back stretch of the Manistique, downstream from M77, when Big Guy brought out his tape recorder: "I had it running last night while we were sitting around the campfire." Wayne loved the idea, "Ok Big Guy, let's hear it." Hearing Wayne call someone two-thirds his size "Big Guy" never ceases to be funny. Biggie turned it on, and we heard incoherent babble, boisterous laughter, and ear piercing shouts. Big Guy looked perplexed, "I can't figure it out." Vid feigned surprise, "Yeah Biggie, we're all stunned." Marquis channeled Coleman Young, "Thas why we don't see no wildlife on these trips."

Jonesey started into some grimacing 'n grunting. Jimmy and Kenny paddled alongside him, "Jonesey, what's going on?" "I think it's the Old Overholt. That rot gut is eating my stomach lining." Gomie guessed "It coulda been the Four Roses." Then Rookie Dave tossed lunch over the side of his boat, and that prompted all sorts of guesses about what cheap whiskey was the culprit. Once the list of what we brought was exhausted, guys started making stuff up...

Biggie "Granny Squat Bourbon?" Chucky "Loose Stool Bourbon?" Johnny "John Beam Bourbon?" Doc "Sudden Spew Bourbon?" Rookie Lutostanski "Why am I behind the smiley face Frisbee?"

23 men, 37 coolers

Day 2 from the livery to Mead Creek is a long haul, a good 4 hours of actual paddling, and there were happy shouts when the concrete access came into view.

Tony Barney was standing at the river's edge when he made the mistake of singing *Take Me to the River*. My reaction was involuntary as I became Bluto at the Delta House Toga Party, Tony became Stephen Bishop's guitar, and *Take Me to the River* became *I Gave My Love a Cherry*. Hearing Tony's tune got me running full speed towards the innocent vocalist. Just before impact, I left my feet and nailed him Chris Spielman-style, burying my shoulder into his side, driving Tony several feet into the Manistique, where I found myself laying on top of him, "Huh, sorry."

Tony wasn't thrilled, barking, "Why don't you pick on someone your own size?" "Tony, you're 6'2" and I'm 6'3". You have to admit, that's pretty close." We didn't see eye-to-eye on this, so I tried to mollify him by asking offensive lineman-sized Wayne if I could tackle him into the river, with no resistance on his part, of course. "No" "No? How about for $5?" Wayne's grin told me this was a horrible idea and best abandoned quickly. I asked Rusty if I could knock his similarly-large frame into the river, in order to make Tony feel better. Rusty lives life at a deliberate speed and, while waiting for his reply, Tony and I both forgot what the dispute was about and slowly walked away.

We awoke Day 3 to steel gray skies and drizzle, with a total of 6 hours to paddle between this morning and the trip's end tomorrow. Some days it doesn't matter what the weather has going on, your spirit is so full of joy that every moment, drenched to the bone or not, is a blessing. This was one of those days. Paddling through the great northern forest, it seemed like all 23 guys were singing along, as one song merged into the next, *King of the Road/I Like Beer/Delia/Men/Sixteen Tons/Fire on the Mountain/Dinah Moe Humm/Rodeo Song* (twice). We called ourselves "The River Dick All-Star Bourbon Band". Even an outstanding ensemble like this one requires quiet time for a few bends to absorb the beauty that we were canoeing through.

Jimmy broke the silence, proposing a toast to the EMU Hurons basketball team, conquerors this March of Coach K and the Duke Blue Devils in the first round of the NCAA Tournament.

Before the game, EMU's sophomore guard and human highlight reel, Earl Boykins, was asked for his thoughts about playing against Duke's point guard, Chris Collins, since Chris is the son of Detroit Pistons Coach Doug Collins. Earl replied, "I play against sons of fathers all the time."

Several hours passed, stomachs were audibly growling, and Wayne laid down the law: "Chow Time is Important! Let's pick one of these sandy beaches we're passing, set-up tents, build a fire, and chow down!" Wayne Thomas Vollmers is wise. As Wayne finished his pronouncement, the day-long drizzle exploded into a torrential downpour. Around the next bend was a sand bar big enough for all 15 canoes. Multiple tarps and painter's drop cloths were pulled out of dry bags, unrolled and held up over our heads to keep at bay the rain crashing down. The singing picked up again as bottles were opened 'n emptied, doobs lit, their smoke swirling under the tarps and cloths, unable to escape the constant shotgun engulfing us.

The loud, pounding rat-a-tat of the rain subsided, the protection above us removed, and the most gorgeous sunshine greeted us. For the first time, we were able to look around to get a good view of the beach we had pulled over on to. Chris shouted, "We're home boys – this is our camp for the night!" This beach was plenty big enough for our tents, with space to drag all canoes out of the river.

The beach happened to be directly across the river from Dugal Creek, a little tributary to the Manistique. The creek ran through a forest in a tableau so pretty that it drew us and a couple of fifths in, before even taking time to eat or set up tents. Big Guy and Kenny walked along the creek first, shouting back to us, "Its real unsteady ground in here, we had to hold on to each other to stand up." Right behind them was Chris, Jason, Johnny, Jonesey, Gomie, Vid, Moth, Jimmy, rookie KB, me – and Frey. It coulda been the Mad Dog/mighta been the Jack/Stroh's/ Dickel, but here comes wild-man Frey runnin' by us on this uneven, tree-stump strewn ground. Frey trips and slams right on his face at Biggie and Kenny's feet. Kenny says, "Damn, and he ain't even bleedin'!" Biggie turned red with laughter, caught his breath and added, "If it were you or me, they'd be helicopterin' us outta this joint." Kenny just shook his head, "But he deserved to bleed... no punctured lung, no nothing".

Jason pointed towards Gomie and Jonesey, "Those Jacksonville Boys look concerned. While we're splashing around the creek without a care in the world, they seem a bit panicky, looking around for snakes 'n gators like back home. Hey! You're in the U.P. guys!"

After we all left Dugal Creek for our camp beach, set up the tents and got a little chow, I paddled an empty canoe back across the Manistique to the creek. Loud splashing from behind got my attention. It was Frey flaying about in the river right behind my boat. "Doc, where you goin'?" "Just goin' across the stream – alone - for a little quiet time, Frey." "Great, I'll come with you!"

The last rays of sunlight lit our beach, the bonfire was now roaring, and Bob Vollmers shouted, "We need somebody to jump over the bonfire!" Colonel looked around for the perfect candidate, "Where's Moth?" Biggie said, "Moth's been passed out for a while. The only way we're gonna get him over this bonfire right now is to pick him up like a sack of potatoes and toss him over."

Chucky always has good stories to share. "I got one for you guys from the Ann Arbor News police beat. About 730AM, this guy walks into the Burger King in Ypsi. He flashes a gun, says give me what you have in the register. The clerk said he couldn't open the register without a food order. The guy ordered onion rings, and the clerk said onion rings aren't available for breakfast. The guy got frustrated and walked out."

Jimmy had another, "This guy's on trial in Pontiac, and complained that he was searched without a warrant. The prosecutor said the cop didn't need one because there was a bulge in the guy's jacket that could've been a gun. The guy says no way, happened to be wearing the same jacket in court, and hands it over for the judge to look at. The judge finds a packet of cocaine in the pocket and needed a 5-minute recess to stop laughing."

Chris mentioned, "Hey Jimmy, Olivia just turned 1, right?" "Yep, just last month, thanks!" Vid said, "And her first spoken word was *SHOTS!*" "No," I said, "I think it was butt-crack. Olivia said butt-crack at the Mobil after softball. She'd heard Maggie read the word from a birthday card and repeated it." "No, I'm pretty sure it was *SHOTS!*" "Well, either way" said Jimmy, "she's her Father's daughter!"

The sounds and smells of breakfast cooking got us moving the final morning. Climbing out of the tents, greeting us was Kenny's smiling face and a hot buffet spread out on a flipped over canoe. God bless that man!

We estimated two hours of paddling was still in front of us before reaching the Cookson Bridge take-out. Rookie Dave spent the better part of his inaugural 4Day drinking, puking, or – upon request – re-enacting each of his vomits, including actual pose 'n placement. With re-enactment requests still pouring in on the 4th day, he asked, "Do I have to recreate *everywhere* I threw up?"

On this final stretch of the Manistique, we passed one beautiful sandy beach after another. The ancient forest we wound our way through had a dark, medieval look about it. With 15 minutes to go and merging from the right, Duck Creek is the last major landmark on the journey, impossible to miss at 20 wide and fronted by a 150' long beach. In a few river bends, we were below the Cookson Bridge, this 4Day's end point.

When livery owner Tom and his big van & trailer arrived to pick us up, he still had the problem of how to get 23 men, one dog, 37 coolers, 15 canoes, and all of our gear back to our vehicles at Northland Outfitters with a minimum number of trips. Tom normally flips the canoes upside down before placing them on the trailer. We suggested keeping some right-side up, and fill them with gear and even one 4Dayer. Tom agreed, allowing the task to be completed in two trips and at the same time giving Rookie Dave the opportunity to ride in a canoe at 40 miles per hour, and heave one more time. Rookie Dave wisely passed.

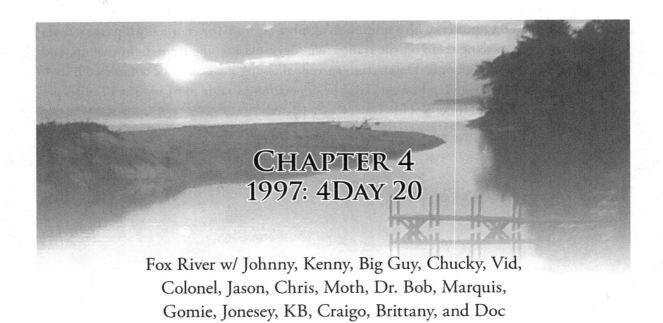

# CHAPTER 4
# 1997: 4DAY 20

Fox River w/ Johnny, Kenny, Big Guy, Chucky, Vid,
Colonel, Jason, Chris, Moth, Dr. Bob, Marquis,
Gomie, Jonesey, KB, Craigo, Brittany, and Doc

*25 years ago, they spoke out and they broke out*
*Of recession and oppression and together they toked*
*And they folked out with guitars around a bonfire*
*Just singin' and clappin', man, what the hell happened here?*
*(Walkin' On The Sun by Smash Mouth)*

Our Mobil Lounge softball teammate and friend, Dave Beers, passed away 3 days before the 4Day. The previous Thursday, at his last softball game, Dave made an incredible stop in the hole from his shortstop position, going all out in a contest we had no hope of winning, because that's the right way, David's way, to play the game. After working all day Tuesday, at dinner he felt a little funny and asked his wife Janice to take him to the hospital. A short period of time later, after being taken to surgery, the doctor came out to the waiting area and told Janice, "We lost him on the operating table." "What?!?" A blood clot took his life. David was angelic, sweet, but a man's man, an outstanding example of how one should live their life, always there for you, whatever time of day, and loved by all who were fortunate enough to meet him. Amazingly, David was hitting .756 when he died, his highest single season average in 6 years with the Mobil Lounge softball team. The softball team and the 4Dayers, two groups with a great deal of overlapping, assembled in honor of David at the funeral home the night before the drive to the 4Day took place.

In celebration of our 20th Up North adventure, Northland Outfitters owners Tom & Carma are throwing a Friday party & dinner in the livery gazebo for the 4Day crew, a wonderful thanks for two decades of business, friendship and memories. At only $6 per man, they provide all the beer and food we can handle, including ribs, smoked turkey, baked potatoes & beans. This is clearly not a profit center for the livery.

Our arrival for this feast was slightly delayed by a break taken less than one hour away at a US2 state park campsite on Lake Michigan. Under sunny skies, and in honor of the Detroit Red Wings last month winning the team's first Stanley's Cup since 1955, Moth unveiled his home-made version of the Cup. The boys posed for photos with this replica, his fine craftsmanship applauded and toasted. Bad craftsmanship would've also been toasted.

To this gorgeous setting overlooking the sun-drenched lake, Moth brought a shoe box of beat up golf balls and an old driver. Soon Johnny, Chucky, Gomie, KB, Moth, and Jonesey are hitting balls into the Big Lake. Big Guy is cautious, saying, "I don't think we should be doin' this, the DNR rangers police this site pretty regularly", but seeing all the fun around him, after several minutes he accepts the next time the driver is offered and tees up a ball. As soon as he finishes his swing, sending a ball far out over the water, sure enough, there is the DNR ranger he warned us about. Although Big Guy received only an admonishment, his situation created quite a bit of laughter among the fellas, who then became the focus of the ranger's attention, "Ok, so what about you guys?" he asked. Vid replied, "We tried to stop him, sir, but he's bigger than us."

Chris arrives at the livery gazebo shortly after the rest of us, holding a new-to-the-4Day whiskey found at a store on the way north: *Jenkins*, sold as 2 bottles shrink-wrapped together along with a fishing lure, all for $7! Jenkins is the first whiskey able to make Old Crow taste, if not good, better. Yes, it's that nasty. Perfect for 4Dayin'.

We hadn't spent 4Day-eve in Germfask since the 1994 night the Jolly Bar blockhead (and his closed kitchen) ran us, our pizzas, and a few hundred dollar potential bar tab out of the pub. However, after this Friday night Germfask livery dinner party and drink-a-thon, it didn't make sense to then drive 10 miles of windy roads to Curtis. So, after sleeping off Tom & Carma's food 'n drink in our beds at the Jolly Motel, we are back at their livery by 10 the next morning, ready to take on the Fox once again.

Surprisingly, the usually slow but steady Marquis is the first to have himself and his gear loaded on to the livery van, ready to be driven to our put-in. It is taking a while for the other brothers to stow themselves & their gear aboard, so Marquis pops out and strolls to the porta john, about 100' away. In the short window of time he is in there, the rest of us board with our gear, close the van door behind us, and away Tom drives.

Marquis finishes his business, opens the porta john door, and sees a van with all his friends, their gear, his gear, and a trailer full of canoes climbing the driveway hill on its way out of the livery and on to M77 headed north. He shouts, "Don't leave me guys!" running the best he can while still pulling his pants up, but sees the van vanish from sight. Marquis has made the mistake today of being first on the van, and never will again.

FOX RIVER
U.P., MICHIGAN

It is a 10 mile walk north along M77 from the livery in Germfask to the launch site upstream from Seney. Marquis begins the trek along M77, hoping his absence will be noticed sooner than later, and Tom will be back to get him in a couple of minutes. However, when doing the 17-man head count, everyone recalled seeing Marquis in the van. The walk will be a little longer than planned.

Tom pulls up to a DNR site overlooking the Fox River, drops us off and, after sharing a little 4Day talk, said he'll see us when we pull into his livery at trip's end. From 12' above the river, the boys walk the canoes and gear slowly down the steep sandy slope to the edge of the Fox.

Once all boats are secured at the shore, we are standing in knee-deep water and toast our dearly departed softball teammate Dave Beers. David always drank Apple Barrel Schnapps, and we down a bottle in his honor. Finishing off a fifth before taking even the first paddle stroke of a 4Day, puts this "earliest-downed-bottle" in a logjam tie for first.

Based on the 4Day personnel with us this year, the time required to complete this task seems to take longer than it should – and that's when the voices begin to ask, "Wait a minute, where's Marquis?" We immediately grasp the situation and begin to plan our next step, when suddenly Tom's van wheels up to the edge of the DNR site, the door flies open, and out steps Marquis. The cheers from the guys and barks from Brittany are deafening. Tom promises to pick up and deliver any more 4Day stragglers found along the highway. Just as we're about to start paddling, an upside down rainbow appears in the sky above us. Absent any rain, we see this smiley face rainbow as David sending his love and telling us all is well.

This is the first year that all 3 of the 4Dayin' Weaks brothers, Marquis, Craigo, and Chris, attend in the same year. Marquis would often look back fondly on the experience, "I love you guys", he'd tell the rest of us, "but my kid brothers mean a lot to me - it was so great when we 3 brothers could be together". Together on one mind-altering side journey, in two canoes, the three brothers explore multiple creeks flowing into the Fox. I love watching the two boats frequently careen off into dark, thickly forested, little tributaries, seeing visions down these black streams that those not peering through the same kaleidoscope can only imagine.

As Marquis recounts it, "I brought along a friend, a plastic squirt toy with the head of my favorite wrestler, Big Boss Man. Of course, Chris and I aren't the best canoers together, but I love my brother. Chris and I flipped over and I'm lookin' for the Big Boss Man, probably washed up somewhere and I'll never find him."

The paddlers in the 3 canoes ahead of the rest of the group pull over to stretch and allow all others to catch up. After a few minutes, Vid is looking back upstream and sounds the alarm, "Oh-oh, someone tipped their canoe." Gear from an as yet unknown boat is floating towards us and we're able to gather everything up before it passes by. After several minutes of pulling in coolers, small dry bags, and seat cushions, there's nothing yet that clearly identifies who the dumped canoe belongs to – and then the laughing spreads among the rescue team as bobbing on the water's surface like he owns the place is a very recognizable plastic squirt toy. "It's Big Boss Man! Marquis flipped!" The happiness etched on Marquis' face as he comes around the bend and hears us yell, "Marquis! We got Big Boss Man!" is one no altered state can enhance.

Shortly after our canoes reach camp at the Seney Township access, a van pulls up. The driver exits the vehicle holding 8 large, white, square boxes. The first ever 4Day pizza delivery to a campsite just took place. For me, what better way to celebrate the 20th 4Day than to make the meal that I sign up for one that requires no preparation except to place an order for my favorite food, pizza. When they heard supplying pizza was a food prep option, Chucky and Jason quicky called me to go in on becoming "chefs" for this entrée.

With the Fox running shallow, the island at the foot of the Seney Township Campground is high 'n dry, allowing us to set up tents on our favorite section of the grounds, where it is the shortest walk possible for carrying gear from the canoes to the camp site.

Big Guy's good golf karma from yesterday on Lake Michigan continues today on the island. After hitting a couple of golf balls into the Fox River, an old timer walks up to Biggie to give him a piece of his mind. Nowhere to run to Big Guy, nowhere to hide.

We saunter into Seney, surprised to find Andy's Bar shuttered. A bright orange sign on the door belonging to the Michigan Liquor Control Commission states they, "have suspended the license of this establishment for 10 days for illegal gambling." (*Author's note:* this sign has since served as wall decor in our home.) We miss our annual Andy's fix, but there are sufficient party supplies back in camp.

Vid, Jimmy, and Johnny are sharing a tent. After the 3 turn in, Gomie and Chris begin gathering frogs – the island is a virtual frog colony. With the stealth of cat burglars, the two slide a half- dozen frogs into the tent, and then wait. It is a short wait. "Hey, which one of you bastards put these 2 frogs in our tent?" "You only found two? Keep lookin' boys!"

The targets for this type of Tomfoolery are easy to find. It is just a matter of choosing which one. Close to midnight found 4 of us standing around a campfire on the Seney Township island: me on one side, on the other, Moth standing between Jonesey & Gomie. Moth will be the target. While his bookends are slightly distracted, I leap over the fire and slam into Moth, taking him quickly to the ground. In the darkness, I can hear the Floridians, "What happened to Moth?" My chortling from a job well done, along with Moth's moans of pain, answer their query and they laugh the laugh of the spared.

Steady rain greets us the morning of Day 2. Building a fire is more work than we want to tackle in these conditions, so leftover pizza from last night will have to serve as breakfast.

Today's first long stop will be within the Spreads at Boot Hill, an hour from breaking camp. At the base of Boot Hill is the same 7' to 8' deep water hole that has existed at least since our first Fox River trip back in '79, but being Craigo's first 4Day in 13 years, I guess he forgot. So, as he floats his canoe towards Boot Hill, when he shouts to the boys gathered on the hill, "Can I get out here?" he receives the same technically correct answer that Captain Johnny did when he asked that question in 1995, "Yes, you can." And, just like Captain Johnny did two years ago, Craigo steps out of his canoe and disappears completely underwater, his baseball cap floating on the surface, outlined by motion rings, the only marker of where he entered the Fox.

The June 1997 issue of *National Geographic* included a story about the Fox River, with several pages of fantastic aerial photos. During our Boot Hill stop, I dug this out of my dry bag and, after showing the guys these photos, read the article's opening lines… *Nearly 80 years ago, young Ernest Hemingway went trout fishing on a remote Michigan river. The fishing was good, the inspiration priceless. From that trip flowed a classic short story titled "Big Two-Hearted River." His story actually describes the Fox, which remains, as Hemingway called it, "the good place."*

Livery owner Tom said that folks from National Geographic rented, for a month, a

Germfask-area house that he and Carma own. The renters had a phone installed, rented a helicopter and hired a pilot for two weeks. During that time, the National Geographic photographer took over 300 photos, of which less than 10 pix, mostly of the Spreads, made it into the story.

Downstream from Boot Hill, we are met by the expected dozen or so major logjams. Including two very long and very badly-needed breaks, it is a 10-hour marathon of fighting to get our canoes over these fallen trees in unrelenting rain. For the first time anyone can recall, these familiar Day 2-on-the-Fox difficulties get the boys talking about spending more time on the laid-back and generally logjam-free, Manistique River. Johnny speculates, "This is no doubt due to some act of nature such as more fallen trees & not due to the fact that we all aged another year."

At the start of the day, we agreed to bypass camping tonight at the High Ground for a 2-night (tonight and Monday night) stay on the Peninsula. Although this creates an extremely long and difficult Sunday, envisioning a Monday spent relaxing in camp on hammocks, reading, story tellin', playing buzz euchre, and in the river only for swimming, Frisbee tosses, or short paddling explorations, well sir, that sounded this morning like another brilliant way to celebrate the 20th 4Day. However, as we pass by the High Ground 8 hours after launching and achingly tired, the realization that two mores hours lay ahead is disheartening.

The Peninsula campground never looked so good. We guess an hour of light is ours to get the tents set up and a big, warming bonfire going. The rain had subsided a couple hours back, dry ground is found for all shelters to be built, and enough dry wood located to get the fire going. There has been little food consumed since this morning's leftover pizza, so when Kenny feeds us all from a big pot of stew he cooked up for us, he makes us a very, very (burp) happy crew.

Monday dawns with a huge breakfast of eggs, sausage, and biscuits 'n gravy, courtesy of Gomie, Jonesey, and KB, a fine start to the day. It takes awhile, but we finally realize today is Craigo's 41st birthday. Shouted birthday greetings, chants, and hugs are all around – and goes both ways. Biggie says, "Although I'm one of the largest 4Dayers, I can regularly be hoisted off my feet the mandatory 5 seconds by Craigoso." A beaming Craigo declares, "Thanks guys! And I'm gonna celebrate the day by serving you ribs tonight." Preparation will be a full day process: the frozen ribs are kept in a cooler without ice to let 'em slowly thaw, then Craigo boils them all day in a big pot. As the hours pass, interest in the ribs grows.

Buzz euchre games are breaking out here 'n there, but the first half of the day is mostly spent swapping 4Day stories. We get to talking about the many great moments experienced on the Peninsula, and Colonel volunteers his favorite, one we never tire of hearing: "It was 3 years ago, but I remember it like it was yesterday. Maybe it was yesterday. Anyways, it was the year that Gomie, Jonesey, and Captain Johnny were rookies – what year was that Doc?" 1994 "Yep, 1994 and the spotlight was on Big Guy." The boys now know what's coming, they're laughing and shouting "Biggie! Biggie!" who's just shaking his head. Colonel starts in on the story…

*Everyone was cocked, telling stories about a great day on the river, and a buzz euchre game was starting up. Well, Big Guy hops into a hammock that someone else set up, and declares he'll throw in his drinkin' lot with the Vid-Doc euchre team. Christened by that lucky star, they get smoked 10 nothing, but they're saying at least they've learned over the years that, when you're playing buzz euchre, to play closer to the tents. So the game is done, and some guys are giving Big Guy a push to get the hammock swinging. He's making yelping noises that we heard as little cries of joy. Apparently that wasn't an accurate reading: a large tree root was directly beneath the hammock, and on each swing Biggie's bottom is getting pounded on this big, muddy root. A person can only take so much of this kind of fun, so Big Guy gets up from the hammock & walks away from us. Watching him amble away, we notice his light gray shorts are 3/4s mud-plastered, the background of a beautiful argyle design, 2 rows of diamonds, each row 4 diamonds wide, and everyone's rolling on the ground, realizing what they're seeing: the hammock's argyle pattern is the only light gray remaining on Biggie's shorts, the rest covered in black from the muddy root-pounding his ass has taken. So Doc starts in about merchandising possibilities, "Argyle Guy action figures – hammock 'n shorts sold separately!" Everyone is cracking up, and Biggie looks back in disgust saying, "Glad I could be your home entertainment center."*

The boys take to the river for a swim, although Vid can't stop shiverin', "Damn this is cold!" "Vid, you're just not drunk enough," Chris informs him, and has a bottle of Mad Dog handy to help Vid get over that hurdle. "If that doesn't do the trick, I'll grab that last fifth of Jenkins for you." "No, the Mad Dog oughta work", Vid assures him.

The Peninsula day of relaxation gives birth to a new 4Day term: *the Council of Elders*. The term originally defined a drunken, confused, blurry moment, and has been recast over the years to reference 4Day veteran wisdom, but its origins were much different…

Chris, Vid, Gomie, and I are playing buzz euchre (again) at the Peninsula's base. Moth, Kenny, Big Guy and Johnny are above us on the hill. Vid directs our attention to that hilltop, "Look at them up there, judging us, lookin' down their noses at us, plotting, like some kind of fuckin' council of elders, passing edicts down on us. We should kick their ass". Johnny says, "We're looking back 'n forth at each other, listening to the guys below, trying to figure out what they're talkin' about. And then they charge up the hill. It would to get ugly for Moth." Chris said, "When I get to the top of the hill, the first guy I see is Kenny. Oh, I can't hit Kenny, so I got Big Guy." So, after the skirmish, the euchre game continues. Some time passes, and Vid looks up, "Those guys on the hill are still looking down and judging us." Chris bolts up the hill where sitting in his chair, chin on chest, Moth is in his traditional pass out pose. Reaching the hill's crest, Chris leaves his feet and linebackers Moth, separating Moth from his chair. The chair is now in pieces. Moth shakes himself out of his stupor, looks at the chair… looks at Chris… then picks up chair, "Damn chair!" and throws it down, as victory is declared for an oppressed world.

It is finally getting near time for Craigo's ribs. The boys are now standing around, watching the artist at work. Craigo had created a homemade barbeque sauce to put on the ribs. To transport the sauce to the 4Day, he filled empty ketchup bottles with it. As Craigo begins applying the sauce to the ribs, Vid only sees paint thrown on the Mona Lisa, "No!!! Not ketchup!" thinking Craigo is destroying his masterpiece. Craigo strings Vid along, telling him, "You'll eat what I give ya!"

*Chow Time!* The compliments flow immediately, and continue years later. An admiring Chucky declares, "Craigie's ribs… what Craigie did with those ribs was amazing, especially when you consider where he was cookin' them at. He was like a machine - I'll never forget it." When anyone mentions, "Those damn good ribs", if the listener is a 4Dayer, he knows exactly what is being referred to. The consensus then and today is that Craigo's ribs on the Peninsula, served on his 41st birthday, were the greatest meal ever on the great northern adventure.

Departing the Peninsula Tuesday morning is a relaxed, happy group of boys. Today's plan is to find one final camp spot somewhere in the 4 hours between the Peninsula and livery. So much fun on the Fox is had this day that it isn't until the canoes are 30 minutes shy of the livery that we realize how close to the end we are. Fortunately, a fine looking, two-tiered piece of land is along the right shore, only 10 minutes from Northland Outfitters. This will be our home for the night.

After the tents are set up, Jason is trying to get Vid and Johnny's attention, "Hey I'm drinkin Jagermeister!" Jason is teasing 'em since Jager has been banned since 1992, when after a long night of drinkin' Jagermeister, Jason slept through his next morning's breakfast responsibilities. Johnny and Vid immediately move towards him and warn, "Then you're going in the river." Jason laughs, "Ha ha, I was just kiddin'. I put Coke in the Jager bottle", which does nothing to slow the boys down. "Don't matter, you're still goin' in the river." Realizing the seriousness of his situation, Jason moves faster than at any time since incurring Jo's wrath when their canoe flipped 4Day '81, today managing to stay just a few steps ahead of lawmen Vid and Johnny.

Around the campfire, it is clear Moth is struggling, so he looks to Marquis, who shares with us the story the next morning. "Moth was asking, 'don't leave me Marquis', hanging on me to stay upright. Well, Moth may have had a little too much to drink last night. He couldn't find his campsite. Hell, the whole campground was only a 20' radius. He kept repeating that he couldn't find his tent. Forget the tent, he couldn't find the campground."

With a campsite so close to the livery, we bring the canoes in mid-morning. This earlier-than-usual arrival works out fine as we have a "celebrate-the-20th bonus day" planned: after a lunch time visit to Betsy and her bar in Curtis, we tool on down to US2 and set-up camp along the shoreline of Lake Michigan. Instead of the usual Wednesday drive home, the 4Dayers enjoy an extra U.P. day of swimming and Frisbee tossin' in the lake, while the DNR rangers enjoy the fact that we kept Big Guy away from the golf clubs.

Back home from the 4Day, a message from Dave Beer's family was waiting for us…

*Dear Mobil Friends,*

*A little note to thank you for sharing in David's life. David's favorite day of the week was Thursday, when he could play ball & share special times with you. Thank you for all your love, prayers, and support thru this difficult time. May you continue to stay close with one another and remember that Dave will always be with you in spirit.*

*Love,*
*Janice, Jennifer, Sarah, & Matthew*

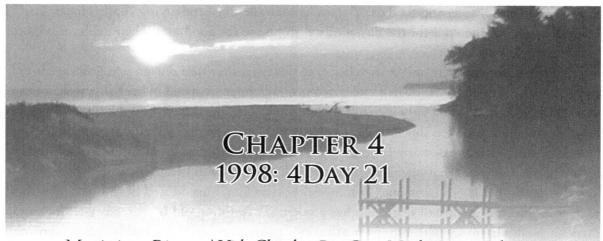

# CHAPTER 4
# 1998: 4DAY 21

Manistique River w/ Vid, Chucky, Big Guy, Moth, Jason, Johnny, Gomie, Chris, Kenny, Huff, Colonel, Brittany, Doc and rookie Ron

*Rollin, rollin, rollin,*
*Though the streams are swollen,*
*Keep them doggies rollin',*
*Rawhide!*
*(Rawhide by Frankie Laine)*

The winter before this year's 4Day, the Colonel and (non-4Dayer) Marty were heading back to Southeast Michigan from an Upper Peninsula snowmobile trip, and stopped in at Andy's Seney Bar. They planned to split a beer 'n a shot, since they didn't have money for one beer each. Andy didn't think it was right for two grown men to have to split one beer, so he bought the boys one on the house. Andy, like a mattress sale, is always on.

Somewhere around that winter day Andy took care of Colonel and Marty, I placed a call to Marcia, the new owner of the Seasons Motel in Curtis, to book our 4Day-eve 'n off the river rooms. She told me that Betsy had been asking "if those 4Day boys had made their plans yet for this year." Marcia said when she told Betsy that we'd made our Curtis reservations, Betsy was all smiles. We must be more charming than we thought or Gomie is quite a dancer.

*The road to the 4Day runs through a Friday night in the U.P. town of Curtis and bellies up to the bar at Betsy's Mc's Tally Ho.*

Arriving in Curtis the night before the 4Day, the boys found Betsy in a particularly reflective mood, her every word soaked up by the enthralled 4Dayers - at least when we weren't yelling *SHOTS!* or singing Roger Miller songs or playing table top shuffleboard or... well, for the most part we were listening. Before tonight, we believed our first meeting with Betsy was 4Day-eve 1994, but as she talked of her time in the U.P., we learned that this was the same Betsy that operated the Jolly Motel & Jolly Bar in Germfask, when we stayed and played there from 1985 to 1987. Back then she was, to us anyway, a fleeting figure we'd only met in passing, with just a few pleasantries exchanged (as she had spent most of her time in Curtis, a town we'd not yet been introduced to). During those 1985-1987 years, Betsy ran the two establishments under the names of the Foxx Motel and the Foxx Bar, in honor of her husband saying "Tally Ho the Fox!" when heading out the door for the day, an English phrase for good luck when fox hunting, i.e. "good bye, we're off".

Betsy is a fantastic lady and story-teller, who always makes sure our grog 'n grub needs are covered, making us feel remembered and welcomed each hour we spend in her bar… well, for the most part. Tonight, she told Gomie that Vid, or as she put it, "the little fella at the end of the bar", has to leave. Gomie looked shocked, "Why Betsy? What did he do?" "Well, he keeps bouncing up and down." Gomie eased any concerns that Betsy may have had by assuming responsibility for any bouncing issues that may arise, but mostly by flirting with her.

This year's rookie class was one: Ron Swiecki. After Chris introduced him to the boys this year, Ron joined our softball team. He has a talent for restoring old homes, story-telling, and carries a small pharmacy with him to treat various pains when drinking bad bourbon won't do the trick.

Last year's long hours of difficulties on the Fox River, fighting our way downstream through one logjam after another, pushed us back to the easy environs of the Manistique River this year. In 21 years of 4Dayin', this is only the 4th 4Day on the laid-back Manistique BUT the 2nd time in 3 years. Some folks press harder on the remote control when the batteries get weak. We just get a new remote control. Is that the smell of Ben Gay in the air?

While floating with extreme lack of speed downstream early Day 1, near the Ten Curves Dam, Vid unveiled a special 4Day brand of blended bourbon whiskey, "4 High". It looks suspiciously like "Ten High", down to the $7.99 a fifth retail, the only apparent difference is that the word "Ten" is crossed out and a "4" hand-written next to it.

The indifferent Colombos cheerfully began to partake of this special 4Day treat, when the fifth, fortunately passed with the cap still on, escaped from Gomie's grasp, sinking to the bottom of the Manistique. Unfortunately, this is a particularly dark 'n deep, about 6' or so, section of the river, with many white pine logs, scraps from the late-1800s commercial timber operations that blanketed the area, littering the stream's bottom, further hindering a whiskey rescue attempt.

While the Council of Elders debated the wisdom of sending Gomie down into the dark depths of the drink to retrieve the drink ("He might get his foot caught between the logs. Why risk it, we have plenty more fifths"), the rookie made his mark. Ron dove in and emerged within seconds with the 4 High, welcomed back with cheers and approving chants of "rookie! rookie!".

Outside of locating a fifth - once thought, though briefly, long gone - few 4Day sights get your heart soaring as does seeing the confluence of the Manistique with the Fox, an hour after Day 1 launching. Paddling the Manistique, the Fox comes into sight as it flows from your right to left. A little under two river hours to the northeast of the Northland Outfitters livery, this junction marks the end of the Fox, an increase in the speed of the Manistique, and – hallelujah! – our arrival at the new steel bridge.

Inspired by Vid's special 4Day brand bourbon, the boys celebrated our arrival at the new steel bridge with a brainstorming session of new bourbon names including:

*Sirhan Sirhan Bourbon Bourbon, Loose Cannon Bourbon, Second Coming Bourbon, Hard Left, Blowing Chunks, Poor Judgment, Foggy Night, Blurred Vision, Train A Comin, Breakfast with Jack Kerouac, Last Chance,* and – although possibly a bit difficult to fit on to a label – *The Police Never Thinks It's as Funny as You Do Bourbon.*

The brainstorming session created a powerful thirst among the 4Dayers. After two fifths worth of quenching, the imbibers wobbled slightly down the steep sandy embankment, stepped into the boats, and pushed off from the ground beneath the new steel bridge. As we floated downstream, little effort was expended. The conversation for those still able to converse roamed to the Eastern Michigan University basketball team and the recently graduated senior class, particularly their amazing point guard, the generously listed as 5'5", Earl Boykins. The 1998 class had a record of 87 and 36, two MAC titles, and a Road to the Final Four tournament victory over Duke in '96. This past February, during the final game played at historic Bowen Fieldhouse, Earl buried a buzzer-beater shot from beyond half court to beat Toledo by one. Two months earlier, EMU traveled to Crisler Arena and defeated Michigan. After the game, Earl was asked if he knew that EMU's all-time record against UM going into tonight had been zero for 20. Boykins replied, "I'm 1 & 0 against 'em."

While we were on the river Day 1, Moth was driving north to meet us, missing the first day of canoeing. He offered to make opening night dinner for us, arriving at Northland Outfitters with the meal about an hour before we wrapped up our paddle, and saw the crew stumble into camp, thinking, "Oh my God, *that's* what we look like?" It was a beautiful feast that Moth spread out before us… two turkeys, baked potatoes, corn on the cob, stuffing, and apple pie.

As we began to dig in, Gomie asked a question that, to all but Moth, seemed innocent, "Moth, where's the gravy?" Moth went ballistic, "F-you Gomie! Where's the gravy? You drunks are having a great time while I did all this cooking, and I get *where's the gravy?*!" This went on for several minutes with Moth barking, Gomie's mouth opened in stunned silence, and the rest of us finding the scene hysterical. It was like a 50s sitcom, the little lady at home not getting sufficient thanks for all that she does. Immediately, "Where's the gravy?" became a 4Day catchphrase.

Although still daylight, as much daylight as could come through the thick cloud cover, Vid had set up his tent and crashed hard. Moth, though stone sober just a few hours ago when aghast at what we looked like post-paddling, had caught up and surpassed us with amazing speed, and was now probably an extra sheet to the wind beyond Vid's 3. Amazingly, Moth could accurately be described as staggering while standing still. More importantly, he was a Moth on a mission, a man prowling the campground with a fifth of Jim Beam in one hand and a shot glass in the other.

The good folks of Clermont, Kentucky once again are selling their Jim Beam fifths complete with a shot glass in the shape of a boot shrink-wrapped to the bottle. Moth wandered the grounds, looking to pour Jim Beam into his next victim, all the while shouting *"BOOT!"* He soon came upon Vid's tent, *"Vid! BOOT!"* *"Go away Moth, I'm trying to get some sleep and sober up."* *"Vid! BOOT!"* *"Moth! Go a-way!"* *"Vid!!!! BOOT!!!!"* *"No Moth, I'm trying to sober up."* *"Vid! (pause) Half-a-boot!"* (Half-a-boot – genius! Those watching this unfold all agreed, what a brilliant tact to take. No wonder Moth considers himself to be the World's Greatest Salesman!)

Vid had no chance against this display of psychology, and agreed, "Ok Moth, half-a-boot." Moth reached into the tent, and poured more Beam into the boot than it could hold. Vid shook his head as he watched the Beam flow over the top of the boot and down Moth's arm. He sighed, took the boot, and drank it down. Not Moth's first sales conquest, and not his last. As the bourbon was oozing through Vid's eyelids, he could make out Moth lurching away, like Godzilla in the mist, in search of his next prey.

Day 2 dawned with a bit of residue about the Great Gravy Affair of the previous night. Shortly after launching our boats downstream, Moth-o-pause took hold and the subject changed from a diner's ingratitude to kibitzing about favorite taverns. The talk turned to the Sidetrack, an old time wonder in Ypsilanti's Depot Town. The Sidetrack opened in 1850, the year after EMU, then known as Michigan State Normal School, did. This is not a coincidence. Ben Franklin passed away 60 years before the bar opened, and the pub owners honored him by posting one of Ben's quotes on their awning: *Beer is the proof that God loves us, and wants us to be happy.* Your kite gets hit by lighting a few times, and you gain a realization of what's really important in life.

The "Driggs River" sign announced the merger of this shallow tributary into the Manistique from the right. Although our Mead Creek Campground destination was now only 15 minutes away, the day was much too gorgeous to pass up this one last river break. Chris opened up his dry bag and brought out the Jim Beam half gallon that wouldn't die. We'd been working on it all day long, and put in another good 20 minutes of effort at this stop, but at least 3 fingers remained at the bottom of the bottle. It was during a momentary hesitation by the 4Day veterans that Rookie Ron stepped up big time once more. With a look of commitment and a belief that this drink had come around one too many times, Ron grabbed the half gallon, stomped its cap into the ground, quadruple bubbled what was left, and threw the empty-vessel-of-whiskey-goodness into the sand. Cheers erupted that we believed were heard 4 hours upstream in Germfask. Were the rook not bigger and us not older than the ideal conditions call for, we would've hoisted Ron on our shoulders and paraded him around. In lieu of that, assurances of his leading position as the lone candidate in the race for rookie-of-the-year would have to suffice.

Shoving off on the 3rd morning, over today and tomorrow were 6 hours of paddling until the trip's end at Cookson Bridge. Camping tonight would be on any sandbar that looked good at any time that we choose. During one of today's river breaks, Kenny told us about his and ex-wife Judy's recent divorce. While Kenny was being questioned by Judy's lawyer, an unexpected opportunity arose for Kenny to invoke Roger Miller into the proceedings. "Mister Umphrey, are you a man of means?" the lawyer asked. When Kenny replied with the *King of the Road* line, "By no means," Judy's lawyer looked confused, but the judge smiled and nodded, clearly a fan of good music (the tight-assed lawyer clearly not). Hearing this story, the 4Dayers exploded in laughter, and spontaneously began singing, shouting really...

*Trailer for sale or rent, rooms to let, 50 cents. No phone, no pool, no pets, I ain't got no cigarettes, ah but, two hours of pushin' broom, buys an eight by twelve four-bit room, I'm a man of means by no means, King of the Road!*

Kenny's story reminded Vid of Alexander the Great's wedding night, when Alexander broke the sad news to his new bride, "It's only a nickname."

The unceasingly gorgeous sunshine took a mid-day hiatus, the rain now pounding us. We pulled the canoes over and took shelter under a large painter's drop cloth. Within moments, making their way among us were fifths of Cabin Still and Heaven Hill as the scent of burning rope surrounded our heads, unable to escape the plastic cover above.

Thus inspired, the fellas picked up where they left off 2 days ago at the new steel bridge, coming up with additional bourbon names we'd like to see…

*Lost Cause Bourbon, Where Am I Bourbon?, Stagger & Lament Bourbon, Detour, Tawdry Acts, One Eye Open, Toss the Cap, Garage Sale, Bob 'n Weave, Fender Bender, Road Closed, Dull Thud,* and - although possibly a bit difficult to fit on to a label - *Burn Down the Mission, Scorch the Moth, But Leave Tate Alone Bourbon.*

*Author's note:* actor David White played the role of Larry Tate, a TV character on the 60s sitcom *Bewitched*. When White died in 1990, Colonel took his obituary photo, enlarged it to the size of a poster that might come with a record album, and brought it to the 4Day. Ever since then, the Tate poster has been a 4Day regular, despite drunken attempts to torch it.

*2nd Author's note:* a record album is a circular piece of vinyl containing about 45 minutes worth of music, played on a record player.

*3rd Author's note:* a record player is… never mind.

With the rain moving on and a new batch of whiskey names created, we were back in the boats when Vid came up with, *There's hair of the dog and there's lickin' the kennel floor bourbon.* This instant classic was versatile, either used as a new bourbon name, or the perfect descriptive statement for excessive day-after imbibing.

Chef Chris was talking about the surf 'n turf dinner he'd planned for the boys tonight, so we were primed to call it a day at the next sandy beach big enough to hold 8 canoes, 4 tents, and a campfire. Such a spot was found around the next bend, with a little under 3 hours of paddling left for tomorrow.

As the evening progressed, Moth was perched 'n weaving on his cooler, with Vid standing a few feet away. "Boy, this scene looks familiar," Vid said, "Last year, Moth was on his cooler next to me, and Gomie & Jonesey were eyeing us, with mischievous smiles. They whispered and then charged. The two slammed into me, lifting me off my feet, and we came crashing down on Moth. Moth was stunned, flat on his back in the dirt, looking up at me, blurting out some kind of drunken mumble, *'Vid, why'd you do that?' 'Moth, don't you see that Southern Scum on my shoulder?'* The triple slam took a bit out of Moth. On hands and knees, he crawled from the wreckage and disappeared into his tent."

Day 4 was about as annoying as a 4Day ever gets. An hour into the paddling, we could hear distant pounding sounds, sounds that grew louder as the day went on. On the last bend before taking-out at the Cookson Bridge, we could finally see the source of our audio discontent: a giant pile driver was pounding large metal abutments into the river floor. The abutments, or pilings, would be supports for a replacement Cookson Bridge that would be complete in the fall.

Leave it to an evening at Betsy's to bring happiness back to any situation. As we entered her tavern, echoes of the pile drivers vanished. Betsy was dancing with some old friends, a sight that brought a smile to us all. The joyfulness she exuded was contagious, and her genuine, heartfelt greeting to the 4Dayers brings a warm glow any time that memory is recalled.

Although Jonesey could not be with us this year, never was his friendship more appreciated than this evening at Betsy's. Gomie was passing out to us 4Day commemorative t-shirts that Jonesey created, picturing the boys camping at the Peninsula, complete with dialogue referencing 16 4Day golden moments. A lot of time, effort, and love was put into this project. A round of shots were downed in honor of our wonderful 4Day brother!

Post-4Day, several of us visited BJay's grave on his birthday, November 13. 7 years had passed since a lightning bolt took his life. We smoked cigars, had drinks, told BJay stories, and left a birthday card, signed by many friends, leaning against his headstone. In December, BJay's folks traveled north to the Lansing grave from their Arkansas home. The birthday card left behind, encased in plastic, was still there. At Christmas we received a note from BJay's Ma & Pa…

*Dear Friends of BJay,*

*What a wonderful surprise we had when we were in Michigan last week. We found a birthday card signed by many very caring people. Do you have any idea of what it meant to us? So many people go through life never knowing one true friend. BJay was blessed with so very many! He had a very rich life!*

*We could not find addresses for all who signed the card, so I'm sending this one thank you to all. We trust that all will be able to read this and know just what it meant to his family left behind.*

*Have a blessed Christmas & Terrific 1999!*

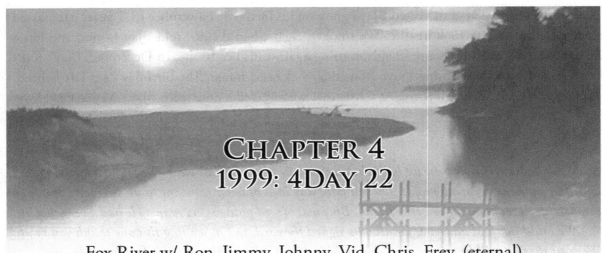

# CHAPTER 4
# 1999: 4DAY 22

Fox River w/ Ron, Jimmy, Johnny, Vid, Chris, Frey, (eternal)
Rookie Dave, Wayne, Rusty, Jason, Captain Johnny, Jonesey,
Gomie, KB, Colonel, Doc, Brittany and rookie Steve

*I hear the train a comin'*
*It's rollin' down the bend*
*And I ain't seen the sunshine since I don't know when*
*I'm stuck in Folsom Prison, and time keeps draggin' on*
*But that train keeps a rollin', on down to San Antone...*
*(Folsom Prison Blues by Johnny Cash)*

The Bird aka Mark Fidrych was in town at the Tiger Stadium plaza, 23 years after his amazing 1976 season, signing autographs and telling stories before the Detroit Tigers-Milwaukee Brewers game, on what was to be the Sunday of 4Day weekend, aka the 2nd day on the river. However, we couldn't miss the chance to see the beloved Bird, especially meaningful as this was the last year of baseball at Michigan & Trumbull, so the annual 4Day getaway was delayed 3 days to Monday, July 12.

We parked, of course, at Irene Sember's lot, 2 blocks east of Hoot Robinson's bar, on Elizabeth Street, our Tiger game lot for the last 15 years. Irene is one spirited lady, and don't even think of pulling into her lot on Opening Day, or for any other big game, unless you're a regular customer. Irene will tell you in no uncertain terms that you are not welcome, with a few adjectives thrown in. She shared with us her thoughts on the Tigers moving one mile east, to Comerica Park, starting in the 2000 season, "Well, they can just kiss my ass!"

How sad it will be to see the Detroit Tigers leave 2121 Trumbull, the oldest address in American Professional Sports, home to Ty Cobb-Al Kaline-Herbie Redmond-Norm Cash-Hoot Robinson-Mark Fidrych-the Brow-Tommy Brookens-Ernie Harwell-Hank Greenberg-Mickey Cochrane-& the Human Earache (a fan who, in the 1934 World Series, was asked by FDR's Secret Service to move his seat and his shouting to the opposite side of Navin Field). The list goes on & on & on.

Houghton Lake's Nottingham Bar, a tavern half-way from Detroit to Germfask and a favorite 4Dayin' stop, has a connection to the Tigers through Hall of Famer Harry Heilmann. Harry played for the Tigers for all but the last 2 years of his career, from 1916 to 1929, and led the American League in hitting 4 times, with averages of .394, .403, .393, and .398. Heilmann would've hit over .400 all 4 times, but his foot speed was a crisp amble in his best days.

Harry was a regular at the original location of the Nottingham Bar, corner of Nottingham and Warren in Detroit. In 1947, the owners closed the Detroit location and moved, along with a number of their regulars, to Houghton Lake, where they immediately reopened the Nottingham that 4Dayers know today. Just like back in the bar's Detroit days, you can always get a Blatz on tap when you walk into the Nottingham. Also brought along from the bar's Detroit location is the signed 8" x 10" photo of Heilmann, looking good in a beer company wooden frame that reads, "Your Goebel Reporter". *Author's note:* Nottingham owner Virgy told us in the mid-2000s some SOB stole the photo off the wall. While writing this book, I came across an online offering of the exact photo with its Goebel's frame in 2016, $60 the asking price by Harris Brothers Auctions.

We lingered a bit longer than usual at the Nottingham this year, celebrating the reunion of the Four Horsemen of Jacksonville: Captain Johnny aka Stench, KB aka Pestilence, Jonesey aka Death and Gomie aka Gomez. This year marks the first time all four have been with us since 1995. Captain Johnny had an outstanding excuse for missing last year's 4Day as he and Mrs. Captain aka Kathy were in China adopting Zhang Zhi Hua, a baby girl they renamed Katrina, or Katie. Traveling with her and her folks from Gatlinburg to Detroit, Maggie and I observed that Katrina's smile lights up a room and her cries can be heard the next holler over.

On the rare year there are no rookies on the 4Day, the (for the most part) good-natured abuse that goes with the title lands on the 4Dayer with the least seniority. With no rookies for this year on the horizon, sophomore Ron suggested to his brother Steve what a fun experience the 4Day will be and how he shouldn't miss it. Wise move, sophomore Ronnie, wise move. Rookie Steve did take the bait, and we're glad he did. Always smiling, he is a fun and likeable fella. The rookie seemed to be everywhere, ingratiating himself to us by offering to assist with just about any task from hauling coolers to tent set-up to schlepping beers for us.

At Northland Outfitters, our favorite employee is Rich. It's always fun to see him at 4Day time, even enjoying his company at Betsy's a time or two. Rich was breaking in a new employee for the 1999 season as our caravan pulled into the livery parking lot for the start of another 4Day fun-fest. Rich told the young man, "Now you watch these guys. Though it's early-morning, they'll be drinking beer." Sure enough, we stepped out of the cars sipping cans of beer. The youngster's eyes got wide as saucers, his head nodding, absorbing this new understanding, saying only one word, and holding that word with involuntary emphasis, "Wow!"

Sadly, 1999 marks the final year of Tom & Carma's ownership of the Northland Outfitters livery, as they have a buyer lined up to take over in 2000. For almost 3 decades, since they opened in 1972, Tom & Carma have assisted countless folks to first meet and then continue to enjoy the beauty of the Manistique and Fox Rivers. They will be missed.

As Tom dropped us off at the Fox River Campground, neither he nor we were in any hurry to see him leave. Tom lingered with us on a bluff above the gorgeous Fox River valley below, while sharing a few laughs and stories. He stayed with us long enough to take a tug off the bottle of Fleischmann's, the whiskey in the honored position of first 4Day fifth this year. Grandpa Daisy, the Grandfather of 4Day brothers Marquis, Craigo, & Chris, passed away last September 2 on Marquis 45th birthday. Grandpa was a gruff, warm-hearted man, who wore his euchre and bourbon well. He began each day at work by knocking down a rock glass of Fleischmann's – and that, fellers, is how you live to an active 93 years old. Grandpa Daisy owned Steve's Bait Shop, the oldest bait shop in Detroit, one block east of Belle Isle, and famous among those who fish the Detroit River.

As enjoyable as it was to share Grandpa's favorite drink with Tom, there was a keen sense of sadness reflecting on Grandpa's passing and our final 4Day with Tom and Carma. The chatter with Tom continued as we launched our canoes into the river, lasting until the final boat disappeared from his view among the pines. As the number of navigated river bends slowly piled up behind us, this poignant feeling disappeared along with the Fleischmann's. The floating party toasted the return of 3 of the 4 Vollmers Brothers, Jimmy-Wayne-Rusty, back 4Dayin' for the first time in 3 years (only Vollmers Brother Bobby listed as MIA).

Those Vollmers Boys kept us laughing. Jimmy told us about a recent Lockhorns cartoon where Loretta and Leroy are in a grocery store together. Loretta is looking at a missing person's photo on a milk carton, and tells Leroy, "If you were ever lost, I'd put your picture on bourbon bottles". Wayne shared the title of what he claimed was his favorite country song, "Get Your Biscuits in the Oven and Your Buns in Bed".

About halfway into today's trip, a couple hours shy of the Seney campsite, we took a break, long even by our standards, at one of the riverside DNR-maintained sites. From 12' above a big bend in the Fox, the site has a commanding view of the narrow river and the forest that surrounds it. The conditions were outstanding: spectacular sunshine, good story-tellin', bad bourbon making the rounds, and then Colonel brought a surprise up from his canoe: the beer pig. Basically, this was a small keg in the shape of a pig. The delivery system was its most outstanding feature with rookie Steve running among us with the pig, making sure that no one went thirsty. The feeling of camaraderie and warmth was incredible, one that no one wanted to see end. It was splendid, in my mind the most perfect moment ever on a 4Day.

Of course, you can't stay at a DNR site above the river forever, no matter how right it feels, 'cause eventually your coolers run empty. So, we paddled to our campsite in Seney, watched rookie Steve set up our tents, ate the pizzas that were delivered right on time, and then took a walk to Andy's for some refueling. Andy was holding court with a few regulars at the bar when we walked in. A big smile spread across his face, "Hey boys, you up here fishin' again?" Chris told him, "Yep, and we caught a Ten High, a Dickel, and a Fleischmann's!" Andy was quiet for a second, and then exploded in laughter like it was the funniest thing he'd ever heard in his life. "Well, we got some more of that kinda fishing here – let me buy you a round."

We'd just downed our Andy shots, feeling good, when KB pointed to a sign behind the bar that read, "Must have been born on this date in 1978 to be served alcohol", i.e. the year of the first 4Day. It led to a collective sigh, shaking of the heads, and thanking of KB for harshing our buzz.

One of Andy's regulars overheard some talk about driving along M28, the road that connects Seney with Newberry, and looked over at us to share some local wisdom. "If you drive 55, they'll know you're drunk." Excellent information to have for future driving in the area.

Sitting in Andy's got Captain Johnny thinking about a guest bar-tending gig he gave me, no pay, just fun, when Johnny was setting up drinks at the Down Under Lounge in St. Clair Shores a few years back. "The party consisted of a few friends when a women's bowling tournament arrived, and I thought it would be a good idea to let Doc handle the crowd. Time after time these ladies would approach the bar and request various mixed drinks, and Docco would simply hand them a beer with a smile. He got away with this for a fucking hour. Tending here regularly, I know how damn picky these gals can be about their lousy drinks and was amazed at how these old babes sucked down the suds they didn't order."

The next morning, we stopped at the Seney party store to pick up ice, beer, and bourbon for the next 3 days. Stocking up today is important, because once we launch on the Fox from Seney, we're in the wilderness the balance of the 4Day, with no chance to restock these critical items. For the last of these shopping list articles, we asked the clerk for a little direction. "What's your nastiest bourbon?" With no hesitation, he replied, "That would be Echo Springs." We found it to be a rough taste, and well below the $9.99 a fifth 4Day ceiling, meeting all of our criteria.

Now supplied for 3 more days of fun, we broke camp, paddling into the spectacular Spreads, with an extended stop at Boot Hill, when Jimmy shared a story with us. He and Lisa took Spencer, who's now 2, to his 4-year old sister Olivia's ballet recital. "Spencer told us in no uncertain terms, *I'm a boy – I like baseball!*" Spencer will make a fine 4Dayer someday.

Colonel took a double-bubbler of the highly-recommended Echo Springs, and began to reminisce about his own childhood, "Growing up in the Thumb, I attended a one-room schoolhouse. There, we tried to blow up the girls' outhouse, but our bomb turned out to be a horizontal rocket. No injury or damage was reported." The Colonel is our resident high tech guru, running a business creating and maintaining websites for businesses, government agencies and individuals. "For this year's Up North adventure, I came up with the *4Day Virus*: launched by *Doc.exe*, it takes 6 days to run, including drive time. Random areas of memory will be deleted, other areas of memory are greatly exaggerated, tries to run once every year, may cause conflicts with spouse programs, and once infected no cure exists".

Back out on the Fox, we put in a good 3 hours of back-breaking work, pulling canoes packed with 3 days-worth of gear over a never-ending series of logjams. Our bodies told us it was time to stop for a bit, so we broke out the river chairs and took a long break. Soon the wonderful *fsst* of beers opening up echoed from shore to shore, bourbon was passed, food was foraged & shared from coolers, and 18 lighters seemed to go off at once, firing up cigars, cigarettes & doobs.

After a few minutes of satisfied silence, I thought I'd share a story that Marquis, who could not be on the river with us this year, had told me about his first rock concert memory...

*Marquis said that his first concert featured Rusty Day & Detroit, Dr. John, and the James Gang back in '69. He swore he was sober when he went in, but must have picked up a contact buzz because on the way out he threw up on the security guard's shoes.*

Well, that got the ball rolling...

*Vid said, "In '66 at Wampler's Lake there was the McCoys, Seger, & Keith. The girls were REAL friendly. Later, I saw the Yardbirds there – best concert ever!"*

*Captain Johnny recalled, "Blue Cheer and the Amboy Dukes, 1968 at the Crow's Nest in St. Clair Shores for $2. When I first walked in I saw this hot babe sitting there. On the way out, she stuck her tongue down my throat, but Blue Cheer stole the show." The boys couldn't figure out how Blue Cheer topped the tongue down the throat, but Johnny confirmed that it was true.*

*Moth said, "Bob Seger for $1.25 at Kimball High School. I passed Dan Carlyle on the way in." Jonesey couldn't resist this one, "So, after Johnny mentioned getting a girl's tongue down his throat, you thought it was important to mention this Carlyle guy?" "The hell with you Jonesey!" was the best that the pleasantly obnoxious Moth could come up with on short notice.*

*While Moth was recovering from the blade of Jonesey, Chucky jumped in, "Van Morrison and the Moody Blues, 1968 at Cobo, $7.50 tickets. Van had just released Brown Eyed Girl. I can't remember the cutie's name that I went with."*

*"Yeah Chucky, I saw Van Morrison, too, a couple of years later", Jimmy said, then smiled with a faraway, satisfied look in his eyes, "I drove my '63 Ford Galaxy ragtop to the Eastowne in 1970 to see Siegel-Schwall, Van, and Alice Cooper."*

*Jason said, "Box Tops & CCR, 1967 or 68 at the Olympia. I was mugged by 3 locals on the way out. It wasn't really a robbery, just a fun beating." KB laughed, "Ok Jason, what's a fun beating?" "One where you live to tell about it and then toast to it on a future 4Day", Jason said, then proceeded to do a double-bubbler of Ten High whiskey to the delight of the crowd.*

The two nights of camping in the wilderness featured wonderful meals, first a Goulash creation at the High Ground by Chris, Ron, & Jason, the 2nd burgers 'n corn-on-the-cob at the Peninsula by them Vollmers Bros. Rookie Steve was a whirlwind each night on tent set-ups, bonfire wood foraging, and beer fetching. With bellies full, both nights we stretched out on the dirt, listening to cassette tapes of Sam Kinison teach us about marriage, religion, homosexuality, & world hunger.

The *Legend of the Confederate Dead* took place on the final day at the new steel bridge. We were over-served to the tune of 3 fifths at the bridge, with the Four Horsemen of Jacksonville in the middle of it all. In the whiskey aftermath, the boys stumbled down from the bridge to a dirt beach at its base, looking to get into their canoes, but coming up short. Some staggering 4Dayers laid down on the ground. Gomie tried to crawl a few inches, then gave up. A sober viewer, had any been among us, would have concluded it looked like a piece of ground fought over during a Civil War encounter. Ron said, "The only thing missing was wisps of smoke blowing over the battlefield and blood among the victims. It was all a blur after that."

Two hours after leaving the new steel bridge, the boys landed at the Northland Outfitters take-out. We gave especially long hugs to Tom & Carma. With the impending sale of their livery, we had no way of knowing when or if we'd ever see them again. For 21 of 22 years, except 1984 when we paddled the Ontonagon River, these two had been an integral part of the 4Day, helping us coordinate trip timing and canoe rental, hauling, & pick-ups. Seeing Tom & Carma meant the 4Day had arrived. Many stories and laughs had been shared with the two of them, and without their presence, the 4Day would never be quite the same again.

15 minutes after departing Northland Outfitters, the 4Day caravan arrived in Curtis. The boys headed directly to Betsy's Mc's Tally Ho pub while I checked us into the Seasons Motel. The craziness of the Confederate Dead drinking levels, calmed during our Tom & Carma good-byes, seemed to re-ignite.

Frey, standing in the middle of Betsy's, was losing what was left of his drunk sloppy mind, growing louder and wild-eyed as he purchased a tray of Jagermeister shots. Figuring it would knock him out, Colonel encouraged Frey to down these as quickly as possible, but the plan backfired, the shots acting like speed on Frey, who slipped out the bar's front door. We now saw Frey through the bar's big front window, spot-lit under street lights, passing doobies to town minors gathered around him. Although we moved quickly to break this up, Frey was now becoming the 90s-version of *the Blob*, not nearly as entertaining as the 1958 Steve McQueen classic, as an alien life-form that grows, figuratively in this case, bigger & bigger, consuming everything in its path.

Within minutes, Rookie Steve rushes in to the bar, "Boss, we got a problem". I run out to see Jason flat on his back at the Seasons Motel courtyard next door with Frey kneeling on top of him, all the while Frey cursing at the top of his lungs while manhandling Jason. Seasons' owner Marcia runs up to me, "Doc, I'm going to have to call the State Police if you can't fix this". Exactly the relaxing scenario I envisioned for our final 4Day evening.

With the assistance of Chris, Jimmy and Wayne-O, 3 of the larger 4Day brothers, we were able to get Frey off of Jason and behind closed doors into one of the motel rooms we'd rented. With those 3 keeping an eye on the amped-up Frey, I stepped out into the darkened motel courtyard, closing the door behind me. Taking only two steps back towards Betsy's bar, something didn't feel right, stopping me in my tracks. Seconds later, the newly calmed night was shattered by a screaming Frey, who managed to slip past his guard detail and burst through the door. That's enough! Our annual Curtis welcome is in jeopardy! I rushed him, grabbed his legs and carried him upright through the still-open motel room door. Two strides inside, I slammed him into the furnace, we spun around to the couch, where I threw him down & sprawled on top on him, lying face-to-face, screaming, *"Frey, if you fuck this up for us, I will KILL you!"* Rising from the couch, I will not forget the stunned looks and open mouths of Wayne, Jimmy, and Chris witnessing this greatly out-of-character scene, like the kids gathered around Ralphie as he flailed away on the bloodied bully in "A Christmas Story".

The guys were able to keep Frey in the room the rest of the uneasy night, although, very sadly, Frey pulled a knife on Chris (thankfully, he was quickly unarmed), his old friend and running buddy from the Navy. Despite Chris' efforts in subsequent years to reach out to his comrade, Frey's warped view of this night's experience has made rapprochement impossible.

Gathered in the motel courtyard the next morning, Gomie, Jonesey, and KB were chatting about the previous evening's mayhem as I walked by. Gomie referred to it as, *"The Night of the Living Frey.* I already saw the movie. I know the book's gonna be good." KB thought it could have all been avoided, "Doc, maybe you could do a little better job of organizing the 4Day in the future." "KB," I replied, "your 4Day invitation for next year will be in the mail with Frey's."

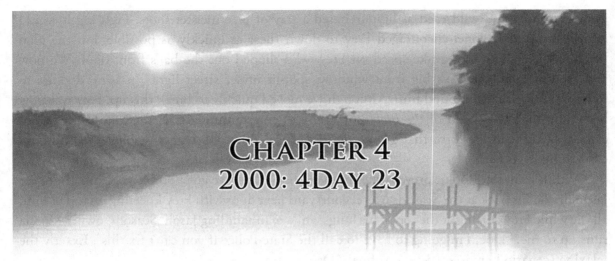

# CHAPTER 4
## 2000: 4DAY 23

Fox River w/ Chucky, Marquis, Big Guy, Ron, Colonel, Jimmy,
Johnny, Vid, Kenny, Gomie, Chris, Brittany and Doc

*Chug-a-lug, chug-a-lug*
*Make you want to holler hi-de-ho*
*Burns your tummy, don'tcha know*
*Chug-a-lug, chug-a-lug*
*(Chug-A-Lug by Roger Miller)*

On Memorial Day weekend in Jacksonville, Florida, Michigan State University-alum Big Guy was in Jonesey's face, hootin' on him about MSU's New Year's Day Citrus Bowl win over Jonesey's hometown Florida Gators. Jonesey is as interested in football as Liberace is in women. After Big Guy walked away, Jonesey asked, "Does this have something to do with sports?"

2 months later, Big Guy came up with a much better use of his time: conducting taped interviews with the 4Day brothers while we gathered at Betsy's 4Day eve. No rookies this year meant no one would feel left out as veterans' memories, while they still existed, are captured for posterity on tape. For some interviewies, it was too late. The only response Vid had for the open mic was a constant stream of, "Ba-ba-loooooo! Ba-ba-loooooo!" Kenny told Biggie, "I been out here 8 years, and I can't remember a thing." Jimmy's lucid recall of 4Days past dissolved into several rambling minutes of deep thoughts about cloning, a lecture I was able to close with the observation, "If we could clone 12-packs of Pabst, we'd be way ahead of the game."

Chris and Ron came blowing through Betsy's front door in the middle of Big Guy's interviews, greeted by a room full of, "Where you boys been? You're 4 shots behind!" Ron said, "Well, we stopped to golf, but we <u>were</u> drinkin' while you guys were in the bar up here. We had a six of Pabst and a fifth of Shillelagh's." *Shillelagh's?* "I don't know either, but it was something cheap & disgusting!" he assured us.

Big Guy figured this was a good time to get a Ron interview on tape, before the Betsy shots piled up, but Ron didn't have much to contribute to Biggie's project. "This is my 3rd 4Day, and I'm still trying to put enough memories together for one of em'." That didn't seem to bother Biggie.

---

150

"Ron, I have to admit, I was a bit jaded at first, but you've been a fine addition to the 4Day. I look forward to seeing you every year. I gotta admit, you're a good man." Ron replied, "Damn it!" since this kind of thinking blows his cover as a self-described asshole. Biggie's compliment came with a P.S. of "No matter how pig headed you are." Ron said, "You're right – we're both stubborn bastards." This unforeseen lovefest continued with Biggie confessing, "And I think you'd go the downs if somebody really needed you." Ron lifted his glass, "Thank you sir."

Chucky leaned in from his bar stool, "You know, my favorite 4Day stories I don't remember 'cause I was part of 'em. That's back when I was drinkin'. Not drinking has saved my memories of the 4Day." Chucky sat back, smiling. "I think I'd like to get into becoming a 4Day historian. You guys are fun when you're drunk. I love coming up here with you – there's nothing better."

The boys were bringing late-arrivals Chris and Ron up to date about our stop earlier today in Mackinaw City at the Keyhole Lounge, where we sang *Sixteen Tons* in honor of a birthday celebrated by some folks sitting nearby, eliciting a standing ovation from several surrounding tables, occupied by people clearly starved for entertainment. Someone asked if we could sing *Happy Birthday* to a member of their group. We had to tell 'em sorry, we don't know that song. Hearing Keyhole Lounge talk, Betsy's ears perked up. She told us, "That bar in Mackinaw City is my favorite tavern." Coming from someone who owns a pub as warm and welcoming as Betsy's is high praise, indeed.

Betsy was now holding court from her favorite bar stool and had our full attention. "It's always special when you boys come up. If I don't get a phone call from you by a certain date, I check with the Season's Motel to see when you'll hit town to make sure I got plenty of supplies on hand." There would not be a repeat of running out of Betsy Burgers as happened when we ordered a second round of them in 1995. Running out of beer and bourbon has never been an issue, despite our prodigious consumption. Betsy took a long sip of her drink before continuing.

"Last year Doc called ahead of time… wanted me to put his G-damn CD in the juke box," she said to laughter all around from the boys, "So I did." Gee, she seemed so sweet when I asked her about this over the phone. Jimmy explained, "Well Betsy, we like to sing along with our favorite songs, like Roger Miller or 16 Tons." Thanks for trying to cover for me Jimmy.

Betsy grew reflective, now staring ahead with a far off look in her eyes. "*Tally Ho the Fox!* my husband would say as he was heading out the door." Thoughts of her beloved Bob McCormick turned the conversation to how the Mc's Tally Ho came to be. "This bar was built in 1940. When Bob and I moved up here from the Lower Peninsula, the 2ⁿᵈ owners had the bar. It was *Burk's Bar* when we bought it in '74. Burk's daughter, Jackie, still lives in town. Jackie told me, "As long as you're alive, my mother will never be dead." Two years after my husband passed away in '83, for some reason, I bought the bar in Germfask and called it the Foxx." Betsy stopped for a moment, then added, "I love seeing you boys. I just hope I'm still here for your visit next year." We assured her she'd be getting hugs and toasts from us for many more years, as if we had anything to do with her, or our, mortality.

The next day marked our first meeting with the new owners of Northland Outfitters, Tom and Sally Kenney. They wisely kept long time N.O. employee, Rich, to help manage their new business. Rich had joined us for a few beers at Betsy's last night. He gets a kick out of our stories, laughs easily, and is a man we're always happy to see.

Although the new proprietors are certainly pleasant folks, the morning – if arriving at noon can still be called morning – held a peculiar feeling in the absence of old owners Tom and Carma. Standing in front of the livery office and opening up a fifth of Beam for our circular firing squad changed the feeling from peculiar to familiar. Handing the bottle to Tom, known to us now as "New Tom", gave him an impression figuratively and literally of what 4Dayin' taste like.

Rich drove us out to this year's Fox River Overlook launch site. As we chatted with him while getting our canoes packed and into the Fox, Rich passed on taking a tug from the fifth making the rounds. "I'm a beer drinker, but I stopped with the hard stuff a while ago. It brings out a side of me that isn't good. But beer I can drink as much as I want." Smart man, not only recognizing but acting on this kind of information.

With the Tigers moving out of Tiger Stadium after last season concluded, favorite stories from the Tigers' days at the Old Ballyard became a topic along the river, spilling out into Andy's Bar that night…

Vid took a double-bubbler of Early Times and, after staggering a step or two, said, "Kaline was telling this story… Ray Oyler came up to bat and McAuliffe, batting behind Ray, came to the on-deck circle carrying his glove instead of his bat." *Author's note*: as the Tigers regular short stop in 1968, Oyler batted .135 for the year, including, famously, "0 for August".

Big Guy said, "My most memorable moment at Tiger Stadium? I went, I got drunk, I fell down, I got back up, dusted off my bloody knee and got back in the beer line."

Colonel thought Biggie might have had the right buzz, wrong locale. "Big Guy, wasn't that at your MSU commencement ceremony?"

Johnny, still laughing from Colonel's comment, jumped in. "Ok, it was Opening Day 1978, and I was going to school at Michigan living in the South Quad dorm. I'd spent the previous

60 hours writing a term paper and… "What? 60 hours?" a skeptical Gomie interrupted. "Yep, 60 hours. I never did like to plan too far ahead. Actually, I was writing, then tearing up, then rewriting the term paper, to be exact. Anyway, I finished typing it about two hours before the bus was to leave for the game, and high-tailed it to my professor's office to turn it in. Although it was pouring out and the Opener was likely to be postponed, I explained to him that I wouldn't be in class today. I'm sure this must have been a great source of amusement to him for many years to come as I was not what you would call a regular attendee. The chances of the Tigers playing in the rain today was about the same as me attending every lecture."

"So, I get back to the dorm to find out that, yes, the Opener was postponed until the next day. Well, I was still a little wired from writing the paper, the eight thousand or so cups of coffee I drank having a little to do with it I'm sure. I stayed up a few more hours before finally crashing at around one o'clock in the afternoon. I finally woke up at one o'clock – 24 hours later! I missed the bus. I missed the game. My best Tiger Stadium story was the Tiger Opener I never saw, but I did get a "B" on my paper."

Chris' proposal of "A toast to our collegiate education system!" was met by a ragged round of "Here! Here!" and a tug from the fifth of Northern Lights enjoyed by all the boys.

"On the subject of education," I began, "Captain Johnny had a story he shared with me from the Old Ballyard on a night the Captain and a Son of Ireland, Michael McBride, attended. Mikey had stowed a pint of whiskey down the crack of his ass to get it past security. It had to be 90 degrees and Mikey, a good 300 pounds, starts to fidget and squirm in his seat, knocking around Captain Johnny in the process. It turned out that the cap on the bottle had cracked and booze was running down Mikey's ass. Here's where the education part comes in, with Mikey learning the effect of alcohol on open pores. After Mikey excused himself, Johnny came upon him in the men's room, seeing Michael's pants down around his ankles and his ass wedged under the running cold water in the sink. Captain Johnny figured nothing like a good alcohol burn to get the hemorrhoids up. Post-game, the two headed to the Anchor Inn Bar, where Mikey perched on a bar stool with his ass up against the cold blasts from the air conditioner."

At Andy's Bar, hours after the Day 1 paddling had come to an end, many glasses were raised as we recalled that Herbie Redmond, the Tiger Stadium dancing grounds keeper & crowd favorite, passed away 10 years ago on, perfectly, Opening Day of 1990.

During our Day Two paddle through the Spreads, we took the traditional break at Boot Hill, celebrating the gorgeous sunshine with two whiskeys, Ezra Brooks and Bourbon de Luxe. Mm. Appropriately, Vid produced *the Boot*, a boot-shaped shot glass from the good folks at the Jim Beam distillery, to maximize our rot gut enjoyment. Beers, cigars, and stories abounded. One story was about another Boot Hill, one that served as the village of Seney's original cemetery.

The Boot Hill Cemetery was first used in 1880, during the height of Seney's wild days, when the town was known as the "Sodom of the North", and the pine forests' loggers filled its (at least) 20 saloons, 5 blind pigs, and 5 brothels. Some died in bar fights and many more were crushed or drown during the spring log drives. The grave situation required a cemetery.

Like the Boot Hill we occupied this day, the Boot Hill Cemetery was on elevated ground, the highest spot around town. Unlike our Boot Hill, the cemetery one is no longer in use, replaced by one opened in the 1920s. At the old graveyard, only a few of the ancient wooden headstones are still legible, marked as "Rest in Peace", "Unknown", or a favorite, "Kilt". It is thought that two of Seney's best known citizens, from the famous Harcourt-Dunn feud, are buried here: Steve Harcourt, shot to death in his bar by Dan Dunn in 1891, and Dan Dunn, killed that same year in revenge by Steve's brother Jim, who pursued Dunn to the Flint-area.

The party at the 4Day Boot Hill lasted for a couple of very fun hours, leaving us in a race with the clock to make it to the High Ground campsite before the sun set. As we fought our way, for the 18th time in 23 years, through the usual Fox River logjams downstream from the Spreads, a quote from Hall of Fame pitcher Lefty Gomez seemed fitting, "I'm throwing as hard as I ever did. The ball's just not getting there as fast."

An unspoken tie, articulated by satisfied smiles, was declared between the evening's dinner of chicken along with cherries soaked in Jack, provided by Gomie, Kenny and Vid, and the next day's roast beef supper served up by Chris, Marquis, and Ron at the Peninsula campground.

Between those two outstanding culinary experiences, and with a fair chance that a 4Dayer would open a distillery somewhere down the road, the brainstorming of names for future bourbons was bandied about on the river including…

*Jack Flatulence Bourbon, Hurly Times Bourbon, Last Paycheck Bourbon, This is Jeopardy Bourbon, and Drunken Gentleman Bourbon.*

The weather for the final day on the Fox River was so stunningly gorgeous, the rainy days of many early 4Days seemed part of a completely foreign experience, except for the similarities then and now in the friendships, the great times, and one story after another. Except for that.

Echoing through the forest, and originating from somewhere downstream, were the sounds of laughs and happy voices. Rounding the bend, the new steel bridge came into view, manned by Chris and Johnny shouting our way and waving us in with fifths and cigars. The mood fit the weather – fabulous – and not one of the 13 4Dayers, least of all the Frisbee-chasing Brittany, was in a hurry to leave the bridge party. At some point between the Four Roses and Kentucky Tavern whiskeys, I had yet another story from Michigan and Trumbull.

"Gentlemen, and you fellers, since we've been talking about Tiger Stadium the last few days, I gotta tell this one. For my final shot at Hoot's, after the final game at The Corner, the tequila shot no sooner hit my stomach when the stomach said *no mas*, and it came back out through my nose, landing dangerously close to Jimmy and Chris. We then strolled down Michigan Avenue to see if I could appease my stomach with a few White Castles. But I digress…

"After that final game, I saw that pizza man and former Ypsi mayoral candidate Faz was interviewed on Channel 4 as the-last-fan-to-leave-Tiger Stadium. *But here's… the rest of the story.* A WJR intern who also worked stadium security told WJR radio host Mitch Albom that someone told security "I'm waiting for Mitch" to avoid getting his butt tossed out. The next day on his radio show, I hear Albom say he wants to know who this person is who used his name to become the last-fan-to-leave-Tiger Stadium. I shout to the next room, "Hey Maggie, Albom wants to talk to Faz!" and I call Faz who says, "Doc who?" I told him, "You know, Maggie & Doc". Faz says, "Oh yeah, I love you bro." "Yeah, whatever, anyway Albom would like to talk to the last fan to leave the Corner." "Really bro? You have WJR's phone number?" "Sure Faz, here you go."

"5 minutes later, Albom says on the air, "We have the man on the line" "Hi Mitch – you the best, bro!" "Faz, you used my name to stay…" "No bro, we're old friends, we met once." "Faz, I don't know you and…" "No Mitch, I know Mother Theresa, and about my new book, *I Love Everyone*…" Mitch and his crew are cracking up, "Do we need anyone in our Marketing Department? We have a real self-promoter here." "No Mitch, you're all wrong, and if you call me at *Hello Faz Pizza*, 734-741-7777, I can prove it." Faz is a genius! Do you have any idea what 30 seconds, let alone 15 minutes, of air time cost on WJR? Faz was able to repeat his pizzeria phone number twice AND was the last-fan-to-leave-Tiger Stadium. Now THAT'S worth a group toast!" Say bye-bye Kentucky Tavern.

Once off the river, we overnight in Curtis. Before settling into a night at Betsy's, a few of the boys grab dinner at the Whitefish Inn. At the Inn, Vid said, "Gomie, if we leave butter on the table too long, we call it going south. What do you call it?" The southerner's answer was as weak as the position he found himself in. "We call it… going north."

A basket was brought to the table. Vid looked in it and said, "Oh, they brought us a northern delicacy." Gomie was interested, "Well, what is it?" "It's cornbread." Gomie looked a bit confused, "I thought that was a southern delicacy." "Well, I think we introduced it to you during carpet-bagging." Gomie's slumped shoulders reflected the score: North 2, South nothing.

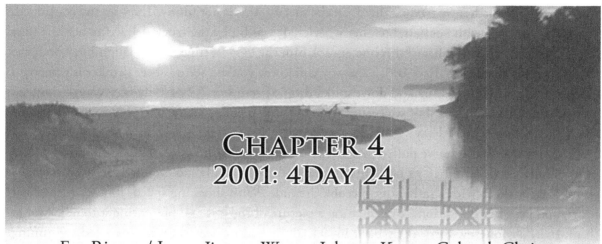

# CHAPTER 4
## 2001: 4DAY 24

Fox River w/ Jason, Jimmy, Wayne, Johnny, Kenny, Colonel, Chris, Vid, Jonesey, Gomie, Ron, (eternal) Rookie Steve, Brittany and Doc

*There's a lake of stew*
*And of whiskey, too*
*You can paddle all around them*
*In a big canoe*
*In the Big Rock Candy Mountains*
*(Big Rock Candy Mountain by Harry McClintock)*

"Come on in boys, the water's fine!"

Could there be a better 4Day line? It was one quoted by 4Dayers in the bars, before and after the paddling, and all up and down the river, one of the classic lines uttered in a great new movie we all seemed to embrace, "O Brother, Where Art Thou?" This story, set in the Deep South during the 1930s, has 3 escaped convicts on the lamb who turn into one helluva bluegrass band, the "Soggy Bottom Boys", a moniker that shouts ***4Day!***

*O Brother*-talk came up on a Pere Marquette River, family & friends, (non-4Day) canoe trip that included Chris' future step-daughter, 5-year old Madelynn. Madelynn tells Gomie he looks like Everett, George Clooney's character in the flick, one of the movie's 3 fugitive convicts, and turns to Vid to tell him that he looks like (the somewhat vacant) Delmar. Young Maddie seems to take special pleasure in teasing Vid. Exhibit 2: On softball "Ugly Hat Night", Madelynn sat in our dugout, staring at Vid and shaking her head, prompting a "What?!" from him. "Vid, how do you expect anyone to ever take you seriously when you wear a hat like that?"

Among 4Dayers, no one's laugh is as contagious as big Wayne-O's. It begins from deep in his gut and is delivered as a booming bass, exploding as it hits your ears and putting a huge smile on the face of anyone within earshot – in other words, anyone within a one-half mile radius of Wayne. Well, there were a lot of huge smiles when we stopped at the Nottingham Bar on the road north, because Wayne was in a particularly great mood.

What got Wayne started was a story Kenny shared, about some older gal who was killed on the way to her 100ᵗʰ birthday party. Granted, on the surface, this is not funny. Then Kenny continued, "Crossing the road with her daughter, her wheelchair was hit by the truck delivering her birthday cake." Well, when Wayne heard this one, it took him the longest time to stop laughing. About the time he caught his breath, Ron said, "The way you know you're a serious beer drinker is when you tumble down a flight of stairs and don't spill a drop of your beer." Not only was Wayne doubled over roaring with laughter, but we suspect one of the 3 regulars at the bar peed himself. Maybe that's why Johnny Cash always wears black.

The sun was setting as we pulled into the Season's Motel parking lot, quickly checking in and proceeding next door to Betsy's bar. On this particular Mc's Tally Ho evening, Betsy employed a young lady barkeep with a rather disagreeable attitude. With shocking speed, Jonesey melted her heart, and later her inhibitions, by sketching a picture of the lass and presenting it to her. And to think that, on Jonesey's first 4Day back in '94, all he had to sleep on was a deflated swimming pool raft.

The morning after Betsy's, gray clouds greeted us as we packed up for the 15 minute drive to Northland Outfitters and the start of 4Day 24. A few of us stopped by the little party store next to Betsy's to pick up some supplies for the river, and ran into longtime livery hand Rich. "Hey Rich, guess we'll see you at the livery later this morning." "Nope, I quit." "What?" Rich's old bosses, ex-owners Tom and Carma, knew the canoe 'n kayak business inside & out, and Rich just did not have the patience for the folks learning on the job, "new" Tom and Sally.

As soon as we launched Day 1 on the Fox, Vid kept saying he needed to pull over, "my legs are cramping up from all the time in the canoe." So, 10 minutes after we shoved off, a small dirt beach was picked for a rest stop. After several jokes and a few stories were swapped to chase the fifth of Early Times making the rounds, I had something to tell the 4Dayers.

"Boys, a toast to Pabst Blue Ribbon Beer. There's some sad news to report. PBR recently closed their last brewery." There was an audible group gasp. "It was in Pennsylvania, of all places. Shouldn't the final Pabst brewery to close have been in Milwaukee?" I thought I saw someone tearing up at this piece of information, but then noticed I was looking at my reflection in the Early Times bottle. "There is some good news, though. Production of Pabst will continue, contracted to Miller Beer, who will follow the PBR recipe at their breweries."

Well, from the group cheer, you'd a thought the Lions won a playoff game. After the initial relief, I was reproached for needlessly scaring the fellas. Chris said, "Doc, it was like telling us there was a terrible car accident and spending time on how it happened before letting us know the driver survived. The only way you can make amends is with a double-bubbler."

This actually played into my hand. After the initial 10 minutes of paddling, resulting in Vid's leg cramps forcing us to pull over, our riverside break had been going on for well over an hour in the hot sun, and I was getting a mite thirsty. The double-bubbler finished off the Early Times, which reminded Gomie of something that Captain Johnny had recently said. "Johnny told me that when the bourbon is gone and the vision is blurring, he refers to it as *Moth's Disease*".

Moth had made the fatal error of not coming on the 4Day this year, which makes you fair game for 4 days of ridicule. There are times when ridicule may be better for your health than attending the 4Day. Case in point: Steve, whose 4Day name is now and forever Rookie Steve, even though this is his 2nd 4Day adventure. Some guys, through their actions or inactions, for reasons hard to put your finger on, wear the rookie nom de guerre as a permanent badge of honor. Rookie Steve is one of those guys.

On Day 2, Rookie Steve, having been thoroughly overserved, was having a hard time staying upright in the bow of the boat he shared with his brother Ron, causing their canoe to capsize a couple of times. To remedy this, Ron used a great deal of electrical tape to bind Steve to the gear directly behind him. A brother's love is hard to endure. While this *did* keep Rookie Steve vertical in the front of the boat, minimizing further tipping, it *did not* allow him to duck when the canoe encountered low hanging branches. This was a particularly brutal experience as 8 major logjams blocked our way. Rookie Steve met the upstream edge of each with jarring force, and was beat to hell all day long. The good news is he was too liquored to realize it.

While the rest of us set up camp for the night at the High Ground, things didn't get much better for Rookie Steve. The whirlwind from the 1999 4Day who put up tents, gathered firewood, and fetched beers, was now an unmoving statue, leaning against a tree while camp was set and dinner served. Colonel was the first to suggest, "I think that something is seriously wrong with him. Alcohol poisoning maybe?" You *think* Colonel?!? Our requests of, "C'mon Rookie, you gotta eat something", started impersonations around the bonfire of Gilda Radner as Beethoven's wife, imploring her husband in a charming Midwestern German, "Lud-vig, you must eat!"

To all of this, there was no response, verbally or physically. After several hours, the statue came down and, without a word spoken, crawled into a tent (set up by others) for the night. Emerging the next morning, Rookie Steve clearly felt pain that we tried to minimize through humor. Jason said, "Don't worry Steve, I'd read that consciousness is just an annoying time between bouts of severe drunkenness." Jimmy reminded Steve of a Sparky Anderson quote, "Pain don't hurt." None of this seemed to help Rookie Steve with his morning agony, which must have been one of the great 4Day hangovers of all time, but it did brighten the morning for the rest of us.

There was no need for Ron to keep the electrical tape handy today. Rookie Steve, one day after his bender, stayed as far away from the whiskey as anyone ever has while 4Dayin'. By the time evening set in on the Peninsula campground, the eternal rookie was feeling good enough to stretch out on a log elevated over the Fox, his look of torture replaced by one of contentedness. By the time we reached the new steel bridge on the next and final day, he was even able to participate, with gusto, in the draining of a fifth of Cabin Still, produced by the good folks of Bardstown, Kentucky. To cheers from the boys on the bridge, Rookie Steve requested, "Give me half a boot please. No wait, make that an overflowing boot. That's better."

Ah, the restorative waters of the Fox.

Marcia from the Seasons Motel called two months after the 4Day, a phone call that was a hard one for her to make and for us to take. On September 23, 2001, at age 72, Betsy McCormick passed away.

The 4Day is a continuous trip, not a destination. The trip is the sum of the people participating. One beautiful trip participant was Betsy McCormick, a lady colorful, fun, and loved. From 1994 to 2001, the eve, the final night, or both of each 4Day was spent in her Mc's Tally Ho Bar in the U.P. town of Curtis. Spending time with Betsy was a special part of each of those 4Days. She was always ready with a smile, a story, an off-color joke, and making a point of knowing when we were coming 4Dayin', so that she could have on hand plenty of beer, bourbon, and - after getting to know our appetites - burgers.

Betsy left on her own terms: spending a night of drinking 'n dancing across the road from her pub, at the Shipwreck Bar, with her closest friends. She had just sat down from a twirl or two across the dance floor with a gentleman, when another fella asked her for a dance. Betsy said yes, stood up, had a massive heart attack, and was gone by the time she hit the floor.

At Betsy's funeral, her daughter said, "Mom couldn't walk into a building without coming out with two new friends".

*There was the night that she wanted to toss Vid from her establishment because he was bouncing too much... or when she told us that "there's no fuckin' swearing in this bar"... or the night Betsy went "dancing" with Gomie... or the night that Jerry Garcia stopped by Mc's Tally Ho and took Betsy, the lone person in her bar who didn't know who he was, dancing across the street. Betsy – the only woman to ever dance with both Gomie & Jerry Garcia.*

A week after Betsy's passing, Colonel reflected on her life. "Very sad indeed. Curtis will never be the same. It's hard to imagine the sorrow of others in that town. We only saw her twice a year, but she was the cornerstone to many of the locals. Take heart though, because she passed on while doing what she loved – living and enjoying life and fellow human beings (Gomie?)."

"Betsy had done something that most will never do – she lived in the Upper Peninsula. I'm sure she had a quick trip to heaven, since the U.P. is as close to heaven as you can get."

"On a slightly lighter side: at least now, when the departed Goobs and B.J. yell *SHOTS!* someone will know what they want."

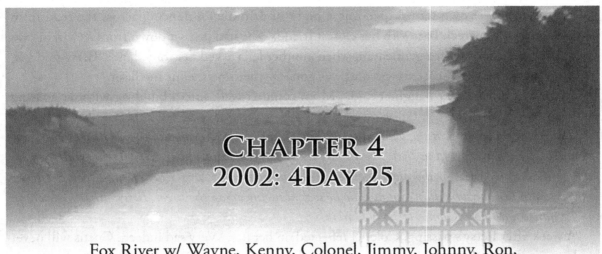

# CHAPTER 4
## 2002: 4DAY 25

Fox River w/ Wayne, Kenny, Colonel, Jimmy, Johnny, Ron,
Jason, Jonesey, Doc, Big Guy, Chucky, Dr. Bob, Vidder, Ricki,
Chris, Gomie, Marquis, Brittany and rookie Dave Mondoux

*You load Sixteen Tons, and what do you get?*
*Another year older and Chucky's in debt*
*St. Peter don't ya call me 'cause I can't go*
*I owe my soul to a barber named Mo*
*(Sixteen Tons – alternate cut, by the Mobil Lounge Softball Team & Beer Swillers Club)*

On the eve of the eve of last year's 4Day24, the boys were in the Mobil Lounge after a night of softball. The beer-soaked chatter about the upcoming 4Day became too intoxicating for never-been-on-one and Beer Swillin' softball teammate Dave Mondoux to resist joining us – just not quite yet. On that night in the bar, June 29, 2001, Dave became the first man to sign a napkin that committed him to a future 4Day, in this case, the 25th 4Day in July 2002.

A couple of months before this year's fun, I called the Mondoux residence and Dave's wife Laura answered. I asked Laura, "Do you think Dave will be 4Dayin' with us?" She answered emphatically, "Oh yeah! He signed a napkin!" The wife of a prospective 4Dayer believed that, if you sign a napkin pledging your participation, then you are committed. This phone conversation is considered the birth of the legally-binding aspect of the signed 4Day napkin.

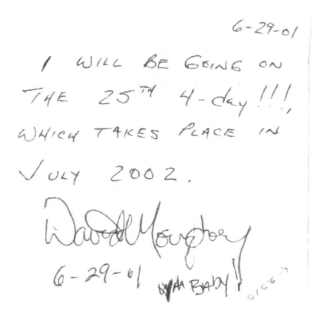

The invitation for this year's trip read, in part, *What began as a summer getaway in 1978 for four of the boys has lasted a quarter century with 45 4Dayers and 25 years of stories to tell and memories to relive with river dicks and corn squeezins waiting for us — we'd best get going.*

The invitation also included some 4Day fun facts…

- 4,000 acres of water are in Little Manistique Lake (south of Curtis)
- 7,000 acres of water are in Big Manistique Lake (north of Curtis)
- 9,000 beers have been consumed by 4Dayers: based on 6 per day x an average of ten 4Dayers per trip x 6 days (4 on the river/2 in the bar) x 25 years (yep, looks about right)

Stumbling into the Nottingham on the road north to order a round of shots, Chucky informed the waitress that, since he's an alcoholic, to pour only a short shot for him. A devilish smile spread across her face, and she poured for Chucky the largest shot of any of ours: one-half of a rock glass filled with Beam. With a resigned, "Oh well", it was tossed down by Chucky. On the road again, Chucky, already an inattentive driver, veered from median to shoulder and back. After a few minutes of this, it occurred to me that not only are our Guardian Angels keeping us safe, but also that the State Police must be giving us a day pass in honor of a quarter century of 4Days.

Also in honor of the 25th, we invited the womenfolk & kids to spend 4Day-eve with us in Curtis. While the boys took all the beds at our usual spot in Season's Motel, families & friends stayed a few hundred feet to the east at Berry's Resort, on the south side of Main Street, in cabins along the shore of Little (South) Manistique Lake.

4Dayers, family, and friends wildly celebrated the 25th 4Day-eve in and around Betsy's old/ new owner Kim's Mc'sTally Ho Bar in Curtis. If raucously singing along with the juke box, shouting "4Day!" n "SHOTS!", or running the tabletop shuffleboard game all night didn't already identify us, our commemorative black t-shirts sporting the number 25 wrapped around 4 fingers did.

Early in the evening, emerging from the east paraded a lady bagpiper in full Scottish regalia, marching down the middle of Main Street towards the bar, and playing songs just for us. Mesmerized, the party temporarily regrouped outside the bar to the lawn in front of neighboring Season's Motel.

The bagpiper stopped in front of our group, where a poster, designed by the Colonel and featuring 4Dayers and friends (BJay, Goobs, and Betsy) who've gone to The Other Side, was unfurled. The piper began to play Amazing Grace. The scene was electric and emotional.

Back inside the pub, Chris, down on one knee and borrowing one of Maggie's many rings, proposed to the unsuspecting Gloria. Her "YES!!!" reply was cheered by both friends and townies, who celebrated together with a round of Beam.

Later, Christine wondered, "Is this typical on the 4Day? I never saw Jimmy so drunk." Quick to clarify, Vid explained, "Chrissie, this is the night *before* the 4Day. When we get on the river, Jimmy will really let his hair down." Chrissie's eyes crossed anticipating what that next level would look like.

Although we had more partying in us, when the beer tap and bar lights were turned off a bit after 2AM, we reluctantly retired for the evening.

With the ladies and kids sleeping in, I knocked first on Rookie Dave Mondoux's motel room door at the promised 7AM time. He was incredulous. "Doc, its 7 o'clock – I'm still blasted. I thought you were kidding last night about starting at 7." "David, I feel as bad as you look." He *did* look awful, pretty much like the guy in my mirror did a couple minutes ago. Laughing at our shared condition, the resulting pounding in my head nipped that laugh-fest in the bud real quick. I assured him, "Forcing myself out of bed to get the guys moving is really, REALLY difficult. But if we're going to get 18 guys to breakfast, packed, and on the road to Germfask, we have to start now." My explanation elicited a weak, "Alright", from the rookie.

Seniority allowed all other 4Dayers to get a few more moments of sleep, but nobody got enough sack time to look like anything other than walking death as we staggered a couple hundred yards east to breakfast at Stamper's Restaurant. Gradually, stories from the incredible evening we all enjoyed last night reinvigorated the boys, their faces soon reflecting the anticipated adventure of the next 4 days.

The Fox was running high and fast this year from the recent heavy rains. As a consequence, Day One ending at the Seney Township campsite only took 90 minutes of actual paddling. It was the 6 hours of party breaks, an impressive display of recovery & recuperation from last night's bender, that had the boys barely to camp while daylight still warmed us.

A few hours before we paddled into our campsite, we had a little fun with Big Guy.

Vid wore his *Yankees Suck* t-shirt on the river today. This induced a few good-natured remarks back-n-forth between New York Yankee fan Big Guy and the rest of us. At what turned out to be a several hour riverbank stop, Gomie borrowed the Yankees Suck shirt from Vid, put it on along with his Confederate kepi hat, a piece of clothing that says "Yankees Suck" in its own special way, and posed for a photo with his arm around Big Guy.

Among several different conversations taking place, a couple of the boys got an idea: let's each put on the Yankees Suck shirt, pose for a photo with Biggie, take it off and pass it on to the next man to be photographed with him. Soon, everyone was involved. So, with Big Guy oblivious to the fact that the shirt was part of each photo, he sat in his beached canoe as one 4Dayer after another leaned in, crouched or sat next to Biggie while Gomie and I shot photos.

After the 4th or 5th such photo, Big Guy said, "I must be the most popular guy on the river." Upon hearing this, in an effort to cloak our intent, Gomie and I immediately swung our cameras away from Biggie and pretended to be taking wildlife and nature pictures. After several others sat with Biggie for a photo, he wondered aloud, "Am I dying?" All 18 4Dayers not named Big Guy, including Brittany the dog (held up by Chris), posed wearing the Yankee Suck t-shirt with him. The shirt was a little baggy on Brittany, but stylish.

Although parts and pieces of the *Yankees Suck* story came up many times during this 4Day, it was never with Big Guy in earshot. The question was how and when will we tell Big Guy?

Big Guy, still without a clue, attended eight months later, in March 2003, our annual softball banquet at the Mobil Lounge bar. I had enlarged to 8" x 10" all 18 Yankees Suck photos, with Big Guy in each one, from the previous year's 4Day. Arriving early to the banquet, I created a

Yankees Suck wall, and hid it behind a black sheet. Soon, the softball team – including the man of the hour – and our friends filed in.

At the end of the banquet, I addressed the still-covered wall. With some embellishment, invoking our dearly departed Goober (4Day class of 1978), I continued, "One of the most beautiful sounds of 4Days past was when Goobs would shout, "Hey Big Guy!" "What?" "The Yankees Suck!" Not only that, but Goobs' dying words whispered to Vid, as he leaned in close, were, "Always remind Big Guy, and never let him forget, that the Yankees Suck." So, in honor of our friendship with brother Goobs, I bring you *the Yankees Suck Wall*."

When I took the black sheet down, revealing the 8" x 10"s, laughter spread across the room, as all eyes shifted to Big Guy. Wondering about his reaction (Happy? Storm-out-of-the-room-mad? Confused?), we watched Biggie walk up to the wall. Studying the photos, not saying anything for the longest time, he then asked, "Did you guys know about this?" Vid exclaimed, "Big Guy, we're the guys wearing the shirt in the photos. Of course, we knew about it!"

Eventually, it was clear that Biggie liked the idea, liked the wall, saw the humor in it all, and was happy to be a central part of such a cool story.

In order to celebrate the spirit of the 25th 4Day with two whole nights at our favorite campsite, the Peninsula, Day 2 would be a physical and mental challenge. We all (well, most of us) agreed to bypass the usual Day 2 High Ground campsite, and add 2-3 hours to an already rigorous 6-7 hours of paddling, to make the Peninsula. With all of our gear weighing the boats down, much of these 8-10 hours would be spent fighting our way over and through logjams, a ball-buster of an effort.

In order to get us on the river as early as possible, as early as getting 18 guys moving who've been celebrating at a blistering pace for two hard days is possible, and at least give us a fighting chance to reach the Peninsula before dark, Rookie David agreed to make his breakfast for us at our annual Fox River break on Boot Hill. Knowing there was no breakfast 'til 45 minutes downstream got us packed and paddling with shockingly speed. A delicious, pre-made, Egg McMuffin-style fare, heated over a small fire, was waiting for us there. Nice job, Rookie Dave.

Everybody likes Rookie Dave Mondoux, and not only because he fed us. We met David in 1998 when he joined our softball team. He's a great shortstop and hitter, but his most endearing traits are his engaging personality, easy laugh, how he jokes around with everybody, and his sincerity. Even though he's spent 5 seasons with our team in the bar post-game each Thursday, and usually is among the last to leave so he knows first-hand our beer 'n shot track record, he keeps saying about our 4Day intake, "I had no idea you guys drank so much."

This day was as brutal as anticipated. About 4 hours into the experience, we'd just dragged our canoes over logjam number six. Rookie Dave said, "You guys know these are out here, and keep coming back each year. If there's another logjam ahead of us, you guys are certified criminally insane." "Not to worry David. There's probably another half-dozen to go." Sure enough, right around the next bend, was number 7. The rookie sighed and slowly shook his head.

Overjoyed to pull ashore on the High Ground, the usual Day 2 camp spot, today's lead canoeists Johnny & Ron jumped, waved, and shouted as other canoes approached. Hearing our yells back that we're continuing the at least two more hours to the Peninsula, the two looked stunned as we canoed by. Guess they were not part of the "most of us" that agreed to bypass the High Ground.

After 9 hours of paddling, plus 2 badly-needed one hour breaks, the Peninsula Campground finally appeared. Hallelujah! My watch read 9PM as the lead boats were pulled ashore. The tents went up and the boys went down – hard. The two days of parties and the fatiguing day on the river today took its toll, as the boys inhaled dinner and slept a deep sleep.

The Day 3 morning greeted us with beautiful blue skies. The reward for yesterday's 9 tough hours on the water was that we would stay in camp all day today. No tearing down tents in the morning and putting tents back up tonight. A day to relax in camp, read, tell stories, and play a serious amount of buzz euchre. We played for hours in the river where it flows around the Peninsula, tossing the Frisbee, floating in the Fox, sipping beer and sharing a fifth or two.

It was great to have the Father of the 4Day, my old EMU roommate and good friend Ricki Rice with us, up from his Asheville, NC home. This was only Ricki's 5th 4Day, his first since 1993. Around the campfire, Ricki reminisced about how 4Dayin' had changed from the first in 1978 to now. "When we went on the first 4Day, it was a raw and unpolished adventure. We weren't sure how much food to bring, we ate our meals individually, and we didn't know if we'd be able to refill our coolers with ice at any time. We weren't even sure where the river went and how long it would take to get to the take-out point. We were just there to have a great time, and we did!"

"Today, you guys coordinate the food, with everyone responsible for contributing to a meal.

There is no doubt that there will be an opportunity to restock the coolers, and there are 25 years of experience to draw on. It's a smooth operation, kind of reminds me a going on a cruise, no surprise, your every need anticipated and provided for."

I pointed out, perhaps unnecessarily, that cruise ships rarely have logjams to navigate. Vid chimed in, "Well, Ricki, we do have one surprise this year – I brought a ladle!"

With a much larger variation of "the boot", the boot-shaped shot glass popular on the 4Day, Vid ran around the Peninsula, pouring bourbon into a metal ladle offered for the 4Dayers' delight or lack thereof. Rookie Dave asked for mercy, "Please Vid, only half a ladle". Vid got a kick out of this since he was pouring out about a quarter ladle for everyone else.

Jimmy added, "Ricki, I got another surprise story for you, well, it was a surprise for one of your old neighbors in Southgate, Mitzi (Mom of 4Dayers Marquis, Craigo, & Chris). One year, BJay mailed a Christmas card to the Weaks' household in Southgate, didn't sign his name, and just wrote "wash yer dick" on it. Well, Mitzi happened to be the one to open the card, and thought it was her ex, Dick, sending a nasty gram. Craigo had to explain BJay's well-meaning vocabulary to his Mom. God bless that boy!"

Back on the river for Day 4, the high and fast-flowing Fox torpedoed us from the Peninsula to the new steel bridge in 45 minutes, two hours short of the livery and the trip's end. Under sunny skies, we stopped here for a two-fifth break, loving the *pfsst* sound of beer cans cracking open, and breathing in the scent of newly lit cigars. Jimmy, who runs the Chemistry Laboratory at the University of Michigan, shared with us a story he'd heard recently at work...

*Scientists at NASA came up with a test to ensure that windshields of airplanes and military jets could stand up to mid-air collisions with birds. They built a gun to launch dead chickens at the windshields, at a speed simulating the aircraft traveling at maximum velocity.*

*British engineers were allowed to borrow the gun to test it on the windshields of their new high speed trains. When the gun was fired, the Brits were shocked when the chickens crashed through the believed-to-be shatterproof windshields, and were embedded in the cabin rear wall.*

*The Brits forward to NASA the test results, including the design of the windshield, and asked the USA folks for suggestions. NASA responded with a one-line memo: "Defrost the chicken."*

That night, we were reunited in Curtis with our families and friends, who had been exploring the Eastern Upper Peninsula and Traverse City areas. As the 4Dayers rolled into Curtis the evening after our final day on the river, some of the wives and lady friends celebrated the spirit of the 4Day by being warned that, should the cabin owners smell any more marijuana, they would be tossed out of their lakeside rentals.

In the bar, Colonel and Jonesey were telling a story about getting to the pub at the end of a 4Day, specifically the drive from Northland Outfitters on the very windy Ten Curves Road to Curtis.

Colonel claimed excitedly, "It at least tied the record for the fastest time from Germfask to Curtis driving a Bronco with a raised suspension and oversized tires. The David Duke bumper sticker provided a kind of parking pass, allowing you to park wherever you like. Good thing YouTube was not around then, or any of my future political aspirations would be shot."

I nodded, "Oh yeah, I remember. I was your passenger for that ride down Ten Curves. It was one of the wildest moments of my life. Both the David Duke bumper sticker and I were holding on for dear life."

Jonesey shivered recalling, "Colonel, you were hitting the curves at 70 mph, bumping the back of my car. In the rear view mirror it looked like your maniacal grin was 2' away. I needed a clean pair of jeans when we got to the Curtis motel. But once in the bar, I saw Betsy's smiling face, got a cold beer and a couple of Betsy burgers. It don't get no better than that."

The night in Mc's Tally Ho bar, now Kim's Tally Ho, without Betsy was fun but a little sad. The late-Betsy's presence was badly missed.

Back home from his inaugural 4Day, rookie Dave Mondoux wrote about the experience…

*When Doc approached me to write down my memories of a rookie's first 4Day, I was wondering what he thought I remembered, because it's not a lot! But, after signing my fate to a bar napkin at the Mobil Lounge, the least I can do is take a ladle shot and try to remember something. Sorry, no such luck. Sorry, no luck on that one either, or that one (stupid Vid). Anyway, a great time was had by all the criminally insane (you had to be there), good food, good party favors, good friends, good bourbon (HA HA HA) and most of all, an absolutely fabulous tradition that I feel privileged to have been allowed to be a part of. Now I know I will live forever, because I survived my first 4Day, well maybe not forever, I probably took a few days off of my life expectancy, but who wants to live forever. 4Day!*

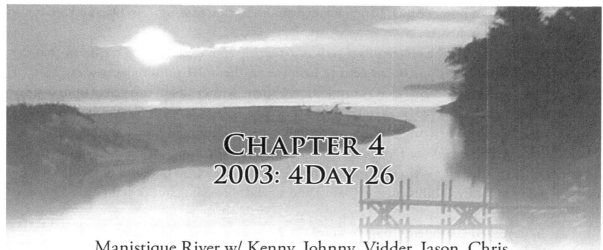

# CHAPTER 4
# 2003: 4DAY 26

Manistique River w/ Kenny, Johnny, Vidder, Jason, Chris, Ron, Gomie, Brittany, Doc and rookies Mickey and Carl

*Come and listen to a story 'bout a man named Jed*
*A poor mountaineer, barely kept his family fed*
*Then one day he was shootin' at some food,*
*And up through the ground came a bubblin' crude.*
*Oil that is, black gold, Texas tea.*
*(The Ballad of Jed Clampett, aka the Beverly Hillbillies theme song, by Flatt & Scruggs)*

Elly May Clampett's Pa died the week of 4Day 26, July 6, 2003.

Two years ago, I was reading a newspaper while flying home from a business meeting, when my eyes landed on a photo of a dancing Buddy Ebsen aka Jed Clampett. The caption read, "Buddy Ebsen, getting Jiggy at 93". The article talked about how, since his acting days, Buddy writes plays for regional theaters, wrote a novel ("Kelly's Quest"), creates oil paintings ("Uncle Jed Country" features the Clampett's cabin and dog Duke's head resting on Jed's knee), is an expert sailor (skippering his 35' catamaran to victories in several major races) and maintains a website.

The Beverly Hillbillies remains my all-time favorite TV show so, once back home, I eagerly checked out Buddy's website. Almost lost among Buddy's oil painting creations on the site was a watch face featuring Jed Clampett delivering his signature phrase, "Weee Doggies!" The watch was available for sale and I placed an order for one immediately.

Within a few days, a package from Buddy Ebsen arrived in our mailbox. Inside the package was the watch with the great picture of Jed next to those classic words, "Weee Doggies!", but it was a ladies watch. The Ebsen assistant reached at the packing slip phone number was very helpful and assured me that a men's version of the watch was on the way. When it arrived, would I return the ladies watch? Of course.

Once again, within a few days, a package from Buddy Ebsen was in our mailbox. Inside the package, though, was not a watch, but a book. The book was entitled, "The Other Side of Oz:

An Autobiography of Buddy Ebsen", and included an inscription reading, "To Dan and Sharon – Good Wishes, Buddy Ebsen".

The staff member on the phone this time was extremely apologetic, letting me know that the 93-year old "Mister Ebsen insists on getting involved in the order fulfillment process, so…" I told her that I was honored Buddy was involved, and that "Mister Ebsen can screw up my order anytime!" The lady said to please keep the book (but how about Dan and Sharon?) and that the correct order would be arriving soon. Sure enough, the men's watch with Jed Clampett's big, beautiful face telling us "Weee Doggies!" was quickly received, along with a bonus gift: an 8 x 10 photo of Jed Clampett looking askance at the telephone receiver in his hand (possibly an irate customer with an order fulfillment complaint) and signed, "To Margaret & Jeff: Weee Doggies! Buddy Ebsen".

Rest in peace Jed Clampett. Thank you for the memories – and the reruns.

For the first time in 5 years, the 4Day will take us down the beautiful, wide, laid-back waters of the Manistique River. Its upper section features gorgeous big bends and fun challenges, portage-free, through debris fields and occasional rapids. Further downstream offers viewings of eagles, loons, and swans as the rivers flows through the Seney National Wildlife Refuge. Beyond the Refuge are enticing sandy beaches, expansive and ideal for breaks and camping.

The last few years have found us on the challenging Fox River.

The Fox is truly fabulous, offering an ever-changing adventure each day. Our traditional Day 1, upstream from the Seney Township Campsite, features a narrow, fast-flowing current, at times barely wide enough to cut a path between leaning tag alder bushes. Soon after Day 2 launches, the exhilarating Spreads branches into multiple fingers, each so narrow that the bushes to the left & right brush against both of your shoulders as the current picks up speed. Boot Hill lies within the Spreads, a wonderful stop with a commanding view of the river. Day 4 from the Peninsula to the livery take-out finds the Fox widening while maintaining a current speed above average for a Michigan river, until it merges with the Manistique for the slower but beautiful final 2 hours of the trip.

What is missing from the paragraph above is that section of the Fox that overlaps days 2 & 3, from the Spreads to the Peninsula campground: 8 to 10 hours of strenuous, exhausting work of pushing fully-loaded canoes over and around major logjams that often number a dozen, plus a slew of smaller obstacles that may require leaving the canoe to push it through. The sense of achievement at day's end does not bubble to the surface while experiencing logjam number ten.

So, between a nod to the aging process, and considering the number of years that have passed since our most recent Manistique experience, the boys looked forward to a return to the river of the very first 4Day back in 1978.

Two rookies joined us this year, Mick Robinson and Carl Verba. We've been friends with Mick for 30 years, Carl for about 20 years. They both play on our Mobil Lounge Softball Team and Beer Swillers Club, great guys and great teammates, just like last year's rookie, Dave Mondoux. And, also just like last year's rookie, a signed, legally-binding napkin conscripted them to a 4Day one year later.

A month before last year's 4Day, we were sipping beers post-game at our sponsor bar, the

Mobil Lounge, encouraging Mick and Carl to come with us on the upcoming trip. Carl had heard the stories of the hard work at the logjams and the hard partying that took place, and was a little nervous about being a part of it all. Certain that Mick would not come 4Dayin', that night Carl signed a napkin for the following year's (2003's) event and wrote on it, "If Mickey goes on the 4Day, I f'in guarantee that I'm going!" Carl was also certain that the napkin would somehow be misplaced over the next 12 months. He was wrong on both counts. Don't worry Carl, it's a 4Day. What's the worst that could happen?

4Day eve found us once again in Curtis, in Betsy's former and now Kim's bar, Mc's Tally Ho.

Rookie Carl seemed to be having a great time, sharing stories and laughs, while knocking down beers and shots with us. Then, another round of shots was set up, and… he was gone. Where did Carl go? "Hey, he's standing outside the bar! Hey, he's puking!" Carl came back in, sat down on his bar stool, and grabbed the filled shot glass in front of him. "Carl", I assured him, "you just threw up. You don't have to do every shot we do." Carl shook his head, "No, it's the 4Day, I'm fine", and he pounded the shot.

Carl seemed ok the rest of the night (maybe we weren't looking that closely), but then morning arrived and he emerged from his room into the sunshine of the motel courtyard. Most of the guys were standing there, getting ready to walk down the street for breakfast. They took one look at this poor soul, and started laughing. "Good God, Carl! What happened to you?" He looked to be near a stage of life's journey when medical personnel go through your wallet to see what organs they can harvest. So long as it's not Carl's liver!

Rookies Carl and Mick had driven together. Carl took what clearly were several painful steps to Mick's motel room. Mick opened the door, and we overhead Carl say, "Mick, its ok with me if you just want to go home." Mick replied, "Carl, we drove all the way here, we're not going to turn around and go home. It's been coming out of me both ways this morning, but we're going canoeing today." Rookie Carl's shoulders slumped as he let out a weak, "Ok".

Chris said, "Rookie Carl, the fun has just begun!" I brought the rookies carryout breakfast from Stampers, and we all assured Carl that he only needed to get some food in his stomach, and he'd be doing much better. We were wrong. On the 15 minute drive to the livery, Mick stopped his car twice so that Carl could toss his cookies on the side of the road.

The only dam on the entire Manistique is a mere 30 minutes into the trip, traditionally the first break on this river. As soon as the rookie canoe of Mick and Carl washed ashore here, Rookie Carl walked slowly but directly to the single picnic table at the site, grabbed a seat, put his head down on the table, and pulled his t-shirt over his face.

Drawing on his 12 years of 4Day experience, Vid immediately diagnosed the situation, and determined that healthy tugs from the Fleischmann's Whiskey bottle would be critical to the rookie's recovery. In other words, hair of the dog was required. As part of a balanced 4Day diet, a Pabst Blue Ribbon beer was opened and placed next to where we believed Rookie Carl's head would eventually emerge from under his t-shirt.

Knowing that any delay in his cure would only senselessly prolong the rookie's pain, and that, at this point, the rookie was an unwilling participant in his own recuperation, Vid opened the fifth of Fleischmann's, placed it under Rookie Carl's nose, waving his hand back 'n forth over the bottle's neck, helping the whiskey's aroma find the rook's nostrils. Jason suggested, "This is akin to banks charging a fee for insufficient funds when they already know you're broke". "Huh?!?!?" was the reaction of several guys, unsure that the analogy fit, but after a few seconds it was felt that whatever the statement lacked in appropriateness, it made up for in cleverness.

Well, hair of the dog definitely worked on this occasion (although Vid himself has been known to say, "There's hair of the dog, and there's lickin' the kennel floor"), as soon Rookie Carl was able to lift his head, smile, separate himself from the picnic table (all good signs), and join the boys as we crossed the pedestrian walk over the dam to the opposite shore of the river.

There we visited a touching memorial that been created since our 1998 Manistique canoe trip. A USA flag was raised over a mound of flowers and stones, in honor of the passing of a member of the Ten Curves Club, a group of local riverside homeowners. One of the stones had an engraving on it to their friend's memory: "If tears could build a stairway, and memories a lane, I'd walk right up to heaven and bring you home again."

It wasn't until 4PM, at our final riverside break, that Carl seemed to fully regain his pep. At that stop, his paddling partner Mick said, "Being a total rookie, I haven't packed anything. I'm just amazed at how prepared you guys are. Look at Chris' cooler – it's perfectly packed with food and drink." Chris shared some cheese and crackers with the grateful rookies, the first thing that either one could keep down all day (Mick suffers less demonstrably than Carl). Between bites, Rookie Mick said, "It's a good thing you guys stop every 20 minutes. It gives us a chance to catch up. Neither of us are very good at canoeing, and we've been going down the river sideways all day." It was fortunate that we were not paddling the more demanding Fox River this year.

Day 2, the 4-hour paddle from the livery to Mead's Creek Campground, was interrupted by canoe vomits 10 minutes apart. Two unlikely candidates fed the fish: first Kenny, then Vid. After Vid cleaned his mouth with a Labatt's, he said it was his first puke since 1978, a full quarter century ago. In honor of this landmark event, Chris passed around a fifth of Banker's Club, for toasts that all partook of, including the four Barf Brothers. Kenny's Confucius-like line bears repeating, "There's those that have, and those that will."

As we floated together downstream, I asked the boys if they'd heard The Legend of Pencil Dick & Mister Weasel. The blank stares said no. "Well gather 'round boys. Last month, we made our trek south to Jacksonville for Captain Johnny & Kathy's annual Memorial Day weekend shindig. One afternoon, Vid and Gomie were playing euchre against my partner Jimmy Harcourt and me. Someone asked who was winning, and I said, "Well, we're getting our ass kicked by Pencil Dick and Mister Weasel." With hardly a moment's hesitation, Vid raised his arm and said, "I'm Mister Weasel." After a few seconds, a look of concern crossed Gomie's face when he realized what was left for him, and said, "Hey!" And that, kids, is how the North won the war."

Day 3 started with a fantastic breakfast, courtesy of Chris and Ron, an egg scramble including sausage and potatoes. Mm, mm! By the time breakfast was finished, the campground picked up, tents taken down, and the canoes loaded, we departed Mead Creek a little before noon.

The Manistique downstream from the livery is wide and obstruction-free, ideal for bringing the boats in close to form a lazy flotilla. Happily passing the time and the whiskey, in a haze of cigar smoke, we came up some new bourbon names...

*You Bet Your Liver Bourbon, Village Idiot Bourbon, Weee Doggies! Bourbon (yeah, that was one of mine), Before & After Bourbon, Unforeseen Consequences Bourbon, Lost Civil Liberties Bourbon, Storm Front Bourbon, Bobby Layne Private Label Bourbon, Timber! Bourbon and, although it may be difficult to fit on a label, Somebody Musta Hit Me in My Face When I Wasn't Lookin' Bourbon.*

Gomie brought it to our attention that it's been 10 years since the final episode of Cheers. That piece of information got the boys reminiscing about their favorite Norm Peterson quotes…

*How's a beer sound Norm? I don't know, I usually finish 'em before they get a word in.*
*How's it going Mister Peterson? It's a dog-eat-dog world and I'm wearing Milk Bone shorts.*
*Whatcha up to Norm? My ideal weight if I were eleven feet tall.*
*What'd you like Normie? A reason to live – gimme another beer.*
*Pour you a beer Mister Peterson? Yeah, but stop me at one – make that one-thirty.*
*What's the story Norm? Boy meets beer. Boy drinks beer. Boy meets another beer.*
*Can I pour you a beer Mister Peterson? A little early, isn't it Woody? For a beer? No, for stupid questions.*

Ron said, "I love Norm, but there was a good one from one of the times that Cliff and Carla were going at it. I don't remember what the subject was, but Cliff said "There are times I'm ashamed God made me a man." Carla said, "I don't think God's doing a lot of bragging about it, either."

Late in the afternoon, we picked one of the many fine, wide, sandy beaches along the river at which to set up camp. After a sweet night around the bonfire and under the stars, sunny skies woke us the next morning, the sun's rays glistening off of the water. The Manistique River never looked so spectacular. Two hours of pure Michigan beauty remained in our paddle until the 4Day came to an end at the Cookson Bridge access.

Post-4Day, rookie Carl reflected on his first 4Day and sent us a note of thanks…

*Hope you (Neanderthal) barbarians made it home safe from the 4Day. Nobody at work believed the debauchery, gluttony, and drunkenness that I witnessed. I was back at 100% by Tuesday morning. By your standards, I am not worthy of a 4Day.*

In reply to Rookie Carl, I wrote…

*Thank you for the extremely flattering letter. On behalf of myself, the Council of Elders, and all 4Day veterans, we appreciate your comments. I'd like to note that you should not sell yourself short regarding your 4Day worthiness – just the fact that you've returned to 100% within 3 days of getting off the river is an accomplishment that puts you in the top 10 percentile of 4Day rookies. Many cannot perform once-simple tasks for up to 1-2 weeks afterward. Please also note that it's only 373 days (should we go back to our normal week after the 4th of July) OR 359 days (should we follow this year's timeline) until the next 4Day, at which time we'll look forward to your sophomore expedition.*

*Regards,*
*Doc*

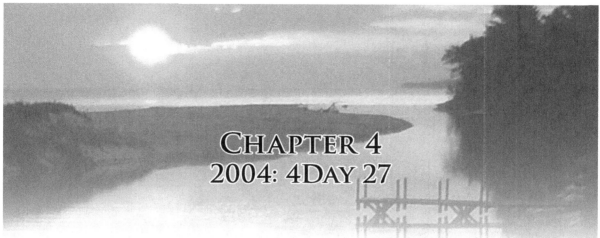

# CHAPTER 4
## 2004: 4DAY 27

Manistique River w/ Ron, Gomie, Huff, Marquis,
Vid, Chris, Kenny, Johnny, Jason, Doc

*I'll never smoke weed with Willie again*
*My party's all over before it begins*
*You can pour me some old Whiskey River my friend.*
*But I'll never smoke weed with Willie again*
*In the fetal position with drool on my chin*
*We broke down and smoked weed with Willie again*
*(Weed With Willie by Toby Keith & Scott Emerick)*

Among 4Dayers, an all-time favorite Rodney Dangerfield joke goes like this…

"You know when you're really getting old? When people talk about you, and you're right in the room. You ever see these families? He's sitting right there, and they're saying, "What are we gonna do about Pop? He can't stay here. We got company coming over, put Pop in the garage." And you see Pop sitting there, drooling."

On the river, Day 1 of the 2004 4Day, I was Pop.

As we were paddling down the Manistique River on this first day of the 4Day, there was a lot of fun shouting back n' forth among the canoes, quoting Rodney lines…

*I'm so ugly, my proctologist stuck his finger in my mouth.*

*Last week I told my wife, if she would learn how to cook, I could fire the chef. She said, if you could learn how to make love, I could fire the chauffer.*

*I bought a used car and found my wife's dress in the back seat.*

*I'm not a sexy guy. I went to a hooker. I dropped my pants. She dropped her price.*

*My dentist said my teeth were brown. I asked him, what should I do? He said, wear a yellow tie.*

*Last night, some guy knocked on our front door. My wife told me to hide in the closet.*

And on and on and on, in a delightful parade of Rodney-isms.

Apparently, I was overserved somewhere between the first to the fifth break along the river. It might have been the fifth of Ezra Brooks at the Ten Curves Dam break, or the fifth of Cabin Still at the new steel bridge or the fifth of Four Roses on that sandy beach on the right shore or the fifth of Kentucky Tavern at the big bend on the left bank or the Stone In Your Shoe Bourbon at — wait a minute. That's not even a real whiskey. And <u>that's</u> when things began to get a little blurry.

Through the haze, I remember sitting on a beach, the boys channeling Rodney, saying, "What are we gonna do about Pop?" Hey, they're talking about me! This was at the end of about a two-hour time period, begun when I mentally took a side journey from the 4Day, entering a strange dream world. I was a contestant on a game show that was slowly coming into view… Hey! It's the Hollywood Squares! I love this show! Peter Marshall is looking at me, saying "Doc, it's your turn." "Peter, I'll take Paul Lynde to block."…

*Paul, it is considered in bad taste to discuss two subjects at nudist camps. One is politics. What is the other? Paul: "Tape measures."*

This is too cool! Paul Lynde, George Gobel, Charley Weaver. Since this is <u>my</u> strange dream, forget the other contestant and the other celebrities in those squares, and forget keeping score in this tic-tac-toe game. Let's just have Peter Marshall keep asking one question after another...

*Paul, if you were pregnant for two years, what would you give birth to? Paul: "I don't know, but it would never be afraid of the dark."*

*George, while visiting China, your tour guide starts shouting "Poo! Poo! Poo!" What does that mean? George: "Cattle crossing."*

*Charley, if you're going to make a parachute jump, you should be at least how high? Charley: "Three days of steady drinking should do it."*

*Paul, it is the most abused and neglected part of your body. What is it? Paul: "Mine may be abused, but it certainly isn't neglected."*

*Charley, you have just decided to grow strawberries. Are you going to get any your first year? Charley: "Of course not Peter, I'm too busy growing strawberries."*

*Paul, why do Hell's Angels wear leather? Paul: "Because chiffon wrinkles too easily."*

Before Peter could ask John Davidson a question (I never cared for the 1980's Hollywood Squares line-up), my Guardian Angel stepped in. Peter Marshall had now been transformed into Kenny – how'd he do that? – and I was sitting on a beach along the river. I celebrated my mind's return to the 4Day with a sandwich and a lot of water.

Vid welcomed me back to the living. "Doc, you were like water going down the drain. We kept asking, "What are we gonna do about Pop?" The first couple of times you answered, "Hey, I'm right here!" After that, when we asked about Pop, you had no answer."

Gomie and I were the lead canoe as we came into view of the Northland Outfitters' campground. I was up front in the bow, Gomie steering in the back. Livery owner Tom was standing along the shore. When we saw him, it was then I recalled that he'd planned to have a couple of beers with us tonight, since we were tenting this evening on his livery grounds.

Rather than traverse the last few hundred feet to the take-out deck, Gomie pulled up to the little dirt slope at the base of a small rise that Tom stood atop. Tom took one look at the state I was in, still a bit musty and careworn, and must have said to himself, "Good God! These guys are the lead boat. What must the laggards behind them look like?" Tom turned and walked away, not to be seen again until the sun rose on Day Two.

Meanwhile, back at the dirt slope, I got out of the boat and, taking a page out of one of Jonesey's favorite movies, "Yellowbeard" (i.e. stagger, stagger, crawl, crawl), I made my way up the slope, across the grounds to the tents we'd wisely set-up that morning, and crashed. Hard. Fortunately for the boys' hunger and my reputation, the dinner that Johnny and I were responsible for was pizzas that were pre-paid, as was the driver's tip, and the delivery time pre-set. As it turned out, my nap ended as the pizza guy pulled up. My guardian angel is getting a workout today.

The next morning, I thanked Gomie for dropping me off at that dirt slope, a quicker river exit that I was all for, rather than paddling the last 5 minutes to the access deck. Gomie laughed. "You said if I didn't drop you off there, you'd kick my ass." "Oh, ah, thanks for taking direction so well."

After my Day 1 bourbon-fueled stint as "Pop", I never enjoyed, nor needed as much, a meal as I did Day 2's breakfast. Jason and Ron had chef responsibilities, and produced a delectable and essential spread of eggs, taters, and bacon.

Today would be a 4-hour paddle to our home for the night, the Mead Creek Campground, about half-way between the towns of Germfask and Blaney Park. Once again blessed with a sunny day, it was a thoroughly enjoyable trip through the Seney National Wildlife Refuge and its fauna viewings, with stops downstream at the merging Gray's Creek, Pine Creek, and Drigg's River, before coming ashore at the campsite landing.

Around the evening campfire, Marquis matter-of-factly mentioned, "I brought Big Boss Man." This news brought cheers so loud that you might have thought were greeting a friend back from the dead. In a way, we were. When Marquis' canoe flipped over on the 1997 4Day, among the gear that went into the river was his Big Boss Man plastic squirt toy. A few bends downstream from his flip, fortunately, some of us were pulled over for a paddle break and able to rescue Big Boss Man before he could float by us.

The Day 3 pancake breakfast created for us by Chris and Marquis got us feeling fat 'n sassy, and also got us to thinkin'. Johnny asked, "Doc, how many total hours of paddling are in front of us today and tomorrow?" Everyone sensed where he was going with this. "About 4-5 hours." "So, if we bust ass tomorrow… we could stay in camp today?" Kenny had a helpful idea, "Maybe if we all take a tug from this fifth of Old Overholt Rye Whiskey, we can find some answers." With nasty whiskey as our advisor, looks like we're staying two nights at Mead Creek.

Now, it's not like we did no paddling on Day 3. That's not it at all. Ten 4Dayers with whiskey, beer, cigars, and a few snacks squeezed into four of the canoes and paddled a good 200 yards upstream to a place now referred to as Drinkin' Beach.

Ron was the first to notice, "Hey! There's a split in the womb: we got both Canada House AND Canadian Mist!" Chris shouted, "Hell, I'll drink to that!" But before he could, Kenny held up his hand. "Let's make the first toast to Z-Bob." The fellas solemnly replied as one, "To Z-Bob."

The boys toasted the loss of a 4Dayer. Kenny introduced us on the 1990 trip to his buddy, Gary Zablocki. Gary, better known as Z-Bob, was the first man to play music on the river during a 4Day. At a Fox River stop just downstream from the M28 Bridge, Z-Bob pulled a cassette player (for those of you under 30, a cassette player is explained in the 1990 chapter) out of his dry bag and popped in Hank Williams Junior's "High Notes" cassette. Z-Bob passed away this January, and as we raised our beers 'n bourbon to him, Kenny and I sang a few lines of Hank Jr.'s "If Heaven Ain't A lot Like Dixie".

Drinkin' Beach had us as residents for about 4 hours before we boarded the canoes 'n headed back to the camp landing. All in all, we got close to 10 minutes of paddling in today. Tuckered out from this prodigious display of loafing, some naptime was required before rising to enjoy the fine spaghetti dinner fixed for us by Kenny and Huff.

Huff packs as if he's going to be far away from civilization for a month, the type of vacation that this man of the woods often takes. He brought along, besides a wide variety of cooking utensils, his tomahawk, knives of all shapes and sizes, and, in case the tomahawk or knives get tossed askew OR some twigs need to be plucked from Moth's gashed forehead (see 4Day 1994), an emergency medical kit.

The Day 4 journey to the Cookson Bridge take-out could only be considered work when compared to Day 3. Expending a minimum of energy, we were floating together and floating lazy. Marquis was entertaining us with his many impersonations, including one of a man named Reggie Harding. It was the briefest of Marquis' impressions, only one line, but a line that had become a 4Day catch phrase, "It ain't me."

Reggie Harding was born in Detroit and didn't stop growing until he was 7 feet tall. Reggie played high school basketball, a center who seriously dominated all opposing centers. The impressed Detroit Pistons drafted him right out of high school in 1963. Reggie was good for a few years, but never became the impact player that the Pistons hoped he would be. His NBA career was done by the time he was 26, and Harding found himself back on the streets. Needing some money, Reggie decided to rob his neighborhood liquor store. Where everybody knew him. A store, owned by the same guy for years, that Reggie frequented for years. The 7' tall Reggie donned a ski mask and pulled a gun on the owner who asked, "What are you doin' Reggie?" Reggie replied, "It ain't me." The police got to Reggie's house before he did.

Indulging in one of his favorite 4Day activities, collecting driftwood, Chris pulled a 4' x 4' x 6' piece, sizeable even by Chris' standards, into his canoe. Reaching today's take-out, Chris loaded the souvenir into his van, a trophy so large that Marquis inquired as to where he should sit. After some reloading, they were able to set up a camp chair, placed next to Chris' treasure from the Manistique, for Marquis' comfort - a temporary comfort until Chris took a sharp curve a little too fast. Marquis harshly awoke from his nap as he executed an unplanned tumble into this massive hunk of Mother Nature's art. Chris quickly pulled to the side of the road, and opened the van's side door to the view of the soles of his dear brother's shoes and the sounds of some intermittent vulgarity. After Chris assisted getting him into a somewhat more natural position, Marquis emerged from the van, glasses slightly askew, with a few more wounds than are normal from a 4Day. The brothers fixed the chair, better secured the gear, and continued home without further incident.

3 months after the 4Day, the boys received the bad news: Rodney Dangerfield had passed away. The laughs go on forever...

*I haven't spoken to my wife for years. I didn't want to interrupt her.*

Thanks Rodney!

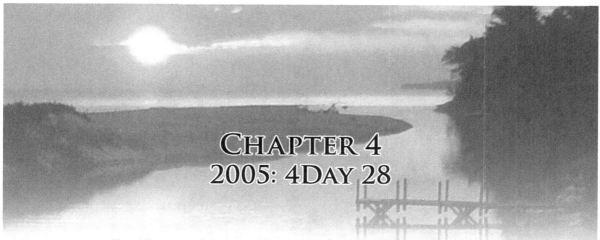

# CHAPTER 4
## 2005: 4DAY 28

Fox River w/ Jason, Jimmy, Johnny, Kenny, Colonel,
Chris, Vid, Marquis, Brittany, Ron, Doc

*Everybody get on your feet*
*You make me nervous when you in your seat*
*Take off your shoes and pat your feet*
*We're doin a dance that can't be beat*
*We're barefootin', We're barefootin'*
*(Barefootin' by Robert Parker)*

"Fat, drunk, and stupid is no way to go through life son." Raise you beer to John Vernon, the man who played Dean Wormer in the all-time favorite movie of so many, the 1978 classic, "Animal House". John Vernon passed away on February 1st of this year. Who will ever forget when he invited the Deltas, after they stole the wrong exam to crib from, to his office for a chat…*"You're not walking out of this one mister. You're finished! No more Delta! You've bought it this time, buster! I'm calling your national office! I'm going to revoke your charter! And if you guys try one more thing, one more, I'm going to kick you out of college! No more fun of any kind!!!"*

Meeting the boys in Curtis on 4Day-eve were a couple of honeymooners, 4Day brother Marquis and his new bride Gilda aka Mister & Missus Weaks. The newlyweds had agreed to separate for one day of their post-nuptial celebration, allowing Marquis to paddle the Fox on the first day of the 4Day. No wonder you married this girl! After Day 1 on the river, Marquis and Gilda camped with us at the Seney Township Campsite. The next morning, when the boats were put into the water, the couple planned to go their own way and the honeymoon would continue.

Standing with us at the Day 2 morning fire, with Gilda still asleep, was the doting husband. Just thinkin' out loud, it was suggested to Marquis that we could quietly pack up camp so as to not wake Mrs. Weaks, and slip away with the kidnapped (relieving him of all responsibility) Marquis before Gilda opened her eyes. You know, just delay the balance of the honeymoon a few days. Gilda could spend some quality time, Sunday through Tuesday, at Andy's Bar and we'd be back before you know it. Marquis decided that, as much fun as he knew he'd have with us, this was not the best way to begin married life. Once awake, Gilda could laugh at this plan since it was not executed.

Waving good-bye as Mister & Missus Weaks drove away, we then launched the canoes into the Fox River as the traditionally long Day 2 began. Sadly, our favorite buck dancer, Gomie, is not 4Dayin' with us this year. He did however, pick up a new 4Day nickname, a process that sprouted last week, the day after Marquis and Gilda entered matrimonial bliss...

On June 18, 2005, Marquis and Gilda were wed along the banks of the Rifle River, in front of a big crowd of family and friends, including many 4Dayers. "Love at the Livery" read the headline in the next edition of the Arenac County News, with a photo of the wedding party, who had canoed in their wedding finery to the ceremony being held at Russell's Canoe Livery in Omer, the self-proclaimed "Smallest City in Michigan". After a hard night of celebrating, wedding attendees camped at the livery, with a Rifle River canoe trip scheduled for tomorrow.

That next day, during a river paddling break, Gomie jumped into the water and stepped on the pointed branch of a fallen tree embedded in the river floor. Due to bad planning, he was barefoot, and the sharp branch punctured the bottom of his foot, slicing deep through the tissue. Ick! We took Gomie to the medical center in nearby Standish. Doctors told him there would be a high risk of infection if he put this foot into a river before the puncture healed. Gomie was assured by the medical staff that the puncture would not be healed before next week's 4Day.

Gomie aka Gomez, birth name Pat Carroll (useful info for this story), had not missed a 4Day since his rookie year of 1994, and sitting out this one was hard on him. To cheer our brother up, we called him from the elevated ground of Boot Hill during Day 2. When he answered, the boys gave him a loud 'n welcoming "Gomie!!!" We really missed our friend, and the phone call raised our spirits as much as it did his. After a few stories & much laughing on both ends of the phone, I said, "Gomie! Gomie! In honor of your foot injury, we got a new 4Day name for you: Shoeless Pat Carroll (Gomie was cracking up at this point; *pause for effect before finishing*)... the hillbilly fuck!" Dead silence on the other end of the line. "Gomie? Gomie? You still there?" After a long spell of quiet, Gomie slowly answered, "Yeah, I'm still here."

On the Day 2 adventure, Boot Hill is an hour downstream from today's launch, and another 7 to 9 hours from our goal this evening, the campground at the Peninsula. Today's plan is the same as 3 years ago, our last Fox River trip. We'll bypass the High Ground camp spot and paddle the extra two hours to the Peninsula, stay there tonight and tomorrow night, refraining from Day 3 paddling as the reward for a grueling Day 2, with 4 hours of canoeing remaining on the final day.

This section of the Fox never fails to be an exhausting, logjam-infested, canoe trip. It cannot be avoided as there is no access point between the Seney Township site and the Peninsula (except at the M28 bridge, but that's only 15 minutes from the start).

Logjams are what we refer to as a complete river blockage, spanning the entire width of the river from shore to shore, with no gaps to pass through. Some may be conquered through a portage: pulling the canoe on to a riverbank and carrying or dragging it to the downstream side of the logjam. If the undergrowth is too thick on or beyond the shore, a portage may not be possible. That leaves 3 remaining alternatives: (1) turn around and head home, (2) cut our way through (usually too time consuming) or (3) go over the logjam.

To go over the logjam, it's best to wait for other canoeists to arrive and work as a team: two guys in the river, one on each side of a canoe, push the nose of the boat out of the water, up and on to the fallen tree(s), where 2 or more waiting 4Dayers balancing on the tree(s) grab the canoe, pull it over the obstruction, and send it downstream to a waiting compadre or two. This process is repeated for each canoe sitting in front of the logjam.

*Author's note:* not posting someone downstream to catch a freed canoe is a mistake, although it can be entertaining watching friends in knee-deep water chasing an unmanned, floating boat.

Balancing on top of a logjam is an experience that ranges from real easy to very difficult. Real easy might be positioning yourself on a single thick, wide trunk that does not move when you stand on it. Very difficult might involve hoisting yourself up onto a tree or trees with many branches that break, give way, or sink under the weight of two men attempting to stand on them.

Of the first 25 4Days, 20 took place on the Fox. However, as the years go by and we get a little older, dragging heavy, fully loaded canoes up & out of the river and over big trees, an average of 12 times a trip, loses a little of its luster while the lure of an obstruction-free float down the wide Manistique becomes more enticing – the main reason it's been 3 years since we last paddled this section of the Fox River.

This year though, we sent in the Marines! From the Halls of Montezuma, to the Shores of… Germfask? Well, one marine and his companion, both seasoned Fox River men: USMC James Joseph Vollmers aka Jimmy (4Day class of 1982) and John Frederick Steck aka Johnny (4Day class of 1987).

A few beers after softball one night, among much chatter about Fox River logjams, Jimmy and Johnny came up with a brilliant idea to attack the problem: they would go to the U.P. a couple of days before the 4Day began, and clear a path through the various river impediments. To do the job, they would arm themselves with a striking arsenal of manual tools including hatchets, axes, machetes, pruners, bow saws, brush saws, and brute strength. Talk of bringing along dynamite and gas or battery-powered tools, despite the pluses of high entertainment value and quicker task attainment, were rejected to reduce the risk of loss of limb or death.

The advantages they would have versus the traditional 4Day journey on these same waters were two: starting early (never happens with big groups) and, despite the impressive catalog of manual tools, traveling light with a minimum of gear, food & drink (minimize drink on a 4Day? Never!). The boys would create a canoe-wide gap through as many barriers as possible, drawing attention to each gap created by marking it with an orange tie. Where practical, they chose to clear an area where the current would naturally push our canoes. By traveling light, they would be able to more easily negotiate river blockages where gaps could not be carved, allowing faster & more efficient movement.

Jimmy and Johnny would be a modern-day "Corps of Discovery", the 4Day version of Lewis and Clark. Not a perfect analogy, but one that felt right. By the time the 4Dayers made the phone call from Boot Hill to the wounded Gomie back in Jacksonville, the fifth of Old Bardstown circulating on the Hill was now gone. It was time to get back into the canoes, the boys eager to spot the first orange tie and witness Jimmy & Johnny's handiwork.

Spirits were almost as high as the sunny skies above as we paddled downstream. Kenny and I sang Jimmy Buffett songs, some of the early stuff, as we canoed together, *"And I'm somewhere, below the sunlight, somewhere upon the sea, you dig deep enough you might find me, find me, cause that's where I'll be" & "Across from the bar there's a pile of beer cans, been there twenty-seven years, imagine all the heartaches and tears, in twenty-seven years of beers".*

The singing was replaced by "Oh shit!" as we raced around a right bend at great speed, and could not avoid a sharpened, broken branch, positioned 2' above and parallel to the water, pointed directly at us, leaning into the river from the left shore. In the stern, I steered Kenny away from it, but I was not as lucky. The honed edge of the branch dug itself 2 inches into my left thigh. "Son of a bitch, this hurts! Damn Kenny, this stick is pretty deep inside me." Kenny looked concerned, "Well, is it wearin' a condom?" I didn't see that question comin' and it immediately changed how I viewed the situation. "I gotta admit, the streaming blood makes it look like the branch struck oil. It's like the bubblin' crude in the first Beverly Hillbillies' episode. Cool!"

Beaching the canoe, I dug out the First Aid kit, cleaned and bandaged the wound, thankful that it was well above the knee. This would improve the chances of keeping the laceration free of river water, aware that there would be times today that we would have to hop out of the boat and get into the river, in order to drag the canoe through areas too shallow or obstructed. Not to mention times required to get into the Fox in order to scramble on top of logjams.

"Orange tie here! Orange tie!" shouts echoed through the forest as the lead canoes arrived at the first tie, a tie that marked an opening created on the far left of a thick barrier of branches bridging the two river banks. The gap created hugged the shoreline and, as promised, was large enough for a canoe to pass through.

In quick succession, several more orange ties were seen, each directing us to a canoe-wide barrier gap we could easily pass through. A few of the larger logjams were not ones that Jimmy and Johnny's pre-4Day work could overcome, but their overall efforts likely saved us a couple of hours of hard labor. It's extremely fortunate that their endeavor was undertaken this year, or we might not have reached the camp until midnight: even with the boys coming up to the U.P. early to open paddling gaps for us, the last canoe did not make it to the Peninsula until 10PM, with barely enough light remaining for a safe landing.

The Colonel and Kenny managed to whip up a full chicken dinner that the half-asleep 4Dayers thankfully ate before collapsing into their tents. There would be a full day in camp tomorrow to resume the party.

The next morning sun's rays broke through the Peninsula's forest canopy, warming tents still-occupied until the scent and sound of sizzling bacon permeated the campground. The chorus of tent zippers sliding down zipper tracks was a promissory note, announcing that soon men with metal, paper, or plastic plates would surround the breakfast fire, waiting their turn to access the pan of eggs, muffins, and sizzling bacon prepared by chefs Johnny and Vid.

Tales were soon being told of, and thanks given for, the outstanding 4Day prep work done by our Lewis & Clark team of Jimmy & Johnny. Their efforts paid dividends yesterday <u>and</u> today: this morning, it prompted a group toast from a fifth of Fleischmann's Whiskey. Vid pointed out that the word "Preferred" is on the bottle's label, so it must be good.

Johnny switched the conversation to EMU 1998 grad Earl Boykins, "The guy is all of 5'5 and 133 pounds, although I read that he can bench press 315, and a few months ago scored 15 points in overtime one night. Earl broke the 21-year old NBA record of 14 points, and basically won the game for the Denver Nuggets. This by the second shortest player in NBA history. Amazing!"

For a few hours of river time sans canoes, we enjoyed diving in the water for Frisbees tossed our way and holding onto floating canoe cushions, with only our head and feet above the waterline, as they carried us around the oxbow-shaped Peninsula. Afterward, buzz euchre games broke out near our tents. Veteran buzz euchre players know hard lessons gained from experience that it's always best to play close to your tent. During one of the euchre games, I told, re-told for some, the story of the horse named Giacomo. "So we're in Loo-ville last month, below the twins spires at Churchill Downs, the First Saturday in May, for the 131st Run for the Roses."

Ron laughed, "Doc, you got a story somewhere in here?" "Yeah, I'm getting to it. So this horse Giacomo is going off at 50 to 1, longest shot in the Kentucky Derby field. I place $20 Derby bets each year for my sisters, their husbands, my folks, and Nona - my Mom's Mom - on whatever horse they want. Coincidentally, my Mom's folks came over from Italy a century ago and their last name was Zandegiacomo. With the family association to the name, my Mom, Nona, and sister Karen all put their $20 on Giacomo. Chris asked me to put $10 on Giacomo, too, for his daughter Madelynn. Maggie and I bet the same $10 on Giacomo."

"So the race starts. From the Derby infield, I can't see the track, but I'm following it on the radio. The horses are at the quarter pole, now halfway, and Giacomo's not even mentioned. I'm figuring he's done. As they're rounding the turn for the home stretch, it gets quiet on the radio for a couple seconds, like the announcer doesn't know what's happening. Then he starts yelling, *"Here comes Giacomo! Here comes Giacomo! Here comes Giacomo!"* I'm going nuts, standing on the infield, the radio on my ear, kinda galloping in place and hitting my leg, screaming "Come on you nag!" over and over. I'm the only one yelling on the infield, because nobody bet on this horse. So Giacomo wins, and pays $1,026 on each of the $20 bets, $513 on the $10 bets. I phoned my Mom and Nona from the Churchill Downs infield with the good news, and they squealed like high school girls. It gives me goose bumps just thinking about it."

"Gomie & Vid walk up to the pay window with me, and I slide the winning tickets to the cashier. Now she's excited. "Oh, I love giving the track's money away. You have a lot coming, so have your friends stand tall behind you to block the view of all this cash." So I look behind me to see what I have to work with in terms of bodyguards. Gomie's starting to stagger from all the Mint Juleps today, and is flat on the ground in 5 minutes, and Vid's saying, "I'm doing the best that I can", being like 5' tall and all. Vid interrupts the story, "Hey! I'm 5 feet 6 inches." That's a valid point you have Vidder. Maggie and I left most of our winnings in Louisville that night, buying dinner & drinks for the group. Back home we thoroughly enjoyed the look on Mom, Nona, and Karen's faces when we counted out each of their $1,026 in winnings for them. It was the second-longest odds for a winning racehorse in the 131 years of the Derby. Giacomo, what a horse!"

Buzz euchre playing came to a stop for the lavish dinner prepared by Chris and Ron, a treat of steak 'n crab legs with veggies. We've come a long way from the wet salami sandwich dinners in 4Days of yore. Warm belly effect quieted the fellas, many lighting cigars and pulling up camp chairs along the river to watch its beauty flow by. After sunset and a little more euchre by table lamp, we stretched out on the ground and listened to a Rodney Dangerfield tape, leading to some good-natured teasing about my drunken sot stint last year as Pop, from Rodney's, "what are we gonna do about Pop?", before one by one the boys wandered off to their tents, calling it a night.

Shoving off from the Peninsula on Day Four, we passed two more of Johnny & Jimmy's orange ties, their work allowing us easy passage at a couple fallen trees. Within an hour, we arrived at the new steel bridge for our first paddling break. Standing on the bridge, looking downstream and to the left, we watched the Manistique River emerge from the forest at its confluence with the Fox. Standing on this familiar spot, our thoughts turned to Chucky, who shared this scene with us many times.

Chucky has been suffering from a debilitating depression for 2 years now. It's so sad that our brother, one of the most endearing people that you'll ever meet, cannot get out of the mental black hole he lives in. The fact that he cannot express the love he's always had for others, and feel their love in return, is maddening. Chris brought out one of his many bottles of Mad Dog, and we all took a pull from it in honor of Chucky. With cigar smoke hanging in the air, the voices soon joined in for a Roger Miller favorite, "Dang me, dang me, they oughta take a rope and hang me. High from the highest tree, woman would you weep for me."

Nearing the end of the 4Day, we floated together sharing a fifth of Early Times and absorbing the beauty of the gentle river and the woodland it flows through. I asked Vid to tell the story of his infamous school bus trip, and he accommodated.

"My Jackson 3rd grade class took a bus trip to the Kellogg's Post Cereal plant in Battle Creek. It was a warm October day, and everybody's excited because you don't have to go to school. All the kids got to eat Coco Krispies, a new cereal being introduced by Kellogg's. Later, the bus stopped at a roadside park so the kids could to eat their lunch. Their attention was drawn to a merry-go-round that sat 20 people, the biggest one I've ever seen in my life. It had double-pumpers, kind of rowing the boat. So we ate our lunch and, in probably 37 seconds, jumped on that rascal. We spun, and spun, and spun. Looking back at it, that was a huge mistake. Everyone got back on the bus. Well, that spinning messed up many stomachs. I think we made it on to the highway before the first kid threw up. You could smell it immediately. Then the second kid threw up, and I went oh-oh. When the third kid threw up, somebody opened a window and then other windows were opened. Normally that's good when the bus is parked, but when the bus is moving, the puke started to whip back in. Now you can't get fresh air from the open window without getting vomit sprayed on you. The vomit is starting to come down the aisle, and I'm on an aisle seat. So I'm looking up and looking down the aisle, wondering where to go. It's gotta be at least 4 kids have vomited now, and the teacher stands up and vomits. When the teacher starts throwing up, every girl and at least half the boys start crying, or vomiting, or both. It's sloshing around on the longest drive ever back to Jackson. I do remember the look on the bus driver's face, and he was just disgusted, like, "Oh my God, get off the bus! Don't ever come back on this bus!" I'm sure he retired. It was the last time I ever had Coco Krispies."

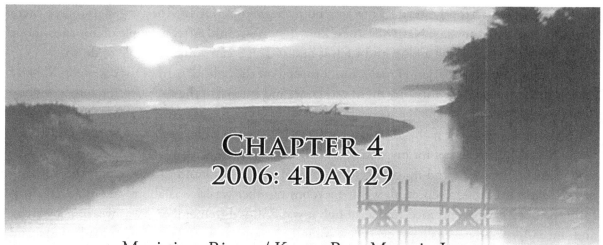

# CHAPTER 4
## 2006: 4DAY 29

Manistique River w/ Kenny, Ron, Marquis, Jason,
Moth, Big Guy, Chris, Vid, Gomie, Johnny, Brittany
(ashes), Doc and rookies Neal and Gillam

*Nashville cats, play clean as country water*
*Nashville cats, play wild as mountain dew*
*Nashville cats, been playin' since they's babies*
*Nashville cats, get work before they're two*
*(Nashville Cats by the Lovin Spoonful)*

Flying in June, I headed to Nashville for the annual National Sales Meeting of my long-time employer, Duracell. This would be the first national meeting since Duracell became a division of Proctor & Gamble. The P&G folks seemed nice enough, and asked me to stay. However, unlike Duracell, they are a Stepford-like conglomerate. Upon their acquisition of my battery company, I decided that we would part ways at the end of September, the 30th anniversary of my hiring by Duracell. 4Dayer Kenny and our buddy Tommy concurred and also planned their departure.

Nashville's Opryland, a bloated, glitzy, Hollywood version of the nearby original Grand Old Opry, hosted the meeting (one Opryland positive: a man-made river flows through it). The gathering's opening night would be a succession of presentations by P&G management, presenting future strategies of which I would not be a part. Without a reason to stay for tonight's speeches, 15 minutes after the program began, Kenny, Tommy, and I slipped out of the large meeting room and caught a cab to Broadway Street, home to Nashville's honky tonks.

What a wonderful decision! Across the alley from the Ryman Auditorium, home to the original Grand Old Opry, sits Broadway Street, one long row of honky tonks, all featuring outstanding country musicians. You don't have to like country to appreciate what's offered here. We checked out Robert's Western World first, where tonight's band was dressed like Hank Williams and the Drifting Cowboys and sounded amazingly like them. After several ole' Hank numbers, they covered the Marty Robbins' song we'd played so many 4Day-eves in Mackinaw City on the Keyhole Lounge juke box, *A White Sport Coat & a Pink Carnation*. Marty woulda been proud.

Believing we'd only been at Robert's for an hour, we were surprised when several Duracell friends who'd stayed for the entire 3 meeting hours began filtering in. They urged us to join them down the street at Tootsie's, Nashville's best known honky tonk. After a couple of Tootsie's shots, the evening was becoming a blur, and I felt it best to hail a cab while still able to do so.

Ambling into my Opryland hotel room, I turned off the light to turn in for the night. When I awoke, it was not yet morning, my room was gone, and I stood in the dark, staring into a brightly lit hallway.

Slowly but surely, the realization of my fascinating situation dawned on me: I stood outdoors, with no clothing on except for my watch, a small watch at that, with a locked door separating me from the hotel hallway, and no pockets where a key might be found to let me into the building or my room, if I could even recall what my room number was! I was about one hundred yards from the hotel's main entrance, and although it was 230AM (remember, I <u>was</u> wearing a watch), and since Opryland never sleeps, every few minutes a tour bus would pull up, unload guests, and depart.

Hiding from the arriving buses, I sat behind an 8' tall row of bushes running parallel to and about 5' away from the hotel wall. Situated bare-assed in the dirt, the thoughts running through my head varied from giggling at George Costanza pretending to be a porn star working under the name "Buck Naked", to asking myself, "How you gonna get out of this one, fuck-head?"

Running perpendicular to the locked door, a metal railing caught my attention. On the other side of the railing sat a loading dock with a light on over both the large bay door and the smaller door next to it. Timing my move around the precise bus schedule, I cupped myself with one hand and sprinted down the sloping concrete dock to the smaller door. Damn, it's locked, too. Had it not been, I imagine late-shift workers busy on the other side of the door might still be telling the story of the night the naked hotel guest paid them a visit.

Retreating to my dirt seat behind the tall bushes, I waited until the next bus drove off. Once it disappeared from view, I stood again at the door separating my darkness from the beckoning hallway light, on the extreme longshot that the door would now be magically unlocked. No such luck. But a hotel employee appeared, walking down the hallway in my direction with a room service tray. I knocked on the door with my one free hand, walking a fine line between not knocking too frantically and awakening the guest in the room nearest this door, but loud enough to be heard. The employee looked my way as I mouthed the words, "I'm a guest! I'm a guest!"

Setting his tray down, the employee walked towards me, opened the door, and asked quite matter-a-factly, "How are you this evening, sir?" How am I this evening, sir? Is nude drunk-walking a common occurrence here? "I'm fine. Thank you so much for letting me in." "My pleasure sir." I asked if there was a house phone nearby, and the staff member (*staff member* – that's funny) directed me to the wall phone down a short hallway to my right. I called the front desk. "Hi, this is Jeff Fletcher, a hotel guest, and I'm locked out of my room without any clothes on." I told them where I was calling from (with no idea of my room number) and asked if they would please bring a key and a towel.

Hanging up, I noticed that the door to the room maybe 20' away from the house phone was not fully closed. Could this *possibly* be *my* room? I knocked on the door to no answer, probably a very good thing ("Hi, did you call the House Dick?"), slowly pushing the door open. There is my briefcase… there is my laptop (idiot)… there are my clothes… this IS my room! Hallelujah!! I quickly called the front desk, let them know I was in the room, cancelled the key and towel, thanked them and their staff profusely, and then hung up. It turns out that I had been drunk-walking, sleep-walking with a great deal of alcohol thrown in. I soon recalled that Opryland room service is 24 hours, so I picked up the phone once more and ordered a celebratory pizza. Apparently the Good Lord has assigned TWO Guardian Angels to keep an eye on my sorry ass.

Thoughts of the previous evening's adventure kept pushing out of my head any attempt to think business thoughts at the next day's meetings. It was a strange and happy day. 20 years prior was the 1986 release of *Ferris Bueller's Day Off*. I suddenly felt a strong kinship to Ferris, finding parallels between his relief at day's end, barely dodging retribution from his principal & getting back into bed before his parents came into his room, and my salvation at last evening's end.

4Day 29 getaway day arrived exactly two weeks after flying home from my naked Nashville adventure. Halfway into the 6-hour drive to Curtis, the boys planned rendezvous found them in mid-Michigan's Houghton Lake for shells of Blatz beer at the Nottingham Bar. Is there anything more-tasty than a fresh Blatz from the Nottingham tap? Mm, yes there is: a Blatz draft with pizza! So, between shells poured for us by barkeep Joanne, I made the 2 mile drive for a Little Caesar's Pizza carryout order.

Hoisting high our Blatz beers, we toasted the companionship of the recently passed puppy, 4Dayer Brittany. This year's 4Day invitation christened the 29th edition of the trip as…

### *The Brittany Memorial*

*4Day fact: 49 folks have joined us during 28 years of 4Dayin'*
*4Day fact: only 14 of the 49 have been on more 4Days than Brittany*
*4Day fact: Brittany had been on nine 4Days ('96–'03 and '05)*
*Now **THAT'S** a Party Animal!*

Honoring his dear Brittany's life, Chris painted her face on to a Frisbee, working some of the puppy's cremated ashes into the artwork, and carried it with him each day on the river. Following the Circle of Life, the 4Dayers mourned the loss of a critter who could always be found near an open can of Pabst, while welcoming two rookies, Neal Linkon and Gary Gillam.

Introduced to the group in his 1970s college days by fellow-Michigan State Spartan Big Guy, is Rookie Neal. A man cerebral, passionate, hard-working, funny, and predictable, the rookie says no 3 times when a fifth is passed his way, and caves the 4th time ("Neal! Neal! Neal!" "Ok"). Rookie Neal wrote a book that was published in 1993, "The Blade", an espionage thriller with ties to the Defense and Space Industry in which he used to make a living. It's a great read, and not just in the vault toilets found at 4Day campsites.

Rookie Gillam defended our country with Chris in the 80s on the U.S. Naval ship S.S. Saratoga. Goofy, good-natured, work-shy, and a joker, the rookie won quite a few bar wagers over the years. "I bet you that I have your name tattooed on my ass." After the bet was placed, he'd drop his drawers and, sure enough, the words "Your Name" were printed on his butt cheeks.

Entering Curtis 6PM 4Day-eve, we grabbed our rooms at the Rally Inn and walked briskly the several feet to Kim's Mc's Tally Ho where plenty of Pabsts, Rolling Rocks, Cuervo, Bourbon, and burgers had been stocked in anticipation of our arrival. Rookie Neal, having driven here from his Milwaukee-area home through the western U.P., had a couple of beers under his belt when the other 12 of us walked through the door. Besides glasses raised to Brittany, many were lifted in memory of the old bar owner, the dearly-departed Betsy. Kim runs a fine pub, but it's not the same without Betsy's presence, laughs, and stories shared from her favorite bar stool.

Rising early the next morning, Wayne's words of wisdom from his very first 4Day in 1986, back when Navy men Chris and Rookie Gillam were keeping America safe, resonated with us: "Chow Time is important". To that end, we wandered down Curtis' Main Street to Stamper's Restaurant for breakfast, while the night before I visited the town's pizzeria, the Pizza Stop, placing an order that would be delivered to the Northland Outfitters' campground later tonight.

Paddling would take place this year on the laid-back Manistique River, traveling through its gorgeous forest of pine and maple trees. We sang Martin Mull's "Men", sipped P.M. Whiskey, and, recognizing 15 years had passed since he left us in 1991, quoted our favorite lines from John Voelker's *Testament to a Fisherman*, "*Because only in the woods can I find solitude without loneliness; Because bourbon out of an old tin cup always tastes better out there.*"

"Since we're noting so many anniversaries this year," I mentioned "how about a few words from a man celebrating his 20th 4Day, Johnny?" When the cheers died down, Johnny said, "Well, I do have a joke that I'd heard. A guy died, went to heaven, and met St. Peter, who asked, "Have you ever done anything of merit?" The guy thinks a minute and says, "Yes. One time I was on my way to Sturgis and came across a group of bikers about to assault this woman. So, I went up to the biggest, meanest one, pushed him in the chest and told them to leave her alone!" St. Peter was really impressed, "When did this happen?" he asked. "Just a few minutes ago."

Driving together and joining us two days into the trip were Moth and Big Guy. It was Moth's first 4Day since 1998, Biggie's first since the "Yankee's Suck" t-shirt year of 2002. They left home Sunday morning, as we began the Day 2 paddle, and planned to meet us late-afternoon when we paddled into the Mead Creek Campground. As Mead Creek came into view, we saw Biggie relaxing in his camp chair on a small hill under some shade trees. Our shouts of "Big Guy! Big Guy!" from the canoes were met by an almost imperceptible nod of the head, a frown, and one finger pointed upward, kinda like, "This level of enthusiasm is all I can muster for you."

Dragging boats and gear ashore, the boys greeted the new arrivals, fully aware that something was not quite right with Big Guy. Helping Moth set his tent up, I asked what was happening with Biggie. "Oh, he's been a pain in the ass all day long. When I drove over to his place to pick him up, I was all fired up shouting *4Day!* He didn't even say hi. Instead, he told me that he wasn't bringing any supplies with him 'cause he was gonna mooch off everyone – his exact words."

Rookie Gillam took the day off from canoeing, spending it at the Mead Creek camp. Vid asked him, "Well, at least you haven't been wasting time gathering firewood. What have you been doing all day?" "I didn't know I could gather firewood." Color the group laughter incredulous. Vid shook his head, "What?! You didn't know you could gather firewood? Look at your rookie brother!" As soon as we hit camp, Rookie Neal was making multiple trips into the woods, each time bringing back deadwood for the evening's bonfire. "What is this, good rookie, bad rookie?"

***"What the fuck is this?!"*** shattered the next morning's early peacefulness. As dawn broke on

Day 3, Moth crawled out of his tent and stood alongside it, pointing to the ground. "Someone took a dump right outside of my tent!"

Labeling this mound *just a dump* is to call Secretariat *just a horse*. The words simply do not do it justice. The sheer mountain-like size of the dump was startling in contrast to the tiny amount of toilet paper sitting perilously high atop it, paling in comparative size. Were it not for the tissue's presence, it would've been fair to assume a humongous and badly-constipated black bear had finally found relief from a long-impacted stool.

The dump's crude proximity was no more than 5' from both the breakfast fire pit and Moth's tent. A tent that he shared with...

### *"Big Guy! Sonofabitch!"*

Realization of the culprit's identity hit Moth like a gash to his forehead (see 1994 chapter Day 4). Now the entire camp, except for Moth's still-snoring tent partner, was up, gagging from the odor while studying the situation from a distance. Exasperated, Moth pointed to the dirt path running away from the river. "And one of the nicest outhouses we've ever seen on a canoe trip is no more than 100' from his dump." Then the really bad news hit Moth. "And I gotta make breakfast by that shit pile!" Ironically, sharing responsibilities for the morning grub with Moth was Big Guy. A fifth of Early Times was quickly located and passed to Moth to put a smile on his pain.

Kenny, venturing a guess, declared, "Maybe Big Guy's sour mood was from a massive crap that needed to come out." Maybe. But what we do know is that Big Guy's overnight dump instantly went down in 4Day lore as the "breakfast surprise".

Woken from his sleep, Bigus' words and manner neither denied nor admitted to the incident. In later years, with the passage of time and brain cells, Big Guy said, "May I say somebody musta hit me in the head when I wasn't looking. I know nothing about this so-called event of when ya gotta go, ya gotta go. Are we sure this wasn't the gravy Moth forgot to bring in stool guise? My memory avoids me."

Subsequent to this extraordinary dump, a one year closure of the Mead Creek campground was ordered by Michigan's Department of Natural Resources. It's possible the closure was due to a reallocation of the DNR's limited funding to a more widely-used campground, but it's also possible, considered likely by those who witnessed Mount Big Pile, that the closing took place to allow sufficient visits by hazmat units until the area could be declared safe for human existence.

*Author's note:* brother-in-law Jeff tells us that, even today, local Potawatomi tribes speak in hushed tones of the dump, whispering of *Big Guy's Day of Deposit*. For area hikers, the dump is referred to as *Cinco dias de Biggie* or *Biggie's Five Day*, due to additional time required to get over or around the snow-capped Mount Big Pile.

Evacuation of camp took place a little sooner than usual this morning, the boys' nostril intake providing some extra giddy-up to their steps as they loaded the canoes and shoved off. Only four hours of paddling, with two days to get there, were between today's starting point and our end point of Cookson Bridge, accentuating the laid-back nature of it all.

Tugging from a fifth of Old Overholt, like clockwork the 4th time he was badgered (remember: "Neal! Neal! Neal!" "Ok"), Rookie Neal opened up about what an incredible adventure this first 4Day was turning out to be, and about one man in particular. "Man, I love Marquis. His statement to me of, 'You ain't no rookie', sure made me feel welcome." We pointed out to him that "Fetch me a beer, rookie!" was a welcome statement in its own way. "That's true," the rook replied, "and making sure that I knew the importance of bringing a good river chair, one with a back on it, for the evening fires was greatly appreciated."

Floating downstream, baseball was as popular a topic as ever, especially with Tigers first-year manager Jimmy Leyland having our Bengals in first place at the just concluded first half of the season. All those firsts got the baseball stories going...

*Chris was telling us about 2 announcers in the broadcast booth. One says into the microphone, "In a surprise line-up move today, they'll be batting the Son of God in the clean-up spot" The other one looks at him, shaking his head, "It's pronounced Hay-Soos... HAY-SOOS!... Geez."*

*Marquis said he saw an interview with Bob Uecker sharing his career highlight, "I walked with the bases loaded to drive in the winning run in an intra-squad game in spring training."*

We stopped early Day 3, a luxury due to the short time remaining to paddle these last 2 days. A gorgeous sandy shore called us in, the canoes beached, emptied, and camp set up. Johnny had needed a fix while waiting for this year's 4Day, and he fulfilled it by going on a shopping spree for new fire gloves, a cooking grate, and a two-burner camp stove. These items were put to good use by tonight's cooks, Chris and rookies Gillam & Neal, for their presentation of an outstanding 4Day stew, a dish rounded out nicely with cold PBRs and a post-supper stogie.

Burping around the campfire under a clear, starry night, talk turned to how amazing it is that 5 years have passed since Curtis bar owner and our dear Betsy passed away. Mentioning that fact stirred up some stories, including a Big Guy recollection from a few years before the 4Day crew initially gathered in her tavern. "My first memory of Mc's Tally Ho was when Goobs and I stopped in for a drink on one of our travels. John was the bartender, and he introduced us to a Rainbow Shot: Cuervo Gold, shot of O.J., and a shot of tomato juice. I also remember him giving me two "mistake" drinks before I ordered my first beer. What a joint, I'm thinkin'. In walks this older woman with a brown bag of groceries in her arms and she says to us, "Would you two boys bring those cases in my trunk inside?" We did as instructed and brought four cases of liquor into the bar. She had disappeared into the backroom, then came out and said, "Thank you boys! I'm Betsy and I own this place." Goobs offered to buy her a drink, but Betsy said, "It's my turn now", as we proceeded to get liquored up with our two new U.P. friends."

Turning over in their sleeping bags, in no hurry to rise Day 4 morning, the boys heard, "Money is no way to ensure wealth, son." Gomie stoked the morning fire while quoting Robert Duvall's character in a new TV western mini-series, "Broken Trail." The boys were excited about this show, being fans of another such series with Duvall, one from back in 1989, "Lonesome Dove". Duvall's portrayal of Augustus McCrae was outstanding, and the gradually awakening fellas starting throwing out Gus quotes...

"Ain't much of a crime, whackin' a surly bartender." "The older the violin, the sweeter the music." "I'd like the chance to shoot an educated man once in my life." After cutting the cards with Lorie to determine if she'll have sex with him or not, she asks him if he won by cheating. "I won't say I did, and I won't say I didn't, but I will say that a man who wouldn't cheat for a poke don't want one bad enough." When Pea Eye asks Gus, "What Indians is we're fightin' anyway?" Gus tells him, "They didn't introduce themselves." On his death bed, Augustus says his last words to his best friend, Captain Call, "My God Woodrow, it's been quite a party, ain't it."

"Augustus is my favorite character", I joined in, "but the best line is by Tommy Lee Jones's Captain Call. When he steps out of the bar with Gus and sees an Army scout whipping his son, Call goes nuts, slamming the scout's head into an anvil, damn near killing the guy until Augustus lassos him to calm things down. A large group of townspeople gathered, kind of in shock at the violence. Captain Call looks at 'em and says, "I hate rude behavior in a man. I won't tolerate it."

Spooning out a hot 'n filling breakfast of eggs 'n sausage from the big pan were today's morning chefs Johnny, Gomie, and Vid. Expressions of thanks congratulated Big Guy for not laying another "breakfast surprise" on us, continuing the serious teasing that was never far from the surface since Moth almost stepped in it yesterday morning. With only 90 minutes of actual paddle time until the 4Day's end, it was a leisurely tearing down of camp before we shoved the canoes into the Manistique, allowing the gentle current to move us southwest, slowly.

Taking a long draw from a fifth of Ten High, Marquis said, "What a shame that they tore down the Lindell A.C. this year." The bar opened 1949 in downtown Detroit's Cass Corridor by the Butsicaris Family, Greek immigrant Meleti and sons Jimmy and Johnny. National newspapers called it the number one sports-themed bar in America, one of the first of its kind. After the Tigers clinched the 1968 pennant, the team congregated there, players going behind the bar to give out free drinks to their deliriously-happy fans packed shoulder-to-shoulder inside. Hundreds more joined the Lindell party on the sidewalks and streets surrounding the bar. Vid had a good Lindell story, "A.C. regular Sonny Eliot had the old TV show, *At the Zoo*, and brought a baby elephant into the bar. Jimmy Butsicaris fed the elephant a Coke, and it shit all over the bar floor. Jimmy B. said he learned to never again let an elephant drink a Coke in his bar."

Big Guy, blistered by mid-day, canoed today with Rookie Neal. Kenny asked, "Neal, why is Big Guy in the front of the boat?" A good question since, generally, you want your girth in the stern, and Biggie outweighs Rookie Neal by 70 pounds. "I don't know why, but he insisted that I be in the back." Between the extra weight up front, and a wobbly Big Guy too drunk to assist in the paddling, the boys zig-zagged their way down the river, banging into trees previously unknown to exist, creating the possibility of a Big Guy dump of a different sort.

Cookson Bridge, materializing around the final bend, arrived much too soon for all except possibly the Big Guy & Rookie Neal boat. Moth started barking about how short a trip this was, and the need for a refund. Vid told me, "Doc, I don't know why you refer to Moth as pleasantly obnoxious. He dropped the *pleasant* years ago".

*Author's note*: during October, the Tigers defeated the Yankees Suck in their first ever post-season match-up! Jimmy Leyland for Mayor!

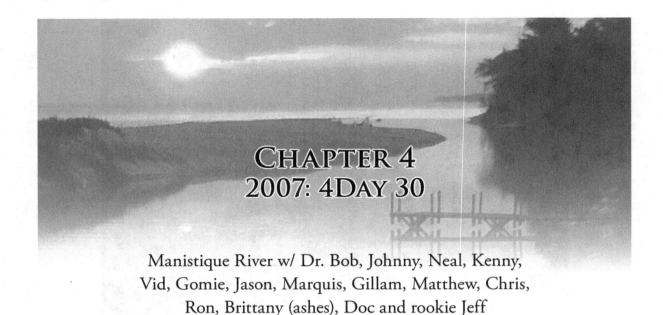

# CHAPTER 4
# 2007: 4DAY 30

Manistique River w/ Dr. Bob, Johnny, Neal, Kenny,
Vid, Gomie, Jason, Marquis, Gillam, Matthew, Chris,
Ron, Brittany (ashes), Doc and rookie Jeff

*I gave my love a cherry, that had no stone,*
*I gave my love a chicken, that had no bone,*
*I gave my love a story, that had no end,*
*I gav... (guitar grabbed, smashed to smithereens; Belushi, "Sorry, huh.")*
*(I Gave My Love a Cherry by Stephen Bishop)*

The 4Day is fondly thought of as *Animal-House-on-the-water*.

4Dayers are a fraternity of brother canoeists. Shouting *"Boot!"* alerts them that a boot-shaped shot glass full of rot gut whiskey is headed their way.

To Dartmouth College's Delta Fraternity, circa 1960-1962, *"Boot!"* meant something a bit different. According to Delta member, National Lampoon writer, and author Chris Miller's 2006 book, "The Real Animal House", to the Deltas "booting" or "to boot" meant a simple vomit, the ability to call up a puke for the sheer joy of it, ideally vomiting for distance. In the basement of the frat house, where the bar was located, guys would step behind a chalk line, chug beers and see if they could "power boot" on to the opposite wall, several feet away. Providing targets and inspiration were large photos on the wall, including one of Arlene Francis (guess they didn't like "What's My Line"). At the end of each night, frat sophomores were required to hose the vomit down into the gutter along the wall beneath Miss Francis and friends.

"The Real Animal House" stories, told for years before the book came out, served as the basis for the 1978 movie "Animal House". Those Dartmouth Delta frat brothers' crazed antics went beyond the pale. It was with great surprise to find that the movie is a timid version of this real, non-compos mentis (i.e. loco), Animal House.

Transformation of the Alpha Delta House from decades as a fairly normal fraternity to a zoo fraternity started with Dartmouth's class of 1956, the first class with a large number of vets from the Korean War. Many of these vets pledged Delta House. Guys who survived all the hell of a war were not about to turn into, to quote the book, "nice, middle-class, college boys." The wildest among them might have been a guy known by his Delta nickname of Rat Battles. One day the frat hosted a faculty dinner, a tuxedo affair. Rat drank 19 glasses of heavily alcohol-laced punch and then, according to the book, power pissed a distance of 20', wayward drops falling on faculty members, into the roaring fireplace. The piss stream smell that rolled out with the smoke gagged everyone present. A frat brother noted, "No one's grades improved that day."

With 2007 marking 30-years-of-4Dayin, it seemed that the proper way to begin the celebration required a visit to our favorite pub-on-the-way stop, the Nottingham. This bar was enjoying their own anniversary, marking 60 years since a 1947 move of the tavern, and many of its patrons, from Detroit to a new home 3 hours north in Houghton Lake.

Drinking Blatz on tap since first spending time in the tavern in 1993, the boys ordered a round of "Milwaukee's Finest Beer" (1950s paid-spokesman Groucho Marx said so himself) as soon as they hit the door. With a grin on her face that hid the awful truth, owner Virgy informed us, "Our beer distributor no longer carries Blatz," prompting gasps from the boys. "Now we have Busch on tap." The baseball analogy would be, "The 1935 Tigers aren't available, but we do have the 2003 version to fill in" OR "Now pinch-hitting for Al Kaline, Ray Oyler." Argh.

A round of shots, "Old Grand-Dad please", was ordered to ease the bye-bye-Blatz news. It is our good fortune that Virgy is a helluva story-teller, and her entertaining anecdotes enabled 4Dayers to stop dwelling for a bit on the sad loss of Blatz at the Nottingham.

Virginia "Virgy" Kalis, 82 years young, came to Houghton Lake in 1980 to stay 4 weeks with her good friend and Nottingham owner Helen. "I liked the area 'n the bar, so I stretched out the 4-week vacation with Helen to 24 years". When Helen passed away in the early-2000s, she left her house and the Nottingham to Virgy in her will. Virgy's comments about her life in Houghton Lake started to wander from subject to subject. "When I joined the bowling league, they typed 'Virgin' on my bowling shirt. A friend walked by and said 'Must be an old shirt'. People wonder if I'm home or at the bar. I tell 'em if they're at my house, ring the doorbell. If it takes 3 rings to get me, I'm home. If you ring 5 times and I haven't answered, I'm at the bar".

Finishing her thoughts before attending to some other customers, Virgy said, "Helen told me Blatz has been on tap at the Nottingham since she and her husband opened it in '47." It's rare to find Blatz on tap anywhere these days, the original draw bringing us into the Nottingham as the place to stop on our way to the U.P. Throwing out a few ideas back 'n forth, Kenny and I put together a brief tribute to the long run Blatz enjoyed here, calling it the *Canoer's Blues*: "Six months shy of 60 years/ Cigarette butts 'n empty beers/ There's no more Blatz/We'll shed a tear/ Six months shy of 60 years".

Maggie, Gilda, Toni, and Mister P drove up to join the 30th celebration festivities taking place 4Day-eve in Curtis. The day before Curtis, the 4 accompanied Gomie, Kenny, Marquis and me on a one day canoe trip down the Two Hearted River, taking it to its rivermouth as it flows into Lake Superior. In addition to the engaging ones mentioned above, Star the Canoeing Dog came dressed in a bikini. Gilda assured Star that, as long as two of her eight mammary glands were covered, there was nothing about which to be embarrassed. Looking at the bikini along with the pink visor Star wore, Maggie assured Gilda, "That ship has sailed."

The Rainbow Lodge livery, at the mouth of the Two Hearted River, is 16 desolate washboard-road miles from civilization. The bumpy drive fried my power locks to the tune of $200, money I found well-spent. For despite Maggie's on-the-river protestation of, "I'm experiencing unruly fly behavior, with an ankle emphasis", we found paddling the river alongside gorgeous sandy beaches and through a thick forest of pine to be delightful. 30 minutes before we even saw the Lake Superior end-point, the sound of the surf crashing on the shoreline echoed through the surrounding forest, a sound only surpassed by Gilda's shouted request to her canoeing partner, "Marquis, would you please wake up and get me back to shore!"

To further our 30th celebration, Kim's Mc's Tally Ho Bar organized a pig roast with 44 pounds of roasted pork, injected with pineapple and barbeque sauce, along with corn-on-the-cob and cole slaw.

Tossing horseshoes on the lawn between the bar and our motel rooms, while knocking down a whole lot of beers, prompted Gomie to observe, "I can argue the score, I just can't keep it".

2007 marks 14 years of making Mc's Tally Ho the centerpiece of either 4Day-eve, the night the 4Day ends, or both. As nice as it was for Kim to make the pig roast happen, under her ownership the tavern gets more foreign to us each year since Betsy's 2001 passing. Kim's done a great job in changing the tavern's atmosphere to attract a larger and younger clientele, and we're happy for her success. The down side is that there's a crowd you have to work your way through and then a line to stand in to get a beer 'n a shot. Roger Miller has been replaced by hip hop music on the juke box, and playing table top shuffleboard requires a wait we're not willing to make. We enjoyed most of the evening hanging outside by the horseshoe pits. For the night's final act, we grabbed the leftovers bagged up for our 4 days on this year's river, the Manistique.

Enlisting into 4Day-hood this year is my brother-in-law, Rookie Jeff Cripe, a deeply-religious man, a thinker, always on the move, one who laughs easily and is sentimental. His internal motor and any car he's behind the wheel of goes one speed: fast. My Dad will tell you that this rookie cooks the best cheeseburger you'll ever eat. Good cooks are very popular on the 4Day.

Day 1, from Ten Curves to the livery, blessed us with sunny skies and much Ten High Whiskey. Recent rains elevated the Manistique River high enough for shallow swimming near the dam, with several boys sunning themselves on big midstream rocks like lizards. Lending culture to the affair, on one large rock Gomie struck a chin-on-fist pose, in honor of Moth's 1996, half-in-the-wrapper, Rodin's the Drinker. The debate whether to continue the fun at the dam a bit longer or head on down to the new steel bridge was ended when Vid jumped into a canoe and took charge, telling us, "There's too many Gilligans and not enough skippers", leading the way to the bridge.

Soon, the air above the former *"Old... Log... Bridge"* was ripe with cigar and marijuana smoke.

Although many memories are happily clouded by the years 'n the beers, commemorating 3 decades of 4Dayin' inspired reminiscing about the early trips. Jason recalled, "All those years of trying to keep our gear dry on the river by stashing the stuff in trash bags, and then Kenny brought waterproof dry bags." Neal observed, "It was like the first caveman to discover fire." Vid thought for a minute, then said, "I have memories I don't even remember," followed-up with his impersonation of Curly Howard, "I keep thinkin', and nuthin's happenin." After a few more seconds, the Confucius in him surfaced, "I can't figure out why we're cloning sheep with all these Playboy Playmates running around."

After 2 more hours of paddling, we spied the livery landing, happy to continue the party there while at the same time being able to satisfying our hunger. After we gathered wood and started up a dinner fire, Chef Ron heated the leftovers from last night's pig roast, while Rookie Jeff and I hoofed it the half-mile to the Jolly Bar to pick up a supplemental pizza carryout order.

There was extra excitement the next morning as we finished off a breakfast of eggs, bacon, and left-over pizza prepared by Gillam, Bobby, & Gomie, packed up our gear and hit the river. In from his Philadelphia-area home to meet us this evening at the Mead Creek Camp to paddle Days 3 & 4 was Matthew Rose, at his first 4Day in 11 years! Matthew is an energy and utility industry consultant, his professional opinion sought after in legal proceedings, and serves on the board of directors of several firms. This business executive keeps a photo on his office wall, positioned so visitors cannot miss it, from the 1983 4Day. Matthew and Chucky pose, both obviously happy and 3-sheets-to-the-wind, Matthew with a Rolling Rock in his right hand and a lit cigar hanging from his left nostril.

Merging into the Manistique River from our right, the landmark that tells us we're halfway into today's four hour journey to the Mead Creek camp, is Pine Creek. We steered the canoes up the creek, running them aground on the muddy bank, where we stayed to empty a fifth of Four Roses. Kenny mentioned he had a story including both baseball AND Pabst Blue Ribbon beer. His audience thus captivated, Kenny began. "There was a Milwaukee Braves' pitcher in the 1950s named Mel Famie. Between innings, Mel would enjoy a bottle or two of Pabst, leaving the empties in the dugout. One day after a few innings of drinking, Mel had a difficult time finding the strike zone, walking quite a few guys, and his team lost badly. After the game, the other team saw the empty Pabst bottles that Mel left in the dugout, and one of 'em said, "Yep, that's the beer that made Mel Famie walk us."

The camp at Mead Creek was a sensory delight: the touch of cool air on sun-heated skin, the alluring sound of deadwood crackling on the evening fire, the nasty taste of the Ten High

Whiskey being passed around, the taste of the multitude of beers drunk in an attempt to cleanse the palette of the Ten High taste, and the enticing smell of the roast being prepared by tonight's chefs, brothers Chris and Marquis. Thankfully, all signs and scents of last year's "breakfast surprise" dump by Big Guy were gone.

Taking some time to relax before the "dinner's ready!" shouts, I dove into my tent to read a few pages from the book, "Lovesick Blues: The Life of Hank Williams". It's amazing to consider that, with all the achievement and pain Hank experienced, he only lived to 29 years old. I lost track of time, absorbed in Hank's story, enough so that Chris called from outside the tent, "Are you ok, Doc?" "Yeah Chris, just reading a little Hank." I returned to the fire barely in time to take the final hit of Ten High. Whew, that was close.

To no one's surprise, based on the culinary history of these two boys, the Weaks' brothers' roast was as flavorful as it was aromatic. Matthew arrived in the sweet spot between the end of the fifth of Ten High and dinner time. The balance of the evening was spent sharing stories, puffing on cigars, sipping beers 'n gagging on Banker's Club whiskey, while watching the Manistique flow beautifully by our campground until, one by one, the boys drifted off to their tents with snoring soon to follow.

Not to be outdone by last night's dinner, the cook crew of Jason, Johnny, and Vid fixed a fine breakfast of biscuits 'n gravy, tater tots, and enough scrambled eggs for seconds all around. Soon, guys were either packing up their tent or were in line at the well-maintained dumper Big Guy took a pass on last year.

Fat and happy and moving slow, the boys had the boats in the water at high noon as we bid adieu to the Mead Creek camp. Downstream from Mead, canoeing flows through the Manistique River State Forest by ancient trees of incredible height. Clouds visible above the tree line give the paddler the impression of viewing a mountain range.

6 hours had passed since the noon departure from the Mead Creek camp, a little under half of it moving downstream in the boats, a little over half of it standing on the shoreline passing

fifths and sharing stories (this was more effort expended than the normal one-third canoeing, two-thirds partying, 4Day split), so we began the process of looking for a big beach to set up camp at for the night. 30 minutes into our search, we recognized the creek merging from our right as one we've camped near many times before, Dugal Creek. From here, about 2 and one-half hours of paddling remain tomorrow until our trip's end.

With the tents set-up and chairs circling the campfire, Neal and Kenny served an evening meal including Neal's favorite brats from Wisconsin. Damn, these are good! Providing a full-service meal, Neal added after-dinner entertainment, sharing a story about the National Transportation Safety Board. "The NTSB recently released the results of a 5-year covert project with USA automakers. Black-box voice recorders were installed in 4-wheel drive pick-ups and SUVs, in an effort to determine, in fatal accidents, the circumstances in the last 15 seconds before a crash. They found in 49 & one-half of the states, 75% of the time the last recorded words were "Oh, shit!" Only in the Upper Peninsula were the majority last words different, where over 90% of the time they were, "Honey, hold my beer, I'm gonna try something."

Day 4 morning dawned to a howling wind, a threat to tents staked to a soft, sandy shore. Sure enough, Johnny's tent was uprooted, and sent tumbling away from our camp down the beach. Johnny sprinted after it and a second before he caught up, the wind changed direction. The next thing we saw was Johnny in full flight coming towards us, the tent in hot pursuit. It was like a Benny Hill episode! Just as the tent was about to roll over Johnny, the wind died down. We quickly tore down camp before the gales returned.

To quote Ron White, "It's not *that* the wind is blowing, it's *what* the wind is blowing".

Back out on the river, we were an hour downstream before we had to break out the ponchos as the rains came down. The rains didn't stay too long, nor hamper our fun when they opened up on us. The flotilla paddled close together, shouting out new bourbon names we'd like to see…

*Say Goodnight Bourbon, Batten Down the Hatches Bourbon, Bleacher Bum Bourbon, Breakfast*

*Surprise Bourbon, Harsh Reality Bourbon, Lights Out! Bourbon, Mass Exodus Bourbon, Cringe! Bourbon, A Trip in Every Sip Bourbon, A Liver Runs Through It Bourbon (yep, that's mine), and –* although possibly a bit difficult to fit on a label – *Drunker Than a Barrel Full of Monkeys Bourbon.*

As we pulled into the Cookson Bridge take-out, livery owner Tom was there to collect our rain-soaked selves and drive us to Germfask, where we dried out at the Jolly Motel, before grog 'n grub at the Jolly Bar. Owner Carol Watson & her right-hand gal, Karen, have ideal personalities for dealing with drinkin' clientele, tough but loveable, reminding us of Irene Sember who used to park cars two blocks east of old Tiger Stadium. They both seem genuine in their happiness to have us spend time in their pub, and Carol makes a really, really good pizza.

Karen took me to task on this night, and she had every right to. Vid's car was parked on the curb in front of the bar, and we walked out to the vehicle to listen to some music, me absent-mindedly with beer in hand. I was in the passenger seat when Karen soon appeared. She leaned in the window, telling me, "Doc, I'll kick your ass you walk outta here with another beer!" I replied, "You're absolutely right Karen. I'm not bein' a jerk, just bein' stupid and not thinkin'." Karen knew my heart, if not my brain, was in the right place, smiled and headed back inside, me right on her heels with a beer mug that needed refilling.

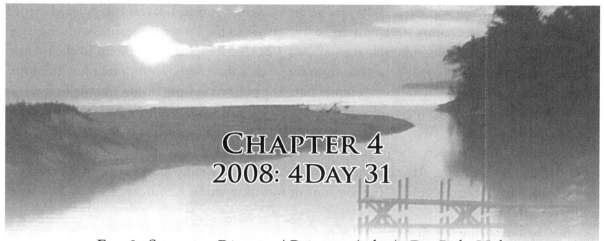

# CHAPTER 4
## 2008: 4DAY 31

Fox & Sturgeon Rivers w/ Brittany (ashes), Dr. Bob, Vid,
Kenny, Gomie, Chris, Johnny, Ron, Neal, Jimmy, Doc

*I'd like to go where the pace or life's slow,*
*Could you beam me somewhere, Mister Scott?*
*Any old place here on earth or in space,*
*You pick the century and I'll pick the spot.*
*(Boat Drinks by Jimmy Buffett)*

My dear Momma passed 4.17.08, only 4 months after being diagnosed with pancreatic cancer. I'd never heard of pancreatic cancer before this, a stark reminder that life is short and not to pass up opportunities to give thanks for what we have & 4Day with your brothers. I love you Mom!

The month prior to this year's 4Day, the Detroit Red Wings were winning hockey's Stanley Cup, their 4th in 11 years. Vid and Big Guy were watching one of the Finals games between the Red Wings and the Pittsburgh Penguins when Captain Johnny, viewing the game in his Jacksonville, Florida home, called. Gomie, also at Johnny's, yelled over the phone, *Go Wings!* Coming from a native southerner far removed from Hockeytown prompted a quick quip from Vid, "Gomie don't know Red Wings from chicken wings." Big Guy, drinking a beer at this very moment, exploded in laughter, beer squirting through his nose. This was not an isolated incident. Previous to the Red Wings/chicken wings evening, Biggie was at Vid's when a TV reporter told of a Chinese wholesaler in New York City, busted for placing tuna fish labels on cans of cat food, inducing Vid to shout, *"That Chink-ee Fuck!"* Big Guy's beer detoured from his throat through his nostrils, the incident christened *Bigus Eruptus*.

For the first time ever, part of a 4Day will be spent on a river south of the Mackinac Bridge. This decision to break protocol was reached over many beers partaken by the Council of Elders, i.e. 4Day veterans, the determination made after guessing input from R.I.P. TV actor David White ("What would Larry Tate do?") of "Bewitched" fame. On such fragile soil are the big issues of the day settled. After two days on the Fox River, we would cross the Mackinac Bridge and travel 30 minutes into the Northern Lower Peninsula to the tiny town of Wolverine. There, a 2-day canoe trip was planned on the Sturgeon River.

The Sturgeon River was scouted the year before by Kenny, future 4Dayers Perry and Mister P, and myself. What an exciting stream to canoe, the fastest in the Lower Peninsula, with the river floor dropping 14' per mile, enjoyable runs of class 1 & class 2 rapids throughout. In the middle of it all is a shoreline bar, easily accessible from the river, a short walk across a meadow from the beached boats, appropriately called Meadows Bar. The pub has seating inside and out.

During the prior year scouting mission, we pulled the canoes ashore and grabbed seats indoors. Mister P asked, "Why are we sitting inside?" I pointed out, "That's where the pizza is." Kenny noted, "That's where the pool table is." Perry chimed in, "That's where the beer is." P nodded, "Stupid question." After finishing a couple of rounds, Kenny shared some of the wisdom he's accumulated over the years, "The toothbrush was invented in Kentucky, elsewise it 'a been called a teeth brush."

But, before taking our first ever 4Day paddles in the Sturgeon, two days would be spent on the familiar waters of the Fox River.

Day 1 launches us into the river at the Fox River Overlook, 150' above the winding river valley below. The only other year we've begun this far upstream on the Fox was 15 years ago, at the 1993 4Day, when we put-in at this same location. Standing atop this majestic cliff, it - as you would guess from its name - overlooks the river below, flowing from your left to right. Looking upstream to the left, the Fox emerges from the shadows as a tight bend, its waters initially flowing towards you before circling to its left, now running parallel to the edge of the cliff you're standing on. The awe-inspiring dark red tint of the Fox cuts a vivid path through the deep greens of the pines on each riverbank, until the angle of the sun turns the river blue as it disappears around the far bend to the right.

Both today and tomorrow's paddles on the Fox, upstream from the Seney Township Campsite, are normally on a portage-free stretch of the river, much different than the logjam fields faced downstream. On Day 1, though, we encountered a great deal of trees recently fallen into or across the river. Within the 4-hour paddle was 1 portage, forcing us to carry canoes through 20 yards of the surrounding forest, 6 deadwood fields requiring us to get out of the canoes and drag them over the debris, and numerous water obstructions testing our steering ability.

The Day 1 half-way point was the Fox River State Forest Campground, today's longest break spot. Here Vid unveiled a fifth of Ten High, with the crossed out "Ten" replaced by a "Four", our favorite number. Hmm, we've seen this movie before. This cringe-worthy Kentucky Sour Mash got the philosopher in Kenny bubbling to the surface...

*"The stages of my life are child, adult, and flood." "My 9-year old grandson, Ethan, wants to move to Michigan. He thinks the whole state is a river & everyone canoes all day long." "I plan to get to my chores once I'm off the river. There should be enough water in the Lower Peninsula alone to keep me away from work for two years." "I don't think in inches, feet, yards, miles, meters, kilometers, or the like. My head tends to calculate in paddle, canoe, or kayak lengths, ever since I had that bad spell of water in my ears."*

The boys may have stayed and listened to Kenny a bit longer, but when Ron noted that, "The mosquitoes are wearing little bibs with pictures of my face on them," we had met the quota of the local skeeter community blood bank, hopped back in the canoes, and continued on.

Day 1 ended where we'd set up our tents this morning, the first of 3 elevated DNR sites along the right bank of the Fox. As our tents were hidden from water-level view, to ensure we stopped at the correct site, I tied a 3' tall poster of Tate to the wooden fence at the hilltop, a work of art that could not be missed from the river.

*The Legend of Tate (expanding on an earlier account)...*

Actor David White played the role of Larry Tate, co-star Darrin's business-world boss, in the

60's TV series "Bewitched". Tate was predictable, pompous, vain, ready to take credit for any of Darrin's ideas, and fun to watch. When David White died in 1990, I brought his Detroit Free Press obituary to the Mobil Lounge for a euchre tournament toast. At that time Colonel, being the mad-tinkerer genius that he is, had developed a copy machine that created high-resolution copies of very small items. Colonel took the tiny obit home, returning with a 3' tall poster we called "Tate". The Tate poster has accompanied us on most 4Days since 1991, including posing for the famous "23 men and 37 coolers" photo from the '96 4Day. In the early-90s, Jimmy felt that we were indulging in Tate idolatry, and tossed the poster into a campfire. Fortunately, the Colonel had created multiple copies. It's vision like that that makes him the Colonel. Once Jimmy learned that David White was a fellow Marine, all other Tate posters were safe.

Flash forward to a 2011 Tate Tale. My book on Wisconsin Rivers had just come out, and, well, let's let Neal tell it. *"So, I'm reading this great new book* (see why I let Neal tell it) *I picked up, while on the bus last night, which is packed with weary office workers quietly making their way home. At one point in the book, I broke out in a huge belly laugh, which drew the attention of everyone on board. The young gent sitting next to me smiles, and politely asks, 'Okay, mind if I ask what's so funny?' So, I read him the passage that makes me laugh still this morning:*

*Peter: "Do you have a lighter in your dry bag?"*

*Doc: "No, but I have a picture of Larry Tate."*

*Of course, I cracked up again. The young gent stared for a moment, and then decided it would be more prudent to stand for the remainder of the trip."*

This DNR site is where, circa 1999, the Colonel treated us to the beer pig, a small pig-shaped keg, an outstanding beer-delivery system. This location is perfect for camping, featuring flat ground, space for several times the number of tents that we have, and plenty of wood on the grounds for our campfires. We spotted our vehicles here so that, tomorrow morning, we can break down camp, load all non-canoe gear into the vehicles rather than weigh down our boats, and drive all of it down to the next night's Seney Township campground before we shove off.

When 4Dayin' in the U.P., we always enjoy daylight for longer hours than we would back home in Southeast Michigan. Day 1 this year falls on June 21, the longest day of the year, and tonight there was enough light to play euchre without a table lamp until 1030PM.

As the "chefs" for this evening, Ron, Vid, & I arranged for livery owner Tom to deliver pizzas & chicken wings from the Jolly Bar in Germfask. It was nice to have Tom hang out with us for a few beers and tall tales, his tip for bringing our dinner.

Around the campfire, I shared a story I'd recently heard about a guy who lost his keys, and got a buddy to help look for them, suggesting, "Let's look under the lamp." The buddy says, "Why, is that where you think you lost them?" "No, but the light's better there."

Neal shared a conversation he'd recently had with Big Guy, missing-in-4Day-action this year, "Big Guy was reminiscing about 4Days past. He said Goobs and he always loved Blatz and Hamm's, according to Big Guy the finest, iciest, most delicious draft beers he'd ever enjoyed, in his entire life as far back as he could remember. Biggie told me about a stop on the way to the 4Day, some year in the Nineties, and repeated rounds of Blatz in icy goblets for 75 cents, served by an older waitress at the Nottingham Bar. Big Guy said, 'Good Lord, I can still taste it'. He believed it was the same year that he and Colonel did a pit-stop flat tire change in a loaded down Chucky-driven Honda hatchback."

Day 2 morning was about as gorgeous as anyone could remember. Guys were leaning against the wooden fence along the edge of the hilltop camp site, watching as the shaded Fox below flowed between tag alder bushes leaning in from the two shorelines, the sunrise lighting tops of the pine trees beyond the opposite shore. Morning cooks Chris, Gomie, and Bobby provided hot coffee, cereal, and fruit to go along with the warmed-up pizza leftovers from last night's dinner.

With another short 2-hours of paddling ahead of us, the breaks today were frequent, long-lasting, and full of stories. Kind of like every other 4Day there's ever been.

Once you have spent time on a 4Day, you don't want to miss the next one. Besides not wishing to be left out of a great adventure, a veteran who then misses a 4Day can have vile things said in his absence. Exhibit A is Jonesey. After being MIA a couple of years, word of his relationship with chickens started working its way among the 4Dayers, summed up in a joke, "Why did the chicken cross the road?" is answered, "cause Jonesey's dick was halfway up its ass."

Now, there is no evidence that such behavior took place, nor does Jonesey seem like the sort who might pine for fair fowl. Nonetheless, this was a story that, unlike the desire of Jonesey's heart, took flight. One of the funniest moments that ever takes place on a 4Day is when Marquis tries to complete the joke. Oh sure, he can ask the question, "Why did the chicken cross the road?" but when it's time to deliver the punch line, Marquis begins to laugh uncontrollably, doubling over when he gets to, "cause Jonesey's…"

On the same early-2000s 4Day, unbeknown to both, Vid brought Jonesey a tshirt and Kenny brought Jonesey a sign, each with the same quote, "I Dream of a Better World Where Chickens Can Cross the Road Without Having Their Motives Questioned."

Too much bourbon and too much sun visited Gomie today, as told by canoe partner Vid:
*Yeah, Gomie had a bit to drink and, ah, that's not the first time, but this time he was just a*

*horrible canoer. I mean, oh my God, he was passing out… he flipped the canoe, it was upside down, and he was just standing there saying, "I don't think I can help". I'm like, 'Yeah, you can help!' That's when I got him into the front of the canoe. He's sittin' up and leanin' left, and I'm telling him, 'Gomie! Get in the middle!' "I'm sorry." 'Ok, but get in the middle!' Then he leans right and sez, "I'm sorry." He didn't want to lay down, but once I got him down, the canoe was stable, but until then… (Vid laughing) he was very apologetic.*

Reaching the Seney Campground island, our home for the night, Gomie staggered from the canoe and passed out. His tent was laying in pieces next to him. I pulled the tent over him like a blanket, where he lay 'til he moseyed over to my van, and spent the night stretched out in back.

Burgers awaited us at Andy's, courtesy tonight's dinner-providers Kenny, Neal, and Johnny. As we were getting ready to walk to town, Vid – not realizing where Gomie had crashed at - was looking in all the tents for him, until finally seeing Gomie in the van. Teens camping at the site asked, "Is your buddy ok?" Seeing an opportunity for payback from "the Great Frog Incident of 1997", when Gomie & Chris tossed about a dozen frogs into Vid, Johnny & Jimmy's tent, Vid told 'em, "Yeah, but I think he likes to play with snapping turtles." The kids didn't toss snapping turtles into the van with Gomie, as best anyone can tell, or we'd likely have heard about it from him. Or maybe not.

Day 3 we headed to the Lower Peninsula for two days on the Sturgeon River. After waking up in my tent, I wandered over to the van to check on Gomie. His condition had improved little from last night. Guess he really hurt himself yesterday. Unable to move painlessly on his own, the boys packed up Gomie's gear for him, allowing the caravan to depart at the scheduled 830AM time. Breakfast at Audie's in Mackinaw City was 90 minutes away, the river livery another 30.

Driving with Gomie reclined as much as possible in the passenger seat, he looked awful, almost as bad as Carl did the first day of the 2003 4Day. You do NOT want to be feeling as bad as Carl did that year, the hangover that all 4Day hangovers are measured against. About 30 minutes into the drive, Gomie finally speaks, "How early can we check into the cabins?" "Do you want to check-in right away?" "Yeah." "Is that what you'd like to do today instead of canoeing?" "Yeah, I do." Unfortunately for Gomie, the cabins were not available early and, even worse, he was paired up with Jimmy as his canoeing partner for the day.

Jimmy is an excellent canoeist, normally the ideal partner for a wounded man. However, Jimmy could not make the Fox River portion of the 4Day, and was trying to squeeze 4 days of partyin' into 2. He would be getting wild on the fastest 'n most challenging river in the Lower Peninsula, with Gomie in the bow. We counted 3 times that their canoe dumped in the first half hour. Flip number 4 for the Jimmy-Gomie boat took place, to no one's surprise, at the 3' drop beneath Scott Bridge. A mere 10 minutes downstream from that 3' drop 'n crash is Meadows Bar. No one was more thankful than Gomie to see us pull the canoes over for a beer 'n pizza break here.

Although my love of just about any pizza makes me the wrong person to give a review of an establishment's fare, I consider Meadow's pizza to be outstanding. Vid laughs every time I give a good pizza review, maybe because he's never heard anything else from me. That's not really true, as I recall a bad pizza 1971 in Toledo (like grease on a cracker), 1987 in Cleveland (despite a severe case of 3AM munchies), and 2012 in Northville (where the server dropped my pizza upside down on to the bar floor). Since that's only 3 out of an estimated 4,500 pizzas, based on a conservative 2.5 per week consumption estimate since going away to college in 1972 (note that I once had pizza, 1 large each time, for 5 consecutive meals), Vid's laughter is probably justified.

Vid told us about the pizzeria with a sign in the window, "Best Pizza in the Country". A 2nd pizzeria opened next door with a sign in the window, "Best Pizza in the World". 3rd pizzeria opens next door with a sign in the window, "Best Pizza on the Block".

Downstream from the bar, we encountered the most exciting and challenging stretch of the Sturgeon, with Jimmy & Gomie's canoe somehow staying upright. In calm patches, we toasted to the 30-year anniversary of the 1978 release of "Animal House", drinking to the classic lines, "Eric Stratton, rush chairman, damn glad to meet you!" and "Knowledge is good – Emil Faber."

This led to calling up a quote from last year's "The Real Animal House" book… *The bourbon flavor made him wince. No wonder the Confederates lost the fucking war, he thought sourly. But the next swallow was better, and after one more Pinto had begun to smell magnolias and hear the jaunty strains of "Dixie."*

Malone's Cabins in Wolverine, where Gomie had hoped to crash all-day long, was our home for tonight & tomorrow night. The setting for Malone's is gorgeous. Below Hemlock trees towering above, alongside each cabin runs the waters of the West Branch of the Sturgeon, a too narrow to paddle, fast-moving tributary of the Sturgeon. It was a short stroll down Old Straits Highway to a fine little tavern, Vickie J's, about the size of a basement rec room. Their sign outside advertised, "Home of the 3" Burgers", food that sent us home to the cabins, happily singing river songs.

Day 4 breakfast at Paula's Café in the nearby town of Indian River may have been too filling. Warm-belly-effect lent an air of indifference to some of the boys about paddling today. For the 4Dayers that wanted to push the group to the river, the towel was thrown in after a post-breakfast visit to the difficult-to-deal-with canoe livery. Apparently, the livery folk felt we had their boats out too long during our Day 3 party on the river and Meadows Bar stop, and today said they'd charge us an hourly rate. Well, as any experienced 4Dayer can tell you, with as many long river breaks as we take, the number of hours we'll be out is an unknown, and keeping an eye on the clock a bother we don't want.

So, after what turned out to be our last-ever visit to this particular Sturgeon livery, we huddled back at the cabins. Over a morning's worth of euchre and beer, alongside the sweet flowing West Branch of the Sturgeon, not to mention story-telling (Norm Cash on his 1,081 career strikeouts: "Pro-rated at 500 at bats a year, that means that for 2 years out of the fourteen I played, I never touched the ball."), it was decided to forego Day 4 canoeing for Day 4 spent at Meadows Bar.

Meadows owner Todd was as happy with our decision as we were. Being a Tuesday, the 4Day crew pretty much ran the place, making the outdoor horse shoe pits and indoor pool table 'n juke box our own. Somehow, Todd had enough PBR longnecks and pizza-makins on hand, and we ordered enough of both that he called in help to handle the orders of 10 thirsty and hungry unexpected mid-week customers.

The next day, since Gomie was staying at our house for a few nights post-4Day, he and I drove south together from Wolverine. Gomie seemed to have fully recovered from his rough day on the Fox River, a very good thing, and was his usual, talkative, self. Arriving home at MagDochaus, after hugs 'n kisses from Maggie, she surprised me with a box from UPS. Inside were the initial copies of my first book, *Weekend Canoeing In Michigan*, sent from my publisher, Arbutus Press. What excitement! My post-Duracell career had launched.

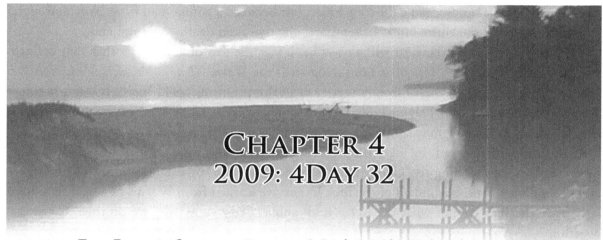

# CHAPTER 4
# 2009: 4DAY 32

Fox, Bear, & Sturgeon Rivers w/ Carl, Moth, Colonel, Jonesey, Captain Johnny, Jimmy, Chris, Ron, Gomie, Vid, Neal, Gillam, Brittany (ashes), Doc and rookies Eric, Gene, and Scott

*Well-a bird is a word, a-well-a bird bird*
*B-bird's the word now well-a*
*Don't you know 'bout the bird*
*Well ev'rybody knows that the bird is a word*
*(Surfin Bird by the Trashmen)*

Mark "the Bird" Fidrych RIP 4.13.09

On April 13, Moth and I attended the Tigers game, and stopped at El Zocalo's Restaurant in Mexican Village afterward to grab a bite. There we saw our friend Roland, who asked if we'd heard about the Bird. No we hadn't. A sad look spread across Roland's face. "He died today." The Bird lost his life due to an accident while working under his truck.

Driving home, Moth kept asking me if I was ok because I couldn't stop crying. The excitement of the Tigers winning the World Series in 1968 and 1984 was goose-bump amazing, but the most wonderful part of being a Tiger fan, in my lifetime, was experiencing the Bird in 1976.

The Bird was everywhere in 1976...

*Got down and did the Gator*, dancing while lying on the floor, at Captain Ahab's Pub in Wyandotte, walking into a party in Belleville with a 6-pack ring of 3 full and 3 empty beers, on the cover of Time/Sporting News/ Rolling Stone, Ernie Harwell's favorite ball player of all-time, beating the Yankees on the Monday Night Game of the Week in front of millions on TV and with Smitty & I watching from the left-field upper deck - two of the last tickets available in a sea of 54,000 bird-lovers at sold-out Tiger Stadium.

For Tiger fans, Mark Fidrych came out of nowhere in 1976. Yes that year he went 19 & 9, yes he had a 2.34 earned run average, yes he started the All-Star game, yes he meant hope to a hopeless team and a struggling city, but the Bird was more than that to Detroit and the state of Michigan. Honest, charming, boyish, goofy, innocent, endearing, unaffected, a bright, glowing meteor that brightened our lives and began a life-long love-affair between a young man from Northborough, Massachusetts and the entire Great Lakes State, one that even death could not end.

But as important as the Bird will always be, it was the loss of a 4Day brother that defined the 2009 trip. This year's 4Day has been designated the *Wayne Thomas Vollmers Memorial*. We lost our dear brother Wayne-O from a variety of health problems on 11.16.08. It was a blessing to have Wayne join Clan 4Day in 1986, the first of ten 4Days that he experienced. His presence was felt through a contagious laugh as booming and as big as he was, by the stories he uniquely told and those he inspired, by jokes unforgettable because they were great or just because they were Wayne's, by teaching us "Chow Time is Important" and, by extension, how to never run out of food on a river. Beyond all of the life's lessons we learned from Wayne, he was able to best articulate the very core of what the 4Day is all about, "You know why we do this? 'Cause it's worth it!"

Wayne's brother, Rookie Gene, rode his motorcycle north from his Bristol, Tennessee home to celebrate Wayne's life with us on the 4Day. Gene and 4Day veterans Wayne, Jimmy, Bobby, and Rusty Vollmers are the only group of 5 family members (just brother Mark missing) to also be 4Day brothers. Like Wayne, Gene is a Vietnam army veteran. I've always enjoyed the rare chances to talk with Gene. We'd first met him when he was a bouncer, along with Jimmy, at Mister Flood's Bar in Ann Arbor. Combining his love of motorcycles with support for fellow vets, Gene is a board member of the Mountain Home, Tennessee chapter of Rolling Thunder. While most Rolling Thunder members are vets who ride motorcycles, neither is a prerequisite to join. With a vow of "We Will Not Forget", Rolling Thunder works to bring full accountability, from all wars, for Prisoners of War and those Missing in Action, as well as visiting vets in rest homes, and providing financial aid to vets and veterans' families in need.

Another 2009 rookie is our Mobil Lounge softball teammate Eric Branny aka E. Rookie Eric joined the softball team in 1985, our first year of play, as one of two, along with 4Dayer Chris, 18-year old, rifle-armed, young guns. When we celebrated Eric's 1988 birthday, post-game in our sponsor bar, Mobil Lounge owner Sharon said, "Let me buy you a birthday drink. How old are you now?" When Eric replied, "21", Sharon hesitated for a moment, a half-smile crossing her face, realizing for the first time that E had been under-age drinking in her bar for 3 years. Eric was recognized as our team's "Sultan of Suds", the Mobil bar version of Babe Ruth's "Sultan of Swat" nickname, as the first Mobil Lounge Beer Swiller to clear the fences with a home run. Eric always has a good joke for us and we consider him our brother.

This 4Day, there was no caravan north as the boys were coming from all different directions, arriving on different days, to paddle 3 different rivers. Organizing so many moving parts makes this the most challenging trip to put together to date. 5 of what would eventually number 16 4Dayers, of which I only knew of 10 until Day 3 (see what I mean), met 4Day-eve at Seney's Fox River Motel. The Day 1 & Day 2 five were Neal, Vid, Gomie, Rookie Eric, and me.

Every 4Day-eve since 1992 has been celebrated in either Curtis or Germfask. However, under Kim's ownership, Mc's Tally Ho in Curtis has become too young and (good for Kim) too crowded, while earlier this year Carol, owner of the Jolly Bar in Germfask, has closed the bar and moved away – very sad news as we thought highly of Carol, her assistant Karen, and the bar they ran. With Curtis and Germfask out, the logical option was to spend 4Day-eve in Seney, giving us an extra night in Andy's Bar. Andy himself was out-of-town this week, but his tavern was still open and still sold beer, bourbon 'n burgers, so we sucked it up and made the best of it.

Day 1… ah, what a gorgeous sun-drenched setting! Those other 5 or 11 later-arriving 4Dayers don't know what they're missing. After grabbing breakfast in the little Seney restaurant, livery owner Tom, as he did last year, dropped us off at the majestic heights of the Fox River Overlook. Although there were only 5 of us on hand, two different gentlemen opened up fifths, Old Grand-Dad and Bourbon (pronounced by the cultured crowd as "ber-bon") deLuxe, clearly anxious for the fun to begin! Noticing our overabundance of good fortune, Tom hung around long enough to join us for a few rounds, enjoying the flexible hours from owning his own business.

Today & tomorrow combined, the actual paddling time is 6 hours. Both nights will find us camping at the Seney Township site, where we have set up our tents this morning. The 6 hours will be split, 4 hours today, ending at two wooden canoe rails running up the hill on the right, where our vehicles wait to take us to the tents, and tomorrow two hours from the wooden canoe rails to our tents.

I paddled solo, Vid with Gomie, Neal with Rookie Eric. Apparently, the fallen trees encountered in 2008 weren't removed by the 4Day fairy in the last year, making for a long, but enjoyable, day of dragging canoes over one tree after another. The enjoyable part of these forced breaks was the shared drinking and stories that ensued at each stop. Eric, as he so often has for us at the Mobil Lounge, had a joke for us at one stop…

"I consider myself lucky, lucky, lucky. Lucky once because I slipped on the ice and a tree fell where I otherwise would've stepped. Lucky twice because I slipped on a sewer after stepping off the curb and a semi blew past where I would've walked. Lucky a third time since a chandelier fell and hit me on the ass while I was making love. I took 36 stitches on the butt." "Ok," Neal said, "I'll bite. Why is that third one lucky?" "Because," Eric concluded, "two seconds earlier and the chandelier would have hit me on the head."

River obstructions and several long breaks stretched the "normal" 4 paddling hours to 8, getting us to our wooden rail take-out near 7PM. We pulled the canoes up the rails to where our vehicles waited and made the 15-minute drive to camp, where we were lucky a 4th time, arriving just 10 minutes before the pizzas, courtesy "chefs" Rookie E 'n me, were delivered by a livery helper.

With food in our bellies and after a little debate (should we stay and party at the campfire or should we go to the bar?), we pushed through the satisfied feeling and hoofed it the 1 & 1/2 miles to the town of Seney, destination Andy's.

This first night off the Fox found us in our comfort zone, tucked between the walls at one of our all-time favorite pubs. Andy's was surprisingly empty for a Saturday evening, and the table top shuffleboard was ours alone for a couple of hours. Shots 1 through 4 had us in a back-slappin' good mood, full of laughs and 4Day tall tales. "What do you think, Eric?" Vid asked. "Oh man," the rookie replied, "this 4Dayin' is something I should've done LONG ago!"

In owner Andy's absence, schleppin' drinks for us tonight was another Andy, who informed us, "I'm Andy #1. The owner is Andy #2." After the 4th round, we asked Andy #1 if he'd like to do a shot with us. He replied, "Hell no! I seen what them shots done to you fellers!"

It was around shot number 5, or maybe number 6, when Gomie slipped into a philosophical mood, *"I do shit, and I think about it later."* That line got us crackin' up. *"A little drizzle is better than a little drool."* Hmm, how 4Day! We'd had drunk just enough bourbon to think Aristotle was among us. *"I never met a river that I didn't like."* Now <u>that</u> statement was one we all agreed worthy of a final shot before taking our leave and stumbling back to the campground.

Day 2 started with no one in a hurry, reminiscent of the "slow Fridays" that followed softball season playin' & drinkin' Thursday nights. It took the aroma of those damn fine brats that Neal brings from Wisconsin, heating up on the grill, to get us out of the tents and into some semblance of movement. Once up, Rookie Eric got the biscuits and gravy going and we soon returned to the well-known 4Day-state (thanks to Wayne-O's teachings) of fat 'n happy.

It was another fantastic day on the Fox, this time free of any obstructions, only a fast 'n easy flow down its narrow, partially-shaded, waters. Paddling alone, at times the only sound I heard was the faint brushing of each arm against leaves from tag alders leaning in from the banks, like the soft *pfsst* of a distant beer can opening. Puffing on a Backwoods Honey Berry stogie, the sweet-smelling trail hit Gomie a few bends back, getting him to holler for an extra I might have.

All 3 canoes pulled over as I dug out a cigar for Gomie. Vid accepted one, too. I was laughing about a recent Andy Griffith Show I'd seen. *"Barney Fife, what a guy! He and Andy were at some Mayberry social gathering. Barney is looking around, disgusted, and says, "Andy, every woman in this room is a dog. If a quail flew through here, every one of 'em would point."*

Maybe it was cigar smoking that got Vid channeling Winston Churchill. "At a social event, a lady said to Winston, *Mister Prime Minister, if I was your wife, I'd poison your coffee.* Churchill replied, *Madame, if I was your husband, I'd drink it.* At another gathering, a woman with a look of disgust on her face told him, *Mister Churchill, you are drunk!* Winston replied, *Madame, in the morning, I'll be sober, and you'll still be ugly."* Churchill likely would've fared poorly in a sensitive diplomatic outpost. Wait a minute – he WAS in one!

At one-half the length of yesterday's Fox journey, today ended at the campsite access at an early 5PM. Tonight, thank you dinner-planners Gomie and Vid, we enjoyed burgers 'n beer at the end of a walk to Andy's. Andy himself was still out-of-town, and the evening was fairly docile by 4Day standards, 2 shots of Dickel, one a toast to today's 30th anniversary of Disco Demolition Night at old Comiskey Park, and a few beers to go with the grub and table top shuffleboard.

*Author's note: for the youngsters, the 1979 Disco Demolition Night was a promotion approved by the Chicago White Sox wonderfully-crazy owner, Bill Veeck, and the brain child of Chicago (formerly Detroit) disc jockey, Steve Dahl, who earned a national reputation for his crusade against disco music. The 7.12.79 promotion was a sell-out at Comiskey Park, 59,000 seats sold, for the evening doubleheader with the Tigers. If you brought a disco album to the game, the ticket price was only 98 cents. After the first game (a Tiger 4-1 victory), Steve Dahl blew up a large crate of disco albums in the outfield. It was then that all hell broke loose, thousands of fans running on to the field, tearing up chunks of the turf, setting advertising signs on fire, knocking over the batting cage, and tossing like Frisbees the disco albums not yet blown up. After the field was cleared and 37 arrests were made, the grounds were considered unfit to play on and the second game awarded to the Tigers as a forfeit.*

The past week's activities were starting to catch up to me. 3 days before 4Day-eve, I'd left home for northern Wisconsin to paddle two rivers for a book I was working on about canoeing and kayaking through the Badger State. Taking backroads near the first river, I passed a farm silo painted to look like a can of Pabst Blue Ribbon Beer. In the bottom left of the silo, where on a normal-sized PBR can it would read, "12 fluid ounces", it read instead "1,500 fluid gallons".

A BIG bag of pretzels will be needed to finish this beer off!

Researching a book sub-titled, "The Rivers, The Towns, The Taverns", is not complete until pubs are scouted post-paddle. After a day on the Little Wolf River in New London WI, we took the stairs from the livery to the conveniently located Upper Deck Bar & Grill. A regular's t-shirt sported the message, "I am not a drunk. I am by nature a loud, friendly, clumsy person". In a move that shouted "Wisconsin!", as we departed for our cars, the waitress ran after us into the parking lot with a tray of shots on the house, ensuring a safe drive home. The next day, after paddling the Wisconsin River headwaters, we tackled the Log Cabin Bar in Conover WI. Great pub, pleasant waitresses, good food, with a wall sign reading IITYWTMWYBTHAD, which our waitress explained to us as, "If I tell you what this means would you buy the house a drink?"

Day 3, we broke down camp early, left the Fox, ate breakfast at the Seney restaurant, and began the 2 & 1/2 hour drive to the Bridge and below for today's Bear River paddle in Petoskey, where we'd meet up with Jimmy, Gene, Chris, Ron & Gillam. Driving along the U.P.'s Lake Michigan shoreline on scenic Route 2, I phoned Moth, absent this year, to see if he'd like something from his favorite jerky store, Gustafson's. "Moth, I'm excited about meeting up with the boys on the Bear today, celebrating Wayne-O, and canoeing the Sturgeon tomorrow, but I'm feeling a little tired. Maybe canoeing the past week is catching up to me." Moth laughed to himself, knowing the party was about to get bigger than I suspected.

Once at the Bear River livery, I was handling miscellaneous, pre-paddle, duties. Walking past a small livery building to grab canoe gear, I was suddenly shocked when two of the 4 Horsemen from Jacksonville, Jonesey & Captain Johnny, who had never said a word about coming, except to at least Moth & my beautiful bride, jumped out from behind the building and grabbed me, shouting *"4Day!"* I seriously thought I was dreaming for a minute. How great is this? Everyone was instantly transformed into 20 year olds, jumping up and down, high-fiving, shouting, and generally going crazy! I was still in a daze as we launched into the mild Bear River current.

The 4Dayers new to this river were struck by how peaceful, green and gorgeous the Bear is, it's slow but steady flow fed by narrow streams winding their way down surrounding hills. The only interruption of the Bear's idyllic setting is the 3 sets of culverts we'll float through.

The shallow 'n sandy Bear waters, flowing through a wide and flat riverbed, provided multiple great Frisbee locations, and we pulled the canoes over to enjoy most of these. While flipping the disc, we tossed around additional Bourbon names we'd like to see…

*Feeble Resistance Bourbon,* (in honor of our suddenly 3 Jacksonville brethren) *Southern Drawl Bourbon, No Sense of Humor Bourbon, Honey I Was Blind Bourbon, Questionable Judgment Bourbon,* (a tip o' the hat to Big Guy) *Argyle Guy Action Figure Bourbon, Moth Lies Bleeding Bourbon, That 70s Bourbon,* and (inspired by the Vollmers 3 of Wayne, Jimmy & Gene, and their service to the nation) - although unlikely to fit the entire name on the label - *Never Tell the Platoon Sergeant You Have Nothing to Do Bourbon.*

The Bear River has, like the Fox 45 minutes beyond Seney, its own version of the Spreads. Several times on today's 2 & 1/2 hours of "actual paddle time", not to be confused with the 6 hours we were on the river, the Bear split itself into multiple fingers, creating channels both long and short, each wrapped around a series of islands. One hour beyond the final set of Spreads, and 5 minutes after paddling through the last set of culverts, the trip ended at the deck on the right, about 100' from our camping area.

Tonight, a camp cookout, hosted by Ron, Chris, Jimmy, and Rookie Gene, served up burgers, chicken, beans, and corn-on-the-cob. Later, among the stories shared and jokes told, the dinner beans made a return appearance, the boys letting 'em rip around the campfire, the River Dick All-Star Bourbon Band playing a tune of farts recalling the scene from *Blazing Saddles.*

The campfire revelry continued way after dark, when a car pulled up in the pitch black. We figured that it might be the livery owners dropping off some more firewood for us. Then we heard a voice lisp an old Mayor Coleman Young classic, *"Who in the fuck are the friends of Belle Isle? All they did was plant a few fuckin' trees?"* It was Moth and the Colonel! What a great surprise! Two more for tomorrow's Sturgeon River paddle. Damn, this 4Day is like a clown bus full of unexpected paddlers showing up.

Moth was cracking up, sharing with the boys the phone conversation he and I had this morning, when I confessed how wiped out I was, Moth all the while knowing there were four surprise arrivals due the last two days that would kick the party up another notch.

Rookie Gene was 3-sheets-to-the-wind, unable to nail down the name of his new friend. "Hey Moss!" Moth corrected him, "It's Moth." "Hey Moss!" "It's Moth." "Hey Moss!" Resigned, Moth said, "We'll work on it in the morning."

Day 4 presented a gorgeous daybreak at our Bear River Campground. With yesterday's out-of-the-blue entrants, Captain Johnny, Jonesey, Moth, and Colonel, all of the paddlers for the final day of the 4Day, to the best of my knowledge, were present and accounted for.

We rendezvoused at noon in Wolverine, a 30-minute drive from our Petoskey-area Bear River camp. In Wolverine, we met the folks from Big Bear Canoe & Kayak, our livery for today's 2-hour journey down the Sturgeon River, the fastest river in the Lower Peninsula. This trip is a repeat of last year's inaugural Sturgeon 4Day experience, minus Gomie's legendary hangover. How ironic, then, that the last (?) surprise 4Day veteran add-on today was Carl aka Doubles, whose 2003 hangover is the one that all 4Day hangovers are measured against, the only one considered elevated above, or below depending on perspective, Gomie's morning-after willies of last year, the arguable all-time runner-up.

It was when we stopped for breakfast, on the road from Petoskey to Wolverine, that Carl called with the unexpected news that he'd join us today. He had a rookie in tow, a pleasant fella named Scott Halloran. To call Carl's participation a surprise is a strong understatement. His massive hangover of 2003, Carl's only prior 4Day participation, and his follow-up letter noting post-trip difficulties with mental acuity and references to us as Neanderthal barbarians, made a sophomore expedition, although welcome, unlikely. Carl sounded nervous over the phone, like someone returning to the scene of a murder they'd witnessed, perhaps bringing his own rookie to use as a human shield to ward off real or imaginary danger heading his way.

Launching for today's Sturgeon River fun run took place at the Trowbridge Road access. The wonderful initial burst of river speed and churning rapids ensured our immediate attention. In a few river bends, the 1' deep stream dials its tempo back ever so slightly while the Sturgeon drops down gracefully over a series of small ledges.

30 minutes from put-in, we pulled over for a paddle break, and a chance to spend a little time acquainting ourselves with Rookie Scott. He was a welcome addition, an agreeable man of good humor, with a ready laugh, so engaging that we questioned Scott about hitching his wagon to someone like Carl. Ah hell, if we didn't like Carl, we wouldn't tease him. Plus, writing his post-2003 4Day "Neanderthal barbarian" letter pretty much ensured he'd be a future target.

Amazing all first by simply attending today, Carl shocked us a second time, grabbing the fifth of Beam at this first river break, and knocking down a double-bubbler. Chris offered Carl a hand shake and admiration, "Carl, you are no longer *Singles*. You're back to being *Doubles*". The "Doubles" moniker earned on the softball diamond, showcased Carl's speed turning singles into doubles. The "Singles" downgrade was fallout stemming from his general demeanor at Carl's one & only 4Day. Chris' statement was supported by a round of "Dah-bles! Dah-bles!" as the recipient of this good cheer took a Beam bonus tug.

10 minutes prior to the trip take-out, we plunged through the 3' Sturgeon drop beneath Scott Bridge aka the "jumpin' bridge". Pulling over on its downstream side, Jonesey, Chris, Ron, & Gomie scrambled to the top of the bridge where they launched themselves, feet first, into the churning river, 10' below. The spectators were happy to see all 4 heads pop up from beneath the river surface, hearing the jumpers "4Day!" yells, 4 sets of eyes squinting to keep the water out, water just deep enough to avoid broken bones.

The Sturgeon trip ended at Meadows Bar, where the livery met us to pick-up our rented canoes. After a beer or 2, we took a brief hiatus to check into our rooms at the nearby & appropriately-named Toasty's Cabins, soon returning to Meadows for dinner, drinks, and pool shootin' over the televised backdrop of Baseball's All-Star game (American League wins their 7th in a row!).

Moth had crammed an entire 4 days of partyin' into this one day, a plan that caught up with him at the bar around sunset. No one really knows why, but one of his last conscious acts was setting his chair just inside the main entrance, facing it out towards the flow of incoming customers (of which there were many), and sitting down just before passing out. For all who served as witness, the image is firmly embedded in their memory of Moth slouched over, mouth open, slight drool, chin on chest, his shirt unbuttoned & belly unleashed, allowing over 3 decades of beer drinkin' to cascade out, like a merging spring bubbling over a broken stone wall, while arriving families ushered in children with eyes shielded, around this cork-in-the-bottle greeting committee of one.

2009 marked Captain Johnny's first 4Day in 10 years, making this his first time on the trip since Mc's Tally Ho bar owner Betsy passed back in 2001. The Captain's family is originally from the Upper Peninsula town of Grand Marais. Although residing in Jacksonville, Florida these days, an unbreakable bond to Michigan and it's "Up North" reaches will always be in his blood. In part because of his family's U.P. ties, Captain Johnny is as responsible as anyone in introducing Betsy to the 4Day, and the 4Day to Betsy. Standing at the Meadows Bar with a PBR in hand, Johnny flashed back to his Betsy McCormick initiation…

"I recall one particular event when 4Dayers were denied bringing pizza into a bar in Germfask

(*Author's note:* the Jolly Bar 1994). Being in a somewhat irritated state of mind, family always said things in Germfask just aren't quite right, I popped into my rental and hit Ten Curves Road remembering Brother Bill saying he had done some time at the Anchor Inn in Curtis. Upon my arrival, the only thing moving at the Anchor were the flies. I decided to stroll across the street attracted by the Johnny Cash booming out the front door and found myself sitting at the Mc's Tally Ho! A nice shot of Jack and a cold beer took the edge off my attitude and lo and behold this pleasant lady plants herself next to me and asks how I'm doing. I tell her my tale of woe and how poorly my friends were treated by the surly bartender in Germfask (*Author's note 2:* never forget what Augustus McCrae taught us, "Ain't much of a crime, whackin' a surly bartender.").

I explained to her that we wanted to bring in pizza and we certainly would drink enough to send his accountant screaming into the night. Betsy, in her best little grin, thought for a moment and said, 'Yeah, I know that guy, we all know that guy. He wanted to work for me but I wouldn't have him.' I ordered us both another drink and got the ten cent tour along with a game of name exchange and it turns out that Betsy had met my cousin Rudy."

"Betsy was a fine lady who was great at engaging conversation, a tavern owner of the old cut who made you feel welcome while at the same time letting you know what the ground rules were for her place. Betsy finished her drink, said she had the late shift that night, and wanted a little nap, so I thanked her for the fine conversation and said I would see her later. Washing down the last of my beer, I turned to leave when Betsy tugged at my arm and said, 'You tell your friends they can bring their pizza or I can offer some of my own, we keep it out back.' The rest is 4Day history and a top notch one it is. I can think of few finer things than ratting on the river for four days then catching a hot shower and strolling into Betsy's and taking in that tavern smell, the juke box thud, and the scent of her great burgers on the grille."

"Did Betsy find me when the timing couldn't have been better for us both? Absolutely. Betsy was one in a million and my time on the 4Day was even better when we were able to stop at her bar and get a hug and a burger and watch her shake her head at Vid. As a side note, I was always let down that Betsy took Gomie dancing and not me."

Driving home the day after it all, our thoughts are with Big Guy, traveling today to Arlington National Cemetery to attend a memorial service for his Navy veteran Father, Woody Alwood, one of the really good guys. God bless!

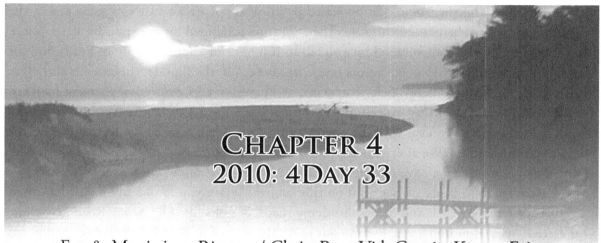

# CHAPTER 4
# 2010: 4DAY 33

Fox & Manistique Rivers w/ Chris, Ron, Vid, Gomie, Kenny, Eric, Johnny, Neal, Brittany (ashes), Rusty, Lutostanski and Doc

*For lo the winter is past, the rain is over & gone*
*The flowers appear on the earth,*
*& the time of the singing of birds has come*
*& the voice of the turtle is heard in our land*
*Happy New Year, Tiger Baseball!*
*(Song of Solomon 2:12, with a tweak, by Ernie Harwell, RIP 5.4.10)*

3 days before Ernie left for the Other Side, Michigan's ban on smoking in bars and restaurants took effect. On ban's eve, the softball team, heavily-4Dayer-populated, gathered at our sponsor bar and unofficial clubhouse, the Mobil Lounge, for a final cigar or two. For the first time in our 25 years at the Mobil, *Sixteen Tons* was not on the bar's juke box. An Internet juke box, one that's supposed to have just about every song ever recorded, had recently replaced the old, trusted, 45 rpm record player. Bar employee Dave tried to help us locate the song on the new- fangled device. After several unsuccessful minutes, he asked if we were sure the song title was *Sixteen Tons*. Yeah, after singing the song an estimated 500 times during a quarter-century of Thursday nights (and a few other assorted evenings), we're pretty sure that's the title.

Without the endearing recording of an Ernie other than Harwell, Tennessee Ernie Ford, to lead us, the boys began to sing *Sixteen Tons* acapella. Vid's critique was kind, "I've heard us do a lot worse." Maybe our voices or his ears were influenced by consumption levels. We established a new all-time Mobil Lounge tab high of $379 this evening, boosting the impending retirement fund of looking-to-sell bar owner and good friend Sharon.

In only two months, we'll get in plenty of acapella time, Ernie Harwell memories, and cigar smoking on the waters of the Fox as we celebrate 4Day 33.

It has been 5 years since we last canoed the Fox River through its most-romanticized *and* most-challenging section, downstream from the Seney Township Campsite. This stretch takes us to some of our favorite spots: the Spreads where the Fox breaks into several narrow, fast-flowing, fingers, on a 30 minute joy ride, followed by a break at Boot Hill, with its elevated, gorgeous view of the river, and then to a location stated by all who put up a tent there to be one of the finest campsites anywhere, the Peninsula. The Peninsula is defined by its expansive flat ground, ideal for multiple tents, surrounded by a thick, lush forest, an endless supply of deadwood for fires, overlooking a big river bend from a fine vista above. On the flipside, this stretch also takes us through a several-hour debris field that spans, in an average trip, a dozen or so major logjams.

6 months before the 4Day, paddling this sounds like a great idea, a dozen or so logjams be damned. Then, as time to deal with the obstructions draws near, bets are hedged, and concerns begin to be heard that, "We ain't kids anymore," and "It's not that we have to drag canoes over all the logjams, it's that we have to drag *fully-loaded 'n weighted down canoes* over logjams."

I sent an email to livery owner Tom on this subject, "Have you found any roads that reach the Fox between Germfask and Seney? Studying maps, it looks like Old Seney Road gets close. Our eternal quest is to find a way to drop our gear off ahead of us on this river stretch to lighten the canoe weights for the inevitable deadwood pull-overs. If no roads in have been found, here's another question: do you know of any trusted young bucks who would be willing to paddle our gear down ahead of us for a fee?" Tom's answer was to the point and funny, "Gee, you don't want much, do you? Just keep the guys at Andy's for 4 days. I'll bring up some pictures and when they come to, we'll tell 'em they had the best time ever!" Tom elaborated, "I've tried hiking in to the river and hiking back out. With a load of gear, you wouldn't want to do it. With *your* load, forget it. Hired paddling would take 6 guys with 3 canoes all day to drop your stuff and come out at this end. It wouldn't be cheap, *if* I could find guys. On second thought, it might be cheaper than 4 days at Andy's!"

Tom's reply was greeted with laughter and helped convince us to revise our canoeing itinerary. Plan B, devised in June during the celebration of Vid's 60th, at Conor O'Neill's, a truly fine Irish pub, just one month before the 4Day, had us paddling all 4 days on the Fox River north of Seney and subsequent big logjams. This would require us to launch upstream from the Fox Overlook, further north on the river than we'd ever 4Dayed before. It seemed like a welcome opportunity to experience a previously unexplored part of the Fox – until we discussed Plan B with Tom.

Tom warned us that the few brave souls putting in at Wagner Taylor Dam Road, the only access north of the Fox Overlook, ran into a stretch of the river so choked with deadfall that they were out of their canoes at every bend. I'm starting to think that Tom is trying to harsh our buzz.

Reviewing the maps, an option appeared. I proposed to Tom putting us in on a tiny tributary to the Fox, one that merges with the Fox upstream from the Overlook, but downstream from the deadfall near Wagner Taylor, the Little Fox River. I was unable to recall either this Tom (since 2000) or old Tom (1972-1999) ever launching anyone into the Little Fox. What a great adventure this could be!

Tom's reply was prudent. He suggested sending his right-hand man, veteran canoeist Phil, down the Little Fox first, to give us a preview. Sound move Tom! Phil underwent *the trip through hades*. Once he could make his way through a tangle of trees and bushes to get from the road to the water, the first 3/4s of the canoe trip, from the Little Fox put-in to the Fox River Overlook take-out, had to be spent bent over forwards or lying on his back, paddling as best he could, in order to pass beneath a solid wall of low-hanging branches forming a virtual low-ceiling culvert.

Tom said when Phil returned to the livery, he and his canoe were covered in mud and leaves. Upon hearing this story, the "no" vote of the Council of Elders was unanimous.

A new plan met with the approval of all: spend a leisurely 3 days navigating the Fox from the Overlook to the Seney campsite, with a 4th and final day on the Manistique River ending at the livery.

4Day-eve, as we prepared to depart from Southeast Michigan for the U.P., Gomie asked Vid a question that seemed strange coming from someone who's going on his 17th 4Day, "How long does it take to get to Germfask from Ann Arbor?" Vid replied, "4 bars."

That 4th bar was actually 7 miles north of Germfask, Andy's Seney Bar, down the street from our night's lodging at the Fox River Motel. After a great deal of carousing, Ron asked if it was too late to revert to Tom's first suggestion, "Just keep the guys at Andy's for 4 days. I'll bring up some pictures and when they come to, we'll tell 'em they had the best time ever!" Support for Ron's suggestion was growing stronger with each beer 'n shot that went down. Finally, Johnny and Neal, the two guys who were only paddling one day before heading home, served as the voices of reason, and Tom's words survived as a fond 4Day footnote.

Day 1 morning is drop-dead gorgeous. That does little to assist us in gathering our wits and gear, but breakfast, a few hundred feet down M28 at the little Seney Restaurant, motivates. After being fed, a final pre-river use of the facilities awaits before checking out of the Fox River Motel. Tents are soon set-up 5 minutes from the motel at the Township Campsite with a half an hour to spare before Tom grabs us up for the noon drive to the Overlook access. Halfway to the Overlook, we drop vehicles at the hill above wooden rails leading to the river, today's end point.

Land-lubbers Rusty Vollmers and sophomore Lutostanski, joining us for 4Day camping only, follow Tom's livery van to see us off. As we start to float away from the Overlook, Lutostanski walks out on to a tree limb that hovers above the Fox, we stretch towards him with our first fifth,

Beam's Eight Star, a big name for rot gut. Reaching for the fifth, Lutostanski drops his phone into the river. We fish it out and hand it back to him. I told him, "Don't worry. Over the years, I've had plenty of electronic devices go underwater. Just remove the batteries, and then bury the phone into a bag of dry rice." Fortunately, he and Rusty have dry rice back at camp. "The rice will absorb the moisture that got into the phone. It may take a few hours, maybe even overnight, but your phone will work again."

I guess that I should've added, "Don't take out the batteries while balancing precariously on the tree limb," since Lutostanski then drops the battery compartment cover into the Fox. Offering a fifth and advice had done enough damage, so we wave good-bye to him and Rusty, rounding the next bend as the two disappear from our sight, assuming that if we see Lutostanski in camp when we get in, that he made it safely off of the tree limb.

First stop, Mad Dog. Eric stands in the river next to his cooler, supporting on its lid E's ever-present 24 ounce Budweiser, as he chugs the Mad Dog bottle that Chris hands to him. These fellers are out of the starting gate fast! Kenny mentions that quick starts like this reminds him of that Wisconsin restaurant we stopped into for breakfast before canoeing the Black River. The waitress greeted us with, "Mornin'! Can I get you a Pabst?"

We know that Neal is serious about partyin' today, his only chance to 4Day before heading back to work in Milwaukee, when he does not need to be asked 4 times to hit any fifths circulating at each stop. His one-day-only brother Johnny is right there, step-by-step with Neal, although Johnny's steps soon became somewhat staggered as he finds difficulty negotiating the flat, sandy, river floor in the shallow, knee-deep water.

Canoeing through the Upper Fox, we encounter the usual series of fallen branches to zig-zag around and occasionally meet up with a river blockage requiring hopping out of the boat to pull it over the debris before boarding the canoe again. Never is there a logjam of the size run into downstream from Seney.

The longest Day 1 stop is at the Fox River Campground, about 2 hours shy of where our vehicles are parked. Chris pulls a fifth of Ezra Brooks out of his cooler. When passed to Vid, he takes time to study the label. Watching him, Gomie starts laughing, "Vid, I thought you couldn't see anything without your glasses." Vid, factoring in the brew he's consumed today, tells Gomie, "Hey, I don't need my glasses. I'm beer-sighted!"

We get to talking about old Tiger Stadium, amazed to think it's been a full decade the Boys of Summer have been playing at Comerica, which we still call Tiger Stadium despite Comerica Bank paying $66 million for the naming rights. Chris starts reminiscing about the final game at the Corner back in '99. *"Gibby and the Tiger broadcast team did their play-by-play about 50' away from us, in an Upper Deck box down the right field line. Jimmy walked over and got Gibson's autograph on his game program. All the players wore the numbers of famous Tigers. Rob Fick wore Norm Cash's number 25, then won the game with a grand slam home run on top of the right field roof, a few feet over our heads, right where Norm hit 3 homers. It was so cool! Jimmy, Doc, Laz, Connie, and I bought a 21-game package to make sure we had seats for this final game at Michigan and Trumbull. Billy Rogell threw out the first pitch, kind of doubtful to even Billy if that would happen, since in the morning he was interviewed saying, **First pitch? Hell, I'm 95! I can barely stand up!**"*

On the subject of barely standing up, I tell a story from college days, *"It was in 1976, when I shared an EMU off-campus apartment with Ricki, Marquis, and Mongo. After an evening of fun, I woke up in bed, still dressed from the night before. Lifting my head, I see a half-eaten pizza lying on my stomach. Something's not right here. Why would half, or any, of a pizza still be left? I don't leave pizza uneaten, especially when I was 21 years old. So I sat up, took a closer look, and started laughing. The remaining pizza was still on the cardboard insert that I heated it up on, and the only part of the cardboard left was right below the pizza. I never took the pizza off of the cardboard. **I ate the cardboard right along with the pizza!** When I lifted the pizza up in the morning, the cardboard* *below looked like a half moon with bite marks on it. I remember thinking, oh yeah, that pizza <u>did</u> taste unusually chewy.*"

As all 4 canoes arrive at the wooden canoe rails about 10 minutes apart, everyone pitches in to pull our coolers, boats, and each other up the hill to our vehicles. Back in camp, we find out that Lutostanski never did find his phone battery compartment cover that had dropped into the river, but he himself did not splash into the Fox from the limb he was wobbling on, a real possibility based on his arc of luck when we last saw him.

Since Johnny and Neal are leaving us in the morning, they signed up with Chris for camp dinner tonight. Neal aka Mister Bratwurst, brought his fine Wisconsin brats, as delicious for dinner as for breakfast, to go along with a delectable stew and after-dinner cigars, all courtesy of tonight's 3 chefs. Post-chow time, some walk and some drive to Andy's for a blurry night of fun and much Dickel, aka George Dickel Tennessee Whiskey.

I crawl out of my tent to find a soundly sleeping campsite, as dawn breaks on Day 2. After getting in my daily 3-mile walk, with a trek to Seney and back, I begin a little camp pick up and take inventory of my gear. Hmm, no sign of my river shoes. Must have left them at our Fox take-out spot yesterday, a couple hundred yards in from Fox River Road.

By now, Gomie and Vid are awake, and they join me for the 10-minute drive to where we left the river yesterday. The 3 of us search the river banks, along trails, under forest brush, and turn up nothing. Fortunately, I packed an extra pair of water shoes for this 4Day. Back in camp, the sweet smell of sausage, scrambled eggs, and bagels that Rusty and Lutostanski put out for us push any thoughts of river-wear out of my head.

The sun shined on us this entire day on the water, the hours on the river flowing by way too fast. A baseball game breaks out, paddles used as bats and a small, plastic football pitched for the ball. Lutostanski decides that this will be the one day he'll paddle with us. His goal seems to be to drink 4 days of bourbon in 1. When he does back-to-back double bubblers, Kenny calls it, "Ill-advised, but impressive."

Paddling into camp, no work is required for the evening as our tents are already up from last night, while Rusty & Lutostanski stockpiled enough firewood yesterday, during the time that the rest of us canoed, to cover us for a full week. The impressive firewood gathering was a huge surprise since in Lutostanski's rookie year of 1996, his only other 4Day appearance, the total lack of effort placed him behind a smiley-face Frisbee in rookie-of-the-year voting.

Right on time, the delivery man from Stop Pizza in Curtis pulls in with the pizzas 'n hoagies that Ron and I ordered earlier in the week. After filling our bellies, we stroll up Fox River Road - except Lutostanski, still passed out on the picnic table, with Rusty occasionally checking his pulse - smoking cigars, telling stories, laughing, and singing *Sixteen Tons & Men* on the half-hour walk to Andy's Seney Bar.

As we approach Andy's, employee Jackie is standing on the bar porch, and asks, "Doc, you gonna get your shoes or you just gonna leave 'em here 'til next year?" Yes, the very shoes that Gomie and Vid helped me look for along the river this morning.

Apparently, after getting off the river yesterday, I took my wet shoes off, changed into the dry shoes I had with me (must have been in somebody's car), and left the wet ones at the bar. The evening of blurry excess had erased any memory of doing this. Gomie seems surprised by what Jackie said, "I don't even remember *going* to Andy's last night."

"Yep," Colonel once said, "it's all now as clear as the mud on the inside of Jimmy's dry shoes."

An older couple across the bar starts waving at me as we played table top shuffleboard. They seem like nice folks, and when I smile and wave back, they walk over. "Are you Doc Fletcher?" Yes I am. "We have your book, and you guys are standing on our bridge!" It turns out that the couple, Mik and Dick, own 1,000 acres along the Manistique and Fox Rivers, including the new steel bridge, formerly home to (and sung with gusto) *the... Old... Log... Bridge.* Mik aka Mikki's granddaughter had purchased a copy of "Weekend Canoeing in Michigan", saw a happy bunch of fellas standing on the bridge, and called Grandma to tell her about it. Mik was happy to hear the bridge is an annual stop for us. Her first husband was the deceased Terrance Carroll, the man that the beautiful tribute of a flower garden and memorial stone tablet, beneath a flag flying high, at Ten Curves Dam is in honor of. Mik and Dick live on the Manistique a couple of downstream bends from the dam, and asked us to look for them when we next paddle through. "Well Mik and Dick, we should be canoeing by your place about noon on Tuesday." "Great, we'll be waiting for you boys!" It's nice to be in your 50s and still be called boys.

Andy isn't at his bar this week, and he is missed. With his 71st birthday coming up July 16, I left a copy of "Weekend Canoeing" (since the book includes plenty of Andy-talk) for him with the inscription, "Thanks for the friendship, good times, & Dickel".

Eric and Kenny prepare a delicious Day 3 breakfast of eggs, bacon, toast, and cereal. Later, Chris, Ron, Eric, Rusty, and Lutostanski decide to head up to Grand Marais for the day, while Gomie, Kenny, Vidder and I re-trace yesterday's river journey, from the wooden canoe rails to our tents. It is one of the milder 4Day afternoons I can ever recall. Under sunny skies there are, like yesterday, only a couple of logs that necessitate getting out of the boats. The hot weather makes plunging into the cool waters of the Fox a very happy experience. Sipping on a few Labatt Blues, smoking a cigar, sharing stories and laughs, all is right in God's kingdom here on earth.

Pulling the canoes ashore at the Seney Township site, we find the Grand Marais Knitting Club back from their side adventure, ready for the Andy burgers that Gomie and Vid are picking up the tab for tonight. At the pub, Kenny gets to talking about some of the Wisconsin rivers we'd paddled the last couple of years, and the interesting characters met on the journey, *"On the Eau Claire River, a deer was running up a side creek towards us chased by a crane swooping in low behind it, eagles were flying overhead, turtles were racing on a beach to the river – I've never seen that one – and there were some wild rapids to steer through. What a great river!"* On the west side of Wisconsin, an older fella named Dave Steele owned a combination canoe livery and winery on the Eau Claire River. *"As livery man Dave drove us to the put-in, he told us it's been his experience in the wilderness that there's not a place on earth you cannot get a beer to."*

On Day 4, Kenny and Eric volunteered to pull double-duty, handling breakfast for the 2nd day in a row. After scarfing down eggs 'n bacon, we break down our Fox River camp. It's been arranged that Tom will arrive with the Northland Outfitters' van at 11, we'll help load the canoes on to his trailer, then transport the boats to the Manistique River. Following Tom south on M77, we will drop our vehicles at the livery, where today's paddle will end, and board the Outfitters' van for the ride to the Ten Curves Road put-in.

30 paddling minutes in, two bends past the dam, we can see in the distance a couple standing and waving on a pedestrian bridge above the river. "Hey, it's Mik and Dick!" This bridge is a few

steps from their home. 20' or so in front of Mik and Dick, we paddle in place, chatting with the nice couple we'd met two nights ago at Andy's. Mik asks about her beautiful bridge down river from where we're at now, where the Manistique and Fox merge, "Will you boys be stopping at our bridge today?" "Mik," I ask, "are you referring to...", and without prompting, the boys sing along, "*the... Old... Log... Bridge?*" The confused look on her face tells me that an explanation is required. "In '91, when you replaced the bridge's old log supports with metal ones, we began nostalgic singing about how the bridge used to be in our early 4Days." Mik kinda gets it, we guess. After a little more pleasant conversing, we bid Mik and Dick adieu, and promise to look for each other at future Andy's Bar visits.

Within a half an hour of saying our good-byes, we arrive at, stand on, and sing *the... Old... Log... Bridge!* I quickly change the topic from Mik and Dick. "Tuesday is pizza night at the Jolly! It's pizza night at the Jolly! It's pizza night at the Jolly!" I'm shoutin' and dancin' here and at each subsequent river break, hankerin' for the great pizza the Jolly has always put out.

The Jolly Bar was not originally in the plans for this year's 4Day. Previous owner Carol had sold the building sometime after our last beer was drunk there in 2008, two years ago, and no new tavern was yet operating on the site last year or as recently as April of this year. However, new ownership has re-opened the bar, and its pizza ovens, just in time for us to enjoy an evening there tonight.

After taking the canoes & kayaks out of the river at trip's end, I visit with Tom at the livery, while the rest of boys hoof it on over to the Jolly Bar for pizza 'n beer. "No pizza tonight fellas, the pizza ovens are down." "Oh, oh," Vid tells the barkeep, "we got a guy who's been doin' the pizza dance all day on the river who won't be very happy."

As soon as I arrive at the tavern, I hear the sad news from Vid who's waiting for the explosion. Instead I calmly ask the waitri what the pizza story is, and she tells me, "We only have one oven working, not enough to accommodate the usual Pizza Night demand. A lot of families come in for Pizza Night only, so we had to send those customers home." "Mm, you say one oven is still working? So, you could make a single pizza?" "Yeah, we could do that." "Great! I'll take one large with mushrooms, thanks!"

My Guardian Angel was working overtime again. If the ovens were running at full capacity, I'd be waiting in a long line for a pie behind the usual turnout of families, but, now I'm the first to put a pizza order in, and the finished product is placed in front of me in 20 minutes. Next, a few of the guys also order pizza, and all is well in 4Day land. Thank you, Guardian Angel!

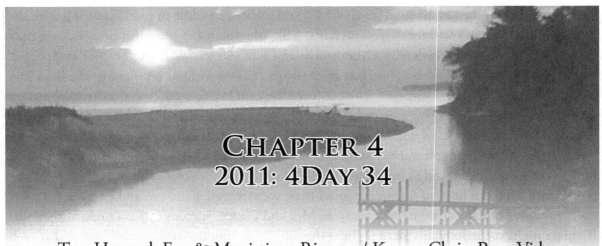

# CHAPTER 4
# 2011: 4DAY 34

Two Hearted, Fox & Manistique Rivers w/ Kenny, Chris, Ron, Vid,
Jimmy, Neal, Eric, Brittany (ashes), Doc and rookie Mister P

*If life seems jolly rotten, there's something you've forgotten!*
*And that's to laugh and smile and dance and sing,*
*When you're feeling in the dumps, don't be silly chumps,*
*Just purse your lips and whistle – that's the thing!*
*And always look on the bright side of life*
*(Always Look on the Bright Side of Life by Monty Python/from the movie Life of Brian)*

For a non-4Dayin' teetotaler, old friend Brian Vittes, a man we immediately renamed Life in honor of the 1979 movie the *Life of Brian*, released the year we met him, shared with us an observation showing keen insight, "I'll say one thing about drinking – it's a good way to get hammered." Affirming the veracity of Life's astute awareness are the experiences of 3 men, dubbed by 4Dayer Rusty "the Illustrious Alumni of the 4Day Fraternity", each celebrating their 20th 4Day this year: Jimmy, class of '82, Chris, class of '90, and Vid, class of '92. Utilizing a six-beer-per-man-per-day baseline established in 2002 by the Council of Elders, including all imbibing on 4Day-eve, Jimmy, Chris & Vid can offer a combined 1,800 4Day beers worth of confirmation to Life's theory.

The 3 veterans will be spending their 20th on this year's expedition down the waters of 3 Upper Peninsula Rivers: the Two Hearted, the Fox, and the Manistique.

2011 marks the inaugural 4Day paddle down the Two Hearted River. Separate from the 4Day, a single afternoon excursion on this stream was taken four years ago. Those on that journey have been looking forward to returning ever since to the beauty of its winding waters, sandy beaches, dunes, and thickly-forested riverbanks.

One of the paddlers from that 2007 day on the Two Hearted is the single 4Day rookie this year, Paul Pienta aka Mister P or the Peester or simply "P". Back in the 70s, P's little black book on the ladies rivaled Sam Malone's. He's the P-nuttiest, a wonderful friend, but a man who tends to see the world in shades of black. What may have finally enticed P to join us on the 4Day was a group effort, a tongue-in-cheek unveiling to him one night at the Mobil Lounge about the typical daily 4Day food plan: "for breakfast we have ham 'n eggs, for lunch big 'ole ham sandwiches, and for dinner thick ham steaks". This menu was presented as a bow to P being a well-known ham-maniac, probably best illustrated by this example: at a New Year's Eve party, P's New Years' resolution was to cut back on ham consumption. No more than 30 minutes after midnight, he had built and was consuming what, to most observers, was the largest ham sandwich they had ever seen. Looking back on it, maybe that was cutting back for P.

4Day-eve is being spent in Seney. After checking into the Fox River Motel, we wander across M28 to Andy's Bar. Andy is in a great mood, "Hey, you boys back here again, eh?" He bought us a round of Dickel, and provided an update on Banjo Bob, BJay's fellow guitar picker during the 1991 4Day. "I book Banjo's band to play here every couple of months. He keeps asking me to bring them in more often, but since the band only knows 4 or 5 songs, I like to wait 'til my customers forget those numbers." "Does Banjo Bob still live in his car?" I asked. "Nah that was another guy. Banjo and his wife live in the woods and I bring them packages of food every few days."

Although the bar is crowded, it's our good fortune that Andy is comfortable letting his help take care of the regulars and our dinner order of Andy burgers, and just hang out with these 4Day fellas from Down Below. After 3 more rounds of Dickel, Andy hits his stride, kicking back with laughs and stories. It is clear he made the right choice back in '78, leaving his job driving a big rig to become a bar owner. Andy tells us he owns 3 homes, one behind the bar, another along the Suwannee River near Gainesville, Florida where he stays November through April each year, and the third on the Manistique River in the Ten Curves Club neighborhood, near Mik 'n Dick's place, two bends downstream from the dam. He sold that third one this year since "I didn't stay overnight one night in the 5 years that I owned it".

With midnight calling and a belly full of beer, burgers, 'n bourbon, we say our good-byes to Andy. "You boys up here all week?" Neal tells him, "We're doing a day on the Two Hearted, and we'll be back in Seney for some canoeing on the Fox in two days." "I'll see you fellas then!"

Day 1 is a busy one, requiring an early start. Before making the 90 minute drive to the edge of Lake Superior at Rainbow Lodge, the livery & cabins for the Two Hearted, we need to check-out of the motel and get some breakfast in us. The little restaurant in Seney is closed this year, its existence is always a crap shoot, so we drive down to Germfask for food at the Jolly Bar. After scarfing plenty at their buffet, we begin the caravan to Lake Superior.

Just north of the town of Newberry, past where we expect that historical markers will eventually be placed in honor of Moth's 1994 head wound & subsequent medical treatment at the Newberry Hospital, two black bear cubs do a little gallop across the road 100' in front of my lead vehicle. Ah, the wondrous sights of the U.P.! Running right on schedule, we pull into the parking lot in front of Rainbow Lodge with 30 minutes to spare before 11AM, when livery owners Kathy and Richard Robinson will take us, our river gear, and a trailer full of canoes to the put-in access. The extra 30 minutes gives us time to sign-in for our overnight stay and toss our bags into the 4 rustic lodges reserved for us.

Launching from the Reed & Green Bridge, we begin canoeing the Lower Two Hearted, the final 11 miles of the 24-mile long river, taking it until it empties into Lake Superior. Downstream two bends, we pull over in order to partake of a gift given to me this past Christmas by my brother-in-law Billy, a gift that he requested we enjoy on the 4Day. The gift comes with the $4 price tag still on it and includes a fifth of Old Forrester, well below our ceiling of $9.99 a fifth, a fact Billy happily pointed out, and a copy of the 21st Amendment. The reason for the tie-in is that this is a special bourbon batch utilizing a 1933 recipe, the same year that Prohibition was repealed under the 21st Amendment.

Old Forrester, established in 1870, claims to be America's first bottled bourbon. Billy suggested we open, sip, and pass this oldest of bourbons as a solemn reading of the 21st Amendment takes place. This was done to shouts of "Hear! Hear!" Jimmy noted that when the 21st Amendment was enacted on December 5, 1933, "The fine gentlemen of the Senate and House were on their game that day!"

The boys love the Two Hearted – and what's not to love! It's a river with multiple runs of light rapids, too many to count gorgeous sandy beaches, pine trees as far as the eye can see, and sand dunes. Plenty of sand dunes, several that Eric the Younger (than the vast majority of us) is taking the time to climb during paddle breaks. Across the river from us, standing 2/3rds of the way up a dune, Eric looks like a 4Day postcard.

The spectacular sandy beaches grow in number and size as we near Lake Superior, drawing us in for several river breaks. It is on the second such break, the break after the 21st Amendment was read, that the Old Forrester nears its end and Ron comments, "The more I drink Old Forrester, the more I miss Dickel. And I don't like Dickel." Yet after sipping the Forrester, Ron is inspired to tell us, "*Reintarnation* means coming back to life as a hillbilly."

Floating downstream together, some traditional teasing of the rookie takes place. I need little prodding, "The last two years, we paddled first the Brule and then the Menominee River with an outfitters out of Iron Mountain. The Toni and P canoe took a flip on the Brule in '09, so when we returned last year for the Menominee, the livery owner handed a life jacket to Peester and assured him, "This is the one you wore on the Brule last year, so it's been tested for floatation."

The dinner crew is two, Kenny and Rookie P. 3 hours into today's 4 hour journey, we took a paddling break on another gorgeous sandy beach. An hour of canoeing from here, the Two Hearted take-out access is a metal ramp 300' before the river empties into Lake Superior. We talk about paddling past that metal ramp and out into the Big Lake's waters, riding the bobbing waves for a few minutes, before canoeing back to the ramp. While we kibitz, it's evident to all that Rookie P is figuratively watching the clock, starting to get nervous about his dinner responsibilities. P abruptly says, "Kenny, we gotta go now!" Kenny assures Peester that all is well, no one is in a hurry (although always willing) to eat, and that the group will likely take another break or two, but the rookie's anxiety wins the day, and the evening's chefs take to their canoe and are out of sight in seconds.

The remaining 4 canoes shove off 15 minutes later, eventually taking the additional two beach breaks that Kenny had forecasted. 2 hours or so after Rookie P and Kenny were last seen, we paddle by the access ramp, see the chefs' beached empty canoe, and continue on into Lake Superior for a little more water fun, before turning for home and chow time.

The finely prepared *Boy Scout Burger* dinners are separately wrapped in aluminum with onions, carrots, potatoes, and seasoning. An evening of drink and cigars around the campfire follow, before the crew drifts off to our cabin beds. Early Day 2 morning, Kenny and I take a walk down by the river mouth, Kenny asking me to point out how far into Lake Superior we canoed yesterday. He sighs at what he missed, "P wouldn't paddle out there. He was too worried about having dinner ready on time." When I say, "Well, that's P." Kenny, always upbeat, replies with a sharp, "Yeah, that's P alright," a fairly normal reaction for most, but about as rough as you'll ever hear come out of Kenny, his disappointment at missing the row into the Big Lake impossible to hide. The canoes had already been picked up by the livery folks, so we could not do a short morning float into Lake Superior, but I promise Kenny that, "We will come back and get you into this lake."

There's no need to push the boys to get moving this morning, 'cause no one eats until we get to Zeller's Restaurant in Newberry, 45 minutes away, prompting us to pack and depart our Two Hearted cabins before 9AM. By noon, we've eaten and stopped at Andy's for a quick post-breakfast shot, no sign of the man himself, and have our tents and Eric's camper set up at the Seney Township site, our home tonight and tomorrow night after two days on the Fox River. Tom Kenney from Northland Outfitters will be by soon with a trailer-full of canoes and a van to transport us upstream to the Fox River Campground launch site.

Tom told us before the 4Day that he and wife Sally sold the livery to another couple, Leon and Donna Genre from Down Below in Clarkston. So, to date, the 4Dayers have outlasted two sets of owners, old Tom & Carma from 1978 to 1999, and new Tom & Sally from 2000 to 2011. Tom has agreed to stay on in the short-term to assist Leon through the growing pains of new ownership.

Kenny brought cherries that have soaked in Jack Daniels since last 4Day. When Tom dropped us off, but before he drove away, he joined us in a couple of cherries each as an edible toast to his decade of being part of 4Day tradition. Neal asked, "Tom, now are you finally going to join us for a 4Day?" Tom laughed, and said, "You boys drink too fast for me!" Neal assured Tom, "The only place that I'm going fast is downhill." We'll have to work on Tom, but his day is coming.

The Fox is its usual fabulous self, featuring the wonderfully familiar quick, tight turns and fast flow through a narrow riverbed. The only downside is that Rookie P headed home after the Two Hearted, sad to see him come all this way north and miss this extraordinary river. Eric was optimistic, "Maybe we'll get both P and Tom for all 4 days next year," an idea met by cheers, suggested by several as worthy of a toast. Within seconds, Vid answers the call of the thirsty with a fifth of Banker's Club pulled from his cooler. Jimmy saw the wisdom in Vid's move, nodding towards him, "Hell hath no fury like a bottle unopened."

At a long riverbank stop an hour downstream from the Fox River Campground launch, Ron talked about truck problems he experienced on the drive north. "The mechanic told me, 'Looks like you blew a seal.' I told him to keep my sex life out of it, and just fix the truck." That story got Kenny to tell us a joke that doubled us over in laughter, one that will be told and retold for many 4Days, "I'm not a gynecologist, but I'll take a look."

Vid and I arranged to have Tom deliver Jolly Bar pizzas to the Seney camp tonight. Just about the time that Tom showed with the pile of pizza boxes, here comes Chris, missing-in-action 'til now, wheeling into the campground to join us for the rest of the trip. After chowing down on the pizzas, the crew headed to Andy's for the evening where Andy was holding court among four buddies. In honor of Andy's 72nd birthday a week from today, we included Andy and his friends in our first round of Dickel shots, raising our glasses to him from across the bar.

Fortunately, the table top shuffleboard game and a nearby table are both open for us. After a couple of games, Vid shared with us a Disney moment, a rare occurrence inside the walls of Andy's Seney Bar. "Mickey Mouse is in front of the court asking for a divorce from Minnie Mouse. The judge tells Mickey, "I'm sorry Mickey, but I can't legally separate you two on the grounds that

Minnie is mentally insane." Mickey says, "I didn't say she was mentally insane, I said that she's fucking Goofy!"

Alright! Here comes Andy over to our table. "I've got a round of shots coming. You fellas like Dickel?" After the laughter dies down, Chris replies, "Yeah, we've heard good things about it." The exception is Ron, who asks if he can substitute diesel fuel for his Dickel shot. Barmaid Jackie says we're out of diesel fuel and brings over a tray with 9 Dickel half-shots. Half-shots? She explains to us under her breath, "We try to keep an eye on Andy's health, and not give him too much to drink." Well, I don't know how the 12 rounds of half-shots Andy joined us on will affect his health, but he was as blistered as the guys walking a broken line back to camp.

Day 3, Eric and Neal got us started on the right foot with a delectable breakfast of eggs, hash browns, and those fine Wisconsin brats that Neal keeps spoiling us with. Chris grabbed an unfamiliar camera to record for posterity a campground scene, "How do you turn this on?" Ron took a stab at it, "Buy it dinner and drinks!"

We launch today at the wooden rails leading down to the Fox from a DNR site. At the first bend, Chris asks that we pull over. When all the canoes are in, he raises a fifth of Fleischmann's. "Gentlemen, and you fellers, my buddy and our 4Day brother, Gillam, passed away a week ago. I'd like us all to drink in his honor." Gary Gillam, one of the most colorful characters to come 4Dayin' with us, passed away July 2. Chris' fellow US Navy veteran was a friendly, eccentric, good-hearted soul. His gentle presence will be missed. Chris brought along on the trip Gillam's old Detroit Tiger hat, charming in its special, very-Gillam-like, tattered and scruffy way.

Today is another in a series of gorgeous moments we've enjoyed on the Fox over the years, with the warmth of the shared experience, full of many stops and many stories…

Jimmy takes a healthy pull from a fifth of Cabin Still, a nice 'n nasty whiskey, before sharing a military tale with us, *"I don't know if this is a true story, but it's a good one. An officer in the U.S. Naval Reserve was attending a conference that included admirals from the U.S. Navy and the French Navy. At a cocktail reception, he found himself in a small group that included personnel from both navies. The French admiral started complaining that whereas Europeans learned many languages, Americans learned only English. He then asked,* 'Why is it that we have to speak English in these conferences rather than you speak French?' *Without hesitating, the U.S. Admiral replied,* 'Maybe it's because we arranged it so you didn't have to speak German.' *The naval group became silent."*

I don't know how we got from the military to my baseball cards, but Cabin Still is magic, so I started in, *"The first pack of baseball cards I ever bought was in the Spring of 1963. I was 8 years old. It was on way the home from 3rd grade. Mrs. Moth, Debbie Boyd back then, was in my class."* Thinking of Debbie stopped me, and we all toasted to such a sweet lady, lost to our brother Moth and all of us much too soon in 2006. *"To Debbie!"* After a minute, I continued, *"We all bought our baseball cards from the truck of Marv the Ice Cream Man, always parked on the same corner. He sold packs of Topps' cards for a nickel each. In each pack was a piece of stale gum and 5 baseball cards. What do I get in the very first pack of baseball cards that I ever purchase in my life? A team photo of the 1963 New York Frickin' Yankees!"* All at once, 8 guys shout, *"The Yankees Suck!"* You bet we finished the Cabin Still on that toast.

It's hard to get 4Dayers off the baseball chatter when it starts. Sparky Anderson passed away since the last 4Day and Jimmy, who attended Sparky Anderson Day at Comerica Park last month, shared some Sparky-isms, *"Rob Deer showed up at camp muscle-bound. He looks like Venus de Milo."* *"I had only a high school education, and believe me, I had to cheat to get that!"* *"The problem with John Wockenfuss getting on base is that it takes 3 doubles to score him."*

The boys were starving when we canoed into camp, and with dinner tonight being Andy burgers, we wasted no time in trucking into town. We walk in the bar, but there's no Andy.

"Where's Andy at?" Jackie shook her head, "You guys hurt him bad last night with all that Dickel. He's been laying on the couch all day, and can't move."

As a bar owner, Andy is free to drink on the job, something frowned upon in his earlier big rig employment, driving 80,000 pounds of metal. Not to imply that Andy qualifies for this joke, but this reminds me of a line by Saturday Night Live comedian Norm MacDonald, "Alcoholism is a disease, but it's a good disease 'cause it's the only one where you get to be drunk all the time."

Day 4 dawns and, oh man, P really should be here for this one! Chris and Jimmy created a breakfast of big, thick slices of ham and taters. Lord almighty, this is good! After the delicious meal and some facilitating, we tear down camp, and wait for Tom to pick us up. Right on time at 11, we help him load the canoes on to the livery trailer, and follow him to Northland Outfitters. There, we drop our vehicles and jump into the livery van for the ride to a different river, shifting gears from the Fox to the Manistique.

Canoeing takes us from the Ten Curves Road access past the dam, where this year there is no sign of Mik and Dick, although we call their names while paddling past their home, on our way to the new steel bridge, formerly known as, and sung with gusto… the… Old… Log… Bridge.

On the new steel bridge, among the sweet smell of cigars 'n bourbon, Eric had a story, *"Adam was hanging around the Garden of Eden, feeling a little lonely. God asked him what's wrong, and Adam said he didn't have anyone to talk to. God said he'd make Adam a companion and that it would be a woman. God said 'She will gather food for you, cook for you, agree with every decision you make, will not nag you, will be the first to admit she is wrong when you have a disagreement. She will bear your children and never ask you to get up in the middle of the night to take care of them. She will never have a headache and will freely give you love and passion whenever you need it.' Adam asked God, 'What will a woman like this cost?' God replied, 'An arm and a leg.' Then Adam asked, 'What can I get for a rib?' And the rest is history".*

Chris asked Kenny how his pet donkey, Wilbur, was doing. Kenny said, "Hee Haw right," getting the laughter started up again. When it quieted down a bit, Kenny asked and answered another critter question, "Where do you find a dog with no legs? Right where you left him."

Exiting the bridge for the final two hours to the livery, I said, *"Boys, hard to believe it's been 30 years, but back in 1981, WRIF's morning guys, Jim Johnson & George Baier, staged a song contest, asking listeners to change the lyrics to top melodies of the day. So I re-wrote the lyrics of Queen's 'Another One Bites the Dust' to 'Havin' White Meat for Lunch', in honor of Uganda's former President, Idi Amin, rumored to be a cannibal and in the news a lot at the time, and sent the re-written song to WRIF. They play the songs that listeners have submitted, but I never heard mine. Ok. So, I attended the Tigers Opening Day '81, and Johnson & Baier are broadcasting live from a booth in Hoot's parking lot. I stop by the WRIF booth and introduce myself to Baier, nice guy, and ask him if he remembered receiving my 'Havin' White Meat for Lunch' parody. He says, 'You're the guy who sent that in? That was the best song we received, but we couldn't put that on the air.' I learned that day what a strong force the cannibal lobby was."*

Among the singing as the 4Dayers slowly paddled their way to the final 2011 take-out, was the first couple of stanzas to "Havin' White Meat for Lunch" aka "Idi's Song", sung to the tune of "Another One Bites the Dust"

*Idi walks quickly down the street, his fork inside his coat*
*The big man's on the prowl for meat, appetite ready to go*
*Are you running, are you running from this, are you stayin' ahead one street?*
*Ahead of Idi a whitey slips, now a lunchtime treat*

*Havin' white meat for lunch, havin' white meat for lunch*
*Yes, he's havin' white meat, he's havin' white meat,*
*He's havin' white meat for lunch*
*Hey, Caucasian stew, havin' white meat for lunch*

*Author's note:* during October, the Tigers defeated the Yankees Suck in their second ever post-season match-up! The Tigers are now 2 for 2 vs. the Yanks in the playoffs! Jimmy Leyland for Governor!

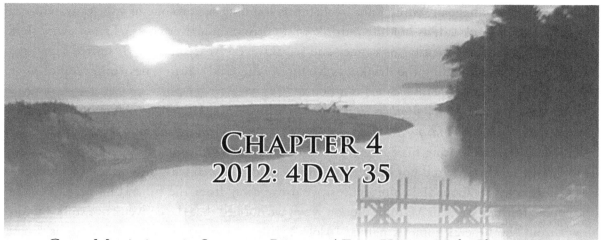

# CHAPTER 4
## 2012: 4DAY 35

Carp, Manistique & Sturgeon Rivers w/ Eric, Kenny, Vid, Chris, Ron, Johnny, Brittany (ashes), Doc and rookies Nick, Dale and Chippy 2Rib

*There is a river called the river of no return*
*Sometimes it's peaceful and sometimes wild and free*
*Love is a traveler on the river of no return*
*Swept on forever to be lost in the stormy sea*
*(River of No Return by Tennessee Ernie Ford) RIP 2012 Marquis, Chucky & my Dad*

On Saturday, July 14, 2012, our beloved, big-hearted, 4Day brother Marquis died.

The following Thursday, the day of Marquis' funeral, Rookie Mark Hayden - 2 days before earning his short-lived 4Day nickname of Chippy and 4 days before earning his permanent 4Day Chippy 2Rib nickname - flew from his North Carolina home to Detroit and into an extraordinary introduction to 4Dayin'. Rookie Mark drove his rental car from the airport to a wake at the Mobil Lounge bar. It was there that the family and friends of Marquis Weaks, all but Maggie and Doc folks Rookie Mark had never met, assembled to play a euchre tourney in Marquis' memory.

The strangest 4Day ever began... strangely. As Maggie and I were about to leave for Marquis' funeral, the phone rang. On the other end was Jeff from Baldwin Canoe Rental. "Doc, did you lose a camera in the river?" "Yeah, a year ago, about one hour paddling time upstream from the Barothy Landing." "Well, I think we found it."

On the morning of Marquis' funeral, a family reunion of people we did not know was wrapping up their vacation at a Barothy Lodge rental cabin along the Pere Marquette River. Just before checking out, two of the family's adult brothers decided on one last river tubing trip. Floating right behind Barothy's Main Lodge, one of the brothers saw the sun glistening off of an object lying on the river floor, and reached down into the cold current to pick up a beat-up camera. One brother owned the *very same* waterproof Olympus camera model. Although the camera fished from the river no longer operated, he withdrew the still dry memory card from it and placed it into his Olympus.

One of the card's last photos pictured a group of people alongside a Baldwin Canoe Rental van. The brothers looked up the canoe rental office number, called, explained what they'd found, and described an image of "white folks in their 50s standing next to one of your vans, while in front of them a black lady is holding a drink while sitting on a river chair." Livery owner Jeff, whose family has been renting us canoes and kayaks every year since 1978, started laughing, pretty sure the lady holding the drink was Marquis' wife Gilda, sitting next to several of us in the photo. And that is when he called our house.

*Something prompted the brothers at this family reunion to take one last tube trip on Marquis' favorite river, the Pere Marquette, behind Marquis' favorite getaway, Barothy Lodge, on the day of Marquis' funeral.* During his eulogy, we shared this story, believing it was Marquis working through the brothers we did not know, assuring us that all is well with him on the Other Side.

Still marveling about the coincidences, we drove away from the funeral home, bound for the euchre tourney wake in Marquis' honor, when we noticed that the convenience store 3 doors down from the funeral home is named "Aloha". This is significant as one of Marquis' finest impersonations was that of the late Detroit mayor Coleman Young, particularly his impression of the mayor, while boarding a flight for Hawaii, replying to a reporter asking if he anything to say to the people of Detroit. The mayor replied "Aloha, mutha-fucker!" As funny as Coleman's "Aloha" comment was, it was hysterical when Marquis mimicked it.

Additionally, Baldwin Canoes gave us the phone number of the brother who found the camera, with an area code we did not recognize. As we neared Marquis' Mobil Lounge wake, Maggie looked up the area code on her smart phone. "You are not going to believe this," she said. "The first town listed beneath this area code is Aloha, Oregon." Today, it felt like Marquis wrapped his arms around each and every one of us.

The next day, Rookie Mark and I departed my Northville home, on our way north to do some 4Dayin'. I first met Mark Hayden in December 2002, when we were both employees of Duracell. Mark and I quickly became friends, sharing a love of people, music, humor, story-telling, and hard work 'n hard play. Mark has heard 4Day tales for years, with an open invitation to join in the fun since we met. His day has finally come.

Maggie sent us off with a batch of her delectable brownies, the car floor soon littered with crumbs from frequent digging into the brownie baggie, as we motored to a 1PM Nottingham Bar rendezvous with Vid, Eric, and Kenny before continuing on to the Upper Peninsula. Chris and Ron will join us two days later, the evening of Day 2, at the Northland Outfitters campgrounds. Besides Mark, two additional rookies will catch up with us tonight, 4Day-eve, in St. Ignace.

Mark's class of 2012 fellow rookies are Dale and Nick. Maggie and I met Dale in May 2011 when, in his duties as an employee of the Port Huron Library, he booked us to share with his patrons some canoeing 'n kayaking stories from my books. While at his library, Dale expressed his love of kayaking, and we encouraged him to paddle rivers with us soon. Two months later, in the days before 4Day 2011, Dale joined us on two U.P. rivers, the Carp and the Indian, bringing along a friend of his, Nick. The group hit it off immediately with those two, and tried to get them to continue the fun by 4Dayin' with us starting the day after the Indian River trip. Although their work schedules wouldn't allow 2011 participation, they did make it this year, and we're happy to have their company. Rookies Dale and Nick brought their kayaks, making 2012 the first year that kayaks are paddled during a 4Day.

The Moran Bay Motel, our 4Day-eve home, is a clean, inexpensive Mom & Pop place just north of the Mackinac Bridge in St. Ignace. The motel sits atop a steep hill overlooking, as you would guess, Moran Bay. The elevated view of the bay from the motel front lawn is outstanding! A local tavern, Timmy Lee's Pub, offers a no charge shuttle van Wednesday through Saturday, 5PM 'til closing, to a coverage area that includes the Moran Bay Motel, 4 miles away. Happily noting that tonight is Friday, a no charge shuttle van day, Timmy Lee's it is!

Boarding the shuttle bus brought back a fond memory from this April at the Pere Marquette River. That day, Mad Dog Chris and his family, including 7-year old son Gus, were with several others on the Baldwin Canoe bus, headed to a river put-in access. Gus had heard the 4Day story from 15 years ago of his Uncle Marquis stepping out of the Northland Outfitters' outhouse as he watched the livery van with all his friends aboard driving away without him. Gus analysis of his uncle's experience reflected the charmingly timeless wisdom of youth, "Never get on the canoe bus early and then leave it to go pee. You might get left behind."

As the shots at Timmy Lee's Pub pile up, Eric informs the rookies, "If you can survive Friday night, you'll know ya made it". All 7 offer two thumbs up to the pub's Friday Fish Fry, Whitefish appetizer and its dip-with-a-kick, pizza, & outstanding burgers. The menu notes the "Brokeback Burger" is a "hunk of beef between two firm buns," not that there's anything wrong with that. The kitchen did a fine job meeting our request to "crispy up the fries", Rookie Nick telling the waitress, "There's a whole crispy society out there." Tonight, the juke box "Born to Be Wild" selection got a workout while the pennant race played out on the bar's big screens, the Tigers whipping the White Sox, before we clear our $299.36 plus tip bar tab and catch the shuttle back to Moran Bay.

4Day-eve stretched long into the night. Once dropped off at our motel, we gathered on its front lawn, enjoying the town's lights twinkling on the bay's waters across US2. Cooler lids popped open and beers are passed around, as stories from 4Days of yore are shared with the 3 rookies. The closest to a 4Day story that a rookie could come up with was when Nick talked about first meeting us on the Indian River last year, "After Ron hit the Mad Dog that Chris passed to him, Ron said, "Too bad Mad Dog bottles don't have a Best-if-Stupid-by-Date on them.""

It was 2AM when Eric asked, "Is anyone still thirsty?" Receiving an enthusiastic response, Eric produced an unopened fifth of Beam. At 3AM, the fifth now empty, the party kicked up a notch as Rookie Nick treated us to a bowl of hashish, an artifact missing on our annual trip for so long, its appearance could be considered the 4Day equivalent of a triumphant archeology dig.

Passing the pipe in almost total darkness had an amusing outcome. Thinking the man to my right was a 4Dayer, it turned out instead to be Tim, the Moran Bay Motel owner and a total stranger until 10 hours ago. He politely declined what I was passing to him, "No thanks, I just want to hang out with you fellas." God bless him.

Day 1 began with overcast skies and a thundering group hangover. Happy 35th fellers! We found breakfast at a restaurant down the road from the motel as step one in the recovery process. One family entering the diner caught a glimpse of the death-warmed-over looks on our faces, and ushered their children back out to the car in search of a less frightening place to eat.

Getting food in our stomachs and the passage of time righted the ship. We stopped back at the motel to grab our river gear, greeted by motel owner Tim, his exuberant attitude and comments clearly indicating how much he enjoyed our company in the early morning hours, a rare breed indeed. This is a very good thing since he gets us tonight, too.

Saying good-bye to Tim, we make the short 15 minute drive up Old Mackinac Trail to the Carp River Campground and a scheduled 11AM rendezvous with Leon Genre. Our caravan arrives a few minutes before Leon, who is in his first year as Northland Outfitters owner, and thus his first 4Day exposure. Last year, several of us took a non-4Day afternoon trip down the Carp and absolutely loved it, listing it among the top 5 rivers any of us had ever been on. Leon is doing us a favor in traveling to the north side of St. Ignace to put us out on the Carp River so we could re-live the 2011 magic in 2012. This is a river neither he nor his predecessors have ever serviced, the access a too-long-to-make-profitable 75-minute drive from his livery.

Soon after launching at the East Lake Road access, it is clear that Carp 2012 will not be Carp 2011. The relatively light St. Ignace U.P. snowfall of the 2011-2012 winter (one-third of the historical 90" average) lowered the water level considerably, and the Carp doesn't have enough merging tributaries to bring it back up to a good, or to even a mediocre, recreational level. In 2011, the 6.4 miles we journeyed down this federally-designated *wild and scenic river* took us just over 2 hours to paddle, the last hour full of excellent rapids, exciting to paddle. In 2012, after barely sufficient water to make an ok first hour, someone pulled the river plug, and we now saw high, dry, & above the water-line the rocky Carp floor that created those rapids. The great final hour of 2011 became, in 2012, 3-hours of dragging canoes & kayaks over rocks & fallen trees.

Although the canoeing 'n kayaking was slow (Vid asked that "From here on out, let's only go on rivers that have water.") the party was in high gear.

Rookie Nick seemed to have an endless supply of hashish, generously sharing it with us at a stop 45 minutes into the Carp. Flashing back to Bill Murray's *Caddyshack* character, Carl Spackler, I answered the calls of "Cannonball!" Taking a hit of what the rookie passed my way, I held the smoke in while taking a double-bubbler of some particularly nasty, cheap & disgusting whiskey before exhaling. Looking back on it, partaking in that third Cannonball of the stop was unwise and, should I wish to have river memories going forward, a recipe I'll no longer follow. On Cannonball number 3, I had not yet finished exhaling when "ahh" became, to quote the Jetson's family dog Astro, "ruh-roh". Shoving off from this stop, I handled paddling chores acceptably from the stern for about 15 minutes, when the buzz raging in my head convinced me to switch places with Rookie Mark, unfortunately for him, my canoeing mate for the day.

Within minutes of Rookie Mark taking over the steering of our boat, the lack of river water forced him to stand up outside of the canoe for an unscheduled dragging of the boat across the dry 'n rocky Carp floor. The rookie was walking in front of the canoe, his legs wobbly from either the excessive partying that had taken place so far OR from pulling both the weight of the canoe and that of his comatose partner, now lying in the ship's stern. Quite possibly, from both.

It was at some point during the 3-hour "walk of hell", while pulling the combined weight of the canoe and its stowaway over a series of rocks, that the boat got away from Mark, slamming into his mouth, chipping a tooth, and earning him his short-lived 4Day nickname of "Chippy". And what a trooper Chippy was, waking me from the cannonball-induced haze only when absolutely necessary to get over or around particularly difficult obstructions. When Rookie Chippy did nudge me awake for assistance, it was with proper respectfulness accorded a trashed veteran.

Rookie Nick experienced his own challenges from what has now gone down in 4Day legend as *the Cannonball! Stop*. Shortly after cannonballing, Nick earned his 4Day nickname of "Chum", his prodigious quantities of puke generously feeding the fish of the Carp. Furthermore, despite being passed out in his kayak, Chum proceeded to chart (in those stretches with water) multiple river banks for future generations, zig-zagging his way down the river, breaking a toe in his explorations. Kenny said, "We enjoyed canoeing with Rookie Nick. Eric and I were following close behind his kayak, talking about how well he was doing after all the partying, seeing him sit upright and steering straight down the Carp. It was then that his torso sagged right, and he started to careen into riverbanks. After Nick crashed into 7 banks head on, we thought we should help."

Leon had agreed to pick us up from the take-out at 5PM. Based on our 2011 Carp journey, that would cover the expected 2 paddling hours plus a little over 3 hours of break time – more than enough time, I figured. However, once you calculate the time required to walk a river without water, drag a Cannonball-impaired veteran downstream, the loss of a tooth, the breaking of a toe, and the earning of two 4Day nicknames, well, this all put a crimp in our timing.

Arriving to pick us up a bit before 5PM, Leon waited 3 hours, his mood turning sour as the clock ticked. When we finally beached the boats at 915PM, the steamed Leon was long gone, only his canoe trailer left ashore for us. Rookie Dale hitched it to his vehicle for hauling the boats back to our Moran Bay Motel rooms. Our second evening at Timmy Lee's is hazy, quieter, and shorter than the first. Despite not arriving at the bar until 1030PM, once we got some food in us, we caught a shuttle shortly after midnight back to the motel, falling exhausted into our beds.

The Day 2 St. Ignace restaurant breakfast has considerably more life than the half-dead one of yesterday, with a lot of chatter about the crazy day on the Carp, assurances to Vid that there will be water in today's river, and predictions of Leon's state of mind when we see him this morning. After the 75-minute drive to Northland Outfitters, we encounter Leon understandably in a prickly mood. He has one of his hired help transport us to the Manistique River put-in, probably wanting to have as little to do with our group as possible, wondering why he ever bought a canoe livery.

Once on the Manistique, all is well. Sunshine glistens off the water, dancing among the non-stop laughing 'n joking. Arriving at the Ten Curves Dam portage, everyone is either certain or at least goes along with the idea that our dearly-departed Marquis is with us: on an otherwise cloudless-day, one cloud is above, impossible to miss, unusually-shaped with fantastic colors like a mid-day Northern Lights, with turquoise, gold (as in "You Got Gold", the John Prine song Marquis asked be played at his funeral) and a pinkish color (maybe the color persimmon from his 2005 wedding party outfits). We figure that this spectacular cloud is a message from Marquis, letting us know not to worry *'cause he's doing great, and we should just keep havin' fun!*

20 minutes downstream from the dam found the boys again out of their boats, spread out in a loose rectangle spanning the river from shore to shore, tossing the Frisbee in the shadow of the new steel bridge. Somehow, a fifth of Canadian Hunter Whisky made its way into a throwing lane, and a toss of the bottle from Vid to Doc went awry, the surprisingly capped, partially-emptied, fifth floating down the river to a seemingly unknown fate.

That's when Rookie Chum took charge. Well, not right away. First, he waited for the Frisbee flipping to wrap up, but THEN he took charge, jumping into his kayak, never wavering in his quest to save the Canadian Hunter. Suddenly, there it was, spotted by Chum as it bobbed in the water along the right bank, the fifth caught up in a debris field. Rookie Chippy picked up the gauntlet, paddling in to rescue the whisky from the tangle surrounding it, and presented the bottle to his 4Day brothers. Kenny watched this all unfold with the perspective of a man who's 4Dayed many a time, "I am glad we got this far into the trip before I got this fucked up."

40 minutes shy of our tents, set-up this morning when we first arrived at a Northland Outfitters' campsite, we beached the canoes 'n kayaks on a shaded, left bank, sandy beach. An unopened fifth was fished out of Vid's cooler, an interesting blend called Kentucky Gentleman. Rookie Chippy was behind Kenny with the Kentucky Gentleman when he leaned over and

nudged Kenny with the bottle. Kenny said, "Sorry, I don't hear out of my right shoulder." The bottle got to Rookie Chum and, after taking a healthy pull, he blurted out an "Ugh" along with a full body shake and a question, "When does the taste go away?" This started a conversation about establishing a rating scale for 4Day liquor based on when the taste dissipates. Agreement was reached on a label of "good rot gut" if the taste left within a half-an-hour, the discussion quickly falling apart when a consensus could not be reached on how to classify a liquor should its taste not go away until the next meal or 'til the next day, etc.

As we cleared the rapids alongside the livery's banks, Chris and Ron announced their arrival at 4Day 35 with greetings shouted from shore. They shared the happy news that the Tigers had completed a weekend sweep of the White Sox, a big deal in this year's tight pennant race. In the excitement of the moment, I in turn shared one of my favorite exchanges from my favorite TV show of all-time, the Beverly Hillbillies, "Jethro, do think this dress shows off my figure?" "Yeah Ma, but I'd wear it anyway."

With the newly-arrived Chris and Ron, we adjourned to the Jolly Bar for a fine night of burgers, singing, Marquis' stories, and pool shootin'. Back at camp, Rookie Dale got his 4Day name, Flounder. The rookie is not overjoyed with the moniker, but he is resigned, knowing that if, like Kent Dorfman in *Animal House*, he asks, "Why Flounder?" he'll likely hear, "Why not!" Contributing in large part to Rookie Dale's "Flounder" christening is the fact that *Animal House* was released on this day in 1978. Timing is everything.

Gathering the fellas late into the night around the campfire creates the setting of what turned out to be Rookie Chippy's grand finale. Chris announces his thirst and directs Rookie Chippy to fetch him a beverage. The smiling rookie replies, "Hey Chris, why don't you go fuck yourself!" The group gasps, the night goes silent, camp chairs move away from the fire, the veteran and the rookie now toe-to-toe. A little rough-housing ensues, and Chris lands on Rookie Chippy. The rookie's next words do not sound good, "Oh oh, get off me man, this is serious".

Chippy eases his way to the tent but, as his otherworldly moaning tells us, lying down brings no relief from the pain. I help him to my van, adjusting the seat setting to find a position that Chippy can best deal with, landing on upright. The campfire mood turns somber, the concern for our brother dominating what little conversation there is. No one is more concerned than Chris.

At 6AM, I step out of the tent to check on Rookie Chippy. Approaching the van, I can see that he is awake. Slowly and painfully he says "I need to go to a hospital." As we prepare to leave, Ron comes over to check on Chippy. "How's he doin'?" "Not so good." Ron opens his ever-present pharmaceutical box, and pulls out a pain-killer. "Give this to the rookie. It will help." Rookie Chippy is hopeful as he consumes the meds Ron offers, and we head northeast for the nearest hospital, located in Newberry, 33 miles away, the same hospital that treated Moth's head wound suffered at the now-famous Moth's Landing, during the 1994 4Day.

Thankfully, Ron's meds are starting to kick in, a blessing to the wounded rookie. On the drive to Newberry, Rookie Chippy is more concerned with Chris feeling bad about what had happened last night then about the pain he feels, and assures Chris over the phone that it was just an accident and "all part of the fun". No wonder I loved working at Duracell with this man.

Pulling up to the Newberry Hospital, though it seems much nicer than it did in 1994, there still is no sign of a "Moth's head wound/Moth's Landing" historical marker, despite this being an incident that cries out for documented preservation. The doctors inform Chippy, "The X-rays confirm two cracked ribs," and continue, "We're prescribing Vicodin and high-dosage Motrin". The rookie takes the news well, likely due to the effects of Ron's medical kit, smiles and proclaims "This changes my 4Day name from Chippy to Chippy 2Rib."

My first thought is we need to fill the scripts and get Mark back home, 'cause we're not going to have a guy sit with two cracked ribs in a tent while we're on the river having a good time. This sparks a sudden and shocking second thought: my 4Day is over. Wow! While driving to get the scripts filled at a St. Ignace pharmacy, C-2rib calls to get his flight moved up to this evening, and I call the boys with an update on the doctor's diagnosis, the new Chippy 2Rib nickname – which is extremely well-received – and tell them that we're driving to Detroit to get Rookie Mark on an early-than-expected flight to North Carolina out of Metro. Turning into the St. Ignace pharmacy for 2Rib's meds, I receive a text message from Rookie Chum, "Leon kicked us out." What!?!

Back at the Northland Outfitters campgrounds, the balance of the 4Dayers had by all accounts a fine breakfast cooked by Rookies Chum and Flounder. It was then that Leon stopped by to let the boys know that they are kicked out of the campground, where we'd planned to spend tonight, because we were too loud the night before, prompting folks renting the 4 livery cabins to check out in the middle of the night, and because we are "too high maintenance". "High maintenance" has never once come to mind when thinking 4Day, except perhaps in 2010 when we sought hired help to lug our gear to the Peninsula. Leon might still have been a bit stewed about waiting in vain 3 hours for us along the Carp River 2 days ago. Maybe.

It was about this time that Vid threw in the towel, "That's it, I'm going home," saying something about having been drinking for 4 days (duh, 4Day) and that he was toast (ironically, a t-shirt from Vid's 4Day collection is a piece of toast; no words, just a piece of toast). Vidder, being a strict man of habit, may have had his equilibrium knocked askew by the strange sequence of events. While breaking down the tents, Kenny gets 3 texts from his housekeeper about a fire in his rental lodge. Yikes! So Kenny says, "Guys, I gotta go," and hits the road for his southern Indiana home. It's the third morning of the 4Day, Ron and Chris haven't yet been on a river, and 4 (there's that number again) guys have left for home. The surviving 5, Eric, rookies Chum and Flounder, Chris and Ron spent the rest of the day on dry land, leisurely roaming the U.P. and its bars, then checking back into St. Ignace's Moran Bay Motel, catching the shuttle once more to Timmy Lee's Pub. Five hours south, the meds have worked their magic on Chippy 2Rib's pain, allowing him to accept a gentle hug good-bye before walking, all smiles, through the Metro Airport gate to his awaiting flight. His 1st 4Day was as crazy as they get. Returning to my house around 9PM, I can't stop thinking how bizarre it is that it's only Day 3 of the 4Day and I'm at home.

In the pre-dawn hours of the next morning, Maggie and I take a 3-mile walk with our neighbor, while I share stories about the strange events of the last few days, and how weird it feels to be missing in action on a 4Day. That's when Maggie makes perhaps the wisest statement ever in 4Day lore, "Why do you have to miss today? The Sturgeon River is only 4 hours away." Mag flipped the light switch on in me noggin'. "Maggie, no wonder I love you! Of course! Was it over when the German's bombed Pearl Harbor? Hell no! I'm going back!"

Before leaving Northville, I call the fellers to make sure there's still some 4Dayers up north. Chris tells me that he woke up to a note from rookies Chum & Flounder that they're heading home 'cause Flounder's back is bad, "so there's only 3 of us left to go down the Sturgeon today". "Well Chris, make that 4, 'cause I'm comin' back, baby!" It was nice to hear that news received with hoots 'n hollers. I stopped by Vid's to pick up my gear left behind in haste at Leon's when I drove Chippy 2Rib to the hospital, and hopefully to talk Vid into returning North with me. I'm unsuccessful on the latter, but, hey, maybe I can talk Johnny into joining me - I'm going right by his house. No one answers the phone. Oh well, solo I go.

On the drive north, I check in with Rookie Chippy 2Rib, now back in his North Carolina home. He was able last night to get 7 hours of good sleepin' in, sitting up in his recliner, his likely bed for a few weeks while the cracked ribs heal. He sounds great! I then call Kenny, and the fire turned out to be, fortunately, a grease fire on the stove requiring clean-up but not replacement, and no flames spread beyond the stove, more good news!

The Day 4 plan calls for us to meet 130PM at a lodge in the town of Indian River. There, the folks from Big Bear Adventures will pick us up for a trip down the Sturgeon River. On my way to the lodge, I get a text: *"Heeeeeere's Johnny! With beers on... at the lodge! 4DAY!!!!!!!!!!!!!!!! Okay, 1 DAY!!!!!!!!!"* Woo-hoo, Johnny's joining us! As I pull up to the lodge, Johnny is sitting out by Old Straits Highway, sipping a beer and ready to go. Eric, Ron and Chris arrive early enough for us to grab our rooms before the livery van arrives. Eric tosses his overnight bag in the room he's sharing with Johnny, and walks out laughing, "There are already 14 empties in the room". I guess Johnny figured since he's just 1 Dayin' that he's got some catching up to do.

We launched at the Meadows access, just upstream from Scott Bridge, aka the "jumpin' bridge". Chris ran to the top of the structure for two, feet-first, 10' jumps into a river with enough water in it to avoid any cracked, dislocated, or broken bones. What a gorgeous day! Even knowing that the riverside Meadows Bar is closed, the *for sale* sign out, couldn't dampen the group's great mood. It was during a stop alongside the old bar, that the boys turned philosophic, first Ron proclaiming, "Tho I canoe through the valley of wetness, I fear no bottle," then Eric issuing a concerning statement, "If you bleed out your ass, you'll know you're having a good time". Before returning to the quick current, Chris unveiled Marquis' boa from the 1986 Mardi Gras attended by all 3 4Dayin' Weaks brothers, and wrapped himself it in as we continue our great run through the always exciting Sturgeon rapids. The river was angry that day, my friends, but fun!

At night, we played euchre, listened to music around the campfire and, unlike yesterday, no one kicked us out. The next morning, we enjoyed a fine restaurant breakfast along the banks of the Sturgeon. After picking up some barbeque jerky for the missing-this-4Day Moth, I cruised backroads bathed in sunshine on the ride home, accompanied by some damn fine music recorded for me by Rookie Chippy 2Rib, including some extraordinary Doc Watson guitar picking.

As we parted ways, the boys started looking forward to 4Day 36 in 2013. All we know for sure is that we won't be camping at Leon's.

*4Day post-script from Rookie Chum...*

4 Day Brothers,

What a great trip! Although it was my rookie year, I can say I was welcomed with open arms, er, bottles! Does anyone know when or how I broke my toe? I can't wait 'till next year, although I am nervous to hear Chris thinks we should be rookies again (I thought my ribs were safe) since we didn't paddle all 4 days. Doc, Kenny, Eric, Chris, Ron, and Vid, I am glad to have met you fellers and can't wait to meet more 4Day brothers!

Chum 7.30.12

*4Day post script 2 from eternal Rookie Steve, making the case for Chippy 2Rib as Rookie-of-the-Year…*

To my Elders (including Brittany, the Frisbee, and the Red Wings Shirt),
Hearing the stories of this year's 4Day brought out some repressed memories (TREE!!!!!) and former fight card play-by-play ("Stop buying Jager shots for Frey, it just encourages him").

My non-binding, no weight vote (like the congresswoman from Washington D.C.) is for Chippy 2Rib for the following reasons:

--Sacrificed part of his body to the River Gods on the first day (do you think someone will call next year reporting they found it?).

--Portaged the ship while his captain was allowed to enjoy his bourbon induced blackout and enjoy the scenery.

--Took part in the rescue of a wanderlust bottle of encouragement with no regard for his own safety.

--Poked The Bear, i.e. Chris, and lived to talk about it (not many people can say they have done that).

Again, Thanks for the stories and the repressed memories (my therapist's kids' college fund thanks you, too), "Rookie" Steve

*4Day post-script 3:*

4Day brother Chucky passed away 8.24.12. The death certificate said Chucky died from heart failure, but he had so many physical ailments, it could have been any number or a combination of things. Chucky went through 8 years of hell, suffering from a debilitating depression that baffled multiple psychiatrists and psychologists, one telling us that Chucky was in the worst 5% he'd ever seen. As best we can tell, the doctors tried close to 20 meds or combinations of meds to get our boy well. All we could do was keep trying, taking him to doctor's appointments and praying that our dear brother could be happy and feel the love of his friends once again. But no matter how bad it got, except for a few of the darkest days, he'd always call or accept our call, and always said "I love you".

It was a real blessing when late last year, Chucky started to come out of it. As terrible as it is to lose Chucky, what a wonderful experience it's been these last 8 months or so – Chucky was happy again, and we got our boy back. Over the past couple of months, he slipped a little after his heart valve replacement and Marquis' passing, but it was still a lot better than those 8 years.

I met Chucky at the start of our freshman year at EMU 40 years ago. Chucky died 40 days after Marquis did. Marquis, Chucky, and my Dad, who all passed within 2 months of each other, had enough experiences to each fill their own book. But this story of Chucky's must be told here...

Brothers-In-Arms, Marquis and Chucky

He had a summer job his junior year, or as he said "years", at EMU, working the graveyard shift at Chrysler's Lynch Road Plant. Chucky's job was to buff and wax the general office area and dust and vacuum the Executive Office (this would be akin to hiring me to service the engine of your car – a very bad idea). Anyway, the buffer was kept in a large storage closet, a space Chucky found perfect for napping during his night shift. He became friends with a small, Italian lady named Gina, who would wake him up in the morning before his shift ended, so he could punch out. One day, Gina forgot to wake Chucky, and instead he awoke to the sounds of typing from the adjoining room – the room he had to exit through. He opened the door a couple of inches and peered out into a sea of secretaries, with no idea what time it was, but definitely the day shift had arrived. How to get out of here? Chucky noticed that the buffer was propped in the corner of his napping room. He plugged it in, took a deep breath, and started it up. The sound of the typing was just enough to muffle the smooth grinding of the buffer, as he emerged from the closet as though this was nothing out of the ordinary. Chucky buffed his way along the side wall, smiling at the only secretary that appeared to have any idea what was going on, and on out of the room. It was 1030AM, good for 3 hours of overtime. The next night there was a note attached to Chucky's buffer, "Thanks for making my day. I hope you keep your job."

*4Day post-script 4:*

My Dad, Herbert Roy Fletcher, passed on Nine-Eleven of 2012. My Papa was a big-hearted man, loving, funny-as-hell, inflexible, hard workin', hard playin', and noble. A story from his 30s, shared with me by his Wayne State fraternity brother, Hank Nickol, bears repeating to highlight his fun-loving ways…

In the early 60's, my Dad and frat brother Hank belonged to a golf league that played 5PM every Monday at the Idyl Wyld Golf Course in Livonia. Heading into the final week of league play, Herb & Hank, two self-proclaimed hackers, had 10 wins and no losses. Another team was also 10 & 0, but they were excellent golfers, one being a former PAC 10 Champion. The two undefeated teams were matched for the championship on the final day, the handicap for Herb & Hank giving them 30 strokes. Herb & Hank won the coin toss and teed off first in front of a very large crowd gathered on the first tee. The first hole was set-up with a knee-high fence running the length of the tee box to keep the crowd back. Herb was up first, and hit a low line drive that rocketed into the last upright on the fence. It ricocheted straight back with tremendous velocity, almost hitting Herb on its way to the middle of the parking lot. The crowd gasped watching this bizarre trajectory. My Dad, cigar in mouth, asked, "Anyone got a rule book?", causing everyone to roar in laughter. Next, he teed off with a two-stroke penalty and partner Hank hit his first shot out of bounds. It all went downhill from there, their entire 30 stroke handicap gone by the end of the 3rd hole. Although the Herb & Hank team lost today, they ended the season 10 & 1, and several celebratory pitchers of beer kept them in the winning spirit!

*Author's note*: during October, the Tigers defeated the Yankees Suck in their third ever post-season match-up! The Tigers are now 3 for 3 vs. the Yanks in the playoffs! Jimmy Leyland for President!

# CHAPTER 4
## 2012 POST-SCRIPT BY MAD DOG CHRIS

Marquis de Stono, Markie, Uncle Marco or as most who met him, brother – and he was mine, in the truest sense. My older brother Marc is an original member of ETT. The fates aligned as he was roomed with a fine young man from Lambertville MI named Jeff Fletcher aka Doc (about the author). Oddly enough, Marc made his first appearance on the 4 Dayyyy in 1992, the 15th year of the trip. As to why it had taken him so long, I can only surmise. He was loyal and dutiful to a fault and had worked almost every day at the family bait shop with our grandfather. Summer time off days were few and far between. It was only when he no longer worked there that he could join us on our northern folly.

Marc was not an ordinary rookie, in fact neither was his rookie brother, Vid. Both had been with the group for a long time before their 1992 rookie year. Several times that year, they were given menial rookie tasks which they refused, turning the table on the would-be hazer. A fine example of this was when someone cracked the cap on a bottle, tossed the cap in the river, and told the rooks to fetch it. They looked at each other, took a pull off the bottle, and handed it to the hazer, telling him to "Drink!"

Marc was a kind and compassionate man. He was not very outgoing, however when you met him, he would always treat you as a friend. Marc was at his very best when working with children and mentally handicapped people. I had the pleasure of watching him in action as we worked together for over 10 years at a couple different jobs in the fields of education and human services. Marc, in his younger days, was surprisingly athletic. He didn't have the build of an athlete but he was strong and smart. In his later years, he was the guy you always wanted on your Trivial Pursuit team as he had a knack for knowing a little something about everything and a lot in the areas of sports, music and movies. He had a robust laugh and a calming sense to him. To most children he became Uncle Marco and loved interacting with them in whatever they were doing. Some of my most cherished memories of him were on Christmas morning, playing with whatever freshly unwrapped gift my children had decided to play with next.

I'd like to take a paragraph or two of your time, dear reader and kindred spirit, as I feel a need to give a little insight to you and perhaps myself. Like the river, life takes on some twists and turns. The water holds dangerous beauty. Obstacles above the water can be tricky but are easier to maneuver around because you can see them. It's the ones beneath that do the most damage. The dangerous beauty for Marc was his childlike innocence. He was very trusting and faithful to a fault. Years of working almost every day at the family business had contributed to drug and alcohol abuse. His obstacle beneath was addiction. Partying with family and friends when he did get some time off was his sense of relief, making it easier to cope with the mundanity of the daily bait shop grind. This led to drinking daily, which led him down some darker paths. I'm not sure when or what caused Marc to realize he was an alcoholic. He did start to change his lifestyle, however it was too late. His liver was shot. Marc was able to have another ten relatively healthy years before passing in 2012. He fought his demons admirably but fought them too late. He had been in and out of the hospital and physical rehab facilities during his last year, as his brain processes would fail him from toxicity related to a poor functioning liver. I remember on one of my last visits with him, he was grinning from ear to ear and whispered to me with a child-like innocence, "Don't tell Gilda (his wife), but I'm gonna go on the 4 Day". Marc was a couple of months shy of his 59th birthday and a week shy of the 35th 4Day when he passed.

In a book that details drunken frivolity of men in one of their somewhat primitive habitats, I debated on sharing the other side of my brother's story. Ultimately, I found it would be a discredit to him, his family and friends if I did not. It would also not give credence to the dangerous beauty and obstacles of life. We all have to face them. The human condition is how we face our trials and celebrate our tribulations. It's how we write the stories of our lives and Marc's is just one of many. His physical time with us on the 4 Dayyyy is over but we have felt his presence and the warmth of his spirit on every trip since his last. I believe this is the message. No matter what demons we have or obstacles we must face above and below our waters, the river continues to flow until its end. What makes the beauty less dangerous and more beautiful is the presence and warmth of the spirits with which we are blessed to share our journey. We have lost quite a few of our 4 Day brothers. Marc was one of the best.

I have Marc to thank for getting me to my first 4DAYYYY. It was in 1990. Three months prior I had been honorably discharged from the Navy and two weeks earlier I had gotten back from a month long adventure to Australia. I decided why not. Although I did not have transportation, I was able to catch a ride to the U.P. with someone if I could get to Doc's house. Marc agreed to take me. Unfortunately I did not know where Doc currently lived and had assumed he was close to his former residence, which was only about 20 minutes away. I also forgot to tell my brother when I needed to be there. When I talked to him I was already running late and he then informed me Doc's new house was a lot further than 20 minutes away. Marc did his best to get me there as fast as he could but I was still over an hour late. Although the boys weren't happy with my tardiness, Marc helped smooth it over and got to send us off with a couple of toasts. Thanks again for looking out for me big brother.

1997 4Day 20 would be the last time I shared a canoe with my brother. One of the things an experienced paddler prides himself on is to not tip. I was 11 years his junior but had a fair amount of time on the water and this was my 6th 4DAYYYY. I'm not sure how much experience Marc had but, as I said earlier, he was a little smaller, athletic and had a pretty good head on his shoulders. I would steer in the back of the canoe, Marc would provide the power from the front. It sounded perfect except I don't think my brother saw it quite the same way I did. He always seemed to counteract my steering along with shifting his weight quite often. To no surprise, it wasn't long before our pride tippith along with the canoe, dumping shortly into the trip. Both of us kind of laughed it off as we gathered our belongings out of the river, emptied the canoe of water and proceeded again, this time with a little clarification on each of our roles in the canoe. However, again I was struggling in the back as Marc seemed to counter act and shift more frequently. I told him to relax that he didn't need to paddle so much and I surmise he probably didn't like being told what to do from his little brother which, of course, led to our second trip into the drink. This time gathering our things and emptying out the canoe wasn't as light hearted. Role clarification was pretty much a moot point. Marc suggested we switch places and I didn't see how that could be much worse. WRONG! I'm not sure what the hell he was doing in the back, however, I was getting sick and tired of eating branches in the front, so

I was trying to compensate. Our conversations were not pleasant. I believe our mother would not have approved of the language we were using toward each other and, of course, we dumped again. No words were exchanged, the glaring eye contact and scrunched faces said more than any dialogue between us could. We went about the duty we were becoming all too familiar with, but this time we had lost quite a bit of our things. One of our items lost was a squirt toy in the shape of one our wrestling favorites from the WWF (now the WWE), the Big Boss Man, making matters worse. We finally caught up to the group at a "rest stop" in the river. As we pulled up, our faces flush with anger from tipping so much, the boys were laughing and said, "We saw stuff coming down the river and wondered who dumped." Then they held up the Big Boss Man and said they knew it was us. This lightened our mood a little, which completely changed by the time we were done partying at the stop with the fellas. We decided to give it one more shot down the river with each other. WRONG!! Shortly after the stop we tipped again. This time we were no longer angry with each other but decided to change up partners and not tempt fate. We never canoed together again. We were both good with that while he was alive but now that he is no longer with us, I would love to have one more trip with him, no matter how many times we tip or how many branches I would have to eat.

There are many other things I remember about my brother on the 4DAYYYY! We usually camped with each other. Marc, along with his other maladies, had a sleeping disorder. We called it Marcilepsy. He could fall asleep at anytime and anywhere. This led to some wonderful photo ops. Marc also talked and snored quite loudly while sleeping. Numerous times when we tried to wake him up, in mid-snore, he would say, "I'm not sleeping". When camping together it was either fall asleep before he did or drink enough so it wouldn't matter. One time when we were camping on Lake Michigan, in the middle of the night, Marc sat straight up in his bed, looked around and shouted, "Merry Christmas". Marc also had an infectious laugh and once he got going, he couldn't stop. He was a horrible joke teller. This was either because he didn't remember many OR those he did remember were so funny to him he would start laughing half way through the joke and couldn't finish. He was wonderful with impressions. Marc did an outstanding Coleman Young, Ed Sullivan, and a man from the inner city named Junior Bird. One Junior Bird impersonation came with a visual as Marc would tilt his glasses crooked on his face and exclaim, "Somebody musta hit me in my face when I wasn't lookin". That was Marc. His gentle soul, compassion and persona would hit you in the face when you weren't lookin'.

My family wasn't very religious while I was growing up. I could count on one hand how many times we attended a church service that didn't involve a birth, marriage or a death. As I grow older, I've become closer to God and realize the importance of faith. Marc had faith. His faith showed in the way he treated others and the love he gave to his family and friends. Marc had many dark times and questioned why this sickness was happening to him, but he never blamed anyone except himself. He accepted his fate as God's will and gave his best to everyone all the way until the end. In turn, I believe God not only blessed us with Marc in our lives but gave us a few signs He accepted my brother with open arms. One of Marc's classic impressions was of Coleman Young boarding a plane to Hawaii. A member of the press asked the mayor if he had anything to say before embarking, to which Coleman remarked, "Aloha muther fukkers". His impression was spot on and would always have us laughing hard. The morning of Marc's funeral, Doc got a call about a camera he lost in the river on a canoe trip a year earlier. The camera was no good but the memory card was salvageable and the person who found it had left their contact information. After the funeral, which ironically was next to the Aloha Liquor Store, while traveling to Marc's wake, Doc's wife Maggie had called about the card. The person who found it was from Aloha, Oregon!

One last sign about the greatness of God and how he allowed our brother Marc to be with us was on the 4DAYYYY. I told you earlier how Marc, during one of our last visits, had told me he was going on the 4DAYYYY. Also at his funeral, we played a song he requested by one of his favorite artists, John Prine. The song is titled, "You Got Gold" (it tells of how love shows us the goodness/gold inside of each other). These two things came together at our first stop on Day 2, a few days after Marc's funeral. It was a beautiful day in the U.P. There was not a cloud in the sky except for the one we encountered as we pulled out to portage over a dam. The dam separates a nice clearing and a memorial for a prominent citizen of the area, built and maintained by his friends. Over this we encountered one singular amazing cloud, containing three magnificent colors; coral, azure and GOLD. With the grace of God, Marc made it to the 4DAYYYY like he said he would. I still feel my brother's presence as well as others who have passed and feel blessed to be with all of those on this wonderful journey that includes adventures like the 4DAYYYY!

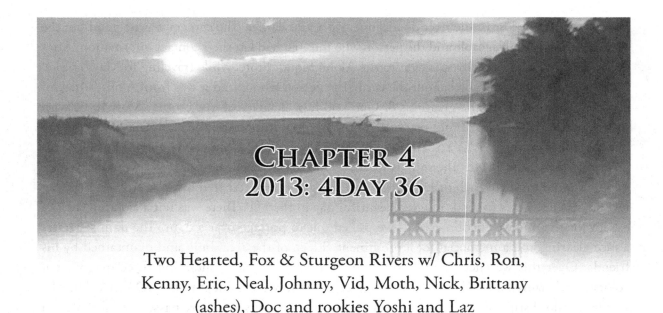

# CHAPTER 4
# 2013: 4DAY 36

Two Hearted, Fox & Sturgeon Rivers w/ Chris, Ron,
Kenny, Eric, Neal, Johnny, Vid, Moth, Nick, Brittany
(ashes), Doc and rookies Yoshi and Laz

*Bring me sunshine in your smile*
*Bring me laughter all the while*
*In this world where we live there should be more happiness*
*So much joy you can give to each brand new bright tomorrow*
*(Bring Me Sunshine by The Jive Aces)*

Tony Battaglia aka Tony B. aka Tony Barney, from the 4Day class of 1995, passed away suddenly February 24.

"There's no way that the 13 of you can throw the 3 of us in the river!" is a 4Day quote made famous by Tony B. in '95. We'd set up camp for the night, and Tony was allowing the bourbon to cloud his choice of words. The "3 of us" that Tony was referring to was himself and his fellow 1995 rookies, KB & Frey, while the "13 of you" referred to everyone else. Immediately after Tony made his statement, KB & Frey slunk off to the surrounding woods, and Chris issued a clear directive, "Tony, put your wet clothes on". After some discussion among a subsection of the Council of Elders, it was agreed that Tony would be spared a dusk swim in the Fox River if, within the next 10 minutes, he could roll a sufficient number of doobies to equal or exceed, when placed end to end, the length of Chris' cooler. With the unsolicited assistance of Chucky, who included dirt in what he rolled, Tony beat the clock and stayed dry.

Moth and I had the privilege of working with Tony at Duracell in the 1980s. He was a man with a good heart, a fine sense of humor, and a ready laugh that made you feel good when you heard it. Toasts will be made in honor of Tony Barney at 3 different rivers this 4Day...

The Two Hearted on Day 1, then two days down the Fox, and the 4th day in the Northern Lower Peninsula on the Sturgeon.

The Two Hearted River was made famous by Ernest Hemingway's 1925 story of the "Big Two- Hearted River". Although he was actually writing about the Fox, the river he loved to camp and fish at as a boy, Hemingway borrowed the more romantic-sounding name of the Two Hearted for his Fox River narrative. Perhaps because of this, my perception for years was that the Two Hearted River was beautiful in name only, a perception corrected during my 2007 inaugural THR trip. It was then I first experienced its sandy beaches and dunes, and the haunting sound of the crashing Lake Superior surf echoing through the dense pine forest.

This beautiful river and its environs were tortured last year by the 3rd largest fire in Michigan's history, the Duck Lake Fire. Lightning strikes ignited the dry pine forest, 33 square miles set ablaze. The geographic equivalent would be if the entire city of Lansing was engulfed in flames. Within the 33 square mile fire zone runs the last 5 miles of the Two Hearted River, and its livery of 30 years, Rainbow Lodge. The livery, its transport bus, vans, and a number of canoes, were reduced to burnt-out shells.

During a September visit to the area last year, I chatted with two volunteers from the 235-man crews who fought the fire daily for the 3 weeks it raged, until contained in June. They spoke of veteran firefighters who said the heat was significantly more intense than any other fires they'd ever fought. The Duck Lake Fire produced an estimated 3 trillion BTUs of energy, the equivalent of 9 of the bombs dropped on Hiroshima, an astounding analogy! Rainbow Lodge's Kathy Robinson said, "We are left with a lot of black ground and burned trees." Amazingly, the Mouth of the Two Hearted Campground, less than one-half mile away from the destroyed livery, was spared by the fire. It is situated on the edge of a rise, several feet above where the river flows into Lake Superior, and where we will camp the evening of Day 1 this year.

With the old Two Hearted livery, Rainbow Lodge, destroyed in the Duck Lake Fire, we arranged to have Ken & Doreen Orlang, owners of the Tahquamenon River livery called *The Woods*, handle canoe 'n kayak renting and transport needs for our day on the Two Hearted. The journey down the last 11 miles of the Two Hearted will be a tale of two rivers: the first 6 miles outside of the land torched by the Duck Lake Fire, the final 5 miles located within the fire zone. It will be fascinating to see the fire's impact first-hand.

Sophomore Chum, formerly known as Nick, brought along a friend this year, Rookie Yoshi. The veterans felt that a 4Day nickname would not be required for the rookie, as "Yoshi" seems to fit nicely the man born as Josh Schlager. Rookie Yoshi is a fine addition to our band of brothers. My view may be colored by the fact that the rook, besides showing a general willingness to pitch in along the journey in any way that he can, set up and took down my tent each night we camped. Rookie Yoshi has a real passion for the 4Day, saying that he's been looking for a group that enjoys experiencing and camping along these remote U.P. rivers. Talking Tigers, family, music, and Marvel Comic Books with Young Yoshi (young compared to the 50/60-something age of most 4Dayers) is very enjoyable, including sharing quotes from the famous philosopher Homer Simpson: "I never felt so accepted in all my life. These people looked deep into my soul and assigned me a number based on the order in which I joined." Yoshi is all-time 4Dayer no. 60.

4Day-eve was spent in the U.P. town of Paradise, 30 miles southeast of the Two Hearted river mouth. A local told us that Paradise has two seasons, shoveling and swatting. We checked into the Paradise Inn, chosen as it is right across the street from a cool tavern, the Yukon Inn, home of the *Yukon Burger* aka the Widow-Maker. This is a third-pound burger topped with a big slab of Canadian bacon, ham, and Swiss & American cheeses. When Chris yelled *SHOTS!* in the bar, it did not bring a waitress to our table to take a drink order, as shouting that word did for years at the Mobil Lounge, but it did draw a nasty look from the owner. Every path has a few puddles.

Day 1 launches on the Two Hearted at the Reed & Green Bridge, where a new, gently-sloping, stairway access replaced the bumpy, tree-root infested, put-in previously contested with. The paddle begins through lush surroundings, in an area untouched by the big fire, where the river runs 30' to 40' shore-to-shore, and the depth varies from 1'- 3'.

At a river break an hour into the trip, Moth shared a story with us, *"An angry wife complained about her husband spending all his free time in a bar, so one night he took her along with him. 'What'll you have?' he asked. 'Oh, I don't know. The same as you I suppose,' she replied.*

*So, the husband ordered a couple of Jack Daniel's shots and threw his down in one gulp. His wife watched him, then took a sip from her glass and immediately spat it out.' 'Yuck, that's TERRIBLE!' she grimaced. 'I don't know how you can drink this stuff!' 'Well, there you go,' said her husband. 'And you think I'm out enjoying myself every night."*

Neal nodded his head knowingly, "I married a Yooper. She would slam the shot and ask for another. That's why I've been with her for 36 years!"

Passing another in a series of sandy beaches, this one a little over 2 hours into the 4 hour paddle, we see the first blackened trees from 2012's Duck Lake Fire. Where the fire was most intense, vegetation burned right up to the river's edge. There'll be some erosion here for a couple of years 'til small willow trees along the river can get rooted and stabilize the banks. Where the tall trees and the shade they provide are lost, fishing is affected as more sunlight will get to the river, warming the Two Hearted and sending brook trout – who like cold water – upstream. Although overall the area is clearly affected by the fire, considering the intensity and reach of the inferno, we were pleasantly surprised by how much green is in the fire zone, and the resiliency of nature.

Within this affected area, what hasn't changed is the large number of gorgeous sandy beaches, one we stopped at for today's final paddling break. Vid recently watched the *Sharknado* movie, & christened it with a 4Day moniker of *Beam-nado!*, a mantra he uses to announce an incoming fifth of Beam is being tossed to you. Rookie Yoshi, not yet familiar with the ways of the 4Day, did not react quickly enough to Vid's shout, the fifth nailing him squarely in the ball sack.

By-passed for now is the campground take-out ramp, so we may continue a couple hundred feet into Lake Superior to bob around in its waters, something Kenny missed our only other trip here in 2011, due to the haste to attend to dinner duties of his canoe partner & co-chef, Mister P. After some play time in Lake Superior, we turn for the campground. There, Chris and Ron produce a ham and mac 'n cheese dinner for us. Outstanding! Moth, although not on the dinner team, brought along a can of gravy just in case Gomie, famous for his *"Moth, where's the gravy?"* quote, showed up this year, the 15-year anniversary of Gomie's ill-received inquiry. After dinner, the fellas wandered down to the Lake Superior beach for cigars while enjoying the awe-inspiring sunset.

Day 2 saw the crew up unusually early and camp broken down with speed rarely seen. A 45-minute drive to breakfast at Zellar's Restaurant in Newberry provides the motivation. Eric is also motivated by the hope that a certain young maiden, whom he tried to entice to canoe with him after our 2011 Zellar's breakfast, is still employed there. Unfortunately for Eric, the fair lass is nowhere in sight, so only one of his hungers is satisfied.

By noon, our stomachs are full, we've made our way the 30 minutes from Newberry to the Seney Township Campground for tent set up (thank you again, Rookie Yoshi!), and driven the short mile & a half to Andy's for a pre-paddling shot and a beer. At 2PM, Leon will meet us at the Seney Township site with a trailer full of canoes, then transport us and the boats to the Fox River Campground launch access. We notice Leon is in a much better mood than when he kicked us out of his livery campground for excessive noise one year ago, but that doesn't change the lifetime ban we're under. "I'll rent canoes and haul you to put-in points anytime, but I can't have you staying overnight at the livery anymore." Until the next owner takes over, we can live with that. After dropping two vehicles at today's end point, a riverside spot approximately halfway between the launch and our tents, we have the rented canoes and the kayaks of Chum & Rookie Yoshi in the water a little before 3PM, a late start even by our standards.

Early into the trip, we encountered the one pretty good size deadwood obstruction we saw today, a fallen tree completely blocking the river. As we worked together to pull each boat through, Kenny shared a story from a paddle down the Prairie River, in the Three Rivers area, a couple of years ago. *"Ernie, the guy from the Liquid Therapy livery, was driving us along the river to the put-in, and we passed an obstruction like this one. Tommy tells Ernie that he's gotta clear that for us. Ernie laughs and tells Tommy, this ain't no Disneyland ride!"*

The 30-something Chum, showing the grizzled veterans a glimpse of the modern world, mounted a video camera on the front of his kayak, preserving a day-on-the-4Day for future viewing. Over the next couple of hours, Chum glimpsed the downside of excessive 4Day imbibing. As a result, the video ends with a 3-minute segment of a close-up of a riverbank tag alder bush he crashed into after an unscheduled careen-right subsequent to passing out in his kayak. This underscores the wisdom of the 4Day rule *never let a solo paddler go last.* The Chris and Ron canoe, piloted with the prudence acquired from, respectively, 22 and 16 years of 4Dayin', made sure to stay behind the increasingly buzzed cinematographer and fished him out of the bushes his kayak plunged into.

The lead canoes and kayakin' Rookie Yoshi pulled over at a riverbank a few bends downstream, waiting for Chris, Ron, and the rope-towed Chum kayak to catch up. Confirming the astute choice of his 4Day nickname, Chum leaned over and fed the fish, then settled back for a nap of recovery during our river break.

Jimmy couldn't be with us this 4Day, but in his honor Vid shared a story Jimmy recently told him. *"Last month, Jimmy and his son Spencer were driving to daughter Olivia's graduation ceremony. Spencer had just been golfing with 2 of his high school buddies, and he told his Dad, 'While we were out there, we were following some guys smoking cigars. My friends both said that the smell really disgusted them, and that it was real nasty. I told them that it kinda smells like a river trip. They asked what I was talking about. I thought about it and then said, you rookies wouldn't understand.' Jimmy proudly told me, "Of course they didn't because none of them have been canoeing with their Dads. That's my boy!"*

Around 7PM, we paddled up to the wooden railings along the right bank of the Fox River, leading to the top of a short hill where our vehicles are parked. While the boys are all pitching in, as each boat arrives, to push everyone's canoes and gear up the railings, here comes Chum kayaking around the bend, bright 'n perky, a big smile on his face, a recovery just this side of the Raising of Lazarus. Ah, the healing waters of the 4Day!

Eric and Moth's dinner creations for the crew were some damn fine soft tacos. The tacos created a warm belly effect that, added to our drunken state and the (for old folks) late hour, made it a struggle to get us up 'n out of our river chairs and walking to Andy's. Eventually, the desire to see Andy and the spreading chant of "We're not dead yet!" pushed us to the tavern. We walked into a fairly empty pub, Andy sitting at the bar, his back to us, chatting with a couple of his regulars. Hearing us enter, Andy spun around on his bar stool. "There they are! How you boys doin' this year?" Andy wasn't present when we stopped at lunchtime earlier today for a pre-Fox River shot, and seeing each other made it a happy moment for all. "Come on, let me buy you fellas a shot!" That declaration has always been well received, but in a shocking development, with everyone so wiped out by the party on the Two Hearted yesterday and the Fox today, the guys one-by-one started mumbling, "No thanks Andy." Andy looked stunned, "But it's my birthday!" It was then that we could hear the spirit of Bluto Blutarsky talking to us, "What the fuck happened to the 4Day I used to know?" Between Andy in the flesh and Bluto in our heads, we accepted Andy's offer and toasted to his birthday. It was the most painful group shot anyone could ever recall. Although Andy was still buying, we shamefully passed on any further shots, and slithered in disgrace out of the pub and back to camp.

Around the dying campfire, Rookie Yoshi and I were the last two still up, celebrating the world's joys and curing its ills, while chatting about the blessings of our 4Day brothers, including Kenny, the man who climbed Mount McKinley and who spent a vacation week flying into the Alaskan wilderness to salvage a buddy's downed and damaged airplane. The rookie guessed maybe Kenny is in his late-40s, no more than 50 years old. When I told him Kenny turns 69 this year, it might have been the first time this trip, except for the long exclaimed, "noooo waaaay!", that young Rookie Yoshi was at a loss for words.

Day 3, the early morning sun broke through the trees shading the campground. The rays warmed our tents and in concert with the aroma of freshly brewed morning coffee and cooking grub, the newly-awaken, with their temporarily-empty plates & cups, stumbled to the breakfast fire. Rookie Yoshi and Chum, having shed yesterday's excesses, with the bloom of youth as an ally, made a delectable feast for us of scrambled eggs, sausage 'n toast.

As dessert to their breakfast, I tossed in a Scottish joke for the boys...

*"I was at the pub the other night and overheard 3 hefty gals talking at the bar. Their accent appeared to be Scottish, so I approached and asked, 'Hello, are you 3 lassies from Scotland?' One of them angrily screeched, 'It's Wales, Wales you bloody idiot!' So I apologized and replied, 'I am so sorry. Are you 3 whales from Scotland?' That's the last thing I remember."*

This story got Kenny's mind to stirring, "Life is simpler when you plow around the stump." When the laughter quieted down, Eric asked Kenny, "Are those cherries you have from a Wisdom Tree? How about sharing some of those with us?" Kenny obliged, and passed around the cherries he'd been soaking in Jack Daniel's since last year's 4Day. This day is starting in fine fashion!

Back out on the Fox, we were pulled over on a left bend bank, talking about how long it's been since 4Day brother Matthew has been on our annual trip. In the finest use of a cell phone since calling for the beer cart from our softball dugout in 2001, we called Matthew and luckily found him at his Philadelphia-area home, ready, willing, and able to do a long distance "SHOT!" of Jack Daniel's with us. We were having so much fun at this break, quite a spell of time passed unnoticed 'til Ron declared, "I could've built a log cabin in the time we've been here."

In the meantime, Chris appeared to be collecting enough driftwood to supply the wood for Ron's cabin. As we paddled downstream, Kenny was teasing Chris about his fondness for collecting big quantities of large river objects. Kenny pointed to a huge midstream rock, poking its head above the waterline, and said, "The unusual thing is that Chris' canoe is underneath that rock."

"Ok fellers," I started, "I have another Scottish 'n Irish joke for you." I'd told this one before to Johnny, and he'd laughed so hard, I was trying to get him cracking up again. *A Scotsman, a Brit, and an Irishman are drinking, when the Scot says, 'As good as this bar is, I still prefer the pubs back home. In Glasgow, there's this wee place called McTavish's. The landlord goes out of his way for the locals. When you buy 4 drinks, he'll buy you the 5th.' 'Well Angus,' says the Englishman, 'At my local in London, the Red Lion, the barman will buy your 3rd drink after you buy the first 2.' The Irishman says, 'Dat's nothin'. Back home in me favorite pub in Galway, the moment you set foot in the place, they buy you a drink and then another, all the drinks you want. Then, when you've had enough drinks, they take you upstairs and see dat you get laid, all on the house!' The Scot and the Brit were suspicious of these claims. 'Did this actually happen to you?' The Mick admitted, 'Not meself personally, no, but it did happen to me sister quite a few times!'"* Johnny doubled-over laughing again, this time almost falling out of his canoe.

Finally, after paddling around a big bend to the right, our tents come into view. Dinner is on everyone's minds. On the menu tonight is Andy burgers, with Vid, Kenny, and me picking up the tab. Within 15 minutes of the last boat pulling ashore, we're walking with purpose to Andy's.

Vid is the first to walk inside the tavern's walls, spying Andy at his usual bar stool perch, and asks, "Hey Andy, is it too late to do some birthday shots with you?" Andy starts laughing, "Hell, no, my birthday isn't 'til tomorrow, anyhow." Chris tells Andy, "Well, after our poor showing last night, tonight we're buying! What'll ya have?" "How do shots of Dickel and Blackberry Brandy sound?" "You mean mixed together?" "Nah, we'll alternate 'em." Ron says, "It sounds awful, but the liver is evil and it must be punished."

I'm amazed. "Hey Ron, does this mean you're finally coming around to the delights of Dickel?" "No," he tells us, "George Dickel is as fine as a 12 minute Carol Channing song. It's like nails on a chalk board, like a kick to your wedding tackle, 2nd only to a jigger of diesel fuel, mixed liberally with the ground, and I have to lick a dog's butt to get the taste out of my mouth. But, it's Andy's birthday, almost, so what the hell."

After several toasts to Andy's birthday, Vid proposes, "Let's drink to Jimmy Leyland. 3 & 0 against the Yankees in post-season play, the Frank Lary of managers!" "Damn," I said, "I can't believe that I never considered the Jimmy Leyland-Frank Lary connection. No one was ever a bigger Yankee-Killer than these two men. Lary was 28 & 13 against the Yankees Suck, his 1960 Topps card my favorite all-time baseball card. On the back it says, in 1958 and 1959 combined,

Frank Lary went 13 & 1 versus the Yanks!" When Johnny said, "Well then, to Frank Lary!", the cheers shook the bar's foundation, unless that was the Dickel 'n brandy making my legs wobble, followed by a short, dear to our hearts, tune taught to us by Captain Johnny Harcourt...

*"The Yankees Suck! The Yankees Suck! The Yankees Suck! The Yankees Suck! They really, really, really, really, really, really suck* (note held with delight)........... *the Yankees* **SUCK!**"

The next morning, with the afterglow of Andy's birthday Dickel and Blackberry Brandy swirling through our heads, we tore down the Seney campsite early to grab breakfast at the little Seney Restaurant. Our Day 4 paddle takes place 2 hours away in the Northern Lower Peninsula on the fast-flowing Sturgeon River, near the town of Wolverine. There we'll meet this year's 2nd 4Day rookie, Lazurus Surabian, better known as Laz, at the ironically-named Toasty's Cabins, our home for the evening.

Rookie Laz is a fellow Eastern Michigan University Huron, a dear brother of ours for 40 years. Laz and wife Connie, aka Caz & Lonnie, are southeast Michigan residents who have a 2nd house nearby, a northern getaway a bit south of Cheboygan, only a 20-minute drive from our pick-up point. Making Rookie Laz the perfect match for the 4Day is that much of his career has been spent as an executive in the beer and hard liquor industry. Working against the rookie is that canoeing and kayaking do not come naturally to him, an issue that magnifies with imbibing, the magnification enhanced on a challenging river like the Sturgeon.

Today, Rookie Laz and I will canoe together.

While I handle the steering in the stern, my slightly-larger partner Laz sits up front in the bow. A certain unsteadiness descends on our boat, one I've not experienced in my 5 prior trips on this demanding river. Laz' center of gravity is not in his seat, but rather hovers a couple of feet above the canoe, creating a *shake* rather that a *flow* downstream. 15 minutes from launching, the 3 canoes and two kayaks pull over for a snack of Mad Dog, Fleischmann's, and Kenny's cherries-soaked-in-Jack.

During this break, we talk excitedly about the re-opening, only 75 minutes down river from where we stand and where we will soon stop, of the old Meadows Bar, reincarnated as the Thirsty Sturgeon. Brandy, a daughter of one of Rookie Laz' cousins, works at the tavern. To commemorate this, Jimmy re-wrote the lyrics of the song *Brandy* by the band Looking Glass...

*There's a bar up the northern way, and it serves a few canoes a day,*
*Lonely 4Dayers pass the time away and talk about their homes.*
*And there's a girl in this river town and she works layin' whiskey down,*
*They say, Brandy, fetch another round, she serves them whiskey and beer.*

The stop was fun, the aftermath not so much. The Mad Dog, Fleischmann's, and Kenny's cherries-soaked-in-Jack has turned Laz into a seat-swaying-seafarer, like one of those dancing windsock guys come to life, amusing from a distance further than the front of the boat I'm in. Twice within the next 15 minutes, our canoe flips over. On the second flip, my jaw meets a tree root imbedded in the river floor, loosening recent dental work. Rookie Laz is very apologetic about it all, and is open to my suggestion that the balance of the trip will be more enjoyable for both of us if he will lower his center of gravity by sitting on the canoe floor. A few minutes into this new dynamic, Laz is excited, "This is great! What a wonderful way to take in the scenery!" I breathe a sigh of relief and we both open beers to salute the revised paddle plan.

Our arrival at the new Thirsty Sturgeon is a mixed bag for me. On one hand, my loose tooth stops me from bitin' off more pizza than I can chew, so that's good. On the other hand, I also can't chew at all without discomfort, so that's bad. Then again, no loose tooth will hamper the downing of a couple of beers and shots in honor of the re-opening of one of Michigan's classic riverside taverns.

The bar is where our Sturgeon trip ends, as we've arranged for Jamie of the Big Bear livery to pick us up here, but only after we get some pub time in. Upon Jamie's arrival, we assist with loading canoes 'n kayaks on to the livery trailer before he transports us to our evening cabins. Once there, Laz phones Connie for a ride home, giggling, "I'm drunk – come get me!" While we wait for the fortunately amused Connie, Laz tells us what a great time he had on his rookie expedition, short as it may have been at one day, and promises to return for future 4Days. My heartfelt response to my old friend is a mumbled "Glad to have you with us, Laz, but maybe not as much as my orthodontist will be".

*4Day 36 post-script...*
August 30, 2013
4Day Brothers,

My brother, Gene, was recently traveling the roads of the U.P., searching out small breweries and sampling their wares. As he passed through the hamlet of Seney, he stopped at a roadside establishment that is familiar to us all, Andy's Seney Bar. We can now add to the line, "Some get there by canoe, some get there by car", *"some get there by Harley"*, too.

During a discussion with a young wench that was tending the serving side of the bar, he asked if she was familiar with the 4Day boys and their infamous leader, Doc Fletcher? She must have been new because she didn't recollect the name. He said, "You'd remember them. They're loud and drink like there's no tomorrow." Her retort, "Like we don't see that every night?" justified her position as having been on a couple rodeos herself.

Shortly thereafter, the proprietor came in and he and Gene got to talkin'. Well, of course, Andy says, "Oh, I know those guys. They're somethin' else."

At any rate, Gene decided that it was time to put his money where his mouth was. Fortunately for us, his mouth was on a can of PBR. Gene thought it appropriate to leave his 4Day brethren a little something from him - $50 in drinking tokens in an envelope especially for the next 4Day sojourn. Stay thirsty my friends!

Jimmy

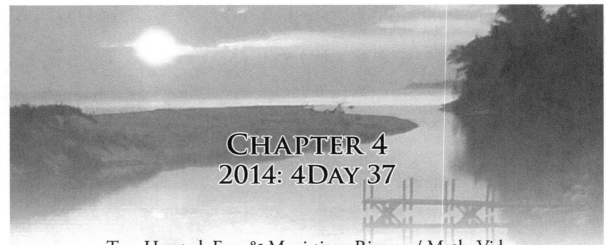

# CHAPTER 4
## 2014: 4DAY 37

Two-Hearted, Fox, & Manistique Rivers w/ Moth, Vid,
Neal, Chum, Kenny, Chippy 2Rib, Chris, Ron, Eric, Laz,
Johnny, KB, Gomie, Carl V., Mister P, Yoshi, Brittany (ashes),
Doc and rookies Carl H., Ken V., Tom K. and Eddie

*I'm going back to the ones that I know,*
*With whom I can be what I want to be.*
*Just one week for the feeling to go,*
*And with you there to help me*
*Then it probably will.*
*(With You There to Help Me by Jethro Tull)*

As the 4Day draws near each year, and the boys' excitement levels rise, the pre-trip email banter grows...

*I heard a rumor that Mad Dog stock has risen at the mere mention of the 4Day. Factories are in full motion in expectations of great sales prior to July 4th. Also sad to report that Dickel will be scarce because the diesel fuel it's made from has skyrocketed. Many rejoiced (at least 1, ME) at the news.*

*Signed,*
*Ron*
*17,228 days without Dickel and counting...*

*Using my Little Orphan Annie Decoder Pin, I was able to read Ron's email and determine his secret message within...*

*"George Dickel Tennessee Whiskey is so fine, it must be created in a special place, and it is, in beautiful Dickel Hollow near Tullahoma, Tennessee. The Dickel distillery was built in 1958 for one purpose: to produce the finest, most flavorful whiskey ever made by man. One taste & you'll agree. Can't wait to sip it along the banks of the Two Hearted."*

*14 days to go,*
*River Dick Doc*

2014 marks the return of two of the 4 Horsemen from Jacksonville, Florida: KB aka Pestilence and Gomie aka Gomez. This is KB's first 4Day in 15 years, and Gomie's first since missing the last 3 trips. In honor of the south once again invading the north, we shared with KB and Gomie a few things you'll never hear a southerner say...

*Oh, I just couldn't, she's only sixteen; I'll take Shakespeare for 1000, Alex; No kids in the back of the pickup, it's just not safe; We don't keep firearms in this house; You can't feed that to a dog; Too many deer heads detract from the décor; Trim the fat off that steak; I just couldn't find a thing at Wal-Mart today; Hey, here's an episode of Hee Haw that we haven't seen; No, I don't live near a Cracker Barrel; Who gives a damn who won the Civil War?*

Gomie confirmed his return through a 4Day history lesson pre-trip email to the group...

*Our prophet & leader - Jeff "Call him Doc, no he's not a real doctor per se, but he can talk his way thru" Fletcher.*

*Our Heretic - Ron "Rookie" Swiecki.*

*Our Seer & part time prophet - Herr Paul "The Colonel" Braun.*

*Our Kraken - Chris "don't make eye contact with him" Weaks.*

*Our Confucius or Confusedius - Johnny "Not the curtains lad" Steck.*

*Our Dalai Lama - Vid "He's a big hitter the Lama" Marvin.*

*Our Wise Man bringing alchemy from afar - Keith "You sure this is Myrrh?" Jones.*

*Our Prodigal Son - Gomez. Can you have Craigo barbeque the fatted calf on the peninsula?*

(Author's note: see 1997 chapter for best 4Day meal ever)

*Our Josephus - Johnny "Asphuck Biggins" Harcourt.*

*Our Lazarus - Keith "Shut up Gomez" Romig (Aren't you glad I didn't put "Cadaver Dick"?).*

*Our Jezebel – Kathy "How many times are you going to watch Animal House?" Harcourt (She's in our brother Captain Johnny's ear; not a believer of the 4-Day, but fears its power).*

*Our leper who hangs around the watering hole begging for shots - describes too many to list.*

*Our Council of Elders - Laying down arbitrary and arcane decisions. Chief Elder Kenny "Rendezvous Lately?" Umphrey.*

*Our Moth – Gary "No gravy" Muir. What happened to you Moth? You were a Pupa w/ promise. Excuse the long winded reply. Consider this my signed napkin. I just wanted to say "I'm in!"*

*Gomez*

Gomie aka Gomez                                    KB aka Pestilence

2014 heralds the return of Mark Hayden, better known as Chippy 2Rib, back for the first time since suffering two cracked ribs and one chipped tooth, all in just two days of paddling during his 2012 rookie year. Chippy brought a bodyguard this year, his son Rookie Carl. The two made the 11-hour drive from North Carolina to my house on Thursday, July 3, the day before we head north. When this Father-Son team arrives, they're bubbling over, ready for action. "What are we doing tonight, Doc?" is more of a starter's pistol than a question. As happy as I am to see them, I have to break the bad news, "Well, it'll be kind of a quiet evening, fellas. Don't think we'll be seein' anyone else until tomorrow at…"

Before I could finish bumming them out, a car screeches into my driveway on two wheels, guys hanging out the windows yelling ***"4DAYYYY!"*** It's KB, Gomie, Moth, and the unexpected treat of the Colonel. Huge grins spring forth from Chippy 2Rib and Rookie Carl. My house goes from zero to breaking the sound barrier in seconds. Guys are jumping up & down, shoutin', huggin', as general pandemonium descends. It's not going to subside for awhile, 'cause Colonel isn't coming north tomorrow. He's on a mission to get a 4Day's worth of partyin' in at my place tonight, and we're all along for the ride. Although there's not a cloud in the sky, we're caught in a rainstorm of cigars, beer, and bourbon, and this front is stationary. Maggie, God bless her heart, makes some appetizers to tide us over 'til the ordered pizzas make their way here. Several party hours later, the Gang of 4 leave for a 4Day shopping run to Meijer, the highly-blasted Colonel's assistance ensuring a grocery list light on food, heavy on liquor. His 4Day worth of partying is an apparent success, as Colonel had no idea he was in a Meijer until presented with photos later.

21 brothers, including 4 rookies, embarked on the 37th edition of the 4Day, paddling the eastern U.P. waters of the Two Hearted, the Fox, and the Manistique from July 5 to 8. Only the

23 men and 37 coolers of the 1996 4Day was a larger turnout. Accommodating the schedules of several of the brothers, 4Day-eve would take place on Fourth of July Friday instead of the usual Friday after the 4th.

It would be unreasonable to expect to show up on the Friday of a major holiday weekend and successfully secure Two Hearted campground space for 21 for two nights. So, Chum, Yoshi, and Yoshi's friend, Rookie Eddie (always wise of a sophomore to bring a rookie in case no other rookies attend and he ends up the de facto rookie), said they would drive up Thursday to hold the needed spots for us. When Kenny heard of a plan consisting of 3 guys looking to hold enough sites for 10 tents, though admirable, he termed the strategy, "rock solid and iffy," and decided to arrive Wednesday and help out. Next thing you know, Chris, who had planned to jump ship in Hong Kong, make his way to Tibet, and get on as a looper at a course over in the Himalayas, decides instead to arrive Thursday to help hold the ground. So now, we have five 4Dayers armed with 18 bottles of Mag Dog, a variety of cheap, rot gut, whiskey, much beer, Kenny's Jack Daniel's soaked-cherries, and another Kenny treat, perfect-for-the-4th of July *Military Bourbon*. These 5 charmers, with a fierce determination to stake out the space we need, can tell somebody to go to hell in such a way that they'd look forward to the journey. The high ground above the Two Hearted river mouth at Lake Superior is ours!

On 4Day eve, with 5 of this year's 21 standing guard at Two Hearted camp, and a surprise rookie who we won't see until Day 4, the remaining 15 drive north for a noon rendezvous at the Nottingham Bar. 90-year old bar owner Virgy is as spry, feisty, and fun-loving as ever, greeting us with the enthusiasm of a woman half her age. "Would you boys like a shot or a beer or both?" "What's the specialty of the house Virgy?" KB asked. "That'd be both!" We toasted to Virgy's health, her one concession to advanced years is that she passed on hitting the whiskey with us. Talking about the old classics like Virgy and her pub got the chatter around to the Oasis Bar. A round of glasses were lifted to the Oasis, a tavern on US10 west of Baldwin, 1 mile north of the Pere Marquette River, that burned down last year when its furnace exploded. The bar had a drink special called *The Osama Bin Laden: 2 shots 'n a splash*. "I had a lot of liquor and a lot of pork rinds, good pork rinds, at the Oasis," Vid said, "unlike the bar that advertised *65% less fat* pork rinds – what else is there *but* fat in pork rinds? What, is the bag 65% empty?"

Ron, Eric and I covered 4Day-eve dinner, a carry-out order at the Newberry Pizza Hut. "Hi, I have an order for 14 medium pizzas." My comment was met with a silent stare from the counter gal, then, "Oh, we don't have a 14-pizza order." My stutter, "But… I…," elicited laughter from the employee. "Just kidding, we have your order ready to go." I laughed back, "That's funny, because you DO have the order, elsewise I was gonna torch this place."

Arriving at the Two Hearted camp, everyone's spirits are sky-high, the excitement impossible to escape. The 5 who arrived 1 to 2 days before us did a great job securing sufficient space for the 20 camping tonight and the next. Scanning the inventory scattered among our sites, we have enough grog, food, and camping gear to support an expedition down the Mississippi River. After pizzas are gobbled down and tents set up, the boys venture down to the Lake Superior shoreline to take in the incredible sunset. Merriment continues into the early morning hours. As Baraboo Wisconsin's Jon Hillmer would say, "If you ain't havin' fun, what are ya havin'?" With the final few around the dying campfire, the pitch black night and empty fifths 'n beer cans surrounding us, I borrow a flashlight so I can pick out my tent among the many squeezed into our camp area. There's a great day a 'comin', and sleep is required before it arrives.

Day 1 breaks as the campground fills with the aroma of coffee and brats, part of a blue chip breakfast prepared for us by Chris and Neal. Though we're camping here again tonight, with no need to pack up the tents, we're still hustling to chow down and exit camp for the 20-minute drive to the Reed & Green Bridge access and a 10AM meeting with livery guy Larry Johnson. Rainbow Lodge is still rebuilding from the big 2012 fire, so this year Lodge customers are being directed to Larry & his North Store Outpost in tiny Pine Stump Junction. Sophomores Mister P and Laz, joining the 4Day this morning, meet us at the access with 20 bags of ice to fortify the depleted coolers.

Only 30 minutes after launching, a sandy shoreline rise beckons us to take an extended river break. Here, using large rocks found in and along the Two Hearted, lugged by rookies Carl, Eddie, and Ken, we directed the formation of a 3' tall by 2' wide "4Day" memo on the river floor.

Rookie Carl "he's a legacy, we gotta take him" Hayden, is the 20-ish son of Chippy 2Rib. He has the soul of an artist, the mind of a techie, and is full of good humor. 30-something Rookie Eddie is pleasant company, though somewhat quiet, perhaps affected by mingling with a group of long-time, older friends. Rookie Ken, another legacy, is the brother of Carl "Doubles" Verba. Ken has played softball with us for a number of years, but is fairly new to this group canoeing thing. He loves to cook and is good at it, traits that guarantee popularity.

A bit downstream, Chris gives us a big scare. We encounter a fallen tree that blocks the entire width of the river. As we work our way through its center, a branch catches one of Chris' eyes. "My eye! I can't see out of it!" Chris immediately shouts, eliciting several "Oh shits!" from the boys, underscored as we see blood running down his cheek below the damaged eye. With no good place to pull over at this point, Chris paddles downstream with Eric to find a beach where we can examine the eye and decide what to do. There is debate whether to paddle upstream, against the current, for the two miles from where we put-in but where we have no vehicle, and then call for a hoped-for ride to the hospital in Newberry, or paddle straight to the campsite, 11 miles downstream where our cars are parked, and speed to the hospital.

As the rest of us make our way through the obstruction, we soon hear laughter downstream, a very good sign. Chris and Eric found a left bank beach and determined that the branch cut above, and not into, Chris' eye. Torn flesh and not a punctured eyeball is the source of impaired vision and the blood running down his cheek. Using the first aid kit, the wound is cleaned and the cut sealed, Chris' sight improves, and a celebratory bottle of Mad Dog is produced to toast his, and our, good fortune.

Hours later, as our tents at the river's edge come into view, "Hallelujahs!" arise from the paddling armada. We are moments from our take-out!

Around the evening campfire, Chris talks about today's battle versus the portage. "My eye was bloodied when I lost my balance on that tree. The markings to my face are reminiscent of my rookie year (*Author's note:* see 1990 when Chris fell off Jimmy's running boards). The portage tried to land the knockout punch early, but I got better. We'll call it a draw." I shout over to Rookie Eddie, "Hey rook, you did a nice job helping get the boats through the debris where Chris was injured," and grab a fifth of Old Overholt from my cooler, "Let's have a drink to that!" As the crew toasts Eddie and pass the bottle, the rookie smiles and says, "I was happy to help." Teasing the rookie, I temper my compliment, "Until that point, I was ready to suggest that your 4Day nickname be Calvin." Rookie Eddie looks confused. "You know, like Calvin Coolidge. He did so little as President that he was known best for his *alert inactivity*."

On this great night along Lake Superior, much of the conversation is about how thankful we our that Chris still has two eyes, and our amazement that so much green has returned to the river's surroundings since the fire of two years ago. The sunlight lasts long enough for us to play euchre without a lamp until 1030PM. Due to extended hours on the water, our day is long, necessitating a campfire-lit, Mexican food feast, by the father & son chef team of Chippy 2Rib & Rookie Carl.

On Sunday, Day 2, morning, we break camp for the 45-minute drive to breakfast in Newberry. After eating, Mister P, Laz, and the Verba Brothers bail out of any more 4Dayin' before they have too much fun. The rest of us begin the 30-minute Newberry to Seney drive and, as the Doc Watson CD plays, *Let it rain, let it pour, let it rain a whole lot more, 'cause I got those deep river blues,* the skies open up. Looking to wait out the downpour so we don't have to set up our tents in the rain, the caravan pulls into Andy's Seney Bar. Although Andy isn't here, $50 in tavern tokens left last year for us by 4Day brother Gene Vollmers are, God bless him, so we get in a couple of rounds on Gene's dime as precipitation pounds the pub roof.

It's only mid-morning, but a bar regular who goes by the name of *Big Foot* has been hard at drinkin' for a few hours. Somewhat hesitantly, we agree to have Big Foot deliver a face cord of wood to our camp a mile & a half away while we paddle. He tells us that the delivery will be made after he knocks down a few more "wobble pops". No hurry Big Foot, you stay and master your craft.

With time running out before the Northland Outfitters van arrives with our canoes for today, we leave Andy's and set up tents in the rain at the Seney Township Campground. With the tents up, we duck into portable shelters provided by Moth and Neal. As the livery van shows to haul us upstream on the Fox River, the rain stops, but dark and cloudy conditions persist. There is a mosquito horde waiting for us at the launch site, and it provides a river escort until we reach the first stop when wind and cigar smoke keep them at bay. Although I was planning to do this on Tuesday, the final day of the 4Day, we need a ray of light through the gloomy sky, so I surprise the boys now with a recording from Baraboo Jon Hillmer. Jon is a wild soul, and his message, with echoes of Robin Williams' "Goood Morning Vietnam!", is short, fun, and to the point, *"Goood Mornin' Muther-fuckers! Happy Fuckin' Tuesday! Ain't nuthin' like bein' up and goin' to fuckin' work on a fuckin' Tuesday! Wooooooooooo!!!!!"*

The effect of Jon's message grips the boys like a lightning bolt. Soon, the beer, Mad Dog, and stories flow on another wonderful river day! Moth shares a tale from his Duracell days, *"I was working with Dave Hitch, and we were stopped at a traffic light. I looked over and saw a dog licking himself. I said to Dave, "I bet you wish you could do that." Dave's response was, "He would probably bite me if I tried."*

As we wind our way through the narrow Fox riverbed, the rain is intermittent, but never enough to put out the paddlers' stogies or light-heartedness. Big Guy's long 4Day absence is noted among the paddlers with shouted flashbacks to Biggie's *breakfast surprise* of 2006. His stanky massive dump, right next to our breakfast fire pit, was one that we would've assumed was left by black bears, had the impressive mound not been topped by a few squares of toilet paper. Johnny adds, "Due to the dump's elevation, it's snow-capped even in summer months." The paddlers memorialize the occasion with a song of tribute, using the melody from "On Top of Old Smokey" for "On Top of Mount Biggie": *On top of Mount Biggie, all covered with snow, we ran fast for cover, but some ran too slow; for dumping's a pleasure, it's chow time's bequeath; from this honking stool, there'll be no relief.*

As the final paddlers land at Seney camp, Yoshi & Rookie Eddie's already bubbling stew for the group dinner beckons with its sweet bouquet. In a happy surprise, Andy's Bar regular, Big Foot, did not let a herd of wobble pops stop him from delivering the promised face cord of firewood. On the down side, Chris ran out of Mad Dog, and says, "Note to self: 18 bottles of Mad Dog only lasts 2 days. Next year bring more." To assuage any sadness Chris may have felt, Gomie opens a fifth of Old Crow and passes it to Chris. With a big grin of thanks, Chris takes a double-bubbler of Crow and, on a day of creating new songs from old favorites, makes Jerry Jeff Walker's Sangria Wine tune his own: *It's organic and it comes from the vine, oh, and it's legal and it gets you so high; I love that Mad Doggy Wine, when I'm drinkin' with old friends of mine; Whoa oh oh, oh oh, I love Mad Doggy Wine!*

The Old Crow is lost in the black hole named Rookie Eddie, who drains the fifth at a pace we warn him is unwise. At the time Chris starts to give his opinion on the rookies, "Rookie Carl has taken a huge lead in rookie of the year consideration. Through his work ethic, service…,"

Eddie, on dinner duty with Yoshi, drunkenly dumps a third of the pot of stew on to the dinner fire. Yoshi minimizes the damage, moving with speed not previously seen, to right the pot before removing the rookie from the area. Plenty of stew remains to feed us. So that the veterans think twice before handing a bottle to a novice, Chippy 2Rib devises a plan to identify rookies through paper plate name tags hung on their camp chairs.

Around the campfire, a cell phone rings. It's Chum's aka Nick's phone and, much to the boys' amusement, it is Nick's Mom calling him. After the requisite teasing of a 4Dayer's incoming Momma's call, it comes out that Nick's Mom is a single parent. Moth pounces on the perceived opportunity with an, "Oh good!" Nick assures him, "She's too old for you Moth." All the boys are now engaged, "Damn, how old is she?" Nick's reply, "She's 55," is met by riotous laughter. KB says, "How old do you think *we are* Nick? Lord, if anything your Mom might be too young for Moth." The 61-year old Moth is now tenacious in his interest in Chum's relatively youthful Mom, "What's your Mom look like? What's her phone number?" Chum thinks he sees an out. "I'll give you my Mom's number if you give me your daughter's." "No problem," says Moth, "its' 867-5309." Good try Nick. Through the night, we kid Chum about the possibility of Moth becoming his Daddy. Chum smiles when this comes up, but it's an uneasy smile. Chris suggests, "Chumley, watch the movie *Easy Money*. There is a scene after Julio marries Rodney's daughter. He smiles and asks Rodney, can I call you Dad? Pray you don't have to do that".

Day 3 we paddle the same stretch of the Fox as Day 2, but today it's 78, sunny, and not a skeeter in sight. Sweet! At each stop today, the boys request a replay of Jon Hillmer's *Happy Fuckin' Tuesday!* message, and I happily oblige.

About an hour shy of the campsite, the Chumley kayak is without a captain, or as Vid would say, "Too many Gilligans and not enough Skippers." Perhaps driven by the fear of Moth becoming his Daddy, Chum has taken to heavy drinking, and is passed out in his boat. The Chris and Rookie Carl canoe are handling safety duties today, making sure that no solo paddler is last in our flotilla. They scoop up Chum, loading him and his gear into the canoe. Rookie Carl paddles Chum's kayak, while Chris transports Moth's future stepson safely back to our Seney camp.

Chum's powers of recovery are amazing, fortunate for a man who relies on them so often, and he joins us for the walk to Andy's for grog 'n grub. It's wonderful that Andy is in the bar tonight! Gomie hasn't seen him in 4 years, KB in 15 years, AND Andy turns 75 this month. After some back 'n forth greetings and gab with Andy, I said, "Andy, we'd like to buy you a birthday shot or two. How does Dickel sound?" Making himself heard over Ron's shout of, "No Dickel!" Andy says, "Dickel would be fine, fellas, how'd you know?" Eric laughed, "Andy, we just got lucky."

After a couple of Andy hours, we retire to our camp for a great bonfire & a first-rate soundtrack of river tunes, ranging from *Country Funk* to the Talking Heads. Rookie Carl flies by camp in his car, channeling Jon Hillmer, shouting out the window, "Happy Fuckin' 4Day! Woooooooooo!" Chris says, "Oh yeah, that's the rookie of the year!" All are in agreement, though I mention, "Yeah, Rookie Carl has it sewn up, but there is a special rookie joining us tomorrow. Finally, after invitations for over a decade, the previous livery owner, Tom Kenney, is paddling with us!"

Before we break camp the final morning, Kenny and Johnny put together a splendid breakfast for us of eggs and biscuits 'n gravy. The hot meal is welcome on a chilly, overcast, morning. As the boys take down the tents, a lot of Monty Python & the Holy Grail jibber-jabber takes place…

*-I fart in your general direction! Your mother was a hamster and your father smelt of Elderberries!* Is there someone else up there we can talk to?

*-Strange women lying in ponds distributing swords is no basis for a system of government. Supreme executive power derives from a mandate from the masses, not from some farcical aquatic ceremony.*

*-What makes you think she is a witch?* Well, she turned me into a Newt? *A Newt?* (pause) I got better.

*-(after all the Black Knight's limbs have been severed) Alright, we'll call it a draw.*

*-Help! I'm being oppressed. Come see the violence inherent in the system.*

*-Old woman!* Man! *Man, sorry. What knight lives in that castle over there?* I'm 37. *What?* I'm 37, I'm not old. *Well, I can't just call you man.* You could say Dennis. *I didn't know you were called Dennis.* You didn't bother to find out, did you? *Well, I did say sorry about the old woman, but from behind…*

*-One day lad, all this will be yours.* What, the curtains? *(smack to the back of head) No, not the curtains, lad.*

*-Please, please, this is supposed to be a, happy occasion. Let's not bicker and argue about, who killed who.*

*-and after the spanking, the oral sex!* Well, I could stay a <u>bit</u> longer.

Young Austin, a pleasant and hard-working sort from Northland Outfitters, arrives to pick up the canoes & kayaks and haul them to today's Manistique River put-in. While we assist loading boats on to the trailer, Chris calls for a rookie to come over and powder his balls, triggering an uneasy laugh from Austin.

It's cloudy and 57 in En-ga-ding-a-ding-a-dine and in Germfask, mighty fine canoeing weather for all but KB, Vid, Johnny, Neal, Ron, Chum, and Eric. These 7 4Day brothers, dubbed by the surviving 9 as "the Vagina Boys", are lost to the comforts of doily-making at the Jolly Motel and Bar. In their defense, Germfask is known for its top-drawer doily-making, and some of the boys <u>are</u> sick, although Neal asks the stricken Vid, "Do I have to be sick to opt out of today?"

Ex-livery owner Tom is the 10th paddler for this final day of the 37th 4Day, traveling from his nearby home in Curtis to, at long last, make his maiden 4Day voyage. We've always enjoyed Tom's company, and are glad to have him paddling with us. As we canoe & kayak along, Tom shares with us U.P. tales of the serpent who lives below the river, the Menni-boujou aka the Mah-Nee-Bozho aka the "pranking deity", who likes to flip over unsuspecting or liquored up paddlers. We believe we've met this feller. It's on to the merger with the Fox and a stop at the new steel bridge formerly, *"the… Old… Log… Bridge",* before paddling the last couple of hours on the most beautiful stretch of the revered waters of the Manistique. We take the opportunity for one last stop on the river's sandy beaches, enjoy one more beer, one more cigar, and one more shared laugh at an old joke, prior to climbing into the canoes for the float to the livery.

Back at the Jolly Motel, we check-in with new owner Rose and meet her dog, Pete Rose. Rose has an upbeat personality, and Chum reports that he shared some herb with Rose this afternoon, information that brings forth nods of admiration from the fellers.

Holy crap, it's Pizza Night at the Jolly Bar! Boy, they do a quality pizza at the Jolly. And Andy is in here tonight, too! I mention to the boys that I love the fact that U.P. bar owners spend their days off at other bars, when an older gal walks by, overhears my comment and says, "Thanks! I have a bar in McMillan." This lady is loudly cheering the Tigers on along with us. The Boys of Summer were losing 5 to nothing when we walked into the bar, before rallying for a 14 to 5 win over the Dodgers. The 4Day karma keeps on flowin'!

Barkeep Glenda, Mom of owner Damion, has a joke to send us on our way...

*It was a young fella's first night at a whorehouse, and he had only $5 to his name. He was told that he can be fixed up with a gal for some 69. While in this position, the gal cuts a stinky one, and says, "Sorry, are you ok?" "Yeah, I'm fine." This goes on a bit longer, then the gal farts again, "Sorry, are you ok?" The young fella answers, "Yeah, but I don't think I can handle another 67 of those."*

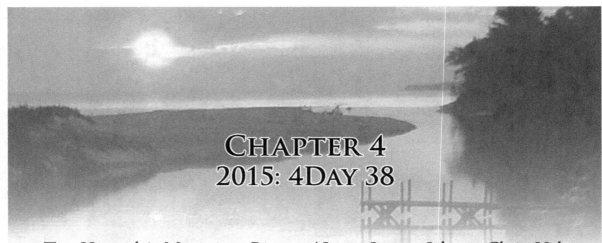

# CHAPTER 4
# 2015: 4DAY 38

Two Hearted & Manistique Rivers w/ Jason, Jimmy, Johnny, Chris, Vid, Moth, Ron, Carl V., Ken V., Neal, Jeff, Chippy 2Rib, Yoshi, Laz, Carl H., Doc, Brittany (ashes), rookies Mailman Kirk, Perry, and Korny

*Before the breathin' air is gone*
*Before the sun is just a bright spot in the night-time*
*Out where the rivers like to run*
*I stand alone and take back somethin' worth rememberin'*
*(Out In the Country by Three Dog Night)*

In honor of Captain Johnny's 62nd birthday, 5.16.15, I mailed to Johnny a 1985 Topps Baseball Card of Detroit Tiger Ruppert Jones. Seeing the card in my favorite baseball card store, it was impossible not to think of that sunny 1984 day at the Corner, our seats positioned in the upper deck front row behind the visitors' dugout, when Ruppert fouled off a screaming line drive headed right for us. Johnny reached out and spared those seated next to us from be-headings. In other words, the 1985 Ruppert Jones card had Johnny Harcourt written all over it. Upon receipt of the card, Captain Johnny sent this reply:

*Docko!!*

*I am a legendary individual. I am envied by many, fish fear me, women love me, and bartenders scurry to keep my glass full. My grass grows in the other direction, my car always starts, my razor is always sharp, and my teeth never need flossing.*

*My canoe never tips, the paper is always on time, street people offer me spare change, and my neighbors always ask me to borrow from them. The cops always let me off and the people at Apple Computer like to ask me what I think. Some say the Big Bang Theory was my idea and the city of Detroit climbed out of bankruptcy because I used to live there. My pencils are always sharp, my batteries never go dead. My dishwasher empties itself and the garbage man comes to the door.*

*My neighbor's dog barks only when I am gone and my cat can kick any dog's ass. I have walked in*

*the rain and stayed totally dry. If I miss my flight, the plane turns around. My brothers say I am the handsome one and my sisters say they can't find a man like me.*

*Tequila make makes me wise and bourbon makes me 2 inches taller. The fact is I have become a very special individual. Those living in the dark ask: what is it? How does he do it? Where does he get his powers?*

*I am all of this BECAUSE!!!!!!...*
*I have a Ruppert Jones Baseball Card*

*I love you Brother*
*The Captain*

"What, no Kenny this year?" was the general reaction. No sir, Kenny won't be on the 4Day with us in 2015. In the first summer after his 70th birthday, Kenny is on a 63-day journey hiking the Appalachian Trail, a 370-mile stretch from Springer Mountain, Georgia, the southern terminus of the Trail, to Roan Mountain, Tennessee. We've had the pleasure of knowing this man since 1977 and he never fails to amaze us. God bless you brother.

Rookie Kirk Coppernoll, better known as the Mailman, descended from French Huguenots who emigrated from Holland into New England. He is the good kind of Yankee. Kirk's previous mail route included Vid's house, a happy occurrence for us all. Like Kenny, Rookie Mailman has a personality that draws others to him, and is an outdoorsman who could adapt just fine to the conditions in any century (to paraphrase Jimmy Buffett, you pick the century, I'll pick the canoeing spot).

Rookie Perry quietly and quickly picked up a 4Day nickname of the Commodore, although my preferred nickname for him is Klink due to his impersonations of Colonel Klink and General Burkhalter from *Hogan's Heroes*. This rookie is low-key, funny, always smiling, and a helluva cook (where were all these cooks in the early 4Days?). I'm honored that he is my brother-in-law.

4Day 2015 begins, as did 2014, with two days of canoeing & kayaking the Two Hearted and 3 nights of camping along that same river. Last year, opening night fell on the Friday of July 4 weekend, and it was critical that some of us go up early in the week to secure our camp space. Although this year's 4Day would begin the Friday after the holiday weekend, a few of the boys still were willing to make the supreme sacrifice and start their 4Day a little early, just to be on the safe side, and stake out enough space for 16 of us to camp Friday, Saturday, & Sunday nights. Moth and Yoshi were the first early arrivals at the Mouth of the Two Hearted site.

Driving north with me this year is Jason Brown, class of 1981, on the way to his 23rd 4Day and first since 2007. In November of that year, Jason had a heart attack, then his heart stopped, and he was declared dead by hospital doctors. Jason is doing surprisingly well for a deceased person. After the heart attack, he suffered a broken back when falling off of his porch. Jason's doctor said had he been drunk, his body wouldn't have tightened up during the fall, and the back break likely wouldn't have happened. Should you have a premonition of falling off your porch and breaking your back, you may want to knock down a few wobble pops beforehand.

With his health issues, friends back home expressed concern about Jason participating on the 4Day. Although using a cane to get around, he seems to be doing fine both physically and mentally. 45 minutes short of the Two Hearted, Jason and I grab Friday group dinner from the Newberry Pizza Hut. Upon our arrival into camp, several 4Dayers jump in unsolicited to assist Jason with tent and gear set-up. Jason's wooden cane is not ideal for getting in and out of canoes. Anticipating this, Yoshi gave Jason the considerate gift of a collapsible metal cane. The entire scene at Friday night camp was one of the most heart-warming times ever witnessed on a 4Day.

Day 1 starts with a big pan of biscuits 'n gravy plus scrambled eggs, thanks to Vid and Moth. The boys chow down healthy portions, anticipating the long stretch of time 'til, other than snacks, their next meal. Actual paddle time from the Reed & Green access to our tents, situated within sight of the Two Hearted flowing into Lake Superior, is 4 hours. Factoring in the usual high number of 4Day river breaks, we'll be out on the water for 8 hours.

15 minutes from launch, our legs tighten up, and we take a 90-minute break. 8 hours 'til take-out may be a bit optimistic. The boys swim, dive in the river after Frisbees and footballs, and swap stories including, "Father Murphy wa*lks into a pub in Donegal, and asks the first man he meets, 'Do you want to go to heaven?' The man says, 'I do Father.' The priest says, 'Then stand over there against the wall.' Then the priest asks the second man, 'Do you want to go to heaven?' 'Certainly Father,' the man replies. 'Then stand over there against the wall.' Then Father Murphy walks up to O'Toole and asks, 'Do you want to go to heaven?' O'Toole said, 'No Father, I don't.' The priest says, 'I don't believe this. You mean to tell me that when you die you don't want to go to heaven?' O'Toole said, 'Oh, when I die, yes. I thought you were getting a group together to go right now.'"*

Johnny pulled from his cooler a fifth with a special message on the label, *"If's" Bourbon, If "If's" were fifths... Cost: way less than $9.99; This is NOT Jim Beam... no, really. Brought to you by the makers of Sirhan Sirhan Bourbon Bourbon, It's Better Coming Back Up Than Going Down Bourbon, and many more!* The back label reads, *Don't look at the back label... Stop it! Stop looking! Turn the bottle around and read the front label... like you're supposed to do. This means you! This is your final warning... alright then, drink two fingers, barf, and then drink two more!*

Having a wonderful time at this stop, Chippy 2Rib falls from the seat to the floor of his beached canoe, laughing at a joke Jimmy tells, *"An Irish priest is driving and gets stopped for speeding. The cop smells alcohol on his breath and asks if he's been drinking. The priest says 'only water officer'. The cop says 'then why do I smell wine'? The priest says, 'Good Lord, He's done it again!'"*

As Jason and I shove off from this break, he demonstrates how well his new collapsible metal cane works for getting in and out of the canoe, and its ease of storage in the boat. Jason smiles, shaking his head, "I am so deeply appreciative of how thoughtful Yoshi is to do this for me." If I wasn't juggling a beer, a fifth, a cigar, and a paddle in my two hands, I'd be wiping away a tear. Sarcasm aside, Yoshi's gift and the crew's overall concern for Jason is pretty cool, especially since its' a warmth shown among brothers whose personalities don't always mesh particularly well.

Floating as a group, we tell the Mailman about the absent Kenny, whom he'd never met, and his story about drinking William Henry Harrison Whiskey. Kenny claimed it was the first Indiana bourbon since Prohibition, and that he and a couple of buddies finished off a bottle while they camped at the Indy 500 a few years back. The whiskey label reads that it is bottled by the W.H. Harrison Bourbon Co. in Temperance, Michigan. Wow! An Indiana bourbon bottled in the small Michigan town where Big Guy, Goobs, and I went to high school! How come we never heard of it? President Harrison died in April of 1841, 31 days after taking office, and what may or may not be true is that he passed after a month-long celebration where participants, including this new President, drank nothing but his namesake bourbon. Maybe it's a good thing this brand is no longer available.

After taking a healthy pull of Early Times with a PBR chaser, I went on, "Last year, Kenny brought a fifth of Military Bourbon to the Two Hearted. This stuff was $5 a bottle, so you figure it's the nasty rot gut we're used to, but I hit it in the morning, at the sober time of day, before alcohol effects your judgement, and I gotta tell you, it was good!" This was met with an incredulous, "C'mon Doc!" "No, it was really good! And you have to like the fact that the bottle comes with a disclaimer on the label: *This whiskey is in no way associated with the U.S. Military.*"

Jimmy said, "Speaking of associations, if all goes well during the courtship of Moth and Ma Chum, we could have our 2nd riverside wedding, 10 years after Marquis' & Gilda's 2005 nuptials along the Rifle River. Andy could preside and his bar could set-up a Seney Township campsite pig roast." Johnny cautioned, "Let's bring other food, just in case." (*Author's note:* see 1991 Andy's pig roast snafu.)

A topic 4Dayers never tire of is Chum last year trying to deflect Moth's drive to the hoop by telling him "my Mom's too old for you." "How old is she?" "55." Kids say the darndest things. I tried to assist Moth's love-life by offering Chum a $5 discount off his 4Day bill if he'd give Moth his Mom's phone number. Chum decided to forgo the savings and, maybe out of fear, this year's trip.

Moth can't stop mulling over the Ma Chum possibilities, "Hmm, a younger woman. I still haven't found out if she can hold her liquor better than Chum. I wonder how flexible she is. I'll have to put my charming personality to work on her. My kids like the idea of older siblings."

Ironically, an anagram of "Mothman and Mom Chum" is *Madman Munch Tho Mom.*

This very fun, long day ended after 10 river hours, including our boats rising & falling the final 30 minutes on Lake Superior's waves. As good a time as we had, this was a hungry crew, and tonight's chefs, the Verba Boys, delivered big time. Ken & Carl made a huge batch of delicious sloppy joes that received rave reviews all around, once we swallowed our food and could talk.

Chatting around the campfire, I passed along a Maggie thought that would definitely apply to us, "With so many in our group at or getting near retirement age, we are still young enough to kayak, but old enough to kayak during the week."

Later, as we play euchre by table lamp, campground neighbors, christened "jackholes" by Chris, shine their car headlamps on us, yelling "Shut the fuck up! We got kids here and we're trying to sleep!" Chris is particularly surprised. He had arrived early this week, chatted and shared fire wood with these same folks. Maybe it is too late for the back 'n forth talking, joking, and laughing at a euchre game, but we definitely aren't the ones shouting and cursing in front of children. Our reply is a relatively calm, "Ok, you let us know that we're bothering you, and we'll keep it down." The next day, other neighbors stop by, kidding around with us about the ruckus, and assuring us that we weren't the problem last night in camp.

The Verba Boys insist, and get no push-back, on providing back-to-back meals, following up last night's sloppy joes with an equally delicious Day 2 breakfast of pancakes. While their cooking preparations commence, and the 1st 4Dayers begin to rise, I take a short hundred-yard walk from camp to the newly-rebuilt Chapel of the Two Hearted, dedicated 9.26.14. This replaces the original chapel lost in the fire of 2012. The spirituality felt paddling waters among the pines and the dunes is echoed within these walls. It is a blessing to have this chapel as part of the Two Hearted experience.

Laz and Rookie Korny, absent until now, arrive shortly before we leave camp for today's launch, bearing the gift of ice for our coolers. Korny aka Mark Kornheiser is an old EMU Huron that we met at the start of freshman year 1972. Korny and I lived on the same dormitory floor, quickly becoming life-long friends. He has been a resident of San Diego for the last 35 years, always making the effort to stay in touch with his Michigan brothers and sisters. In the 90s, Korny started a company that automates, assisting the disabled, doctors & attorneys, most interestingly through voice recognition, allowing a person to verbally dictate directly into their computer.

"Korny," I ask, "Vid was at the White Castle drive-through once, well maybe more than once, when he slurred his words to the point that the person taking orders didn't know what Vid wanted. Would your company's technology have been able to help in this instance?" "No, that's next generation technology stuff. One day, though, we'll be able to help Vid and those like him."

Day 2 is 90 minutes of actual paddling, launching at the access known as the Old Campground, ending once again at the Lake Superior rivermouth. Laz and Rookie Korny are canoeing partners today. Carrying their canoe down the steep and rotting stairs of the Old Campground access, Korny steps on a plank that gives way. The Crash-Bang-Boom Team of Laz & Korny goes, as my Dad would say, ass over tea kettle. We all turn towards the crashing sound, and see Korny lying, banged up but ok, on the ground next to the flipped over canoe, but where's Laz? Suddenly, from behind the rubble, a hand is seen… it grabs the side of the canoe and now, coming into view like a rising sun, is someone's hair, a set of ears and eyes, a nose, and… to cheers from the boys, it's the battered but alive Laz.

As yesterday, Jason and I are canoe partners again today. What is different from Day 1 is that

Jason, even though dosing with morphine as needed for pain, is drinking from the fifths that make the rounds at our first stop. Raising an eye-brow Belushi-like (yeah, I wish), I ask, "Jason, didn't you say that morphine and alcohol is a dangerous mix?" "Yeah, but I did fine yesterday, better than anticipated, plus today's a short trip, so why not?"

Jason seems ok, so maybe he's right. As we leave the beach break, it all falls apart. Jason has become Mister Gumby, his bones now Jello, turning him into 150 pounds of a dead-weight human S-curve. Pushing off from shore, Jason tries to stay upright in the bow, but sways wildly back-n-forth, my partner now a dancing windsock guy on steroids. "Jason! Sit down in the bottom of the boat!" "No, I'm fine" "Jason – you're going to flip us. Bottom of the boat!" "No, I can do this." "Jason! The only thing you're capable of doing is arguing with me – bottom of the boat!"

He either can't or won't make the move I request. Fortunately, another beach is a couple hundred feet ahead, and we intentionally run ashore there. Seeing a bad moon rising in our craft, Laz and Korny close in quickly on us, beaching their canoe as we did, and assist in getting Jason off of his seat. The 3 of us set up a comfortable floor seat for Jason, cushions below him and between his back and the cooler. We throw a towel over his head to ward-off sunburn.

All 11 boats pull over to check on Jason and, although we've just taken an hour plus break one bend ago, the Frisbees and fifths come out again. Moth tells us about a cooler that holds 95 beers, or as he put it, "You know what that is? 4 cases minus the one in my hand." Moth truly is the World's Greatest Salesperson!

The rest of today, over & above party stops, I pull over frequently to check on Jason, keep him comfortable and ensure all is well. It's amazing how a 90-minute paddle can turn into a 5-hour experience. As a result of the frequent stops, our canoe is one of the last to reach the take-out.

*The Tale of Good Carl/Bad Carl...*

As we paddle into camp, the boys tell me the DNR man – now departed - had been here to talk to us about last night. Apparently, one of our neighboring campers contacted the Newberry DNR office to complain about the noise from last evening. It didn't matter that the cursing jackhole campers, who left earlier today, are responsible for most of the disturbance, the DNR fella wants to talk to us and, thanks to Carl Verba, me specifically.

Moth and Yoshi, as the earliest-in-the-week campground arrivals, were the ones whose names are listed on the camp board reservation slips. The DNR agent asks to speak to them, making sure they know that, if further complaints prompt one more visit by him from Newberry (a 50 minute round trip, much of it over rough dirt roads), we will be tossed. Before the agent can get back in his vehicle, Carl Verba comes racing out of the vault toilet he's been busy in. Pulling his pants up and shouting, "Wait! Wait!", Carl breathlessly runs up to the DNR guy to make sure that he knows "Doc Fletcher is the guy who organizes this group." Why Carl felt it was necessary to pass on this tidbit of information remains a mystery to all of us.

Now the DNR guy is eager to talk to me, still out on the river with Jason. Maybe it is a good thing that Jason is having a rough reaction mixing morphine & alcohol, making me take a bit more time out on the water. The DNR guy kept asking, "When do you expect Doc to get in?" Anybody familiar with the 4Day knows the answer is, when asked about any of us, "We have no idea." After waiting around for a while, he departs about 30 minutes before Jason and I make it back to welcoming shouts of, "Hey Doc, the DNR guy was here, and wanted to talk to you!", and being brought up to speed about our special visitor.

I feel compelled to give Carl Verba a verbal swirly. From this moment on, he will be known as "Bad Carl" and Carl Hayden as "Good Carl".

The sun has not yet set as we sit around a big bonfire, recounting the day's excitement from the Laz-Korny Crash-Bang-Boom comedy show to Bad Carl pulling his pants up and flagging down the DNR guy. After his self-induced, exhausting day, Jason is passed out sitting in his captain's chair. Moth lurches over to Jason to give him a drunken hug, but in his embrace the two begin to totter. Before anyone can reach them, they crash together, Moth landing on top of Jason. Now Jason awakes, making noises that indicate intense pain. We help him to his tent, thankful that there is enough morphine & alcohol still coursing through Jason's veins that he blessedly soon passes out again.

Emerging from his tent the morning of Day 3, to no one's surprise Jason says he feels pretty beat up, and will pass on paddling today. As we break camp this morning for today & tomorrow's Manistique canoeing & kayaking, the roughed-up Jason gets a great deal of help from the guys to take down his tent and pack all of his gear.

As we caravan from the Two Hearted camp to our Zellar's Restaurant breakfast in Newberry, this seems like the perfect place in our 4Day narrative to insert a few paragraphs from a 1999 book Maggie directed my attention to, "The Devil's Workshop", authored by Stephen J. Cannell, the man who brought us, from 1983 to 1987, one of my favorite TV shows, *The A-Team*. Perhaps my love of the *A-Team*, and belief in the 4Day wisdom of alcohol as a cure for what ails you, was transmitted telepathically to Cannell when he wrote this scene. To set the stage, a man named Lucky is a handcuffed hobo suffering from the D.T.'s…

*Roscoe was knocked back by the ferocity of the hobo's scream and the violence of his actions. Lucky was yanking his handcuffed wrists so hard that blood was squirting from cuts where the metal shackles dug into him. "Shit!" Roscoe said. "Stop it!"*

*Roscoe was panicked; he didn't know what to do. He grabbed a phone off the counter and dialed. "Gimme Doc Fletcher," he said to the nurse. "'Mergency!" After a minute, the doctor came on the line. "What can I do for you, Roscoe?" Roscoe explained the problem, and when he was finished, Lucky was pulling his handcuffs so violently he was deeply scarring the wooden arm of the bench. "OHHHHHH, GOD… PLEEEASE," he wailed.*

*"Go to the liquor cabinet, get some liquor, and pour it in him till it stops. That's all I can tell ya t'do for now," the doctor said. "Other than that, leave him be till he comes out of it."*

*Roscoe hung up and ran and got his bottle of Scotch off the store shelf. He opened it and poured four shots into Lucky, who swallowed them like a man parched on a desert. The effect was like cold water going into an overheated engine. Lucky started to calm down as the whiskey hit his bloodstream and sedated his rioting nervous system.*

Before the rest of us head to the river, Rose at the Jolly Motel readies a room as an early check-in for Jason. He needs a long, healing sleep to recover from yesterday's one-two punch of a morphine-bourbon mix on the river & Moth crash-landing on his back in camp.

It is an unhurried Manistique float on a gorgeous day, with stories going back 'n forth. I told the boys about Marty's Bar, a tavern in Mount Pleasant frequented by townies & CMU students alike. Maggie, Toni, Mister P and I were in Marty's, doing pub research near the Chippewa River for my *Canoeing & Kayaking College Campuses* book. *"So we sit down, and P asked the waitress, 'Do you have Pepsi?' She says, 'No, Coke.' He asks again, 'Pepsi?' She replies, 'Pabst?' They have Pabst on tap for $1.50 a shell (4Dayer nods of admiration are all around). Our waitresses are Tracey & Lacey. I'm not making this up. Owner Marty tells us he's owned the bar for almost 20 years, and that's after owning a bar in Mecosta for 7 years. Maggie compliments him, 'You're holding up well for a guy who's owned a bar for that many years.' Marty says, 'A friend told me it looks like I haven't aged.' I told him that drinking McMasters Whiskey all these years is the reason, and he said, 'Oh, you mean you're pickled.'"*

Since this 4Day began, Vid has been warning Rookie Mailman, "Watch out for the 3rd day! It'll sneak up on you!" Sure enough, on the new steel bridge, formerly *the… Old… Log… Bridge*, after fifths of Fleischmann's and Heaven Hill are drained, the rook starts repeating, "Vid tried to tell me about Day 3," giggling and staggering while he recounts the cautionary advice. Rookie Mailman is in a semi-comatose state the balance of our time on the river, but within 15 minutes of checking into his Jolly Motel room, he bounces up and joins us for a night at the bar next door. What amazing restorative powers the descendants of the French Huguenots have!

Tonight, the boys are shuttling back 'n forth from the bar to the spaghetti and garlic bread being prepared outside of the Jolly Motel by Chris and Ron. Not only does it taste great, but it goes well with beer, bourbon, and Jolly Bar pizza!

Bright & early on Day 4, there's a knock on the door of the room I'm sharing with Jason.

Chris walks in and says, "Jason, today you're going canoeing 'n fishing with me!" After his bad day and bad night, the thought of finally getting in serious fishing time puts some giddy-up in Jason's step and a day-long smile on his face. It's a 4Day miracle, with love from a brother.

Day 4 on the Manistique, as Day 3, was the same 3-hour trip ending at the Northland Outfitters' livery. 30 minutes after put-in, we stop for our usual party break at the Ten Curves Dam portage. Chris and Jason use the opportunity to break out their fishing gear, and have a successful time catching small mouth bass at the dam. The group conversation roams to 4Dayers absent this year. Jimmy asks, "Hey, when are we gonna get Colonel back 4Dayin' with us?", a frequent question about our brother who's been missing-in-action since '09. I tell him, "Jimmy, it's not the same as having the Colonel telling this while standing next to us, but we'd talked on the phone not too long ago, and Colonel recounted his 1990 rookie year encounter with Wayne...

*Upon our first meeting, I gave my best firm handshake to this large stranger. He paused, raised an eyebrow, and we preceded to have a short Indian arm-wrestling contest. I locked my arm in position, and he preceded to slide me around the sand like a plastic soldier. Then he turned on the big Wayne-O smile and said, "I like you, you're durable."*

You can feel the warmth settling over Jimmy, hearing this great story about his big brother Wayne, 7 years after his passing to the Other Side.

Ron has been struggling for years with back pain, more so lately, but pushed through it enough to paddle this one day with us. On today's last stop, I see an opening to tease him about his well-known distaste of George Dickel Tennessee Whisky, "Ronnie, I know that you're always looking for new ways to enjoy Dickel, so on a recent paddle down the Pere Marquette, I created "Trickel", a mix of Ten High, Buffalo Trace, and Dickel. It was every bit as tasty as it sounds."

Ron shows concern, "As your friend, I discourage this form of franken-bourboning. At best, you may be surrounded by friends and jocularity and at worst you might incite "the Chris", a beast rumored to follow you around with a "chaser" to then be followed by the dreaded "double-bubbler". He can be identified by his rainbow, not judging, of colorful beverages and his distinct call "Rookie! We need a bottle!" Wait, on second thought I can't come up with a reason not to franken-bourbon."

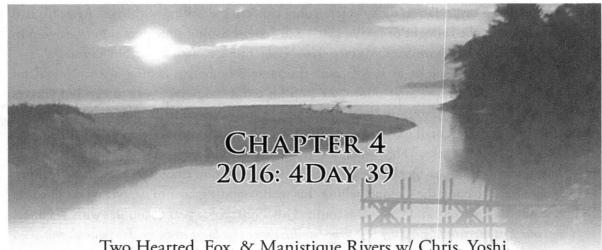

# CHAPTER 4
## 2016: 4DAY 39

Two Hearted, Fox, & Manistique Rivers w/ Chris, Yoshi,
Mister P, Eric, Mailman, Vid, Johnny, Carl V., Ken V.,
Jason, Ron, Brittany (ashes), Doc, rookie Crow

*Rock & Roll Music gets out and gets into your head*
*Rock & Roll Music is saying what's left to be said*
*Rock & Roll Music is all that you need to be free*
*(Rock & Roll Music by the Frost)*

Glenn Frey of the Eagles passed away on January 18, 2016 at age 67. Among the quotes attributed to Glenn was one that could have been the title of this book, "Some people call it history. I call it evidence."

Along this vein, quotes among the 4Day boys are flying back 'n forth, as they get fired up about the upcoming July trip Up North. Johnny forwarded 2 quotes, "In dog beers, I've only had one," signed anonymous & "In a few short weeks, I plan to have several dog beers," signed me. Ronnie sent simply a signature, Ron "I'm just dippin' a toe & refusing Dickel" Swiecki.

It's June, and I'm at the Houghton Lake Library, sharing canoeing & kayaking stories with their patrons. Being in Houghton Lake, my thoughts turn to the town's jewel, the Nottingham Bar, so I decide to stop in for a shell of beer. An email to the crew sums up the visit…

*There's sad news to report: the Nottingham, site of so many on-the-way-to-the-4Day-memories, has closed their doors. A family friend moving some bar items out told me 92-year old Virgy is slipping physically & mentally, has had enough – she's moving in with her daughter - and this Saturday there will be an auction of her home and the bar (Maggie told me, "Don't even think about it," damn voice of reason).*

*The news gets the fellers to thinking. Jimmy recalls the wall photos of Lolich and Fidrych, signed to the previous owner, both saying, "Helen, keep a cold one ready!" Johnny changes his name to Johnny "I miss the special happy hour Blatz half shells (.65 down from .75)" Steck. Chris sees the sunny side, "NottingHAM? Isn't Mister P, a well-known ham aficionado, retired? This is a very interesting opportunity, not to mention timely. Imagine Mister P's NottingHAM Palace, Home of the Ham Slider, and back by popular demand, Blatz on tap! Throw in a couple of Mad Dog buzz euchre nights... gentlemen & ladies, I think we have ourselves a winner! I've got a couple of bucks and some elbow grease... LET'S DO IT!!!!!!!!!!!!!!!!!!!!!!!!!!!!!!!!!!!!!!!!!!!!!!!"*

Maybe we'll get this year's one rookie to throw some cash towards Chris' plan. Rookie Evan is a friend of 2nd year man, the Mailman. Once again, a sophomore wisely brings a rookie along as insurance in case no other rookies are present and the sophomore gets stuck serving as de facto rookie. Rookie Evan has some top notch stories, laughs a lot, takes classes at EMU, alma mater of several 4Dayers, pitches in without being asked, fetches beers when asked and, from his work on a fifth of Old Crow, earns a 4Day name of Crow. We like this rookie.

Jason and I drive north together again this year. Once over the Mackinac Bridge and on to US2, a nasty storm rolls in, knocking out the cell towers. That's too bad, since we agreed with Marissa, owner of the Pine Stump Junction Cook Shack & Drinkery, that when we cross the bridge, we'll call in our pizza order for the group dinner. The tiny town of Pine Stump Junction and this tavern is about 20 minutes from our home for the next two nights, the Mouth of the Two Hearted River State Forest Campground. With no U.P. phone connection, Jason and I decide to drive to the pub and place our order upon arrival. Although the storm clears, not only are the cell towers still down, but the bar's power is out. This doesn't stop a dozen or so locals from bellying up to the bar, intent on sucking down beers from the pub's fridge before they go warm. It's a thankless chore, but these folks seem up to the challenge. Late-afternoon sunlight seeps into the pub, illuminating the beer-drinking efforts, but cannot power the pizza ovens for this evening's camp meal. So we switch gears, hope that power returns tomorrow, and give Marissa money to cover pizzas and a drivers' tip for dinner to be delivered in 24 hours.

Sacrificing for the fellas by going Up North 2 days early to snag an excellent Two Hearted campsite are Chris & Yoshi. By the time that Jason and I wheel in, Mister P and the Verba Boys have also arrived. Ken & brother Bad Carl Verba had signed up to cook tomorrow's dinner, but with our pizzas delayed 24 hours, they agree to cook, along with Chris, tonight.

The Mailman and Rookie Crow nee Evan soon arrive. The rook tells us of an interesting incident that took place while he was a passenger in Mailman's car on the drive up. As they parked in front of a store in Clare, Rookie Crow was taking a tug off of a fifth. A note was waiting for them on Mailman's vehicle when they returned: *Hello Sir, I know this is none of my business. I have no intention of calling the police, but I noticed you take a drink of whiskey before you got out of your car. I wouldn't be able to handle it if I heard on the news that people in a blue Chevy got into an accident & killed themselves or others. This world has enough bad in it. Please keep this in mind the next time you decide to have another drink while in a car. Enjoy your road trip! Please be safe. Signed, Concerned Human (smile face).* Our Guardian Angels are both above us and among us.

4Day-eve, we get liquored like days of old, torn-up, with pieces of memory tossed into the Two Hearted. Among the party potpourri this evening, Chris gives me the gift of a giant flask, embellished with "Doc's 4Day" printed above a canoe on the front, in back written "About the Author" with an engraving of me in a canoe. The flask is filled, emptied, and refilled through the night, an ever-changing blend of LTD Whiskey, Tullamore Dew, Jack Daniel's, Canada House, Fleischmann's, and, for an extra taste treat, 8 cherries. Enough refills take place that this gift is received twice, once 4Day-eve and then again the next morning, when I awoke, saw the flask, and asked Chris, "Wow! Where did this come from?" Chris laughed when he thought I was kidding, then laughed much harder when he realized I wasn't. *I stood on the bridge at midnight, and somebody moved the river.*

Day 1 morning, Mister P heats up coffee when the Coleman stove he borrowed from Jimmy catches fire. In his best Japanese-ruling-warlord voice, P says, *"Must study situation!"* The fire rising, his mind races as fast as his feet (Go Shogun! Go Shogun!) as he moves his car away from the flames. Peester then locates a pair of pliers and disconnects the stove's propane source, thinking aloud that he won't dock Jimmy for loaning the defective merchandise to him.

The caravan departs camp 1030AM for our scheduled meeting with livery guy Larry at the Reed & Green bridge launch site. Sunny skies bless us as the last boat enters the waters of the Two Hearted ten minutes after 11. Rookie Evan shows the 4Day wisdom of a veteran, reflecting on the spectacular cathedral we're floating through, "The great thing about rivers is they're all different and they're all beautiful." It is in the early stages of the trip that Rookie Evan gains a 4Day name of Crow for his mastery in administering the coup de grace to a fifth of Old Crow. Rookie Crow becomes the 70th 4Dayer since the initial journey was taken on July 21, 1978.

While the flotilla heads downstream, the Mailman begins to converse about his Sugar Shack. "Mailman," a couple of guys ask, "what's a Sugar Shack?" So he explained, "My Dad told me stories about when he was a kid in the 50s, growing up on a farm in Grass Lake by Jackson, tapping the Maple trees on the property. It always intrigued me, so when Dad decided to buy some horses and go back to farming, on the land in '07 I built a shack with poles and baling twine, wrapped it in tarp and visqueen, and put a barrel stove in it in which we cooked the sap to make Maple syrup. In 2013, we built the real Sugar Shack, an upgrade to the tarp shack. In this Sugar Shack, we have a firewood box with a door on it, on top of that a metal pan for boiling sap to syrup. The trees are tapped for about a month, beginning early-March, until the night time temps are too warm and cause the sap to rise too far up the tree trunk. A good, hard winter increases the sugar content in the sap, yielding more syrup from each gallon of sap. A 50 to 1 - gallons of sap to syrup - ratio is a good year."

The Mailman continued, "The first full moon in March is the Sugar Moon, and that's when we have a big party." Hearing the word "party" brought back day-dreamin' 4Dayers to Mailman's story. Chris asked, "What's this about a party at your Sugar Shack?" "Oh yeah, it's a BIG celebration! You guys should come over for it." "What do you do between seasons?" "Well, when the tree-tapping season is done in April, and the last of the sap is boiled down, we celebrate mushroom hunting season with another party. After that, we celebrate drinkin' at the Shack, but without the side distractions."

Late in the day, wrapped in an aura of cigars, beer 'n whiskey, we come up with some new bourbon names we'd like to see…

*Erratic Behavior Bourbon, If the Enemy Is In Range So Are You Bourbon, Run Aground Bourbon, Against the Current Bourbon, Last Drop Bourbon, Senator & Mrs. Blutarsky Bourbon, Lights Out! Bourbon, Future Stories Inside Bourbon, The Pope's Private Stash Bourbon, Lower Crust Bourbon, After the Spanking Bourbon, Lost Paddle Bourbon, Trailer For Sale or Rent Bourbon, Tsunami Force*

*Bourbon, Old Crotch Rot Bourbon, and,* although it may be difficult to fit on a label, *Face It Kent, You Threw Up On Dean Wormer Bourbon.*

We paddle into camp at 8PM, nine hours from launching, and two hours after the Pine Stump Junction pizzas arrived. These pies taste much better fresh, but we're just happy to have dinner waiting as we arrive. A happy, warm feeling envelops us this evening. Instead of the black flies that occasionally inhabit the Two Hearted site, we've been invaded by a gaggle of chipmunks. The boys are hand feeding peanuts to the cute little critters.

Even better camp company is our neighbors, Chet & Debbie, with whom we enjoy swapping stories and jokes. They are nice, down-to-earth folks who love to travel the state. Chet & Debbie live in Jackson and, like us, are huge fans of that town's Klavon's Pizza. On the drive north, Chris called and gave me a heads up on the couple, so we added a pepperoni pizza to our order for them. Maybe we should've ordered one for the chipmunks, too. Those hungry little buggers chewed away at the cup holders built into my cooler.

Day 2 features the short Old Campground to Lake Superior stretch, a laid-back float down the Two Hearted. Its 90-minutes of actual paddling, plus twice that for the usual tomfoolery. The view from the top of the Old Campground hill is fantastic, overlooking the river, forest, & dunes. The aged, rotting steps down to the river, the same steps that gave way in 2015 to the Crash-Bang-Boom Team of Laz & Korny, have been replaced by firmly embedded logs. The walk down, though still steep, now offers safer footing and a new & improved flat landing at the river.

A historical marker added at the hilltop recognizes that the Two Hearted was designated a "State Natural River" in 1974 and details the Nature Conservancy's work on the river's behalf. The new log steps were installed, in a wild coincidence, just before August 2015 when Governor Snyder paddled the stretch we'll be on today. To his credit, Rick Snyder was a Conservancy member before becoming Governor.

Chris, Yoshi, & the P-nuttiest took the day off from paddling, driving to the knitting symposium in Grand Marais. They dodged being tagged with a nickname like the 2014's Vagina Boys or the *Housewives of the U.P.* by informing us that several hours of their time today would be spent preparing a delicious pork & collard greens dinner for the group. Oh, you sweet-talkers, you.

It is a lazy, short trip today, those 4Dayers not going to Grand Marais floating downstream in no particular hurry, passing fifths of Early Times and Four Roses between the canoes, drinking beers, singing Martin Mull's "Men" and the Thunderbird Wine commercial from the 60s, and searching for water-based answers that have eluded mankind for decades...

*If the professor on Gilligan's Island can make a radio out of a coconut, why can't he fix a hole in the boat? Do one-legged ducks swim in circles? If so, how about old time Red Wings' announcer and one-armed man, Budd Lynch? If Milli Vanilli fell in the river, would someone else make a splash? Why is it that when a person tells you there's over a million stars in the universe, you believe them, but if a fellow 4Dayer (probably Ron) tells you that Dickel tastes awful, you have to taste it to make sure? Seeking these answers concluded with one definitive statement we all agreed on: timing has a lot to do with the outcome of a rain dance.*

With plenty of time on our hands before the promised supper, side explorations on Two Hearted backwaters allow us to paddle near the base of hilltop rental homes built post-2012 fire by the folks at Rainbow Lodge. It is late-afternoon when we reach the take-out access, allowing time for several euchre games before dinner.

The pork & collard greens meal taste like a great deal of time went into the preparation, so we abandon any teasing of the 3 who bailed out of paddling today. After dinner, we assemble on the edge of our campground for tonight's incredible view of the sun setting over Lake Superior.

Day 3 finds us departing Two Hearted camp at 9AM for our day on the Fox River, 90-minutes away, with breakfast in Newberry and then a shot at Andy's on the way. The Mailman might be the single greatest packer of vehicles in the country, at the very least the greatest in 4Day history – and that includes the impressive stowing job that Jimmy performs each year. Hmm… Mailman and Jimmy are both Marines. The Mailman credits honing his craft during years of handling the packing for his family of 5 on month-long cross-country vacations. This morning, he packs into a 2-door Chevy Cobalt gear for two, a tent, and a field kitchen that could serve a platoon. Incredible!

We set-up tents at the Seney site a few minutes before the Northland Outfitters' van arrives to haul us to the Fox River launch. Today is 2 hours actual paddling and, based on past history, 4 hours of breaks. Though once you've paddled Hemingway's river, you know it's wonderful, it comes back with a delightful clarity when you're actually on its waters, a clarity that overwhelms you as you fly down the winding, narrow stream, sometimes so narrow that tag alder bushes from both banks brush against you. It is a joy to hear the comments of Fox first-timers Mailman and Rookie Crow, beaming as they canoe, "This is like the Amazon!"

Today starts with Jason dosing himself with bourbon and falling out of his canoe. It is assumed by at least a few of us that Jason enjoys hanging off the back of the canoe Chris captains, suspended there for a good hour or so while traversing down river. The noises coming from Jason, when his mouth isn't below the water line, sounds as best we can tell like a "Whee!" Watching the submerged Jason give a full-body embrace to the river, reinforces the truly healing powers of the Fox. After that, Chris notes Jason, "Is right as rain, and has a little extra pep in his step. It's another 4Day miracle!"

The Mailman is asked to pass a fifth to another canoe. He overcomes his first instinct before sending it along, "I've been a civil servant for 30 years. You don't get that way by helping out."

Life sucks when (1) the Yankees win OR (2), as in the case tonight, when Andy's not in his bar. He does, however, have a bumper sticker on the wall, advertising a Kenai, Arkansas pawn shop that entertains us, "If you don't like our prices, bring your girlfriend by & we'll dicker." Once we are finally able to stop laughing, Ron suggests that we put this bumper sticker quote on the cover of the 4Day book, right under the retail. The last time I remember laughing this hard was when Marquis was impersonating Ricki Ricardo, and we got to talking about an *I Love Lucy* scene in which Ricky and Fred Mertz are trying to cook dinner. Ricky asks Fred, "What do you know about rice?" Fred replies, "I had some thrown at me on the darkest day of my life." (Although previously referenced in the 1992 chapter, a line worthy of repetition)

Day 4 starts just after 7AM, with the boys heading in twos and threes for breakfast 7 miles away at the Jolly Bar in Germfask. Leon arrives 10AM at Seney camp to pick up his livery boats for transport to our Manistique River put-in at the Ten Curves Road access. While we assist in loading the canoes & kayaks on to his trailer, Leon tells us about a "new" '97 Dodge for his Northland Outfitters livery with 43,000 miles on it, purchased online this morning for just under $4,000. The burgundy 1983 Dodge Ram Prospector, transporting 4Dayers since old Tom in the 80s, is to be put out to pasture with a quarter-million miles on it. By the end of the day, perhaps with an eye towards transporting an anticipated large number of 2017 4Dayers, Leon decides that keeping both the '83 van and the '97 van makes sense.

"Old Tom" is Tom Gronback, who ran the livery from our first 4Day in 1978 until he and wife Carma sold it in 1999 to "New Tom" & Sally Kenney. Today, we heard from Barry at the nearby Big Cedar livery that Tom Gronback died of cancer 2 years ago, very sad news. Barry also informed us that Tom's right-hand man, Rich, a guy we've had a few beers with and who we last heard from in 2001 as he was about to get married, has 3 kids, is living in Manistique, and does some work around Germfask. We'll see if we can track Rich down and hoist a toast with him to Tom's memory at the July 2017 40th 4Day.

While the rest of us launch into the Manistique on Day 4, Ron see us off, his chronically-aching back keeping him out of a canoe. Although not paddling today, he discovers the roads leading to both the Ten Curves Dam Bridge & the new steel bridge, meeting us at each. This marks the first time ever a 4Dayer drove up and joined in on a 4Day paddling break along the river.

Vidder told us about the 1896 discovery of a cryptic tablet by two woodsmen clearing land north of Newberry, the clay tablet found when the two uprooted a tree. Both the Smithsonian Museum and the University of Michigan were informed, but neither could translate the tablet. In 1905, archeologists discovered on the island of Crete an ancient script known as Minoan, with the same language as that found on the tablet in 1896 Newberry, but it wasn't until 1988 that the dots were connected from Crete to the U.P. The Minoan people had a monopoly on bronze from 3000 to 1200 B.C., but did not have enough local sources to meet European Bronze Age demands, so is it possible they somehow they crossed the Atlantic and mined in the U.P. 5,000 years ago? To my question, "Vid, to have first-hand knowledge of this, just how old are you?", I received in reply a sharp, "Hey Mister, that's enough of that!"

Enjoying Ten High Whiskey and Mad Dog Blue Raspberry, both as tasty as they sound, at today's final stop along the Manistique, 30 minutes from take-out, Chris proclaims, "It takes a village to have a 4Day." When one considers the number of boat builders, cigar rollers, brewers & distillers we keep busy, it *does* take a village to have a 4Day.

*4Day 2016 post-scripts one & two...*

#1 November 6, 2016/250 days 'til 2017 4Day40...

One week ago today, Captain Johnny, Kathy, Maggie and I stopped in at Andy's Seney Bar on our way up to Grand Marais. Andy himself, the man who opened his pub in 1978, the year of the 1st 4Day, was bellied up to the bar. Maggie and Kathy had heard the legend, of course, but were meeting the man for the 1st time.

We always knew that there was a Missus Andy, since his daughter served us beers 'n burgers back in the 80s, but didn't know anything about Andy's wife. As I told Maggie, whenever we see Andy, his marital status never seems to come up; it's pretty much us sayin', "Hey Andy! Let's do some Dickel!", or Andy sayin', "Hey fellas, good to see you! Let's drink!" Today that changed. Missus Andy's name is Betty. She was shelpin' drinks, cookin' burgers, and generally being fun 'n feisty, "I could put Andy down faster than my two dogs." Betty & Andy were married, took a few years or so break from each other, which may be why Andy is still with us today, and have been back together the last 15 years.

Andy told us that he's planning a pig roast (I think I heard Vid & Johnny Steck start laughing - see 1992 pig roast that wasn't) next year on July 15 - the first day of 4Day40. With Betty's presence, I have some confidence that the pig roast will actually take place. In part, the pig roast celebrates Andy's 78th birthday, on July 16. Andy & Betty told us that it will probably be $15 per person, and that they are bringing in 300 pounds of pork and 100 pounds of chicken. I don't know what their regulars are going to eat, but that oughta take care of 30 or so hungry 4Dayers!

#2 As Christmas 2016 approaches, the sign-up sheet for the 2017 4Day40 has grown to well over 30, the largest number of 4Dayers yet, including a dozen rookies. A note to the boys is in order:

Gentlemen - and you fellers,

With so many first-timers scheduled to join us for the 40th 4Day in July 2017 (July 15-18), I thought it educational to bring up a point of 4Day doctrine. To preface this point, I should mention that I love women. I even married one. But the 4Day is a guys' thing. There are another 51 weeks a year that we can be blessed with the fairer sex - and then there's the 4Day. No chicks on the river or camping overnight with us. They might hog all the bourbon.

207 days to go,
River Dick Doc

*The fellas replied…*

*Chris asked, "Are you making an exception for KB?"*
*Moth had an inquiry, "So if I get lucky at the Jolly or Andy's, I guess I'll have to go back to her place? That would be awkward if her husband or boyfriend is home. I'm not into that kind of threesome."*
*Moth's note allowed me to open the floodgates. "Moth, if you get lucky at the Jolly or Andy's, we'll put up a historical marker and then pay for your motel room rendezvous."*
*Jimmy contributed, "I'm pretty sure that any woman (?) that Moth picks up at the Jolly or Andy's, would not, in most men's opinion, be considered getting lucky."*
*Prompting Colonel to ask, "Jimmy, aren't you forgetting about the one-eyed, one-armed lady named 'Lucky' that frequents the place?"*
*Jonesey brought up an interesting point, "But what if Moth picks up KB?"*

Class of 2015 Perry aka the Commodore had words of support for Moth, "Don't worry Moth, most of the women that frequent the Jolly or Andy's could pass for men. No one will know."

But what if Moth picks up KB?

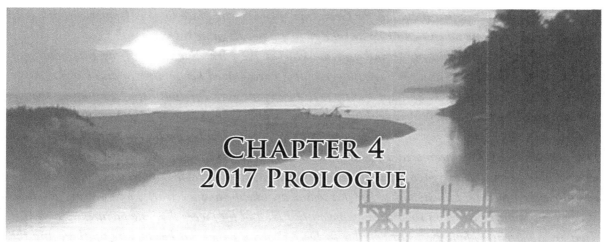

# CHAPTER 4
## 2017 PROLOGUE

On 1.27.17, our dear Aunt Mary Weider passed away at the age of 105. At her 105th birthday party in December 2016, she was a little quiet until I mentioned that I had a bottle of Rolling Rock beer in my cooler. Well, Aunt Mary's eyes got big, an ear-to-ear smile widen across her face, and she knocked down that bottle in 3 minutes. And that, folks, is how you live to 105.

Aunt Mary was the baby sis of our wonderful Nona, aka Grandma aka our Mom's Mom. The sisters spent most of their childhood in Auronzo, Italy, including the last years of World War I, when German troops entered their home with only the 8 and 6 year-old sisters present. The soldiers didn't want trouble - they were starving and looking for food. They came to the right place. Nona and Aunt Mary were the two most incredible chefs I've ever known (tortolinni, ravioli, oh my my) and it's a wonder that the Germans ever left the house.

After emigrating to America, Aunt Mary fell for the Detroit Tigers like a 4Dayer falls for a day in the U.P. wilderness. She attended at least one Tiger game every year from 1927 to 2016, a string of 90 consecutive years, starting one year after Ty Cobb's last as a Tiger & 6 years before Mickey Cochrane's first. Once she celebrated her 100th birthday, Aunt Mary would bring a sign to 2012 games, signs updated in 2013, 2014, 2015, and 2016, starting with "I'm 100 years old and I love my Tigers." Among 90 years of Tigers, Aunt Mary's favorite was that nice Italian boy, Rocky Colavito. Her grandkids Lorna and Mark made their home her home, and took her to as many games as she wanted. On Labor Day of 2015, at 103 years old, Aunt Mary threw out the first pitch at the Tigers' First Annual Grandparents Game, and was voted 2016's Detroit Tiger Fan of the Year by Major League Baseball.

Aunt Mary was a person easy to love. Gordie Wykes met her while working as an usher for the Tigers in 2012 and wrote 3 years later about the impact that Aunt Mary, or Nona, had on him...

*While I love my new full-time job, I do miss being at the ballpark all the time. The thing I miss the most is not baseball, but seeing my regulars. I don't have that many, but my favorite is a woman I met my first year working. I love flirting with older women because they think I'm handsome, sweet, and charming; whereas women my age tend to think I'm hideous, shady, and creepy. This woman I met my first year initiated flirting with me, sharp as a tack, and hilarious. She gets up out of my wheelchair and points to the "00" back of her custom made jersey, "You see that, that's my age, I'm 100 years old." She told me stories of when she was growing up as an immigrant in Detroit. She told me to call her Nona, which is Italian for Grandma. My favorite place to go is Comerica Park so it means the world to me when I can help anyone go to a baseball game there.*

*I encountered her again my second year working at the park. She came in my gate holding a sign that said, "I'm 101½ and the Tigers biggest fan." I recognized her coming in and loved that my Nona was able to come back, and apparently so did everyone else. They put her picture up on the big screen. Some of my co-workers were making fun of me, simply calling her my girlfriend, based on how I talked about her. One of my supervisors even called over the radio, "Gordie your girlfriend is ready to be picked up." Which prompted a few baffled co-workers to text me simply, "Girlfriend?" When I was pushing her out people gave her a standing ovation. Multiple people stopped us rolling down the concourse for a picture. I always asked her if it was okay, like she was a celebrity with a time schedule. When I got home I flipped on the Braves game on ESPN, and they were showing pictures across MLB Twitter. Apparently Nona isn't just popular in Detroit because they put her picture up there and the Internet rejoiced.*

*This year I heard my girlfriend had been back a few times. Unfortunately I didn't get to see her because the games I work are few and far between. So few and far between that I've taken a lot of flak for attending almost as many games as a fan as I have worked as an employee this year. The other day my friend with a 41-game season ticket package game me four pairs of tickets. Because of all-day rain, I was worried it wasn't going to happen, but I was pleased that tonight turned out to be a perfect night for baseball. We got there a little late and in a few innings I see a beautiful woman on the big screen holding a sign indicating she's 102. I already know where she's sitting and was made fun of for how fast I jumped up from my seat to go see her. It is halfway around the stadium and I give her a huge hug. I asked her how she's doing and she tells me honestly she's not doing well, "Oh, my boy. This is going to be my last time I come here." I tell her I'm sorry I missed her the other times she came this year. I tell her I'm going to miss her. I tell her I love her. "I love you too, you look just like my boy. I'm going to be with him soon." She outlived all her sons. I didn't cry then, but I'm crying now, and I was wiping away tears at my seat later when it was still 2-1 in the Tigers favor. I give Nona one last hug, if this was truly going to be her last time at the park, I didn't want to bother her. Her great-granddaughter, who I'm assuming is about my age says to me, "We asked for you at the gate. They said they hadn't seen Gordie in a while, but this must have been the beautiful young lady he was always talking about."*

*I know deep down I shouldn't be sad about this. She lived an amazing life and she had to know the true meaning of heartbreak outliving all of her sons. It is the assumption when starting a relationship with a hundred year-old woman that you are going to outlive her as a 27 year old man. In my heart I'm a teacher and I know that when the world loses someone like Nona, we are losing one of our greatest teachers. The amount of history she has lived through is remarkable. In terms of Tigers baseball years she has been around for each of the World Series the Tigers won in 1935, 1945, 1968, and 1984. She was already 20 years old when "Take Me Out to the Ballgame" was sung for the first time at a ballpark. The official Detroit Tigers' page posted her picture with the caption, "Meet Mary. Her first Tigers' game was in 1927" (They must not be on the same Italian Grandmother-name basis as I am with her). After six hours it has over 100,000 likes and more than 8,000 shares. Maybe she can get a few more?*

*I originally offered my friend money for the tickets. I know there's a dollar amount printed on each one, but after this priceless experience tonight, I'm really not sure how to compensate him. I hope that the next time I sing "Take Me Out to the Ballgame," there will be no tears streaming down my cheeks, but in the same way people sing religious songs to rejoice, I will be looking up at the clouds on another perfect day thinking of my beautiful Nona's smile, that she was able to show me one last time, even when she was telling me this was the last time she would be taken out to a ball game.*

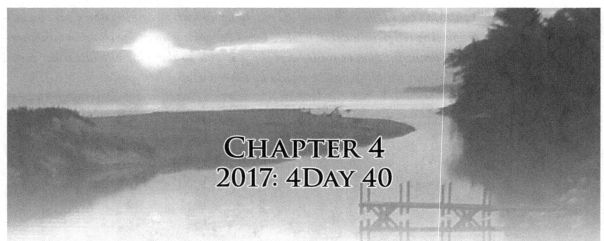

# CHAPTER 4
# 2017: 4DAY 40

Manistique & Fox Rivers w/ 40 on the 40th w/ Kenny, Colonel, Vid, Chum, Mad Dog Chris, Craigo, Mailman & son Rookie Thomas, Ricki (Father of the 4Day) Rice, Eric, Mister P, Chippy 2Rib, (and friend) Rookie Terry, Good Carl, Jonesey, Perry, Neal & son Rookie Adam, Verba Brothers Ken & Bad Carl, Rookie Matt, (and friend) Rookie Jeff, Moth, Johnny, Ron, Jimmy & son Rookie Spencer, KB, Rookie Ken & son Rookie Jordan, Laz, Yoshi & brother Rookie David & puppy Rookie Aurora, Rookie Billy & son Rookie Chris, Rookie Rich (1990s Northland Outfitters employee), Jason, Gomez, Brittany (ashes) & Doc

> *Trailer for sale or rent, rooms to let, fifty cents.*
> *No phone, no pool, no pets, I ain't got no cigarettes*
> *Ah, but, two hours of pushin' broom*
> *Buys an eight by twelve four-bit room*
> *I'm a man of means by no means, King of the Road*
> *(King of the Road by Roger Miller)*

In the winter of 2017, Jason checked into a hospital for a variety of health issues he was dealing with. While Jason lay in a University of Michigan hospital bed, feeling like crap, he flips around the channels on the TV in his room, and lights on something totally unexpected that immediately lifts his spirits: *I Dream of Seney*, part of a video travel series entitled "All Over the Map".

In *I Dream of Seney*, Jason sees a section of the Manistique River, that as a 24-year 4Day veteran he knew well, the waters downstream from Northland Outfitters. Here you paddle through the Seney National Wildlife Refuge, home to (anything but) Common Loons, Bald Eagles, and (the largest water bird on earth) Trumpeter Swans. Creation of the Wildlife Refuge System is another brilliant idea by President Teddy Roosevelt. Bully!

Like the Loons, 4Dayers return to their northern nesting grounds each year. This year, though, there will be one very important member of the U.P. welcoming committee missing...

*Gentlemen - and you fellers,*

*It is with great sadness that I let you know that Andy Stachnik, friend of 4Dayers and owner of*

*Andy's Seney Bar, passed away yesterday, April 21, 2017. Andy died at the Petoskey Hospital, his family at his side. Thanks to our old friend and ex-Northland Outfitters owner Tom Kenney for passing the word.*

*In the 70s, Andy drove a big rig, transporting logs, power poles mostly, from Traverse City up to Munising, work he liked less and less. Then one memorable day, Andy's Guardian Angel stalled his truck just down the road from a bar in Seney, a bar near the Fox River with a "For Sale" sign out front. Andy jumped at the opportunity to change his life, and bought the bar in 1978, the same year as the first 4Day - how perfect. Though we'd canoed & camped nearby during 6 of the first 7 4Days, it would not be until 1985 that 4Dayers first stepped into Andy's Seney Bar.*

*The news of Andy's passing feels a bit surreal. Andy seemed immortal. Our thoughts go to his wife Betty, and all the family and friends who loved him. Every year since 1985, Andy was part of the 4Day experience. There was no re-entry with Andy - he always had a big ol' hearty greeting for us, and made us feel as though we'd just been together the day before, though it usually had been a year since we'd last seen each other.*

*In October 2016, Kathy & Captain Johnny Harcourt, Maggie 'n I stopped in the bar on our way to spreading Jim Harcourt's ashes in Grand Marais, and had a wonderful visit with Andy and his wife, Betty. It was the first time the ladies had ever met Andy, and the first time the boys could recall meeting Betty. Andy told us about a planned July 2017 pig roast, on 4Day 40 weekend!, and we looked forward to celebrating Andy's 78th birthday with him at the roast. God bless his soul. I know right now he's offering the Lord some fine George Dickel Tennessee Whiskey. When Andy & the Lord heard Ron gag at the thought of Dickel, they laughed and said, "More for us!"*

*83 days to go,*
*River Dick Doc*

Preparing for the upcoming 40th, with Andy in mind, I filled the extra-large flask that Chris gave me 4Day-last with a blend called "Trickel", featuring Andy's favorite, George Dickel Tennessee Whisky. With Dickel as the given, the other ingredients constituting Trickel may vary. This time around, Dickel was mixed with a cast of nasty including just the right amounts (I actually have no idea - it's all a crap shoot) of Buffalo Trace, Kentucky Tavern, and Canada House. Here's to you, our old friend Andy!

In the week leading up to the 40th, an email arrived from oldest-4Day-rookie ever and brother-in-law Billy, with a tempting proposition, "the Jeppson's Malort Challenge". According to Billy, in the interest of sociological exploration and medical science, he will arrive at the 4Day bearing one unopened bottle of Malort's liquor for everyone - except him, 'cause you don't get to 69 by bein' no fool – to share. Billy passed along some of Malort's fan-created slogans...

*Malort, kick your mouth in the balls!*
*Malort, when you need to unfriend someone in person.*
*Malort, tonight's the night you fight your dad.*
*Malort, the Champagne of pain.*
*Malort, turning taste-buds into taste-foes for generations.*

*Drink Malort, it's easier than telling people you have nothing to live for.*
*Malort, what soap washes its mouth out with.*
*Malort, these pants aren't going to shit themselves.*

Malort means "wormwood" in Swedish, the country from which founder Carl Jeppson hails. Interestingly, the Russian translation of the word is "Chernobyl." The original label ended with what sounds like a gypsy curse: "The first shot is hard to swallow! PERSEVERE. Make it past two 'shock-glasses' and with the third you could be ours… forever."

Billy is one of 13 rookies this year, an astounding number considering we've never had more than four (there's that number again) in any one year. Billy is one of Maggie's two big brothers, along with Tom. Besides being my brother-in-law and someone I love, I've always had a great deal of admiration for Billy. He rode a motorcycle into his early-20s, when Retinitis Pigmentosa closed the curtains on his vision. That did not slow Billy down, nor did it dull his sense of humor: around the campfire, Billy noted a chill in the air & fellow rookie Matt aka Hawkeye loaned him his hoodie. Once Billy slipped it on, Matt said he hoped Billy didn't mind that it was pink and advertised "I Like Men" across its front – Billy almost fell out of his chair laughing. Billy worked 37 years for the Department of Labor in both Washington, D.C. & then Milwaukee (a town he likes, but locates it as being "behind the cheddar curtain"), ensuring businesses were OSHA compliant. Billy has a larger record (yes, vinyl) collection of albums than 99% of the world, is a ham radio aficionado, is very funny (see "cheddar curtain" comment), has paddled Michigan & Wisconsin rivers with me for over 20 years, and will most likely kick your butt in a game of Trivial Pursuit. Billy quickly earned from the boys a 4Day name of "Billy Wonder".

Billy & Cheryl's son, Christopher, better known as Chris, is one of our wonderful nephews. Rookie Chris lives in Utah, and for the last 4 years has been part of the Alta Hotshot crew, fighting wildland fires in the Western states – although his crew has been as far east as Minnesota, where they had to canoe each day from base camp to the fire zone. Last year, Chris was Alta's "Sawyer of the Year". Hotshot Sawyers run the chain saw, often up to 16 hours a day, the most physically-demanding crew job. In an impressive lack of creativity, Chris has picked up the 4Day name of "Sawyer".

Two missing-in-action-since-2009 veterans, the Colonel and Jonesey, celebrated their return to the 4Day by introducing some bourbon names that ought to be…

*Technical Difficulties: Please Stand By Bourbon, When There's Nothing Else in the House to Drink Bourbon, Rusty Flask Bourbon, and Whiny Prick Bourbon.*

Colonel has a series of ideas ready to go for a possible Whiny Prick Bourbon ad campaign…

*Whiny Prick Bourbon: preferred by city-slickers and dandys the world over.*
*When I retreat to my safe-space, I always drink Whiny Prick Bourbon.*
*When my husband starts acting like a whiny prick, I give him a shot of Whiny Prick Bourbon, and send him to bed early.*
*Whiny Prick Bourbon – strong enough for a man, but distilled for a woman.*
*Whiny Prick Bourbon – when there's nothing else in the house to drink.*

And finally, a special batch of Whiny Prick Bourbon with a higher alcohol content, but with a name that may be difficult to fit on the label…

*If Ya Learned It Drunk, Ya Need to Remember It Drunk, Science Says So Bourbon*

Early in the year, Herr Colonel sent to me a photo of his eldest son, Eric aka Milford Slim, standing next to his Dad. I replied to Colonel, "I didn't know that you had a twin brother" and that I was struck by how the 17-year old Eric is maturing as I hope to someday. The Colonel replied, "It reminds me of a conversation I was having the other day with (12 year old son) Joe. Somehow I referred to gay guys as butt-buddies. Then Joe stated 'if you ever mature beyond a five year old, please let me know.' I told him not to hold his breath".

One 40th rookie is a blast-from-the-4Day-past, Rich Parker. Rich was on the Northland Outfitters' staff for 12 years, transporting our boats 'n us to & from 4Day access sites throughout the 90s 'til he left after the 2000 season, last seen by any of us in July 2001. Tracking Rich down was time well-spent. Out of his Manistique home, Rich runs a lawn care biz with 60 clients, all who found out about Rich by word of mouth. He and his wife Jackie have 3 kids, the oldest going off later this year to Law School. Rich's better half told him to make sure to let us know that his family is NOT the cause of his gray hair. I assured him that all the wives say that. Rich is responsible for a 4Day story favorite, this one from '99…

Rich was breaking in a new employee for the 1999 season as our caravan pulled into the livery parking lot for the start of another 4Day fun-fest. Rich told the young man, "Now you watch these guys. Though it's early-morning, they'll be drinking beer." Sure enough, we step out of the cars sipping cans of beer. The youngster's eyes got wide as saucers, his head nodding, absorbing this new understanding, saying only one word, and holding that word with involuntary emphasis, "Wow!"

Rich is attending this 4Day in the midst of a family reunion weekend. His wife Jackie insisted that he break away from that in order to join us for at least one day, and that she'd drop him off Sunday morning and pick Rich up that evening so that he could drink beer all day & not have to worry about driving. Rich married well.

### 4Day40-eve (Friday, July 14)

It's another 4Day miracle! Last-minute add-on Gomez aka Gomie, dear 4Day brother and best buck dancer we've ever met, made it 40 fellers for the 40th!

The U.P. will be well-protected during this 4Day, as our group includes 3 Marines (Jimmy, Rookie Spencer, Mailman), and one representative each from the Army (Chumley), Air Force (Rookie David), Navy (Mad Dog Chris), and Coast Guard (Rookie Terry), as well as one unaffiliated Colonel.

On this day, rain blankets the northern Lower Peninsula as vehicles containing a majority of the 40 converge for a lunch-time rendezvous at the Keyhole Bar & Grill in Mackinaw City. A tavern celebration ensues of huggin', back-slappin', laughin', story-tellin', and grub 'n grog. As number 40 features a horde of friends-of-friends' rookies, many first-time introductions take place.

Crossing the Mackinac Bridge, the gray day is magically transformed into gorgeous sunshine, as the boys head for a long-due visit to Betsy's old tavern, Mc's Tally Ho. Although the time shared between these walls today is special, since our last group 4Day visit here 10 years ago, the bar is unrecognizable. Where'd the table top shuffleboard go? Where'd the flag painted on the ceiling go? The cozy bar we once bellied up to has expanded, like our bellies, to twice the size. This metamorphosis of the bar is nice, but we're happy we experienced what used to be when we did. Thank you Betsy. RIP.

Pulling into Germfask, gotta attend to the checklist before I can exhale and enjoy the evening… stop by the Jolly Bar to pay for the pizzas that will be delivered to our camp Monday, pay for Tuesday night motel rooms at Rose's, pay for two face cords of firewood to be delivered today to our campsite (thanks again Rose), check-in at the livery office to review Day 1 launch timing & get cabin keys. As I walk from the office to the campsites, Ricki drives by shouting something out his window about my Mom. Can't make out all the words, but the tone leads me to believe that it's not "Happy Mother's Day!" Apparently, on the way to Mc's Tally Ho in Curtis, he wasn't given directions, could raise no one on their cell phone, and drove around aimlessly during our time in the bar. 5 days from now, when we depart from this poor cell reception area and can once again pick up messages on our phones, it will be fun to listen to Ricki's frustration growing on each of today's 3 missed calls.

Illuminating the greetings, laughs, and warmth taking place below, late-day sun-rays poke their way through the canopy created by trees towering above the Northland Outfitters' campground. Tents pop-up like dandelions after a summer rain, the cooking fire-soon-to-be-bonfire has been set, chairs arranged in a circle around it, while a steady stream of nasty bourbon is circulated among the group. *4Day40 Town* is in full swing.

Damn, those are fine dinner burritos the chef crew of Chippy 2Rib, Good Carl, Perry aka Klink and Rookie Terry feed the 4Dayers! Food intake for some, though, lost the battle in providing a sufficient base for imbibing Five Star, Barton's, Colonel E.H. Taylor and other bargain booze making the rounds. For those boys going down prematurely, Moth came up with a new slogan for one of the whiskeys, "There's good times & then there's Early Times". For most, though, the 4Day-eve party went on for hours, until – at 1AM - I found myself the last to leave the now extinguished campfire.

For the first time ever at the Northland Outfitters campground, I rented a cabin. Being the 40th, I thought it'd be cool to write the final 4Day book chapter as it happened: the cabin provided a bed, desk and a lamp, allowing me each morning-after the chance to transcribe the previous-day's notes from my digital voice recorder, augmented with still fresh-in-my-mind thoughts, to the laptop. My cabin was one of 4 and, as I tried to key in at 1AM, someone had the correct key and it wasn't me. Several unsuccessful attempts to enter the cabin with the wrong key concluded with a series of 14 "fucks!" - basically "fuck! fuck! fuck!" followed by 11 more - in a little-late night venting. After a surprisingly good night's sleep in my car's front seat, at 8AM I was able to retrace the likely location of the correct key to Gomez & Jason's cabin, thanked Gomie profusely for digging around and locating the key, and got in just a few minutes of working on the book in my cabin, concluding the 4Day-eve section with this tale of "The Night I Slept in My Car," before the scent of breakfast drew me outdoors.

## *4Day 40 Day 1 (Saturday, July 15)*

Invading every tent, trailer, and cabin was the sweet aroma of breakfast cooking. After going at it hard 4Day-eve, the boys were more than ready for the chow served up by Vid, Mailman, Moth, Jason, and Rookie Thomas: honey baked ham, scrambled eggs, fresh Clementines, apples, and pancakes dished-up with Mailman's home-brewed maple syrup.

Before today's paddle down the Manistique, I swore-in the 13 rookies, including Rookie Dave's 14-month old puppy Rookie Aurora, on the Northland Outfitter's river side wooden deck...

*(Doc) I, state your name; (Rookies) I, state your name*
*(Doc) Do hereby pledge allegiance to the 4Day; (Rookies) Do hereby pledge allegiance to the 4Day*
*(Doc) Er, with beer and bourbon for all; (Rookies) Amen*

After boarding the livery's shuttle vans, we soon arrived at the Ten Curves Road access, 2 & 1/ 2 paddling hours upstream from the 4Day40 Town camp. Launching under sunny skies, we found ourselves in a river running a foot & a half above its normal depth, due to the deluge that had pounded the U.P. for the last several weeks, including rain storms 25 of 30 days in June.

Arriving at the Ten Curves Dam 20 minutes after launching, for the first time ever on a 4Day there is enough water in the river to skip the normally-required portage and instead, for those interested, paddle over the dam. Whether portaging or paddling over, all boats beached for the traditional dam break. Johnny "I have just enough liver for one more 4Day" Steck sat in solitude across the river from the gathering. Observing him, Vid said, "Johnny looks a bit rough. Last night he ran with the big dogs & got fleas." Inspired by the natural beauty surrounding us, Vid turned spiritual, "The Dali Lama walked into a pizza joint and asked if they could make him one with everything."

Kenny's 5-year-old great grandson Landon asked him last week what he was doing. "I'm going 4Dayin". Landon said, "Well can you wait? I'm out of summer school in 3 days!" Kenny said no but promised him a canoe day together when he gets back home.

Eliciting an incredulous look 'n laugh from the young rooks, when we were about 90 minutes into our paddling break at the dam, I told 'em that we'd best be heading downstream for the 10 more minutes to the new steel bridge, "And that's where we'll take our *long* break, boys".

Boarding our boats, we looked back at Rookie Ken still on shore, dancing with his oar like a drunken Moth weaving on a barstool. Mad Dog Chris provided us with the play-by-play: "Rookie Ken weebled and wobbled, but gravity did win when Ken made the mistake of moving his feet." With the Father-Son rookie team of Ken & Jordan in their canoe, Colonel observed that, "For Ken's ability to sit upright in a canoe and not fall over, thanks to counterbalance mastery by son Jordan, the two should be designated *Timber & Steady*." And so it shall be.

The first arrivals at the new steel bridge climbed atop the structure and poured bourbon in the general vicinity of the mouths of those later-arrivals who paddled 6' below. The accuracy rate was 50%. When two unopened PBRs were jarred from the bridge rail, falling into the water, the ever-alert USMC Spencer, marvelous Godson to Mag 'n me, dove in without hesitation. He broke the surface holding the two cans high, to cheers cascading down on him from above. The fact that Spencer was planning to drink one of those delicious Pabsts to get the taste out of his mouth left by some crap beer, did not lessen the adulation. From his dive 'n PBR rescue, another 4Day name was born: Rookie Spencer is now Otter aka River Otter.

Otter's Cool Papa Jimmy shared a recent conversation with an old acquaintance…

"I was talking about gaining maturity and wisdom as we grow older and how we don't put ourselves in as many bad situations as we might have in the past. He responded, "I have a different take on that. I figure that I don't have as much time as I used to have, so I should take every opportunity to do stupid shit. My wife knows who she married." I did have to rethink my stated position and it made me wonder when I became the voice of reason."

*"Moth down! Moth down!"* Moth's kayak drifted into a river dick and flipped over, kinda like the whiskey was steering the boat. Rookie Christopher beached his Dad, Billy Wonder, on a little sandbar, righted the Moth & his kayak, getting them on their way in under a couple of minutes.

Docking their boats at the take-out earlier than most was the dinner crew of Neal, Herr Colonel, Yoshi, and Rookies Adam & Jeff, getting a leg up on preparing a fine chili feast for all to enjoy.

Cheap whiskey and stories from the first day of the 4Day flowed deep into the night, interrupted only by the snores of the early campfire departures. Guys sitting around the fire suggested, "What happens on the 4Day, stays on the 4Day!" Kenny said, "Then why's Doc writing a book about this? You just *thought* you were gettin' away with it."

## 4Day40 Day 2 (Sunday, July 16)

Knowing that this Sunday morning was a big one, as dawn broke I fought the urge to stay horizontal. Not only did I need to get my writer's time in on the book and get some food in me - the Verba Boys & Rookie Dave served up a delectable breakfast of French toast, bacon, blueberry pancakes, and sausage – I needed to be on the lookout for a surprise arrival.

Unbeknownst to the fellers, bagpiper Pierre O'Gea was driving in from Marquette this morning, a 90-minute excursion, to assist us in a memorial service for our dearly-departed 4Day brothers and other dear friends. In the livery store, Vid was the first to spot Pierre, who was dressed in full Scottish regalia. Vid asked, "You're not a male stripper are you?" to ensure Pierre was at the right location and to avoid an unwanted embarrassing situation.

With Pierre's arrival, the boys gathered where photos of those who've gone to the Other Side before us were unveiled, and stories told of each. Kenny said, "This is like every 4Day I've ever been on wrapped up into one. Even the guys that aren't here are here." After the memorial, as Pierre played a bagpipe medley including, of course, *Amazing Grace*, shots of Malort (thanks again Billy) were passed out to each brother. Upon hitting our taste buds, the solemn nature of the event was interrupted by a series of audible groans and yucks! Colonel noted that, "Malort's sets up shop on your tongue and just keeps fucking you." Rookie Terry rinsed his mouth out with Listerine, but the Malort taste would not go away. The inspiration behind slogans created by Malort drinker's, such as *Malort, kick your mouth in the balls,* became painfully clear to all.

Blessed with another beautiful day of sunshine & high 'n fast water, we bid adieu to Pierre O'Gea and launched at the Northland Outfitters' dock, beginning a 4 hour journey down the Manistique to a take-out we haven't paddled to in ten years, Mead Creek.

Paddling breaks along the river were much fewer than anticipated, but not due to any intent on our part. The stretch of river from the livery to Mead Creek usually shows over a dozen wide, sandy beaches along the water, each ideal for pulling the boats ashore for a break. With the river running so high from the recent rains, we estimated 2/3rds of these beaches were underwater.

4Day rookie nicknames are sometimes given just because and sometimes earned: during today's 2nd river stop, Rookie Thomas, the Mailman's son, took a big tug from a fifth, then began to vomit. Chumley assured him there's a first for everything, at which point the rook says he was puking while in the canoe before this stop. When Rookie Thomas then pukes into the river, and while bent over catches a frog, he immediately is christened "Frog". Even though the rook only seems to take breaks from puking to lend a hand wherever needed – and can't seem to do enough to help out – the "Frog" name wins out over "Great White Spewer" or some such.

Adam is christened Guppy, Matt is Hawkeye, Spencer is Otter or River Otter, Billy is Billy Wonder, Chris is Sawyer, Terry is Scruggs, and Jeff is Beach Ball (Chippy 2Rib said, "Comin around the bend, I saw the belly first."). The rookie Father & Son team of Ken & Jordan are Timber & Steady (see Day 1), Rookie David is Sven (great red, Viking beard) and his puppy Aurora is Dog Meat. Just when you think Aurora couldn't get any more adorable, she walks by and around her neck is a koozie holding a beer. My paddling partner today, Rookie Rich, had many good 4Day names proposed for him, but the one with the most support is "Radar", honoring his past Northland Outfitters' days of alerting new employees about 4Dayers soon arriving with morning beers in their hands.

Yogi Berra once said, "You can observe alot just by watchin'." Observed during one joyful river break was Gomie telling someone in the crowd, "I don't need you how to tell me how to drink too much," Yoshi sayin', "I liquidated all of my assets and drank 'em on the 4Day," & Chumley addressing no one in particular, "You're short and we're stupid – we're all fucked." Jonesey suggested promoting next year's 4Day with a "Blazing Paddles" promo 4Day41 poster, and then started describing a "Blazing Saddles" scene, where the cowboys arrive on horseback at a toll booth in the middle of the desert, one they could easily go around, "Has anybody got a dime? Somebody's gotta go back and get a shitload of dimes!"

Paddling through the beauty of God's Cathedral, one visual delight today was man-made: with the boats beached, the sin of Rookie Adam sassing some veterans (example: calling Good Carl "Mediocre Carl") ended in his airborne cartwheel toss, from shore to river, courtesy of Chumley. Plunging into the water as Adam, he emerged soaked with the name Guppy. Bad rookie behavior often brings down the wrath of Mad Dog Chris, but his attention was diverted to the Northern Lights Whisky, a rot gut of which there are so many bottles, Chris asked if Northern Lights is a 4Day40 sponsor. Motioning down the beach to Rookie Terry aka Scruggs, Chris poetically notes that the rook, "Embraces the essence of our folly and the whole time appears jolly!"

Excitement awaited our boats, 30 minutes shy of the Mead Creek landing. Funneling all canoes & kayaks to the left one-third of the river was a large fallen log, that – to add to the challenge - the current would like to push you into. Just ahead of Rookie Rich & me, the Rookie Father & Son team of Billy & Chris caught enough of the tree to flip over. No sooner were they rescued by 3 canoes of fellow-4Dayers, and their canoe pulled ashore and drained of water, than a non-4Day family flipped at the tree and Chris was right back in the Manistique, helping pull them to safety.

All this dampness brought a joke to mind: A police officer called the station on his radio, "We have an interesting situation here. An old lady shot her husband for stepping on the floor she just mopped." "Have you arrested the woman?" "Not yet – the floor's still wet."

Arriving in a later wave of canoes at a sandy beach stop, we were told of Rookie Spencer/Otter rescuing a kid that flipped his kayak, in part, because he focused on texting instead of paddling. When asked about this, young Otter brushed aside the text story line, stating, "You never leave a fellow paddler behind, whether it be a friend or stranger, rookie or veteran." Now *there's* a welcoming river presence!

With all safely on dry land and back in camp, on this, the 20th anniversary of Craigo's famous ribs-on-the-Peninsula, brothers Craigo & Chris joined with Cool Papa Jimmy, & rookies Spencer & Matt to create yet another classic dinner, "Chicken Drops", chicken breast wrapped in bacon with hickory rub. Mm, mm! Amid the post-grub stories, laughs, burping 'n farting, it seems every time you looked towards the river, you'd catch a glimpse of Chumley chuckling while pissing on Moth's truck.

## *4Day40 Day 3 (Monday, July 17)*

Stepping 8AM into the livery office, I greeted co-owner Donna, who was overjoyed to see me. "We heard so many good things about you guys yesterday!" *Really? Us?* "Oh yeah! People said how nice you guys were, how you helped rescue folks when their boats flipped over. You guys were stars! I had warned people before they started canoeing, you know, that there are 40 guys out there, but don't be concerned, they might be in the water, or on the shore, 'cause there were families & couples, some young, but they all thought you guys were the best! Some even wanted to meet you when you got out of the river at Mead Creek."

One such rescue was early in the previous day's paddling. A young man with two older ladies had their canoe capsize in deep water. Laz said, "It was so deep there, I don't how in the hell he got out of his canoe, rescued the 3, helped them get the water out of their boat, but Rookie Chris somehow did it!"

Office accolades were not expected, but yesterday it <u>did</u> seem like we joyously greeted, with unusual enthusiasm even for us, everyone we encountered on the water *(the 4Day Welcome Wagon, bringing bourbon 'n cheer to you!)*, and eagerly extended a hand to those in need, 4Dayers and all others, righting flipped boats & pulling each other through obstructions. And in this sea-of-neighborliness, the two that seemed to be everywhere at once were rookies Otter Spencer & Sawyer Chris.

How times have changed. 5 years ago on this same spot, Donna's husband Leon tossed us out of the campground ("I'll put you on the river, but you can't camp here anymore"), declaring that it was to be a lifetime ban, upset that folks renting all 4 of his livery cabins had checked out in the middle the previous night, due to the noise (including the cracking of two of Chippy's ribs) we were making and the late-hour we made it at.

Ensuring we were off on the right foot today was a "Mountain Man" breakfast created by Laz, Jonesey, KB, and the father-son rookie team of Ken & Jordan: scrambled eggs, sausage, bacon, shredded cheese, hash browns, grits, and burritos to wrap it all in. Damn good! The boys were looking for a dutch oven for the cooking process, until Jonesey said he'd only heard of a dutch oven described as "the act of trapping a person under bed covers after releasing vile gas fumes." Unable to get the stinky mental picture out of their heads, the chefs opted instead for a large pan.

Rookies Matt and Jeff, as expected, had to pack up this morning, sadly heading home as work called. There were hugs around as Jeff wished us well, "It was good meeting all you fellers. The only thing missing were togas. Thanks for everything, even the shot Sunday morning, whatever the hell that shit was." *Malort, it leaves a taste in your face & a stain on the brain.*

Lookin' a little rough around the edges this morning, Gomie said that he's had hardly any sleep while sharing a cabin with Jason. Hmm, you better play that back in your head Gomie, it doesn't sound quite right. "No, no, no. Every time that Jason moves, he's moanin' in pain from his cracked ribs." Pre-4Day week, Jason had taken a fall on his sidewalk, cracking some ribs, but figured he'd rather be in pain on the 4Day than at home. Good for Jason, bad for cabin-partner Gomie. "You know Gomie," Vid said, "you're just one pillow away from a good night's sleep."

You know Gomie, you're just one pillow way from a good night's sleep

Day 3 on the Fox found our paddling numbers cut to less than half from the previous day, as the brothers' work schedules allowed some, like Matt & Jeff, to only 4Day a couple of days, while several *Housewives of the U.P.* skipped paddlin' for the pursuits of golf, sight-seeing, or relaxing in camp. As a result, the 16 canoes of Day 2 were reduced to 6, along with the 4 kayaks.

Warnings from the livery office that "up to 12 portages" and "a real mess with beaver dams" awaited us on the section of the Fox upstream from the Seney Township Park, thankfully, were unwarranted. Never was a portage in the true sense of the word - pulling canoe or kayak overland - required. Rather, the Fox here ran like the Fox here usually does, as the narrow river's tight turns combine with fallen branches or trees and force paddlers to get out of their boats 2 or 3 times to pull the craft through or over the obstructions. We handled this the way we often do: the first couple of paddlers to reach the impediment beach their boat or boats, and push or pull all trailing craft through the snags. Canoeing alongside the remains of an old beaver dam reminded me of a Martin Short story told about a visit to Bea Arthur's dressing room.

Rare is it that bulls and bullfighters are the subject of a fine joke, but Good Carl had exactly that for us on the river...

*A couple goes to a bullfight, then into an adjoining restaurant for dinner. The neighboring table of guests are eating huge mounds of meat. "What's that?" "Oh, that's the bull's balls," the waiter explained, "You need a reservation to dine on those." They make reservations for next week's post-bullfight dinner, attend the match, and then enter the restaurant announcing, "Hey, we're here for the bull's balls." When dinner arrives, it's only two small mounds of meat. "What the hell is this?" The waiter replies, "Senor, sometimes the bull wins."*

Sweet music, including the Talking Head's "Take Me To the River" and Charlie Watt's greatest-drumming-ever-on-a-45 rpm on "Paint It Black", floats with us, emanating from Good Carl's cool inflatable kayak, which Carl referred to as a "fat, nimble guy."

I ask, "That was a really good one – what was it?" 4Dayer chorus replies, "I don't know" with roaring laughs at the situation. Sometimes the amount of time that elapses from hearing a great joke or line to digging my recorder out of the dry bag to capture it, is longer than my – or, it seems, that of any other 4Dayer's - memory of what was said. Chippy sez "I dunno" should be the new 4Day motto. Amid the good humor, Good Carl says, "The world would be a much darker place without the 4Day."

Jonesey asked, "Doc, how much further do we have to go?" Answer, "We're two fifths from the end." When Jonesey shot back a quizzical look, I told him, "Hey, I don't make the news, I just report it," adding some mythical fifths that could take us home: *Shoddy Workmanship Bourbon, Lickin' Yer Chops Bourbon, Huge Mistake Bourbon and,* although too long to fit on the label, *When the Radical Priest Come to Get Me Released, We Were All On the Cover of Newsweek Bourbon.*

Concluding Day 3 on the Fox River, the boats ground ashore and Northland Outfitters dispatched two vans to pick up the boats, our gear 'n us. Two minutes after departure, the lead van pulled up to the M28 stop sign, with Andy's Seney Bar a quarter mile to the east. A debate ensued about continuing directly to our livery camp, where we knew the first round of pizzas had just been delivered – with round two due in 30 minutes – or turn left to the bar and raise a glass to the recently departed Andy. Although some grumbling was heard over the growling stomachs, even the dissenters acknowledged the answer was obvious. Hungers were put on hold, and in minutes we were inside the hallowed walls where so many 4Day evenings, and even a few late-mornings & afternoons, were spent. 15 shots of Andy's favorite, George Dickel Tennessee Whiskey, were distributed & raised to our friend's memory. After the shots were downed, Jonesey stepped outside to fulfill his recent prophesy of puking next to Andy's Seney Bar.

Exiting Andy's for the waiting vans, we were told that had we not stopped for the shots, allowing time for the livery drivers to check and manage one van's temperamental coolant system, the van would have broken down somewhere shy of our Northland Outfitters' destination, 7 miles away. Andy as Guardian Angel, who'd thunk it? Up went the cry, "It's another 4Day miracle!"

Today's paddlers arrived in camp just as the 2^nd & final pizza delivery was made. Excellent! When I asked Billy if I could bring him another slice, he said "No thanks, I've had two." I laughed and slapped his shoulder, "Two? Hell, I've had 8!"

Nick aka Chumley was one of the boys who took the day off from the river. He told us, "I rolled into the Jolly Bar about 11AM. They asked, "Do you need a menu?" I answered, "No just a shot of bourbon." They replied, "Oh, you must be with those 4Day people."

Making its way around the campfire is a bottle of Orange Mad Dog. With about half remaining, KB asks Eric if he can have a pull. E replies, "Not outta this bottle!" and polishes it off. About dark-thirty, KB was heard to wrap up a conversation with, "Anyways, that's my version of it." Jonesey said, "KB pulled that shit on me several times."

Among the fireside laughing at yet another story, Jonesey recalled once asking me, "Doc, really? Did that happen?" and I replied, "Well, it's been embellished." This conjured up another tale…

*An Amish boy and his father were in a mall. They were amazed by everything they saw, but especially the two shiny silver walls that could move apart and then slide back together again. The boy asked, "What is this Father?" Never having seen an elevator, the father said, "Son, I have no idea." While the two watched, an obese older woman in a wheel chair moved up to the moving walls and pressed a button. The walls opened and the lady rolled between them into a small room. The walls closed and they watched the small numbers above the walls light up sequentially. They continued to watch until the last number lit and then the numbers began to light in reverse order. Finally, the walls opened again and a gorgeous 24-year old blond stepped out. The father, not taking his eyes off the young woman, told his son, "Go get your mother."*

Johnny & I considered ways to get Vid up out of the tent and back to the fire with us. Gomie suggested we throw frogs in the tent. Johnny pointed out, "Hey, I'm sleepin' in there, too."

### 4Day40 Day 4 (Tuesday, July 18)

The Final Day, the Final Day, the Final Day of 4Day40 started with a breakfast buffet at the Jolly Bar, financed by "chefs" Mister P, Kenny, Gomez, Johnny, and Father-of-the-4Day Ricki.

The original 4Day40 40 were by now reduced to 28. Day 4 would repeat the paddling trip of Day 1, with trimmed numbers, launching at the Ten Curves access.

Downstream at the dam, Rookie David aka Sven, addressed us, sharing a few words and a bottle in honor of his fellow Air Force 23rd Special Tactics Squadron based in Hurlburt Field, Florida.

There, local pizza parlor "Helen Back" hired a distiller to create, specifically for the 23rd, the bottle of bourbon David now shared with us. Combining the mottos of the Air Force Special Ops & the Medical Pararescue team, the label reads, "First there, that others may live." From David's Squadron, 8 brave souls have lost their lives in the defense of our country.

Taking the traditional long break at the dam, a whole lotta swimming and Frisbee tossing is taking place upstream and downstream from the dam. Puppy Aurora is intently watching 4Dayers jump into the river off the pedestrian bridge located above & parallel to the dam – including David doing an amazing back-flip from the bridge railing, David's Special Ops' training ensuring pre-flip that water depth was sufficient for such an activity. Vid shouts, "If Good Carl jumps in, Bad Carl will call the cops."

Aurora follows her Dad David into the river, and gets pulled underwater from the churning hydraulics at the base of the dam. David, Mad Dog, and Good Carl jump in the water, racing towards the dam, with many more rushing to be of help. David, the first on the scene, pulls his dog to safety. An anxious moment that got everyone's attention and adrenaline going ends in audible sighs of relief.

Downstream at the new steel bridge, Moth shouts something to Jonesey, who starts laughing, "With my hearing and his slurring, we got a real communication problem." Moth replies, "I'm not slurring, I'm speaking in cursive."

*Special Forces Dive Team!* In what was derided by the boys on the bridge as an amazing display of bad judgement, Chippy tossed a bottle of Benchmark whiskey across the water to Terry aka Scruggs. The throw fell short and, to no one's surprise, the fifth plummeted straight to the river floor. Rookie David dove in the river, disappeared underwater, instantly emerged with the bottle, and was christened with a second 4Day name of David Booze-Finder.

As the flotilla meandering resumes, Moth recalls a Two Hearted River story, "After the first stop where many bottles were flowing, Good Carl paddles the prone Chippy 2Rib into stop 2. Good Carl asks *who wants to help me clean puke out of the boat*?" Vid was curious, "Who answered?"

Talking of getting back on the Appalachian Trail in the fall, Kenny reminded us that his Trail name is "Tree". He'll be joined by a lady with the Trail name of "Red Squirrel". When it was pointed out that squirrels love to climb trees, Kenny smiled the smile of the knowing. We could not be sure, but he seemed to be humming a John Prine line, "cause I knew that topless lady had something up her sleeve."

Pulled over on to a fine sandy beach at one of this year's final river stop's, Mailman watches Good Carl jump up 'n down on a big tree branch that lies across the river, breaking branches left & right, and sez, "I smell a puncture wound." Mailman told the story of a man on a street corner shouting, "All lawyers are assholes! All lawyers are assholes!" A guy comes up and says "I take offense at that." "Are you a lawyer?" "No, an asshole."

## 4Day40 the day after (Wednesday, July 19)

Milling about outside the Jolly Motel the morning after the 4Day, the fellers gradually load up their vehicles for the ride home, dragging out the good-byes. Each year, this day-after departure morning is the 4Dayer's Groundhog Day, with the same strange feeling of being so close to the rivers that were our home for the recently concluded adventure, yet knowing we would not be on them together again for a full year.

As the well-spaced caravan turned south from the motel lot on to M77, heading to a final group breakfast at the southern base of the Mackinac Bridge, Yoshi sat outside of room 1, isolated from the dwindling gathering. "Yoshi, stow your gear and share some chow with us at Audie's!" The chance to spend a few extra minutes reliving 4Day moments with the brothers broke his distant gaze, bringing a smile at the possibilities of extended group camaraderie. Then Nancy & Larry Schlager's oldest snapped out of it. Yoshi shook his head, "No, I have to go north." He planned to soon make the solitary drive to the Two Hearted River camp along Lake Superior, and get in a day or two on that great stream before returning to the rude intrusion of the real world, but camaraderie won out and Yoshi's two Upper Peninsula bonus days were greatly enhanced when Kenny decided to spend some Two Hearted time with the lad.

The pull to continue paddling the U.P. is a strong one, the words of John Voelker calling to us…

*"Because I suspect that men are going along this way for the last time, and I for one don't want to waste the trip;*

*Because only in the woods can I find solitude without loneliness;*

*Because bourbon out of an old tin cup always tastes better out there.*

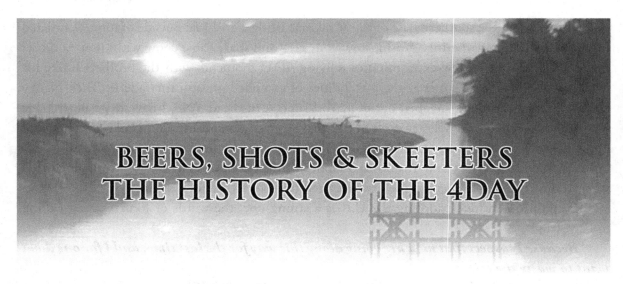

# BEERS, SHOTS & SKEETERS
# THE HISTORY OF THE 4DAY

1978 #1 Manistique River: Ricki, Goobs, Stover, Doc

1979 #2 Fox River: Ricki, Doc & rookies Chucky & Big Guy

1980 #3 Fox River: Chucky, Ricki, Doc & rookies BJay, Matthew & Craigo

1981 #4 Fox River: Craigo, Matthew, Goobs, Chucky, Doc & rookies Butchy, Jason, Jo, Ellen, Geno & Sid

1982 #5 Manistique River: Chucky, Jason, Matthew, Doc & rookies Jimmy & Patti

1983 #6 Fox River: Craigo, Goobs, Matthew, Chucky, Doc & rookies Slovik, Schmidt, Clevidence, Timko & puppy Casey

1984 #7 Ontonagon River: Butchy, Goobs, Chucky, Craigo, Big Guy, Doc & rookie Tom

1985 #8 Fox River: Jimmy, Goobs, Chucky, Big Guy & Doc

1986 #9 Fox River: Jason, Goobs, Chucky, Big Guy, Jimmy, Doc & rookie Wayne

1987 #10 Fox River: Slovik, Jimmy, Wayne, Jason, Big Guy, Goobs, Chucky, Doc & rookie Johnny

1988 #11 Fox River: Wayne, Goobs, Matthew, Jason, Big Guy, Jimmy, Johnny, Chucky, Doc & rookies Rusty & Bob V.

1989 #12 Fox River: Chucky, Johnny, Jason, Big Guy, Wayne, Rusty, Bob V., Jimmy & Doc

1990 #13 Fox River: Johnny, Goobs, Wayne, Jimmy, Jason, Chucky, Big Guy, Doc & rookies Kenny, Chris, Colonel & Z-Bob

1991 #14 Fox River: BJay, Big Guy, Kenny, Chucky, Goobs, Johnny, Jimmy, Colonel, Wayne, Doc & rookie Doctor Bob

1992 #15 Fox River: Big Guy, Jimmy, Johnny, Dr. Bob, Jason, Colonel, Doc & rookies Vid & Marquis

1993 #16 Fox River: Kenny, Chris, Marquis, Johnny, Vid, Jimmy, Rusty, Jason, Colonel, Ricki, Doc & rookies Moth & Huff

1994 #17 Fox River: Chucky, Huff, Kenny, Chris, Marquis, Big Guy, Jimmy, Johnny, Vid, Moth, Jason, Colonel, Doc & rookies Gomie, Jonesey & Captain Johnny

1995 #18 Fox River: Gomie, Jonesey, Captain Johnny, Jason, Colonel, Marquis, Dr. Bob, Chris, Moth, Johnny, Vid, Chucky, Doc & rookies KB, Tony Barney & Frey

1996 #19 Manistique River: Big Guy, Chucky, Jimmy, Vid, Marquis, Johnny, Moth, Matthew, Jason, Colonel, Chris, Frey, Tony Barney, Wayne, Rusty, Bob V., Gomie, Jonesey, KB, Kenny, Doc & rookies Lutostanski, Rookie Dave & puppy Brittany

1997 #20 Fox River: Johnny, Kenny, Big Guy, Chucky, Vid, Colonel, Jason, Chris, Moth, Gomie, Dr. Bob, Marquis, Jonesey, KB, Craigo, Brittany & Doc

1998 #21 Manistique River: Vid, Chucky, Big Guy, Moth, Jason, Johnny, Gomie, Chris, Kenny, Huff, Colonel, Brittany, Doc & rookie Ron

1999 #22 Fox River: Ron, Jimmy, Johnny, Vid, Chris, Frey, (eternal) Rookie Dave, Wayne, Rusty, Jason, Captain Johnny, Jonesey, Gomie, KB, Colonel, Doc, Brittany & rookie Steve

2000 #23 Fox River: Chucky, Marquis, Big Guy, Ron, Colonel, Jimmy, Johnny, Vid, Kenny, Gomie, Chris, Brittany & Doc

2001 #24 Fox River: Jason, Jimmy, Wayne, Johnny, Kenny, Colonel, Chris, Vid, Jonesey, Gomie, Ron, Steve, Brittany & Doc

2002 #25 Fox River: Wayne, Kenny, Colonel, Jimmy, Johnny, Ron, Jason, Jonesey, Big Guy, Chucky, Dr. Bob, Vid, Ricki, Chris, Gomie, Marquis, Brittany, Doc & rookie Mondoux

2003 #26 Manistique River: Kenny, Johnny, Vid, Jason, Chris, Ron, Gomie, Brittany, Doc & rookies Mick & Carl

2004 #27 Manistique River: Ron, Gomie, Huff, Marquis, Vid, Chris, Kenny, Johnny, Jason & Doc

2005 #28 Fox River: Jason, Jimmy, Johnny, Kenny, Colonel, Chris, Vid, Marquis, Ron, Brittany & Doc

2006 #29 Manistique River: Kenny, Ron, Marquis, Jason, Moth, Big Guy, Chris, Vid, Gomie, Johnny, Brittany (ashes), Doc & rookies Neal & Gillam

2007 #30 Manistique River: Dr. Bob, Johnny, Neal, Kenny, Vid, Gomie, Jason, Marquis, Gillam, Matthew, Chris, Ron, Brittany (ashes), Doc & rookie Jeff

2008 #31 Fox & Sturgeon Rivers: Brittany (ashes), Dr. Bob, Vid, Kenny, Gomie, Chris, Johnny, Ron, Neal, Jimmy & Doc

2009 #32 Fox, Bear & Sturgeon Rivers: Carl, Moth, Colonel, Jonesey, Captain Johnny, Jimmy, Chris, Ron, Gomie, Vid, Neal, Gillam, Brittany (ashes), Doc & rookies Eric, Gene & Scott

2010 #33 Fox & Manistique Rivers: Chris, Ron, Vid, Gomie, Kenny, Eric, Johnny, Neal, Rusty, Brittany (ashes), Lutostanski & Doc

2011 #34 Two Hearted, Fox & Manistique Rivers: Kenny, Chris, Ron, Vid, Jimmy, Neal, Eric, Brittany (ashes), Doc & rookie Mister P

2012 #35 Carp, Manistique, & Sturgeon Rivers: Vid, Eric, Kenny, Chris, Ron, Johnny, Brittany (ashes), Doc & rookies Nick, Dale & Chippy 2Rib

2013 #36 Two Hearted, Fox & Sturgeon Rivers: Chris, Ron, Kenny, Eric, Neal, Johnny, Vid, Moth, Nick, Brittany (ashes), Doc & rookies Yoshi & Laz

2014 #37 Two Hearted, Fox & Manistique Rivers: Moth, Vid, Neal, Nick aka Chumley, Kenny, Chippy 2Rib, Chris, Ron, Eric, Laz, Johnny, KB, Gomie, Carl V., Mister P, Yoshi, Brittany (ashes), Doc & rookies Carl H., Ken V., Tom K. & Eddie

2015 #38 Two Hearted & Manistique Rivers: Jason, Jimmy, Johnny, Chris, Vid, Moth, Carl V. aka Bad Carl, Ron, Ken V., Neal, Jeff, Chippy 2Rib, Yoshi, Laz, Carl H. aka Good Carl, Brittany (ashes), Doc & rookies Mailman, Perry & Korny

2016 #39 Two Hearted, Fox & Manistique Rivers: Chris, Yoshi, Mister P, Eric, Mailman, Vid, Johnny, Bad Carl, Ken V., Jason, Ron, Brittany (ashes), Doc & rookie Crow

2017 #40 Manistique & Fox Rivers: Kenny, Vid, Colonel, Chumley, Mad Dog Chris, Craigo, Mailman & son Rookie Thomas, Ricki, Eric, Mister P, Chippy 2Rib, (and friend) Rookie Terry, Good Carl, Jonesey, Perry, Neal & son Rookie Adam, Verba Brothers Ken & Bad Carl, Rookie Matt Sawyer, (and friend) Rookie Jeff, Moth, Johnny, Ron, Jimmy & son Rookie Spencer, KB, Rookie Ken & son Rookie Jordan, Yoshi & brother Rookie David & puppy Rookie Aurora, Laz, Rookie Billy & son Rookie Christopher, Rookie Rich (1990s Northland Outfitters employee), Jason, Gomez, Brittany (ashes) & Doc.

# 84 4DAYERs LISTED IN ORDER OF FIRST APPEARANCE

| | | |
|---|---|---|
| Ricki | 6 years | '78 – '80, '93, 02', '17 |
| Stover | 1 year | '78 |
| **Goober | 10 years | '78, '81, '83 – '88, '90, '91 |
| Doc | 40 years | '78 – '17 |
| **Chucky | 20 years | '79 – '91, '94 – '98, '00, '02 |
| Big Guy | 17 years | '79, '84 –'92, '94, '96 –'98, '00, '02, '06 |
| **BJay | 2 years | '80, '91 |
| Matthew | 7 years | '80, '81, '82, '83, '88, '96, '07 |
| Craigo | 6 years | '80, '81, '83, '84, '97, '17 |
| Butchy | 2 years | '81, '84 |
| Sid | 1 year | '81 |
| Joanne | 1 year | '81 |
| **Geno | 1 year | '81 |
| Ellen | 1 year | '81 |
| Jason | 25 years | '81, '82, '86 – '90, '92 – '99, '01 - '07, '15 – '17 |
| Jimmy | 22 years | '82, '85 – '94, '96, '99 – '02, '05, '08, '09, '11, '15, '17 |
| Patti | 1 year | '82 |
| Slovik | 2 years | '83, '87 |
| Schmidt | 1 year | '83 |
| Clevidence | 1 year | '83 |
| Timko | 1 year | '83 |
| ***Casey Timko | 1 year | '83 |
| Tom S. | 1 year | '84 |
| **Wayne | 10 years | '86 – '91, '96, '99, '01, '02 |
| Johnny | 30 years | '87 – '08, '10 – '17 |
| Rusty | 6 years | '88, '89, '93 (brung a deer), '96, '99, '10 |

| | | |
|---|---|---|
| Bob V. | 3 years | '88, '89, '96 |
| Kenny | 22 years | '90, '91, '93, '94, '96 – '98, '00 – '08, '10 - '17 |
| **Z-Bob | 1 year | '90 |
| Colonel | 16 years | '90 – '02, '05, '09, '17 |
| Chris | 26 years | '90, '93 – '17 |
| Dr. Bob | 7 years | '91, '92, '95, '97, '02, '07, '08 |
| Vid | 26 years | '92 – '17 |
| **Marquis | 12 years | '92 – '97, '00, '02, '04 - '07 |
| Moth | 12 years | '93 – '98, '06, '09, '13 – '15, '17 |
| Huff | 5 years | '93, '94, '98, '04, '05 |
| Captain Johnny | 4 years | '94, '95, '99, '09 |
| Jonesey | 9 years | '94 – '97, '99, '01, '02, '09, '17 |
| Gomie | 19 years | '94 – '10, '14, '17 |
| KB | 6 years | '95 – '97, '99, '14, '17 |
| **Tony Barney | 2 years | '95, '96 |
| Frey | 3 years | '95, '96, '99 |
| Rookie Dave | 2 years | '96, '99 |
| Lutostanski | 2 years | '96, '10 |
| ***Brittany | 21 years | '96 – '03, '05, (ashes) '06 – '17 |
| Ron | 20 years | '98 – '17 |
| Rookie Steve | 2 years | '99, 01 |
| Mondoux | 1 year | '02 |
| Mickey | 1 year | '03 |
| Bad Carl | 6 years | '03, '09, '14 - '17 |
| **Gillam | 3 years | '06 – '07, '09 |
| Neal | 10 years | '06 – '11, '13 – '15, '17 |
| Jeff | 2 years | '07, '15 |
| Gene | 1 year | '09 |
| Eric | 8 years | '09 – '14, '16, '17 |
| Scott | 1 year | '09 |
| Mister P | 4 years | '11, '14, '16, '17 |
| Chippy 2Rib | 4 years | '12, '14, '15, '17 |
| Nick | 4 years | '12 – '14, '17 |
| Dale | 1 year | '12 |
| Yoshi | 5 years | '13 – '17 |
| Laz | 4 years | '13 - '15, '17 |
| Good Carl | 3 years | '14 – '15, '17 |
| Ken V. | 4 years | '14 – '17 |

| | | |
|---|---|---|
| Eddie | 1 year | '14 |
| Tom K. | 1 year | '14 |
| Mailman | 3 years | '15 – '17 |
| Perry | 2 years | '15, '17 |
| Korny | 1 year | '15 |
| *Seiko | 1 year | '15 |
| Evan | 1 year | '16 |
| Spencer | 1 year | '17 |
| Billy Wonder | 1 year | '17 |
| Chris M. | 1 year | '17 |
| David S. | 1 year | '17 |
| *Aurora | 1 year | '17 |
| Terry | 1 year | '17 |
| Thomas | 1 year | '17 |
| Matt S. | 1 year | '17 |
| Jeff T. | 1 year | '17 |
| Ken R. | 1 year | '17 |
| Jordan R. | 1 year | '17 |
| Adam | 1 year | '17 |
| Rich | 1 year | '17 |

*puppies
**R.I.P.

# In Memoriam

1991 BJay (Class of 1980)

1991 John Voelker (Testament to a Fisherman)

1994 Goobs (Class of 1978)

1997 Dave Beers (dear brother)

2001 Betsy McCormick (Mc's Tally Ho Bar)

2004 Z-Bob (Class of 1990)

2005 Brittany - puppy (Class of 1996)

2006 Debbie Muir (Love of Moth's life)

2008 Wayne-O (Class of 1986)

2009 Jimmy Mong (dear brother)

2009 Mark the Bird Fidrych

2011 Gillam (Class of 2006)

2012 Marquis (Class of 1992)

2012 Chucky (Class of 1979)

2013 Tony Barney (Class of 1995)

2014 Geno (Class of 1981)

2014 Tom Gronback (Northland Outfitters original owner)

2017 Andy Stachnik (Andy's Seney Bar)

Printed in the United States
By Bookmasters